'David
2008

Shakespeare's Visual Theatre

In this study of Shakespeare's visual culture Frederick Kiefer looks at the personified characters created by Shakespeare in his plays, his walking, talking abstractions. These include Rumour in 2 *Henry IV*, Time in *The Winter's Tale*, Spring and Winter in *Love's Labour's Lost*, Revenge in *Titus Andronicus*, and the deities in the late plays. All these personae take physical form on the stage: the actors performing the roles wear distinctive attire and carry appropriate props. The book seeks to reconstruct the appearance of Shakespeare's personified characters; to explain the symbolism of their costumes and props; and to assess the significance of these symbolic characters for the plays in which they appear. To accomplish this reconstruction, Kiefer brings together a wealth of visual and literary evidence including engravings, woodcuts, paintings, drawings, tapestries, emblems, civic pageants, masques, poetry and plays. The book contains over forty illustrations of personified characters in Shakespeare's time.

FREDERICK KIEFER is Professor of English at the University of Arizona, Tucson. He is the author of *Fortune and Elizabethan Tragedy* (1983) and *Writing on the Renaissance Stage: Written Words, Printed Pages, Metaphoric Books* (1996).

Shakespeare's Visual Theatre

Staging the Personified Characters

FREDERICK KIEFER

PUBLISHED BY THE PRESS SYNDICATE OF THE UNIVERSITY OF CAMBRIDGE
The Pitt Building, Trumpington Street, Cambridge CB2 1RP, United Kingdom

CAMBRIDGE UNIVERSITY PRESS
The Edinburgh Building, Cambridge, CB2 2RU, UK
40 West 20th Street, New York, NY 10011–4211, USA
477 Williamstown Road, Port Melbourne, VIC 3207, Australia
Ruiz de Alarcón 13, 28014 Madrid, Spain
Dock House, The Waterfront, Cape Town 8001, South Africa

http://www.cambridge.org

First published 2003

Printed in the United Kingdom at the University Press, Cambridge

Typeface Minion 10.5/14 pt.   *System* LATEX 2$_\varepsilon$ [TB]

A catalogue record for this book is available from the British Library

Library of Congress Cataloguing in Publication data
Kiefer, Frederick, 1945–
Shakespeare's visual theatre : staging the personified characters / Frederick Kiefer.
  p. cm.
Includes bibliographical references (p.) and index.
ISBN 0 521 82725 6 (hardback)
1. Shakespeare, William, 1564–1616 – Stage history – To 1625 – Pictorial works.
2. Shakespeare, William, 1564–1616 – Dramatic production.   3. Shakespeare, William,
1564–1616 – Characters.   4. Shakespeare, William, 1564–1616 – Symbolism.   5. Costume –
History – Pictorial works.   6. Personification in literature.   7. Abstraction in literature.
8. Symbolism in literature.   9. Gods in literature.   I. Title.
PR3095.K54   2003
792.9′5 – dc21   2003043506

ISBN 0 521 82725 6 hardback

In memory of my father
Frederick P. Kiefer

Contents

Illustrations

Acknowledgments

Three institutions, all located in London, proved indispensable to the writing of this book. The Warburg Institute generously welcomed me and offered an opportunity to make use of its materials in art history; the folders in the photographic archive provided a starting point for research. The nearby Print Room of the British Museum made available its unrivaled collection of engravings, woodcuts, etchings, and drawings; the personnel there were unfailingly helpful, going out of their way to locate the prints I sought. The British Library, a model of efficiency in its new home, provided the literary materials I needed.

I also owe debts of a more personal kind, particularly to Judith H. Anderson, Carl T. Berkhout, Clifford Davidson, F. J. Levy, Peter E. Medine, Robert S. Miola, and Leslie Thomson, who generously assisted me at various stages. I am grateful to Martin White, a reader for Cambridge University Press, for his valuable suggestions. Larry Evers, my department head, helped secure the funds necessary to publish the illustrations. I especially want to thank A. R. Braunmuller for his counsel and support.

I am also grateful to the editors of *Comparative Drama*, *Renaissance and Reformation*, and *Allegorica*, who published earlier versions of my work on, respectively, Spring and Winter, Time, and Rumour. Finally, I wish to thank Thomas Moisan and Douglas Bruster, editors of a Festschrift for G. Blakemore Evans, for granting permission to reprint my work on The Five Senses.

Introduction

I

When Queen Elizabeth visited St. Paul's cathedral on New Year's Day, 1562, she found a newly bound prayer book on her customary cushion. Opening it, she discovered unfamiliar pictures of various saints and martyrs interspersed with the Gospels and Epistles. Far from being pleased, she frowned and blushed, shut the book, and asked for the one she had previously used. Following the service, she sought out Dean Nowell to inquire about the new book. He explained that he had purchased some prints from a German visitor and had had them bound into the prayer book as a New Year's gift. "You could never present me with a worse," replied the queen, and she went on to declare her "aversion to idolatry, to images and pictures of this kind."[1] In his defense the surprised Nowell said that he meant no harm, that his mistake sprang from ignorance. Elizabeth accepted the apology, but the incident had wide ramifications: "This matter occasioned all the clergy in and about London, and the churchwardens of each parish, to search their churches and chappels: and caused them to wash out of the walls all paintings that seemed to be Romish and idolatrous; and in lieu thereof suitable texts taken out of the Holy Scriptures to be written."[2]

Elizabeth's preference for words over pictures, at least in the ecclesiastical sphere, suggests a major direction of sixteenth-century culture in England. Creative impulses that in another country issued in frescoes and oil paintings, woodcuts and engravings, were diverted to other forms, especially those employing the written word. Artistic expression in England did not have the prestige it enjoyed in both the Catholic and the Protestant nations of Continental Europe. The training and traditions that nourished Dürer and van der Leyden, Titian and Rubens, Maarten van Heemskerck and Hendrik Goltzius, did not exist in England. Indeed, Richard Haydocke reports in 1598 that the English purchaser of a painting may fail "to bestowe anie great price on a peece of worke, because hee thinkes it is not well done"; the painter, for his part, may reply "that he therefore neither useth all his skill, nor taketh all the paines that he could, because hee knoweth before hand the slendernes of his reward."[3] Henry Peacham provides a telling indication of his countrymen's jaundiced attitude toward art: seeking to extol its value, he resorts to cataloguing the sums of money that Italian princes and popes spent hiring artists.[4] When Elizabethan writers describe the work of artists, their language betrays disapproval: "the very terms used commonly to refer to painting – cunning, shadowing, counterfeiting, and tricking – carried the negative connotations of inauthenticity and moral baseness."[5] As late as the Caroline era, Edward Norgate could describe "the end of all drawing" as "being nothing else but soe to deceave the eyes, by the deceiptfull jugling and witchcraft of lights and shadowes, that round embost, and sollid bodyes in Nature may seeme round embost and sollid in *plano*."[6]

The finest painting in England was confined chiefly to portraiture, and the artists who executed portraits were either visitors or immigrants or descendants of immigrant families: Hans Holbein, Nicholas Hilliard, Isaac Oliver, Marcus Gheeraerts, Daniel Mytens, Wenceslaus Hollar, and Anthony van Dyck. On those occasions when new buildings required adornment, Continental artists and artisans were likely to be awarded commissions demanding expertise, especially in the final stages of decoration. Thus to complete Nonsuch palace, begun in 1538, Henry VIII invited "at the royal cost, the most excellent artificers, architects, sculptors, and statuaries of different nations, Italians, Frenchmen, Hollanders and native Englishmen."[7] What the king did, evidently, was to hire "native artificers to raise the building according to their own unschooled notions of the Renaissance style and then, at huge cost, persuade the foreigners to apply to it a plethora of ornamental detail."[8]

No Maecenas followed Henry to the throne: "Edward, Mary, Elizabeth, James, who succeeded him, all failed to engage in active artistic patronage. After Henry's death in 1547 no new palaces were built, no major additions were made to those that already stood, no important commissions from the Crown were given for furniture, tapestries, paintings or any other art form."[9] This diminishing interest in artistic endeavor may well have resulted from the depredations of the iconoclasts, unleashed by Henry's break with Rome and unrestrained during the reign of his son.[10] Iconoclasts not only destroyed much of England's religious heritage but also inhibited the development of young artists and artisans, familiar with the expertise of their Continental counterparts. The effect was insidious, crippling English artistry at precisely the moment that the Italians, French, Germans, and Dutch were moving from strength to strength. Not surprisingly, when the Whitehall Banqueting House, the most important structure of early seventeenth-century London, neared completion, Peter Paul

Rubens received the commission to paint the ceiling panels, and Gerrit van Honthorst painted the large allegorical canvas that decorated the wall facing Whitehall.[11]

Similarly, English country houses were adorned with materials designed and, in some instances, purchased abroad. The tapestries for the High Great Chamber at Hardwick Hall, Derbyshire, for instance, were made in Brussels. Designs for windows, doorways, fireplaces, hall screens, and fountains in this and other houses were inspired by the pattern books of Sebastiano Serlio, Jacques Androuet du Cerceau, Wendel Dietterlin, Cornelis Floris, and Jan Vredeman de Vries, as Anthony Wells-Cole has demonstrated.[12] Leonard Barkan does not exaggerate when he says, "by any European – and not only Italian – standards, the real level of visual culture in Elizabethan England was astonishingly low."[13] The English themselves acknowledge the deficiency. Henry Peacham, for instance, laments, "I am sory that our courtiers and great personages must seeke farre and neere for some Dutchman or Italian to draw their pictures, and invent their devises, our Englishmen being held for vaunients [good-for-nothings]."[14] How, Peacham must have wondered, would English artists grow in sophistication without gaining the practical experience that would stretch and enhance their talents? The commissions that sustained Ghirlandaio and Piero della Francesca, Pinturrichio and Giovanni Bellini, were unavailable in England. Instead of financing the creation of architecture, sculpture, and painting, the English church branded the arts an impediment to salvation. A homily read in all Elizabethan parishes condemns any sort of ecclesiastical art as tantamount to the idolatry of pagan religion: "better it were that the artes of payntynge, plasteryng, carvyng, gravyng, and foundyng, hadde never ben found nor used, then one of them, whose soules in the syght of God are so precious, shoulde by occasion of image or picture peryshe and be lost."[15]

The cultural climate fostered by such judgments proved inhospitable to artistic innovation. The English lacked even a vocabulary for discussing developments on the Continent. Lucy Gent observes, "The desperate shortage in sixteenth-century English of terms to do with art is a clear index of a lack of contact with works of art being produced, or recently produced, in Italy and France."[16] On those occasions when local artisans produced *objets d'art* for English houses, the results could be clunky; witness the fountain of Venus at Bolsover Castle.

Although their painting and sculpture were impoverished by Continental standards, the English nonetheless delighted in those kinds of artistic representation that escaped the label "Romish and idolatrous," as the contents of their houses attest. Writing in the 1570s, William Harrison offers eyewitness testimony to a growing interest in what might be called conspicuous materialism: "the furniture of our houses . . . exceedeth and is growne in maner even to passing delicacie: & herein I do not speake of the nobilitie and gentrie onely, but even of the lowest sorte that have any thing at all to take to."[17] Harrison's remark is tantalizing: we should like to know precisely what he had seen or heard about. But he fails to describe a single identifiable artifact. He does, however, at least name the kinds of works that impressed him: "tapistrie, Turkye worke, pewter, brasse, fine linen." Tapestries were likely to be the largest and most expensive artifacts in a room.[18] Often these were made on the Continent and shipped to England for installation, though many were designed and made at the workshops founded by William Sheldon at Barcheston, Warwickshire, and at Bordesley, Worcestershire. In the early and mid-seventeenth century, large numbers of tapestries were also made at the factory in Mortlake, near London.[19] Families with modest resources made do with painted cloths on their walls; Falstaff refers to such cheap artwork when he describes his soldiers: "slaves as ragged as Lazarus in the painted cloth" (*1 Henry IV*, 4.2.25–26).[20] We know that appliqué wall hangings also adorned private homes, as did illustrative panels painted on paper and attached to walls. Little Moreton Hall, in Cheshire, contains a rare surviving example: the painted frieze depicts the story of Susanna and the Elders (in Elizabethan dress).[21] By "Turkye worke" William Harrison refers either to the carpets displayed in so many Elizabethan portraits (too valuable to be walked upon, they were customarily displayed on tables), or to the textile panels used for upholstering chairs and stools.[22] Harrison's references to pewter, linen, and brass describe objects used at mealtime: when the carpets were rolled up and stowed,[23] tables might be set with pewter goblets, plates, and other implements, and with damask linen napkins; at night brass candlesticks held the source of lighting.

Shakespeare's *Cymbeline*, acted by the King's Men in 1610, allows us to amplify Harrison's account, for the play contains the rare description of a room's contents. Jachimo, emerging from the trunk in which he has hidden, carefully surveys the bedroom of the sleeping Imogen and describes what he sees: "Such and such pictures; there the window; such / Th' adornment of her bed; the arras, figures" (2.2.25–26). The "pictures" are evidently paintings; the "figures" are carved in wood, probably on the bed frame or headboard. The word "arras" may denote either the embroidered curtains that hang from the upper frame of a tester (i.e., four-poster bed), providing shelter from drafts, or the wall-hangings described in more detail later: the chamber "was hang'd / With tapestry of silk and silver" (2.4.68–69).

(In England's cold, wet climate, tapestries, which prevent warmth from being dissipated, substitute for the frescoes that adorn Italian houses and palaces.) Jachimo also reports that "the chimney-piece" (above the fireplace) is decorated with a scene of "Chaste Dian bathing" (lines 81–82). Since Jachimo refers to the "cutter" (line 83) of that scene, we surmise that this chimney piece has been made of either stone or wood, though molded plaster was the more common material in Shakespeare's England. The andirons in the fireplace "were two winking Cupids / Of silver, each on one foot standing" (lines 89–90), and although Jachimo doesn't mention a fireback, we know that iron shields, with designs impressed in the metal, ordinarily protected brick from the fire and directed heat into the room. Finally, "The roof o' th' chamber / With golden cherubins is fretted" (lines 87–88). Here Jachimo refers to a ceiling "with interlaced designs of raised plaster."[24] Such ceilings, typically characterized by geometric patterns and even pictorial scenes, adorned virtually all substantial Elizabethan and Jacobean houses. Some twenty designs adapted from Henry Peacham's *Minerva Britanna* (1612), for example, decorate the ceiling of the long gallery at Blickling Hall, Norfolk, while Old Testament scenes adorn the plaster ceiling of the gallery at Lanhydrock, Cornwall.

Jachimo's account of Imogen's room, together with the evidence of surviving buildings contemporary with Shakespeare, suggests that English houses were filled with embellishment of all kinds. Hugh Platt provides a glimpse when he writes about "The Art of Molding or Casting" in 1594. Platt offers detailed practical instruction on creating molds "of carved or embossed faces, dogges, lions, borders, armes, &c, from toombes, or out of noble mens galleries: as also of pillers, balles, leaves, frutages, &c, therewith to garnish beds, tables, court-cupboords [movable sideboards or cabinets used to display plate], the jawmes [jambs] and mantletrees [beams across the opening of fireplaces, serving as lintels] of chimnies, and other stately furnitures of chambers or galleries."[25] John Ferne, writing in 1586, urges that "al men embrodure [embroider], depaint, engrave, and stampe, upon their hanginges, walles, windowes, and other domesticall acconstrainmentes [accoutrements?]" the natural heraldry of Adam.[26] The embellishment described by Ferne and Platt was carried out on a palatial scale at Audley End, Essex, built between 1603 and 1616 for Thomas Howard, Earl of Suffolk.[27] Orazio Busino, chaplain of the Venetian ambassador, visited the house in 1618 and undoubtedly saw the immense hall screen still on view today: carved in oak are pairs of terms (pedestals merging into human forms at the top), male and female, garlanded panels and arches, Ionic volutes, decorated squares and rectangles, and elaborate strapwork. No longer surviving, unfortunately, are the "handsome halls" and long galleries that Busino admired. Those galleries (one measured 226 feet in length) displayed portraits mostly, members of the family and social connections. The Italian visitor also remarks that the house was "richly ornamented with the most sumptuous furniture embroidered in silk and gold."[28] Not until the reign of Queen Victoria would English interiors again be treated to such density of decoration.

The everyday objects that people wore, handled, and used in their homes also reveal a delight in the visual. Women wore earrings, pendants, chains, brooches, bracelets, clasps, rings, hairpins, and pomanders, some of these based on patterns engraved by Hans Collaert or René Boyvin. Men too sometimes wore earrings, and both sexes carried decorated handkerchiefs of the kind that Othello gives to Desdemona. Both men and women also wore around their necks starched ruffs of intricate design; they wore hat ornaments and carried scent bottles; they used decorated combs and manicure tools.[29] Their hands, festooned with rings, wore gloves with embroidered cuffs. Garments of men and women featured aglets, glittering ornaments usually made of metal, attached to large skirts or sleeves or hats.[30] Purses, which hung from belts, were similarly worn by both sexes; the purses might be embroidered, and the belts were often woven and cinched with metal buckles.

Miniature portraits, which could be employed as jewelry, were highly popular in Tudor and Stuart England and justly famous. In fact, Peacham celebrates the miniatures of Hilliard and Oliver as "inferiour to none in Christendome for the countenance in small."[31] Such paintings were often worn on chains around the neck: in the birth-to-death portrait of Sir Henry Unton, who served as ambassador to France and as warrior in the Netherlands, a miniature painting of Queen Elizabeth hangs from the neck of the sitter.[32] Miniatures also made an appearance on the stage. They were almost certainly used in one of the early scenes of Marlowe's *Edward II*, when the king bids farewell to Gaveston: "Here, take my picture, and let me wear thine" (1.4.127).[33] The so-called closet scene of *Hamlet* also probably features miniatures when the prince challenges his mother to see the contrast between his father and uncle: "Look here upon this picture, and on this, / The counterfeit presentment of two brothers" (3.4.53–54). Today miniature paintings are on view at the Fitzwilliam Museum, the Victoria and Albert Museum, the British Museum, the National Portrait Gallery, and the Wallace Collection.

Other sorts of pictorial display adorned Elizabethan and Jacobean homes too. Needlework cushions of the kind still extant at Hardwick Hall provided visual interest while making benches, chairs, and stools more comfortable. Coverlets and pillow covers, sometimes made of linen, were worked with stitching to represent flowers or geometric patterns. Marquetry chests, painted hall chairs, and joined armchairs with elaborately carved backs (made by skilled joiners) were among the furnishings to be found in aristocratic houses. Wainscot panels, usually painted, were often embellished with carving; the long gallery built c. 1520 at The Vyne, Hampshire, displays not only the familiar linenfold motif but also flowers, royal badges, and cardinals' hats.

To walk into an Elizabethan interior was to experience what Eric Mercer has called "an uproar" of color: "Throughout the greater part of the period the only reason for leaving anything unpainted seems to have been the physical impossibility of reaching it with a brush."[34] Not even windows were exempt: some contained coats of arms in colored glass; others contained the stained glass that had become available with the dissolution of the monasteries or that had originally belonged to Continental churches;[35] Felbrigg Hall in Norfolk contains both native and foreign glass. Designs copied from books were used as models for painted plaster figures: for instance, on either end of the long gallery at Little Moreton Hall we find representations of Fortune and Destiny copied from the title-page of Robert Record's *The Castle of Knowledge*, published in 1556. Books of the well-to-do might feature embroidered covers or gold-tooled leather bindings, even polychrome decoration, and those same books sometimes contained engraved title-pages along with additional engravings or woodcuts illustrating the text.[36] Queen Elizabeth herself wore a girdle book, a miniature prayer book with a spectacular cover that dangled from a chain encircling her waist.[37]

Compared with Palladian structures like the Villa Barbaro, adorned with frescoes by Veronese and filled with artifacts that flowed through Venice from all over the Mediterranean, English houses and their contents may fall short in aesthetic excellence.[38] But it would be a mistake to think that spare simplicity or blank surfaces represented the epitome of English taste.[39] Indeed, as the clothing visible in aristocratic portraits suggests, the English probably took as much pleasure in pattern, shape, and color as did their Italian, French, or German counterparts. Like them English men and women lived in a culture that relished display, whether in the form of a civic pageant, royal entry into a city, public entertainment, or funeral. Everyday life, moreover, presented a world of richly decorated surfaces. Pictorial or sculptural detail adorned dishware and drinking vessels, ewers and basins, jugs and platters, vases and tankards, cutlery and glazed earthenware plates, saltcellars and caudle cups, watches and clocks, embroidery and carpets, tapestries and painted cloths, pillows and bolsters, overmantels and fire-backs, wainscoting and plaster friezes, newel posts and firedogs, ceiling boards and hall screens, molded bricks and stove tiles, internal and exter-nal porches, tombs and monuments, swords and pistols, armor and shields, musical and scientific instruments, inn, alehouse, and shop signs, even pas-try and sugar-work.[40] Nor were such artifacts reserved only for the socially privileged. William Harrison remarks that, although in times past "costly furniture" was largely confined to aristocratic houses, "now it is descended yet lower, even unto the inferiour artificers and most fermers," who have learned "to garnish their cubbordes with plate, their beddes with tapistrie, and silke hanginges, and their tables with fine naperie."[41] Admittedly, ordi-nary laborers did not possess either the means to acquire the materials that Harrison names or the leisure to contemplate them. But even apprentices and illiterate servants accumulated a substantial visual vocabulary by virtue of living in a world where no object was deemed too large or too small to embellish.

II

If there was any place in Renaissance England that managed to combine, on the one hand, the word (spoken and written) so prized by Queen Elizabeth, and, on the other, the visual display enjoyed by so many, it was the theatre. Perhaps because most of us read plays rather than see them performed, we have a tendency to think of theatrical experience as consisting chiefly of listening. Visual aspects of play production are commonly ignored or deprecated: "The Renaissance was a time in which sight and visibility had an uncertain and less central place in the culture. People still *heard* plays in the Renaissance, while we *see* them today."[42] Admittedly, sixteenth-century writers characterize playgoers as "auditors" (from the Latin *audire*, "to hear"), and playwrights sometimes speak of playgoers as listeners: "Would you were come to hear, not see, a play," writes Ben Jonson with typically highbrow condescension.[43] But this usage reflects disdain for the multitudes who, missing a playwright's profundity, find more entertainment in what they see than in what they hear. Perhaps more typical is John Marston's apology to the reader of *The Malcontent*. He expresses the hope that "the unhandsome shape which this trifle in reading presents may be pardoned for the pleasure it once afforded you when it was presented with the soul of lively action."[44]

By the early years of the seventeenth century, references to spectators and to seeing plays become far more plentiful, as Andrew Gurr has demonstrated, and, in any event, counting the number of references to "audience" as opposed to "spectators" is hardly a reliable guide to understanding theatrical experience, for the English Renaissance "never managed to evolve a term encompassing the feast of the conjoined senses which drama began to offer in Shakespeare's time."[45] The notion that the theatre was inattentive to visual display cannot be sustained. Indeed, the theatre stands at the intersection of a culture that, while investing the word with supreme (religious) importance, simultaneously finds both pleasure and edification in what the eyes behold.

Students of Renaissance drama make grand claims for the language of Shakespeare and his contemporaries in the theatre, and deservedly so. But when it is said that "the extraordinary power Shakespeare attributes to theatrical representation...does not reside primarily in the visual images of the theatre, but rather in the words that interpret and enliven them,"[46] we are in danger of forgetting that the plays touch us deeply not only by their language but also by the sheer force of their spectacle: a god descends from the heavens; a statue comes to life; a father and daughter, long separated, are finally reunited. Those Elizabethans hostile to drama, moreover, argue that what the playgoer sees constitutes the greatest source of appeal and thus of moral peril. Stephen Gosson, for instance, decries theatrical showmanship: "For the eye beeside the beautie of the houses, and the stages, hee [the playwright] sendeth in gearish apparell, maskes, vau[l]ting, tumbling, daunsing of gigges, galiardes, morisces, hobbi-horses; showing of judgeling [juggling] castes, nothing forgot, that might serve to set out the matter, with pompe, or ravish the beholders with varietie of pleasure."[47] Similarly Philip Stubbes excoriates "bawdry, scurrility, wanton shewes, and uncomely gestures, as is used (every man knoweth)" on the stage.[48] Even the theatres themselves come under attack for their physical appearance. T. W. [Thomas White?] in 1577 writes, "beholde the sumptuous theatre houses, a continuall monument of Londons prodigalitie and folly."[49] And John Stockwood, in a sermon of 1578, complains that the Theatre built in 1576 was a "gorgeous playing place."[50]

When Elizabethan and Jacobean playgoers approached a public theatre, they would first have encountered a painted sign identifying the structure, and when they walked inside, they discovered a combination of textiles and painted wood intended to provide visual delight. Although the sole surviving depiction of a theatrical interior (in an outdoor playhouse) contemporaneous with Shakespeare shows a building with little adornment, the artist's accompanying comments indicate that the decoration was splendid. The covering over the stage of the Swan theatre, Johannes De Witt reports, was "supported by wooden columns painted in such excellent imitation of marble that it is able to deceive even the most cunning."[51] Another record (of a trickster who promised an entertainment at the Swan and then absconded with the money) tells us about some of the interior furnishings: "the common people, when they saw themselves deluded, revenged themselves upon the hangings, curtains, chairs, stooles, walles, and whatsoever came in theire way."[52] This account fails to specify exactly where the hangings and curtains were located, but the title-pages of *Roxana* (1632) and *Messalina* (1640), admittedly plays printed not long before the closing of the London theatres, depict hangings stretching across the tiring-house wall at the back of the stage.[53] Playgoers saw other sorts of decoration too. The contract for the Fortune theatre calls for carved satyrs to be set atop posts of the structure's frame and stage.[54] The drawings by Inigo Jones of the Cockpit in Drury Lane depict statues within niches on either side of the main opening onto the stage; the arch above the doorway is supported by two Doric columns; and draped above the two subsidiary doors are festoons of foliage.[55] The underside of the superstructure covering the Globe stage was painted to simulate the sky, probably the stars, possibly even the signs of the zodiac. The rebuilt Globe theatre in London, with its carved figures over the stage, brilliantly painted tiring-house, and decorated ceiling above the playing area, today provides some idea of the splendor that must have confronted Shakespeare's playgoers.[56]

That splendor extended to the costumes on which acting companies spent lavishly.[57] Worcester's Men, for instance, paid more to purchase a black velvet dress for the chief female character in *A Woman Killed with Kindness* than they did to buy the script from Thomas Heywood.[58] Thomas Platter, who visited London in 1599, reports that "actors are most expensively and elaborately costumed."[59] He explains that noblemen typically bequeathed clothes to their serving men, who sold the (perhaps out of fashion and soiled) attire to actors. Theatrical companies also commissioned artisans to produce the costumes of ancient, mythological, and fantastic characters. Such costumes could be a valuable asset in a theatre that, lacking painted scenery of the kind common today, needed to establish a sense of locale quickly and effectively. Costumes were also a practical necessity in a theatre requiring actors to play more than one role in a drama, for costuming allowed the illusion that playgoers saw a different character when an actor re-entered in a different guise. It was costuming, of course, that transformed apprentice (youthful) actors into the semblance of adult women onstage. And costumes registered characters' occupation, social status, and nationality. Costumes, then, represented a major investment for any acting company,[60] as the hundreds listed in Henslowe's *Diary* attest.

Also crucial to performance were theatrical properties that could be carried or thrust onto stage, instantly establishing a setting and creating an effect. Henslowe's list of such properties includes a hellmouth, Phaeton's chariot, and a tree of golden apples. Some of the most memorable scenes on the Elizabethan stage enlist such properties. In *The Spanish Tragedy*, for instance, a sensational murder occurs in a place of retreat and recreation: four killers enter a garden in the middle of the night and proceed to hang a man whose body they repeatedly stab. What established the setting was not just the language of the characters but also the bower from which the dead man was hanged. This scene must have electrified playgoers, for when the play was printed years later, the title-page featured a woodcut showing the discovery of the body in the arbor.

III

Visual aspects of theatrical performance not only satisfy the playgoers' desire to see action rather than merely hear declamation but also furnish playwrights a way of conveying meaning both economically and powerfully. Staging in Renaissance England frequently achieves its effects by sight, when actors handle objects invested with the associations conferred by society's experience, attitudes, and values. Playwrights, then, depend upon much the same ways of seeing that painters depend upon, and Elizabethan portraits are filled with symbols requiring interpretation.[61] "Scattered over the portraits of this period are little inset allegorical scenes," writes Roy Strong.[62] To signal the majesty and virtue of Queen Elizabeth, for example, painters render on canvas an array of artifacts and natural objects. Without knowledge of their iconographic significance, viewers of her portraits will likely remain baffled. Lucy Gent observes that "portraits of the quality of the 'Sieve' and 'Ermine' portraits encourage one to read as much as to look."[63]

On the stage even the most ordinary things may possess symbolic import. Consider the hand props that figure in dramatic action: goblets, swords, lutes, letters, candles, handkerchiefs, purses, keys, flowers, and other everyday items. Although these objects lack a voice, they can nonetheless be charged with significance. Anyone who has seen Shakespeare's *Richard III* will recall the moment when Richard of Gloucester stands between two bishops, a book in his hand (3.7.94.s.d.). That prayer book is an outward sign of piety, intended by Richard to hoodwink his subjects. Playgoers see something else too, for, privy to the king's shenanigans, we know that the display is utterly fraudulent. The prop, then, becomes an eloquent revelation of the king's duplicitous nature. Another instance of a symbolic hand prop is the mirror that figures in the deposition scene of *Richard II*. Having requested the object, Richard stares into it before shattering it on the floor (4.1.288.s.d.). The modern playgoer needs no special knowledge to grasp the overall significance of the scene. But it must have had added resonance in the Elizabethan theatre, for the mirror was a familiar symbol of vanity; in fact, personified Vanity virtually always holds such an object. A mirror, however, could also symbolize an effort at self-knowledge, for mirrors also belong to representations of Prudence. The genius of Shakespeare's staging is that the visual image alerts the playgoer to both meanings simultaneously.

A habit of mind accustomed to seeing symbolism in physical objects will also find symbolic meaning in situations that point beyond the immediate circumstance.[64] When in *King Lear*, for instance, Kent is put in the stocks, Jacobean playgoers saw not just an outspoken and loyal friend of the king being mistreated by his enemies but also something more. For in the moral interludes that precede Shakespeare's play, as well as in sixteenth-century prints, representations of virtue are confined in stocks by their evil adversaries.[65] The specter of an individual merging with a type is again apparent later in the same play when the Fool observes, "Now a little fire in a wild field were like an old lecher's heart – a small spark, all the rest on 's body cold" (3.4.111–13). Just then he points to a character entering the stage – "Look, here comes a walking fire" – and in walks Gloucester, the father of an illegitimate child, carrying a torch. What we hear combines with what we see and, for a moment, the character verges on becoming an abstraction.

In theatres that relied upon character types (the Vice, tyrant, scheming servant, and so forth), upon actors assuming different identities by donning different costumes within the same play, upon characterizations, especially in the late 1590s and afterward, based on some ruling "humour," and upon larger-than-life gestures of the kind that Hamlet deplores in his advice to the players, theatregoers were accustomed to look for visual paradigms. What Scott McMillin and Sally-Beth MacLean write about one of the major Elizabethan acting companies applies to virtually all the actors in London: "Behind the Queen's Men ... lay a system of acting by brilliant stereotype."[66]

IV

The fullest dependence upon visual expression in the Renaissance theatre is to be found in the literal abstractions we encounter on the stage. From the time of *Everyman* to that of Shakespeare, the drama employed personifications as characters; in the moral interludes such symbolic figures mingle with historical personages. As late as the 1580s Robert Wilson could populate his plays with characters named Ambition, Conscience, Desire, Fame, Fraud, Shame, and the like.[67] Although personified characters become less common in the 1590s, we continue to encounter them in dumb shows, choral prologues, and occasionally even in the midst of the dramatic action.

Lacking naturalistic status, these walking, talking personifications dwell in the realm of the symbolic.[68] To us they seem relics of a distant age, the survival of an earlier dramatic mode featuring a hybrid mix of the conceptual and the palpably human. These days, eager to identify theatrical features as specifically modern, we shy away from that which seems old-fashioned. Even editors of Renaissance plays pay scant attention to personified characters. A little embarrassed by the very existence of such figures, we brand them naive or quaint and move on. Yet if we are fully to enter into the experience of Renaissance theatre, we need to come to terms with those abstractions. After all, the most accomplished playwrights give them life. Marlowe brings the Seven Deadly Sins to the stage in *Doctor Faustus*. Kyd has Revenge preside over the action of *The Spanish Tragedy*, while Love, Fortune, and Death serve as chorus in *Soliman and Perseda*. Jonson creates a character named Iniquity in *The Devil is an Ass*; Envy appears in *Poetaster*; and the symbolic characters of *Cynthia's Revels* include Phantaste and Arete.

This study of Shakespeare's visual culture looks at the personified characters he creates, figures that achieve a theatrical effect chiefly through visual form and whose meaning involves symbolic interpretation. The exploration has a threefold purpose: first, to reconstruct the appearance of the personifications; second, to explain the symbolism of costumes and props;[69] and, third, to assess the significance of such symbolic characters for the plays in which they appear. The project is predicated on the conviction that Renaissance drama, while concerned with social and psychological realism, has "an equally strong impulse towards symbolism and myth,"[70] that much of the symbolism is visual, that personified characters, by how they look and what they say, contribute significantly to the meaning of their plays. By reconstructing Shakespeare's personified characters, we may recover the knowledge necessary to present them in performance; we may better understand what led Shakespeare to create them in the first place; and we may deepen our feeling for the pictorial dimension of Renaissance theatre which, George Kernodle observes, is itself "one of the visual arts."[71]

V

The chief problem posed by this effort of reconstruction is that we have largely lost the visual vocabulary of Elizabethan England. Most painted cloths, tapestries, embroidery, carved overmantels, plaster ceilings, majolica, and other artifacts have disappeared, the victim of decay, neglect, and change in fashion. Even when contemporaries of Shakespeare write about personifications, they are apt to be frustratingly incomplete or even silent about details of appearance. Thomas Heywood, for instance, in the description of his lord mayor's pageant for 1631, writes, "I have forborne to spend much paper in needelesse and impertinent deciphering the worke, or explaining the habits of the persons, as being freely exposed to the publicke view of all the spectators."[72] Similarly, Thomas Dekker explains his failure to describe an abstraction in a civic pageant by saying, "Having tolde you that her name was Justice, I hope you will not put mee to describe what properties she held in her hands, sithence every painted cloath can informe you."[73] Thanks to statues of Justice on courthouses across America, the modern reader knows that Justice typically holds a sword in one hand and scales in the other. But we no longer live in a society where personifications take visual form on household artifacts or in public celebrations. And so when we encounter Spring and Winter, or Rumour, or Revenge in a printed play, the chances are that no vivid picture takes form in our mind's eye. Extant stage directions, alas, are of little help, for they usually describe personified characters in the most cursory way or not at all. We are left to wonder how those figures were costumed and what props they carried. Bewildered, we may cease to think about them at all. Even the 500-page *New History of Early English Drama* (1997), which seeks to treat comprehensively every aspect of the drama, devotes only a brief essay to costumes and props, and that essay gives scarcely two paragraphs to the look of personified characters.[74]

How, then, may personified characters be reconstructed? In *The Compleat Gentleman* Henry Peacham outlines a strategy when he advises readers on learning about the deities of Greece and Rome. Statues, he suggests, offer the most direct source of information. Ideally, people should journey to France, Spain, and Italy, where they may see classical statuary in profusion

not so comprehensive

but, if travel proves impossible, they should resort to "the gardens and galleries of great men"[75] at home, and Peacham singles out the collections at Arundel House and Somerset House in London. "It is not enough," he continues, "for an ingenuous [i.e., noble] gentleman to behold these [statues] with a vulgar eye: but he must be able to distinguish them, and tell who and what they be."[76] To this end Peacham proposes four steps. A gentleman should acquire "generall learning in history and poetry. Whereby we are taught to know Jupiter by his thunder-bolt, Mars by his armour, Neptune by his trident."[77] He should also study the images on ancient coins; peruse the woodcuts of ancient statues in a work called *Icones statuarum quae hodie visuntur Romae*; and view statuary in the company of a knowledgeable acquaintance. Virtually any literate person with access to a book collection might follow Peacham's first suggestion, but one wonders how many of his contemporaries could adopt the others: numismatics,[78] then as now, was an esoteric field of study; copies of *Icones statuarum*[79] must have been scarce; and knowledgeable guides must have been similarly hard to find. Peacham's fourfold program, however, is exemplary in emphasizing the value of bringing together different kinds of materials. In the spirit of his interdisciplinary approach, this reconstruction of Shakespeare's personified characters includes not only the statuary and literature of antiquity but also a range of artifacts popular in the sixteenth century.

A treasure trove of information is at hand in texts of civic pageants that employ personifications alongside mythological figures and historical personages.[80] These pageants were, for the most part, conceived and written by dramatists who worked in the theatres of Elizabethan and Jacobean London. Of particular interest are the lord mayors' pageants, which were held in London every October and which became increasingly elaborate in the early seventeenth century. The playwrights responsible for the pageants – some so prolific as Thomas Heywood, Anthony Munday, and Thomas Middleton – wrote descriptions that were published in pamphlet form. Also extant are accounts by Ben Jonson and Thomas Dekker of the single most important pageant of Shakespeare's lifetime: the coronation procession of King James I in 1604. Seven triumphal arches were constructed on the streets of London, and those structures were filled with personifications of all kinds: most were painted or sculptural but professional actors (e.g., Edward Alleyn) represented some.[81] Augmenting these written records are pictures: the arches were engraved by William Kip and published in Stephen Harrison's *Arches of Triumph* (1604). No similar visual record exists of Queen Elizabeth's coronation procession,[82] but a detailed written account survives, as do reports of her entry into other cities and her visits to the nobility at their country estates. Collectively, this material brings to life a world where personified figures were as commonplace as billboards and neon signs today.

Although the creators of civic pageants were highly inventive, they depended upon traditional representations, and those writers had at hand a rich fund of symbolism in the form of what they called "devices." This catchall term designates a symbolic design, especially of a witty nature, and they appeared everywhere. As Henri Estienne observes, "a devise presents it selfe to the eyes of all the world, in being placed upon frontice-pieces of houses, in galleries, upon armes, and a thousand other places, whence it becomes a delightfull object to the sight."[83] Coats of arms, consisting of a symbolic picture and a brief motto, are a species of device.[84] They identify an individual or a family and they frequently appear in Renaissance portraits of aristocrats. Shakespeare himself was paid to compose an impresa (to use the Italian term) for the Earl of Rutland in 1613. Imprese find their way onto the stage too. In Marlowe's *Edward II* the barons express their hostility toward the king by describing the devices painted on their shields (2.2.11–46). And in Shakespeare's *Pericles* knights at a tournament present decorated shields to a princess, who describes the symbolic pictures and reads aloud their Latin mottoes (2.2.16–47).[85]

A close relation of the impresa is the emblem, a tripartite artifact consisting of a symbolic picture, motto, and explanatory poem. William Camden explains that while an impresa is "borne by noble and learned personages to notifie some particular conceit of their owne," emblems "propound some generall instruction to all."[86] The emblem's picture takes the form of an engraving or woodcut on paper, and these emblems were gathered together and published as books. Compared with their Continental counterparts, the English produced few such collections. The most important, Geoffrey Whitney's *A Choice of Emblemes*, did not appear until 1586, fifty-five years after Andrea Alciato began the vogue with his *Emblematum Liber* (1531). Significantly, Whitney's book was published in Leiden rather than London, and it is a derivative work, recycling pictures and ideas from Continental emblem books. We may be tempted to dismiss Whitney's book as yet another indication of a dependence bordering on literary and pictorial theft. A more benign view sees in *A Choice of Emblemes* evidence of the extent to which emblems and visual symbols in general transcend national and linguistic boundaries. Inevitably such emblems find their way into English decorative schemes. Thus around the borders of William Sheldon's tapestries of the Seasons at Hatfield House near London, one can still see pictures and mottoes lifted from emblem books. Even more important, emblems infiltrate the drama. Dumb shows on the stage, Rosemary Freeman points out, are "in both form and function only a much more elaborate version of the pictures in an emblem book."[87] The dialogue in plays also finds inspiration in emblems: in *The White Devil*, for example, two characters describe an emblem, translate the Latin verse, and explicate its meaning (2.1.323–31).[88]

The English masque, peopled with mythological figures and abstractions, draws upon the same sources of symbolism as emblematists used. In fact, Allardyce Nicoll observes that spectators "looked upon the masques as nothing but a series of living emblems."[89] Writers of such masques ransacked books of mythography, ancient histories, and various artifacts for their symbolism. The foremost practitioner of the genre, Ben Jonson, was also one of the most learned men of his time, and the printed texts of his masques explain in elaborate detail the roots of his symbolism. Unfortunately, masques were as ephemeral as they were expensive to produce, and no pictorial record survives of their performance, save for the painting of Sir Henry Unton and his family in London's National Gallery. What have survived are most of the costume and scenic designs by Inigo Jones, Jonson's partner. Jones's draftsmanship is superb, and some pictures are in color, allowing us to imagine how the figures looked in performance. The populace of London did not, of course, have an opportunity to see masques at court, but playwrights, especially in the early seventeenth century, began to include in their plays scenes inspired by masques, thus democratizing this most aristocratic of genres and allowing for the dramatization of specifically political points.

More numerous than costume designs or devices or pageants are the prints produced during Shakespeare's lifetime.[90] Woodcuts, engravings, and etchings survive on every imaginable subject, from religion to sex, and they include a multitude of personifications. Prints are plentiful because it was so very profitable to make them (fig. 1). Albrecht Dürer once complained that his paintings, while much coveted, required huge investments of time and failed to provide him a satisfactory living. To a correspondent in 1509 he wrote: "No one shall ever again compel me to paint a picture entailing so much work...from now on I shall stick to engraving. If I had stuck to that, I would now be 1000 fl[orins] ahead."[91] Rewarding for artists and publishers to produce, prints were affordable to middle-class buyers in a way that oil paintings were not. Engravings and etchings could be purchased singly or, by the well-to-do, in book form; they were

1 Interior of a business where prints are made. Engraving by Philips Galle after Jan van de Straeten (Stradanus)

And it could be meant to run as a re-strike

sold in markets (fig. 2) and booksellers' stalls. Single-leaf woodcuts, even less expensive, were hawked by peddlers. Prints, moreover, could enjoy an exceptionally long life, for although particular exemplars were susceptible to destruction by fire or water, a print could be issued and reissued for decades, until the metal plate or woodblock that produced it finally wore out.[92] Because so many prints were made and because they were easily portable, they circulated throughout Europe. Those that so offended Queen Elizabeth when she discovered them in her prayer book had been bought from a German traveler. It was through such foreign prints that the English came to know not only the paintings, buildings, and gardens of the Continent but also the visual symbols that were the common property of European culture in the Renaissance. In the aggregate, those prints acquaint us with the range of possibilities for the artistic rendering of abstractions.

Prints, pageants, devices, emblems, and masques, along with plays and poetry – these are the raw materials of this study. Before we look at specific instances, however, we need to consider the extent to which people could decode the symbolism they saw in various artifacts and entertainments.

2 Merchants selling prints at an indoor market in Prague. Print by Aegidius Sadeler II

VI

Courtiers who witnessed or participated in masques represent one end of a spectrum: presumably they had a fairly high degree of visual sophistication if only because they were familiar with heraldry and other sorts of witty devices. Participants in Elizabethan and Jacobean tournaments, Alan Young reminds us, needed to possess not only armor, weaponry, and horse but also "an appropriate impresa."[93] Even courtiers, however, could not immediately have understood all the symbolism of Ben Jonson, Thomas Campion, Francis Beaumont, Aurelian Townsend, and other masquemakers.[94] Jonson in particular delighted in the learned and the arcane, and it was not in his nature to make things easy for spectators. Discussing his *Masque of Queens*, he writes of the witches, who appear in the antimasque:

> to have made themselves their own decipherers, and each one to have told upon their entrance what they were and whether they would, had been a most piteous hearing, and utterly unworthy any quality of a poem, wherein a writer should always trust somewhat to the capacity of the spectator, especially at spectacles, where men, beside inquiring eyes, are understood to bring quick ears.[95]

Jonson assumes that spectators will be equipped with a certain degree of acuity, but they will need to listen closely as well as observe. This does not mean that Jonson spells everything out, for the effort to comprehend the symbolism of a masque constitutes a source of delight. As Stephen Orgel notes, "we must not underestimate the Renaissance's love of mysteries and enigmas. To find oneself in the presence of mystic and impenetrable truths afforded considerable pleasure."[96]

Those mysteries flattered the erudite, who knew that visual symbols enjoyed a prestige conferred by classical antiquity. John Ferne observes that "domb signes and pictured formes" had their origin in Egypt: "this did that wise nation, to the intent their sacred misteries should not be prophaned or contemned of the ignorant & untaught multitude."[97] Symbols that resist easy interpretation also helped preserve distinctions in social class. The contrast, for example, between courtly sophisticates and the "untaught multitude" is dramatized in John Ford's *Love's Sacrifice*. When Mauruccio devises a picture of himself containing a "most rare transparent crystal in the form of a heart," intending it for the woman he desires, his puzzled servant asks the meaning: "But now, sir, for the conceit" (2.1.62–63, 67).[98] Mauruccio's reply emphasizes the gulf separating master and servant: "Simplicity and ignorance, prate no more! Blockhead, dost not understand yet?" (lines 68–70).

If courtiers represent a sophisticated sensibility, the groundlings who surround the stage at public theatres represent the other end of the spectrum. Yet Hamlet, in his advice to the players, pays them a compliment even as he disparages them: "O, it offends me to the soul to hear a robustious periwig-pated fellow tear a passion to tatters, to very rags, to spleet [split] the ears of the groundlings, who for the most part are capable of nothing but inexplicable dumb shows and noise" (3.2.8–12).[99] Such dumb shows may telescope the action,[100] as the show preceding the play-within-the-play in *Hamlet* does. Or dumb shows may present a situation in symbolic terms, as they do in *Gorboduc* or *The Spanish Tragedy*. Whatever the show's function in a particular play, Hamlet suggests that the most humble playgoers possess at least some ability to make sense of those pantomimic actions.[101] If the groundlings did not possess that capacity, why would Shakespeare create such a show in this very scene of *Hamlet*, where the prince instructs the visiting players?

Groundlings at the Globe were among the same people who witnessed street pageants; and creators of such pageants were mindful that spectators might need help in understanding what they saw. In *Sidero-thriambos*, a pageant for the ironmongers in 1618, Anthony Munday writes, "For better understanding the true morality of this devise, the personages have all emblemes and properties in their hands, and so neere them, that the weakest capacity may take knowledge of them."[102] We detect impatience in Munday's acknowledgment that certain figures might not be instantly explicable to all – hence the need for those "emblemes and properties." But even spectators of greater sophistication must have had their powers of understanding challenged by the sheer profusion of personifications in Elizabethan–Jacobean culture.[103]

Whether aristocrat or plebeian, a viewer would more readily identify some symbolic figures than others. Consider, for instance, a print designed by Maarten van Heemskerck and published by Philips Galle in 1563 (fig. 3). One in a series of six known as *The Wretchedness of Wealth*, this particular print, representing the means by which wealth may be acquired, deploys six standing figures, who form part of a procession. At their front (and on the extreme left) stands Fortune: winged, wearing a blindfold, and sporting a forelock, she holds in her right hand a purse bulging with money and, in her left, a beggar's shallow bowl. In all likelihood she would have been instantly recognizable to everyone, for she is a favorite of Renaissance artists.[104] At the far right side of the print is a fierce muscular figure in Roman armor: he holds a torch in his left hand and an unsheathed sword in his right. The print labels him Violence (Vis), and what he embodies must have been apparent to most observers.

Between these two figures stand five others, whose symbolism is more problematic. Next to Fortune stands a poorly dressed man striking a stone with a flint. The caption calls him Labour, and next to him walks Diligence, a woman who holds a distaff and spindle; set in the distaff is a candle, "presumably signifying that she works deep into the night."[105] Their characteristic activities help us understand the identities of these two figures.

3 *The Wretchedness of Wealth*, one in a series of six prints by Maarten van Heemskerck

Further to the right stands Deceit (Fraus), whose two faces (masks) signal a duplicitous nature; she holds a pair of spectacles, which she means
to sell.[106] Again, a thoughtful observer would almost certainly guess the
meaning. But the woman between Diligence and Deceit is more difficult to
interpret. Named Frugality (Parsimonia), she has her shoes on her hip; she
"walks barefoot to save her shoes and stockings."[107] Her nature may have
been apparent only to the most alert observers. Finally, the shadowy figure of
Mendacity, who lacks either a symbolic object or significant activity, would
almost certainly have remained mysterious without the identifying label. A
single picture, then, confronts the beholder with multiple personifications,
at least a couple of which elude easy identification.

The range of challenges posed by Heemskerck's engraving characterizes virtually every pageant, masque, and emblem book. Of these the last
places the greatest demand on the acuity of observers, for the symbolism
of emblems can be extraordinarily obscure; hence the need for explanatory
poems explaining the designs. Similarly, imprese depend for their meaning
on the interplay of word and picture. As Samuel Daniel says, "the figure

without the mot [motto], or the mot without the figure signifie nothing."[108] In masques the meanings of personified figures may become fully apparent only in the masquers' speeches, the counterpart of an emblem's descriptive poem or an impresa's motto; and perhaps only the *readers* of Jonson's masques find sufficient explanation (in the form of the author's elaborate notes) to comprehend fully what spectators beheld in performance. Civic pageants and plays may present a somewhat lesser degree of difficulty, for their symbolism tends to be less arcane than that of emblems or masques. The devisers of such entertainments, appealing to a broad cross section of the populace, resist a penchant for the outré. But they are careful to identify symbolic figures not only by costumes and props but also by spoken words. In all of these cases, it is the combination of word and visual image that ensures accessibility of meaning. Even Shakespeare takes no chance that playgoers will remain baffled by a symbolic character. Thus when a personification walks onstage, he identifies himself: Time in *The Winter's Tale* may carry an hourglass but he announces his name nonetheless.

Although the modern reader or playgoer may not be accustomed to envisaging the look of personified characters or identifying similarities between artistic representation and stage presentation, Henry Peacham reminds us that his countrymen were thoroughly at home in a world of symbolic personages. Discussing classical deities and mythological creations, Peacham cannot restrain his enthusiasm: he speaks of "the pleasure of seeing and conversing with these old heroes."[109] For Shakespeare's England, moreover, the study of deities and other symbolic figures represented a shrewd investment, one that had considerable practical value: "the profit of knowing them redounds to all poets, painters, architects, and generally to such as may have occasion to imploy any of these, and by consequent to all gentlemen."[110] Finally, Peacham, who drew what may be the only contemporary sketch we possess of a Shakespearean play in performance,[111] explains that iconography has specific relevance for theatrical entertainment. Knowledge of pictorial symbols, he points out, will benefit "poets for the presentation of comedies, tragedies, maskes, shewes, or any learned scene whatsoever."[112]

My purpose here is not to posit a connection between any particular entertainment or artifact, on the one hand, and a personification of Shakespeare's, on the other. After all, we can never know with certainty what the playwright had seen.[113] Nor can we know what playgoers encountered in their daily lives. What we can do, however, is recognize that certain personifications were commonplace, appearing in a variety of art forms, and that playwrights could presumably have depended upon playgoers to make a connection between what they had previously seen at home or in the streets and what they were seeing on the theatrical stage. In fact, playwrights creating symbolic characters needed to assume the playgoers' familiarity with visual symbolism and a readiness to be intrigued, delighted, and moved by that symbolism.

The concluding speeches of *Love's Labour's Lost* present a puzzle, for neither the 1598 Quarto nor the 1623 Folio indicates speech prefixes for the songs of Spring and Winter. Since we don't know the identity of the speakers, or singers, we also don't know what the actors looked like. Were they represented on Shakespeare's stage as male or female? Young or old? How were they costumed? And what hand props may they have brought onto stage?

Modern editors have for the most part sidestepped these questions, though some have conjectured the singers' identities. John Kerrigan, noting Armado's query – "will you hear the dialogue that the two learned men have compiled in praise of the owl and the cuckoo?" (5.2.885–87) – identifies the singers as "Holofernes and Nathaniel. No doubt the pair take the parts of the owl and the cuckoo in the *dialogue* which follows."[1] G. R. Hibbard is only a little less certain: "Since no entry is provided for either Spring or Winter, these parts may have been represented by Sir Nathaniel and Holofernes."[2] H. R. Woudhuysen believes that "the singers are presumably *the two learned men*... who compiled the dialogue, in which case they are Holofernes and Nathaniel."[3] These views are perfectly plausible. It's not illogical to suppose that the makers of the songs should give them voice. The songs are so brief, moreover, that they hardly warrant the introduction of actors who are not already in the cast.

Productions of Shakespeare's comedy, however, rarely follow the suggestions of editors. As Hibbard notes, "Most directors have preferred to hand these lyrics over to the rustics, but there have been occasions when the entire cast has joined in."[4] The performance history of *Love's Labour's Lost*, first acted c. 1594, reveals an almost bewildering variety in the presentation of the songs. In John Barton's Royal Shakespeare Company production of 1965, villagers recited – rather than sang – in front of wicker figures representing a cuckoo and an owl. David Jones, directing the RSC production of 1973, gave Spring's song to Nathaniel, while an unnamed villager sang Winter's. In John Barton's 1978 production for the RSC, Nathaniel, his head adorned with a green laurel wreath, held a glove puppet of a cuckoo during the song, while Holofernes, wearing a brown and red wreath, held the glove puppet of an owl. In Barry Kyle's 1984 staging for the RSC, Spring was represented by Jaquenetta, Winter by other villagers. And in the BBC television production, directed by Elijah Moshinsky and broadcast in 1985, a woman dressed in yellow sang the song of Spring while another woman, in gray, sang Winter's.

We can never know, of course, how closely any of these stagings resembles Shakespeare's. Nevertheless, in the belief that conjecture may prove fruitful, I should like to suggest that Shakespeare was inspired by the representation of the seasons in the pictorial arts of his time. Popular subjects, the seasons were depicted in paintings, tapestries, woodcuts, etchings, and engravings. The last three categories are the most useful for our purposes, for many more people had an opportunity to see prints than ever had a chance to view a particular painting or tapestry. Since woodcuts, etchings, and engravings were relatively easy to produce, convenient to transport, and inexpensive to purchase, they were both plentiful and widely dispersed in Renaissance Europe. Prints of the seasons, which typically appeared as sets of four, allow us to see how Shakespeare's contemporaries commonly envisioned Spring and Winter.[5]

Spring

Perhaps the most iconographically interesting pictures of the seasons are those depicting a triumphal chariot, or wagon. Typically, a personification of the season rides in the wagon, surrounded by other symbolic figures. For example, the Dutch Monogrammist AP, who worked about 1536/7, presents Spring as a woman standing atop a wagon and holding a basket of flowers (fig. 4). Around the wagon appear mostly classical figures, including Apollo, the Nine Muses, Orpheus, Pan, and Dionysus. And participants hold aloft banners with symbols of the months – March, April, and May. Although the iconographically complex program may seem to have little significance for a staging of *Love's Labour's Lost*, at least two nineteenth-century productions employed processions at the play's end. At Covent Garden in 1839, Madame Lucia Vestris represented the "Emblem of Spring," accompanied by wildmen, huntsmen, shepherds, and shepherdesses; the "Emblem of Winter" was accompanied by wild-men, woodcutters, logbearers, and lords of misrule.[6] At Sadler's Wells in 1857, Samuel Phelps staged processions for the seasons, each of whom rode in a chariot.[7] Although Shakespeare may have emulated the processions of the Dutch Monogrammist (and anticipated the strategies of Vestris and Phelps), such staging would not only have been cumbersome but also

4 Spring in her chariot, by Monogrammist AP

would have suffered another disadvantage: it would have necessitated the hiring of many additional actors (along with the provision of costumes) to fill out the processions, a considerable expense for the sake of a single scene. The complication of a symbolic procession, moreover, might have detracted from the simplicity and charm of the songs themselves.

Shakespeare did not need to resort to a panoply of rustic folk in the fashion of Madame Vestris, or to a panoply of mythological figures in the fashion of the Dutch Monogrammist, for he had at hand a tradition of genre scenes, employed to depict Spring in the later sixteenth century. Invariably these have an outdoor setting, frequently a garden. For example, an etching by Hessel Gerritsz after David Vinckboons depicts the paraphernalia of a Renaissance garden (parterres, fountain, wooden railing) against the background of a great house surrounded by tall trees; aristocratic men and women are at leisure while gardeners wield shovels, rake, and wheelbarrow.[8] A representation of the season by Johannes Barra after Pieter Stevens depicts another large garden with a palace in the background; in the foreground, men and women enjoy music.[9] An outdoor scene by Jan Saenredam after Hendrik Goltzius also makes music central to seasonal activity: a man plays a lute while, next to him, a woman has an open book (perhaps of music) on her lap.[10] In a garden behind them couples stroll, while another man and woman, mostly hidden by foliage, embrace. Hieronymus Cock, in a rendering of Ver (Spring) after Lambert Lombard, makes explicit the romantic love evident in such depictions: a partly nude woman holds flowers in her hand while winged Cupid touches her shoulder and breast; in the background men and women enjoy food, drink, and music.[11] Especially later in the Renaissance, genre scenes became increasingly simple and spare. Herman Saftleven, in a print dating from the early to mid-seventeenth century, depicts several youths swimming in the sea,[12] while his contemporary, Jan van Almeloveen, evokes spring by a man with a fishing pole.[13] Such scenes could have furnished hints to a playwright who meant to evoke the season by the appearance of an actor. But swimming would have been difficult if not impossible to depict onstage; and neither a lone fisherman nor musician would necessarily have been sufficient to signal a particular season.

More useful to Shakespeare would have been personifications of the season, for he could emulate these by a single actor whose significance would be easily recognized. Fairly typical is a print by Jan Sadeler after Dirk Barentsz (Theodor Bernards). Dominating the composition is a seated woman with flowers in her hair (fig. 5). She also holds a pot of flowers on her knee, while her other hand grasps the branch of a tree. Still another pot of flowers sits on the ground nearby, underscoring her identification with a nature coming to leaf and life. In the background the artist includes activities proper to the season: a hunting party, a hawking expedition, and lovers in an arbor. An engraving by Philips Galle after Maarten de Vos personifies Ver as a young woman with flowers in her hair; in her right hand she holds a bouquet and, in her left, she holds the long stems of other flowers (fig. 6). Next to her is a vase containing a single flower and a smaller pot with another kind of flower. Various garden implements – rake, shovel, watering bottle – fill the foreground while gardeners work in the background.

Jacob Matham, in contrast, represents the season as a nude young man with a drapery tied loosely over his shoulders, long hair, and a physique suggesting androgyny.[14] He holds a pot of flowers while, in the background, couples take their leisure in a garden. Vegetables and flowers fill the decorative border of the print, along with the zodiacal symbols of Gemini, Taurus, and Aries. Yet another rendering of the season by Matham, after Hendrik Goltzius, depicts a mostly nude youth who has leaves in his hair and who holds a basket of leafy branches.[15] In the background young men

5 Spring, with flowerpots, by Jan Sadeler after Dirk Barentsz (Theodor Bernards)

and women sit at a table outdoors and listen to musicians, while other couples stroll or embrace under huge trees. Again, the appropriate zodiacal symbols appear in the sky.

The prints described here indicate that, although no single formula was used to depict Spring, artists frequently employed a personification, which they supplemented with inset genre scenes. The personification of the season usually consists of a young woman or, less often, an adolescent male. If female, the figure is dressed in a simple light tunic. Whether male or female, the figure is readily identifiable by the flowers and leaves worn in the hair, held in the hand, or contained in pots.

The evidence of courtly and civic entertainments amplifies the information gleaned from prints.[16] In *The Spring's Glory* by Thomas Nabbes, a masque published in 1638 but probably never performed, Spring wears "*a green robe*" (line 223),[17] while her garment in Francis Kynaston's *Corona Minervae*, a masque presented before Prince Charles in 1635, is "*of greene taffata, fringed with silver.*"[18] In *Chloridia*, a masque performed "by the

6 Spring, with flowers in her hair and her hands, by Philips Galle after Maarten de Vos

queen's majesty and her ladies, at Shrovetide, 1630," Ben Jonson describes
Spring's upper garment as green, while "*under it* [she wore] *a white robe*"
(lines 28–29).[19] In similar fashion, Henry Peacham, describing the month
of May, says that the figure "must be drawne … clad in a robe of white and
greene."[20] Flowers invariably adorn the personification of Spring. In *The
Triumphs of Peace*, John Squire's pageant celebrating the inauguration of
the lord mayor in 1620, "*Ver was suted in greene taffety, a chaplet of flowers in her hand.*"[21] In *The Spring's Glory* Nabbes describes the garment as
"*wrought over with flowers*" (line 223), while Spring's outfit in *Chloridia* is
similarly "*wrought with flowers*" (line 29). Peacham specifies "daffadilles,
hawthorne, blewbottels" on the embroidery of May's robe, "a garland of
white damaske & red roses" upon May's head.[22] In *The Masque of Flowers*,
performed in the Banqueting House at Whitehall, 6 January 1614, Spring's
elaborate attire includes "*a high tire* [headdress] *on her head, antic with
knots of fair hair and cobweb lawns rising one above another, garnished with
flowers to some height … a kirtle* [gown] *of yellow cloth of gold, branched*

7 The triumph of Spring, by Virgil Solis

with leaves; a mantle of green and silver stuff cut out in leaves; white buskins, tied with green ribbons fringed with flowers" (lines 89–95).[23]

Such flowers are the single most important iconographic attribute of the season: in an entertainment by Middleton, the Seasons "call up Flora, the goddesse of the Spring."[24] Significantly, triumphal processions commonly locate Flora in Spring's chariot. The woodcut by Monogrammist AP, discussed above, places Flora, her hair adorned with flowers, in the coach (fig. 4, p. 27 above). In a somewhat simpler composition by Virgil Solis, Ver sits atop the chariot and plays a musical instrument while Flora, a garland in her hand and flowers in her hair, sits below (fig. 7). And a procession by Antonio Tempesta seems almost to conflate Flora and Spring, for the latter not only has flowers in her hair and left hand but also, in her right, four garlands of the kind that Solis gives Flora.[25] Three putti seated in Tempesta's chariot, in addition, hold aloft garlands containing the zodiacal symbols of March, April, and May. Perhaps the sort of flowers depicted in these and other prints adorn a character in Shakespeare's *Pericles*, for when he beholds the daughter of King Antiochus, Pericles says, "See where she comes, apparelled like the spring" (1.1.12).

Of the characters in *Love's Labour's Lost*, Jaquenetta would most suitably represent the season. A pregnant young woman (5.2.672–77), she suggests the fertility implicit in evocations of the season by Virgil Solis and others. Solis' triumphal procession (fig. 7) includes three figures conventionally identified with sexuality: a monkey sits at the rear, a satyr walks alongside, and Cupid, bow and arrow in hand, hovers above the chariot.

Winter

Representations of Winter, like those of Spring, take many forms; they range from complicated iconographic programs, to genre scenes, to personifications. The Dutch Monogrammist AP depicts a triumphal wagon:

standing atop is Winter with a pot containing a smoking fire balanced on his head.[26] Below sits two-faced Janus, and accompanying the cart are Aeolus, Vulcan, and such personifications as Horror, Paupertas, and Defectus; banners representing December, January, and February are held aloft. This elaborate symbolic program gives way in the later Renaissance to genre scenes chiefly. Aegidius Sadeler, in a very early seventeenth-century engraving after Pieter Stevens, depicts Winter with a picture of men cutting blocks of ice and gathering firewood.[27] In an etching by Hessel Gerritsz after David Vinckboons, men and women skate on the ice surrounding a great house.[28] And Hans Bol represents the season by a man putting on his skates while, in the background, others are already skating.[29] Jan van Almeloveen depicts a man cutting firewood while others skate.[30] To such conventional activities Dutch, Flemish, and German artists sometimes add the slaughtering of a pig.

For all the popularity of genre scenes, artists continued to personify Winter throughout the Renaissance. Typically, the personifications appear as part of a series portraying the four seasons. For example, in a print by Jan Sadeler after Dirk Barentsz, Winter is a seated and bearded old man who wears a long fur-trimmed garment and a similarly trimmed hat.[31] He stretches out one hand and foot toward the warmth of an open fire, while he holds a tankard containing a warm drink with the other hand. Near his chair a dog lies curled up, observed by a cat, while outdoors are the ice skaters common to genre scenes. Balthasar Jenichen, who also made a series of four prints representing the seasons, varies the type. In a print after Jost Amman, Jenichen represents Winter by two seated men warming their hands before a fire indoors, while outdoors a horse draws a sleigh through the snow.[32] The bearded Winter by Philips Galle after Maarten van Heemskerck wears fur-trimmed garments, holds a staff (presumably for support), and clasps a pot containing a smoking fire; in the background people huddle next to a fireplace and, outdoors, men and women skate on a frozen river (fig. 8). The zodiacal symbols of Pisces, Aquarius, and Capricorn appear above. Finally, the depiction of the season in a print by Philips Galle after Jan van de Straeten (also part of a series of four), places near its center a seated old man with his hands held over a fire; other figures perform such seasonal activities as carding yarn and hauling wood.[33]

Although personified Winter usually appears as male, there are exceptions. In a print by Philips Galle after Maarten de Vos, Winter is a woman who holds a bridle (a common symbol both of Nemesis and Temperance); beneath her feet is an anchor, symbolic of hope, a herald of the coming spring.[34] Galle combines this personification with genre scenes: in the

8 Winter, with a pot of fire, by Philips Galle after Maarten van Heemskerck

background people ice skate, ride in a sleigh, butcher a cow, and roast a pig. Wenceslaus Hollar in the mid-seventeenth century made several series of etchings in which Winter appears as female.[35]

Most personifications, however, represent the coldest season as an aged man[36] warming himself; and the source of that warmth is usually a pot containing a smoking fire. Jacob Matham, for example, pictures a stooped and bearded figure whose hat and coat are trimmed with fur and who rests his weight upon a T-shaped cane (fig. 9). With his other hand he holds a pot from which smoke rises. In still another representation of Winter (after Hendrik Goltzius), Matham shows a similarly bearded and attired old man, who warms himself by the fire contained in a pot.[37] This and other pictures dating from the late sixteenth century recall the much earlier figure of Winter by the Dutch Monogrammist AP.

Winter also makes an appearance in courtly and civic entertainments. Along with the other Seasons, he has a featured role in Thomas Nashe's *Summer's Last Will and Testament* (performed c. summer 1592);

9 Winter, with fur-trimmed garments and hat, by Jacob Matham

unfortunately, the surviving stage directions fail to tell us anything specific about his costume.[38] In *The Masque of Flowers*, however, we find a detailed description: Winter is "*attired like an old man, in a short gown of silk shag* [cloth having a velvet nap on one side], *like withered grass all frosted and snowed over, and his cap, gown, gamashes* [leggings] *and mittens furred crimson, with long white hair and beard, hung with icicles*" (lines 71–75). Francis Kynaston, in *Corona Minervae*, adds a garland appropriate to the season:

"*Winter* [enters] *in a long gowne of freeze, his haire and beard all made of icicles, a garland of hollies and ivie intwin'd upon his head.*"[39] In Ben Jonson's *Masque of Beauty*, presented at Whitehall, 10 January 1608, the character named Januarius appears in a "*robe of ash color, long, fringed with silver; a white mantle*" (lines 15–16).[40] In John Squire's *The Triumphs of Peace*, Winter appears "*in a furred gowne, and in his hand a pan of burning coles.*"[41] Finally, Winter's facial expression must be the antithesis of Spring's: Ulpian Fulwell speaks of "horie Hyemps frowne."[42]

On Shakespeare's stage it would have been easy to evoke such figures by giving an adult actor a beard, dressing him in a fur-trimmed coat and hat, and by putting in his hands a smoking pot and, possibly, a cane or staff. The beard would be "clogd with iseckles," as Peacham describes personified December and January; makeup could supply the requisite "nose redde."[43] Spectators accustomed to seeing representations of Winter would quickly have made a connection between the appropriately garbed actor and the season.

Of the characters in the cast, the most suitable for this role is Dull. The advantages of employing the constable are fourfold. First, it seems appropriate that the characters enacting the two seasons be of roughly the same social status. There is less of a disparity between Dull and Jaquenetta than, say, between either Holofernes or Nathaniel and the maid; Dull and Jaquenetta share an unlettered, unsophisticated, and humble condition. Second, Dull and Jaquenetta enjoy roughly the same theatrical prominence: they are onstage together in two scenes (1.2 and 4.2); and although he is onstage in two additional scenes and she only in one, they speak about the same number of lines overall. Third, Dull is specifically identified with music when Holofernes, looking forward to the entertainment, says, "we will employ thee," and Dull replies, "I'll make one in a dance, or so; or I will play / On the tabor to the Worthies, and let them dance the hay" (5.1.152–54).[44] Fourth, although the stage directions of neither the Quarto nor the Folio indicate the presence of either Dull or Jaquenetta in the play's final scene, and although this may seem to argue against their performance of the songs, these two characters are not necessary to the resolution of the plot and thus the actors are free to take on additional roles at the play's close. All they need do is don the appropriate costume, carry the requisite hand prop, and enter to sing the songs.[45]

There is a sound theatrical reason for assigning the songs of Spring and Winter to actors who differ markedly in appearance, even if other actors join in the singing.[46] Those songs form, in Armado's expression, a dialogue; they represent disparate seasons of the year and of life. Accordingly, their tone is different – exuberant versus restrained. In a theatre where ideas necessarily take physical form, it makes sense to assign the songs to characters dissimilar in age, sex, and demeanor. The physical appearance of Spring as a nubile woman and Winter as a bearded old man would complement the content and mood of the songs. And the appropriate hand props – a pot of flowers in the one instance, a pot of fire in the other – would underscore the contrast.

Cuckoo and owl

Armado introduces the songs, saying, "This side is Hiems, Winter; this Ver, the Spring; the one maintained by the owl, th' other by the cuckoo" (5.2.891–93). Despite the contrast, each song enthusiastically embraces the delights of its own season. Spring, especially through the evocation of flowers and birds, conjures up a pastoral setting, a world of shepherds and ploughmen, as well as maidens bleaching smocks in the sun:

When daisies pied, and violets blue,
    And lady-smocks all silver-white,
And cuckoo-buds of yellow hue
    Do paint the meadows with delight,
The cuckoo then on every tree
Mocks married men; for thus sings he,
             "Cuckoo;
Cuckoo, cuckoo" – O word of fear,
Unpleasing to a married ear!

When shepherds pipe on oaten straws,
    And merry larks are ploughmen's clocks;
When turtles tread, and rooks and daws,
    And maidens bleach their summer smocks,
The cuckoo then on every tree
Mocks married men; for thus sings he,
             "Cuckoo;
Cuckoo, cuckoo" – O word of fear,
Unpleasing to a married ear!   (lines 894–911)

Winter, while acknowledging cold and ice, manages to find comfort in mundane seasonal activities – bringing firewood indoors, stirring a pot, roasting crab apples:

When icicles hang by the wall,
  And Dick the shepherd blows his nail,
And Tom bears logs into the hall,
  And milk comes frozen home in pail;
When blood is nipp'd, and ways be foul,
Then nightly sings the staring owl,
      "Tu-whit, tu-who!" –
A merry note,
While greasy Joan doth keel the pot.
When all aloud the wind doth blow,
  And coughing drowns the parson's saw,
And birds sit brooding in the snow,
  And Marian's nose looks red and raw;
When roasted crabs hiss in the bowl,
Then nightly sings the staring owl,
      "Tu-whit, tu-who!" –
A merry note,
While greasy Joan doth keel the pot.

        (lines 912–29)

The owl's song may confound our expectations since it makes no apology for the obvious discomforts of short days and frigid nights. Instead, it cheerfully accepts its place in the rhythm of the year.[47]

 Together, the two songs celebrate what C. L. Barber has called "the going-on power of life."[48] That vitality is epitomized by the two birds, with their symbolic associations. The cuckoo suggests the powerful impulse to propagate; it implies a primal sexual energy, as we learn from Michael Drayton's "The Owl," where the bird of spring's song is described: "His song still tends to vanitie and lust, / Amorous deceits, poligamies unjust" (lines 1025–26)."[49] The bird mocks married men because "its cry is so reminiscent of *cuckold*, and its habit of laying its eggs in another bird's nest resembles the behaviour of a man who seduces another man's wife or of a married woman who couples with a man other than her husband."[50] The cuckoo's vitality makes it virtually synonymous with the season: "The cuckoo was by almost universal consent the sign of spring."[51]

 The owl, for its part, has implications for human sexuality too, though these are less immediately apparent to the modern playgoer. Today we are likely to recall that the owl is the symbol of Athena, classical goddess of wisdom, and that the bird was particularly associated with melancholy and death in the Middle Ages and Renaissance.[52] (Lady Macbeth calls the owl "the fatal bellman" [2.2.3].) In fact, Catherine McLay finds meaning in this very cluster of associations: "the concluding song of the owl epitomizes Wisdom because it takes account not only of Life but also of Death."[53] Shakespeare's audience may well have felt this, but, given the context of the dramatic action, that audience would almost certainly have seen another significance as primary, for the owl is "sometimes used to refer to the specific sin of lust."[54] The sound of the owl's cry, moreover, may have a specifically sexual meaning, as Peter Holland suggests: by "Tu-whit, to-who!" the owl "may be calling 'to it,' an encouragement to have sex (for, as King Lear will remind us, birds, as well as bees, do it: 'the wren goes to't'" [4.6.112]).[55] And the owl, like the cuckoo, is closely identified with folly, especially in matters of the heart.[56]

Today we have largely lost the visual vocabulary represented by the bird on the title-page of *The Owles Almanacke,* a satire aimed at astrologers, published in London in 1618.[57] This owl, dressed in ruff and gown, and perched on a chair, is busy in his study: he draws symbols in a book resting on a lectern. Far from representing wisdom, this owl embodies the opposite value. The comic implications are suggested not only by the absurdity of situation but also by the work's subtitle: *Found in an Ivy-bush written in old Characters, and now published in English by the painefull labours of Mr. Jocundary Merrie-braines.* The birds represented in Ben Jonson's *Masque of Owls* (performed 19 August 1624) are, similarly, all objects of scorn.[58] The particular application of the owl in the realm of romantic love is apparent in a print by Cornelis Claesz Clock, an artist who worked in Leiden and Gouda c. 1600–10. This engraving exemplifies folly by depicting a disorderly domestic interior wherein cooking implements lie strewn on the floor, and a man with horns seemingly growing out of his shoulders scratches his head in a gesture of bewilderment (fig. 10). In the background his wife embraces another man, while in the foreground sits an owl on his perch, staring imperturbably at the observer. Another artifact from the sixteenth century – a German flagon in the shape of a standing owl – underscores the significance of this bird in matters of love. On the owl's breast are two lovers holding hands while a man in a fool's cap laughingly gestures toward them, suggesting that this match is not destined to endure.[59] Finally, the owl and mirror appearing behind the bride in *The Peasant Wedding,* painted by Frans Verbeeck in the mid-sixteenth century, suggest that "the people at the wedding feast are 'owlglasses,' foolish, intemperate buffoons and, by analogy, that the viewer who behaves like them should see himself as an

10 Domestic interior, an owl in the foreground, by Cornelis Claesz Clock

owl in the mirror, not just literally, but also in the moral mirror held up by the painting."[60]

We should not be surprised to discover that the songs of both Spring and Winter have in common an acknowledgment of human folly, for the songs seem to have been intended as a mocking complement to the Pageant of the Nine Worthies.[61] Don Armado tells the princess and Navarre that the entertainment of the songs "should have followed in the end of our show" (5.2.887–88). By delaying the songs until the play's closing moments,

Shakespeare extends the gentle mockery beyond the Worthies of the past to include the would-be lovers of the present. The dialogue, observes Francis Berry, "sets the affectations and self-deceiving aims of Navarre and his academy in perspective."[62] If those who earlier joined Navarre in his doomed academic scheme were foolish in turning a blind eye to human nature, so too are the earnest young men even now. In undertaking to fulfill the strictures demanded by the women and forsaking all else for the imagined bliss of wedded love, they ignore the biological imperative epitomized by the lustful cuckoo and the foolish owl, an imperative that knows nothing of oaths and customs, nothing of the institution of marriage.

Theatrical directors responsible for the most compelling revivals of *Titus Andronicus* in the past fifty years have been mindful of the play's potential for generating striking visual images. The single most acclaimed twentieth-century production was Peter Brook's at Stratford-on-Avon in 1955. Inspired by Renaissance art, Brook paid careful attention to what playgoers saw. According to Jan Kott, Brook used a Renaissance palette in costuming his actors: "He has freely taken a full range of yellows from Titian, dressed his priests in the irritating greens of Veronese. The Moor, in his black-blue-and gold costume, is derived from Rubens."[1] Surrounding the actors was a set calculated to disturb: it evoked "fluting pillars or a vast ribbed cage"; theatregoers saw it "tinctured with the wash of blood-red lights."[2] Through the combination of set, lighting, and costumes, Kott concludes, the director managed to create "sequences of great dramatic images. He has found again in Shakespeare the long-lost thrilling spectacle."[3] Seeing that spectacle, Kott reports, was akin to watching a film.

Playgoers at the 1967 production in New York's Delacorte Theatre in Central Park similarly witnessed a series of stunning images. Gerald Freedman, the director, looking for a way to engage an audience surfeited with violence in daily life, decided to distance the dramatic incidents from any particular time and place. He sought to "shock the imagination and subconscious with visual images that recall the richness and depth of primitive rituals."[4] Masks and patterned movement took the place of naturalistic action.

What Brook and Freedman discovered was that the way to stage the play effectively was to exploit the stylized nature of the action. Or perhaps it would be more accurate to say that they accentuated certain aspects of the dramaturgy and suppressed others so as to render the visual stylization more vivid and thus more affecting. When, for example, Brook staged the meeting between the raped, mutilated Lavinia and the garrulous Marcus, the director drastically cut the long Ovidian speech of description. The focus of the scene became the sheer spectacle of desolation: "Lavinia's wounds were ritualised; long crimson scarves hung from her sleeves, symbolising blood."[5] In effect, Brook substituted "visual for verbal effect – the transforming power of costume and lighting for that of metaphor and simile."[6]

What playgoers saw in this production, as in Freedman's, was evidently more important than what they heard, and what they witnessed were characters achieving a status transcending that of individuals: "The actors in both productions were praised for pushing their interpretations into the realm of the heroic or of the personification of abstractions such as evil, revenge, or grief."[7] Titus, played by Laurence Olivier at Stratford, became, in Anthony Quayle's words, "madness itself."[8] Muriel St. Clare Byrne commented of the raped Lavinia at Stratford, "Vivien Leigh, utterly motionless, fixed in despair, seemed the very incarnation of woe."[9] In New York, similarly, Olympia Dukakis as Tamora was "an almost impersonal force."[10] In short, the characters took on the role, in Gerald Freedman's words, of "poetic abstraction." Visual symbolism became the means of generating emotional power.[11]

Such reliance upon visual effect almost certainly characterized the production of *Titus Andronicus* in the 1590s. This, at least, may be gleaned from the record of a 1596 performance at the estate of Sir John Harington, Burley-on-the-Hill, Rutland. On New Year's Day some two hundred of Harington's family and friends watched the play, which was probably performed by the Lord Chamberlain's Men. Jacques Petit, hired to tutor Harington's son, was among the spectators, and he wrote of the experience in a letter to Anthony Bacon. That letter, while revealing no particular detail of performance, contains Petit's overall assessment: "la monstre a plus valeu q[ue] le suject."[12] Although we cannot know precisely what caught Jacques Petit's eye at the 1596 performance, it may well have been a combination of costume, stage action, and special effects.

Modern Shakespeareans, seeking to discover the play's inspiration, look to Elizabethan genres that depend upon visual display. For example, M. C. Bradbrook, recalling Elizabethan civic pageantry, wherein personifications describe themselves and others, observes that *Titus Andronicus* is "more like a pageant than a play."[13] Nicholas Brooke compares the combination of words and spectacle to another Elizabethan form, one that combines symbolic pictures with explanatory poems: Lavinia, raped and her tongue cut out, is "dumb and unmoving like the wood-cuts in an emblem book, while Marcus provides the interpretative verses that were usually printed beneath."[14] Similarly, Ann Haaker, exploring "the extensive pictorial ingenuity of *Titus*," locates correspondences between the dramatic action and specific emblems: "To a symbol-oriented Elizabethan audience, *Titus* is a spectacle consisting of a series of graphic pictures which, like those

in the popular emblem books, offers yet another way to express a view
of the world."[15] Similarly, Michael Hattaway calls the opening of *Titus* "a
very emblematic pageant."[16] Lawrence Danson identifies still another cor-
respondence between the play and the visual arts, calling the entry of the
disguised Lavinia and her sons at Titus' door "a masquelike device."[17]

What all of these Shakespeareans register is the extraordinary significance of things seen in *Titus Andronicus* and the resemblance to genres that
combine words with visual images. I should like to extend this approach by
considering one possibility – that the original staging of Tamora's visit to
Titus' house in the final act involved characters whose identities, through
a change of costume, took on the status of personifications.

Revenge

When in the last act of *Titus Andronicus* Tamora calls on Titus, he recognizes
her at once: "I know thee well / For our proud Empress, mighty Tamora"
(5.2.25–26). She, however, claims another identity: "I am Revenge, sent
from th' infernal kingdom / To ease the gnawing vulture of thy mind, /
By working wreakful vengeance on thy foes" (lines 30–32). Titus seems
initially to balk at accepting her assertion: "Art thou Revenge? and art thou
sent to me, / To be a torment to mine enemies?" (lines 41–42). "I am," she
replies, "therefore come down and welcome me" (line 43) and he does.

This exchange leads us to wonder what Titus – and the playgoers –
actually saw when Tamora turned up at his door.[18] Was there something
about Tamora's appearance that made her claim to be Revenge at least
plausible? May Shakespeare be evoking a specific personification known
to his playgoers? Frances Teague suggests that, in presenting Tamora as
Revenge, Shakespeare uses "an emblematic costume or property to establish
the identity of a symbolic character."[19] We know, of course, that abstractions
commonly mingle with people on the Elizabethan stage, and, as Alan Dessen
observes, "the presence of a figure of 'Revenge' in the 'real world' of Titus'
Rome was at least possible in the theatre of the early 1590s."[20] There would
be nothing outré about such dramaturgy. In fact, the playwright could
actually intensify the theatrical effect of the scene by employing a strikingly
costumed figure as Tamora/Revenge. How, then, was Tamora costumed?

Although the play lacks detailed stage directions, there is, at the beginning of the scene, one tantalizing hint about costuming: "*Enter Tamora and
her two sons* [Demetrius and Chiron] *disguised*" (5.2.0.s.d.). This direction,
which appears in both the Quarto and Folio versions of *Titus*, must mean

that the Gothic queen has changed her appearance since she was last on-stage. Her first words confirm the alteration: "Thus, in this strange and sad habiliment, / I will encounter with Andronicus, / And say I am Revenge" (lines 1–3). That she has donned a "sad" garment but left her face un-covered explains why Titus recognizes her so quickly. No subsequent stage direction or reference in the ensuing dialogue, however, adds substantially to our understanding of her garb as "strange and sad."

There is one other indication, early in the scene, of something unusual in Tamora's appearance: the suggestion that she arrives at Titus' door in a chariot. Titus refers to her "chariot-wheels" (5.2.47), "vengeful waggon" (line 51), "car" (line 53), and "waggon-wheel" (line 54). Collectively, these references suggest to Eugene Waith that "Tamora is drawn on stage like Titus" in the play's opening scene.[21] Jonathan Bate demurs: "Revenge tra-ditionally rode in a chariot, so it can be assumed rather than shown, and the sustained references from [lines] 47 to 55 seem to work to supply in the imagination what is not physically present on stage. If there were a chariot, Chiron and Demetrius could draw it on, but since they do not exit with Tamora there would be no way of getting it off."[22] This practical point is well taken: who would haul the chariot offstage? Waith is forced to posit the presence of additional, silent figures: "Since her sons remain with Titus when she leaves, some attendants would have to be provided to draw the chariot."[23] If we assume that Tamora arrives in such a chariot, Waith must be right in his supposition. But the ensuing dialogue provides no evidence of unnamed figures onstage.[24]

What lends credibility to Tamora's identification as Revenge is that both she and the personification are female. Since classical antiquity embod-iments of revenge belong to that sex. Alison Findlay, who observes that "Revenge tragedy is a feminine genre in spite of the fact that the revenge protagonists are usually male, and female characters appear to play more passive roles," explains: "The feminization of revenge stems immediately from the feminine Latin noun 'Vindicta,' but links back to figures from an older classical tradition: the Furies, the figure of Nemesis, and ultimately the life-giving and consuming earth."[25] The most familiar revengers of classical mythology include a panoply of females: Juno, Medea, Artemis, Hecuba, Althea, Procne, and Philomel.[26] Juvenal, undoubtedly speaking for contemporaries in ancient Rome, observes that "no one so rejoices in vengeance as a woman."[27]

For the Greeks and Romans, the goddess Nemesis embodies retribution, and in the Renaissance Nemesis remains female. Thus in *Respublica*, per-formed by the Chapel Children c. 1553–54, Nemesis is called "the mooste highe goddesse of correccion" (line 1782),[28] and in *Locrine*, performed c. 1590–94 possibly by the Queen's Men, she is "the mistress of revenge" (5.3.45).[29] Nemesis is sometimes conflated with Fortune, who is herself female. Richard Linche, in his adaptation of Vincenzo Cartari's *Imagini de i dei*, says that "Among the ancients and among the old writers, Fortuna and Nemesis were oftentimes taken to bee all one."[30] Albrecht Dürer conflates the two in an engraving known as "Das grosse Glück," wherein Fortune holds the bridle of restraint.[31] When personifying the abstraction, poets too identify Revenge as female. Thomas Sackville in his Induction to the *Mirror for Magistrates* (1563 edition) writes: "fell Revenge [sat] gnashing her teeth for yre, / Devising meanes howe she may vengeaunce take."[32] Incidental references in the drama similarly conceive of this figure as female: in *The Revenger's Tragedy*, performed c. 1606–7 by the King's Men, a character urges, "give Revenge her due" (1.1.43).[33] In *Histriomastix*, performed 1598–99?, a character metaphorically compares his vengeful impulse with childbirth: "My soule is bigge in travaile with revenge, / And I could rip her wombe up with a stabbe, / To free th' imprisoned issue of my thought."[34]

Also female are the Furies, and when Titus addresses Tamora, he evokes those mythical figures: "Welcome, dread Fury, to my woeful house" (5.2.82). The ballad of Titus Andronicus, which probably derives from the play,[35] also compares Titus' visitors with Furies:

The Empress thinking then that I was mad,
Like Furies she and both her Sons were glad,
So nam'd Revenge, and Rape, and Murder, they
To undermine and hear what I would say.[36]

The Erinyes (to use the Greek name for Furies) are spirits who originated, according to Apollodorus, when "Cronos cut off his father's genitals and threw them into the sea; and from the drops of the flowing blood were born Furies."[37] Ovid calls them "sisters born of Night, divinities deadly and implacable" (4:451–52).[38] Aeschylus in *Eumenides* says they are "loathed of men and of Olympian gods."[39] The Furies are three in number and their names are symbolic, Pierre Le Loyer explaining, "the one was called *Alecto*: that is *uncessantly tormenting*. Another was named *Megera*: which signifieth *enraged*. And the third *Tisiphone*, which is as much, as to say, *the avenger of murther*."[40] On the Elizabethan stage, as in antiquity, the Furies function as agents of punishment. In *Tancred and Gismund* (acted by the gentlemen of the Inner Temple in 1591), for instance, Megaera announces, "Vengeance and death from foorth the deepest hell / I bring" (4.1.862–63).[41]

The most distinctive features of the Furies are the snakes that curl about their limbs and heads (in lieu of hair). Abraham Fraunce reports that Furies' garments are also "girt with a snakie girdle."[42] In addition, Ovid relates, Tisiphone has "a torch which had been steeped in gore," and she wears "a robe red with dripping blood" (4:481–83).[43] Michael Drayton describes this same Fury as bearing a whip in one hand, a long knife in the other (lines 87–88).[44] A dumb show in *Gorboduc*, performed by the gentlemen of the Inner Temple in the Christmas season of 1561, assigns snakes, whips, and torches to the Furies: "*there came from under the stage, as though out of Hell, three Furies – Alecto, Megera, and Tisiphone – clad in black garments sprinkled with blood and flames, their bodies girt with snakes, their heads spread with serpents instead of hair, the one bearing in her hand a snake, the other a whip, and the third a burning firebrand*" (dumb show preceding act 4).[45] Similarly, George Peele's *Battle of Alcazar*, performed by the Admiral's Men c. 1588–89, includes this stage direction: "*lying behind the curtaines [are] three Furies, one with a whipp, another with a blody torch, and the third with a chopping knife*" (2.300.s.d.).[46] Designs by Inigo Jones for William Davenant's *Salmacida Spolia*, a masque performed in 1640, show the Furies, who are naked to the waist, carrying snakes and torches.[47]

Titus refers to Tamora as a Fury because Furies are creatures who avenge wrongs, especially the murder of blood relatives, and because Tamora has just aligned herself with the principle of retribution by calling herself Revenge. Alan Hughes, commenting on Titus' welcome to Tamora, writes: "Perhaps Titus recognises that the function of Revenge resembles theirs [the Furies], rather than believing that she is actually one of them. This may suggest what Tamora's 'strange and sad habiliments' looked like."[48] Hughes does not venture further in speculating about the nature of those habiliments, but Titus' evocation of the Furies could imply something about the color of her costume. Since the Furies are conventionally garbed in black and since Tamora describes her attire as "sad," it seems likely that she wears black, as Jonathan Bate has suggested.[49] Elsewhere Shakespeare associates this color with revenge: Othello speaks of "black vengeance" (3.3.447), and Nemesis is described as "black" in Shakespeare's *1 Henry VI* (4.7.78), which was first performed in 1592. If Tamora's garments were flecked with red, this color too would evoke the Furies whose clothing in *Gorboduc* is "*sprinkled with blood*" (dumb show preceding act 4).

Were the actor playing Tamora to have long, shaggy hair,[50] like Revenge in a dumb show of *The Misfortunes of Arthur*, performed by the gentlemen of Gray's Inn in 1587–88, the hairstyle would suggest the snakes that cover the heads of the Furies.[51] In Anthony Copley's *A Fig for Fortune* (1596),

Revenge's hair is described as "snake-incurl'd, Medusa-like."[52] In Marston's *Antonio's Revenge*, performed by Paul's Boys in 1600–1, a character speaks of the "curled locks / Of snaky Vengeance" (2.1.7–8). As for hand props, Tamora may have a whip.[53] In one of the scenes probably added by Ben Jonson to Thomas Kyd's *Spanish Tragedy* in 1602,[54] Hieronimo says, "there is Nemesis and Furies, / And things call'd whips" (lines 41–42).[55] In *Antonio's Revenge* a character speaks of the "steel whips / Of knotty vengeance" (2.3.127–28). And Otto van Veen's depiction of Punishment puts in her hand three snakes, which she wields like a whip.[56]

If we knew exactly how Revenge looked elsewhere in Elizabethan tragedy, we could add significantly to our knowledge of Tamora as Revenge. But an examination of other plays yields surprisingly little information.[57] John Pickering's *Horestes*, performed c. 1567, features a Vice who announces his name as Patience to one character (line 100) and as Courage to another (line 241), but to the playgoers the Vice reveals his true name and nature: Revenge (line 795).[58] Representing himself as a messenger of the gods, he encourages Horestes to take revenge on Clytemnestra for killing his father Agamemnon. Although Revenge is onstage for much of the play, neither the dialogue nor the stage directions specify costume or props.[59]

Thomas Kyd's *Spanish Tragedy*, first performed c. 1587 (possibly by Strange's Men), also makes a character of Revenge, and Alan Hughes, noting Kyd's creation, suggests that the costume worn by Shakespeare's Tamora "might have been available" in the company's inventory.[60] But Hughes draws back from speculating about the particulars of costume or props. Like Hughes, Philip Edwards believes that Shakespeare, in costuming Tamora, was inspired by Kyd's example: "It seems likely that the 'strange and sad habiliment' which she wears was a direct allusion to the costume Revenge wore in *The Spanish Tragedy*."[61] This may well be true, but although Kyd's Revenge remains onstage throughout the entire play, we learn nothing of the character's appearance. The only action we actually see Revenge perform is falling asleep.[62] Most readers of *The Spanish Tragedy* and *Horestes* envisage Revenge as male, and the immensely effective National Theatre production of Kyd's play in 1982–84 employed a male actor in the role.[63] The only evidence in the text, however, is a single masculine pronoun in the chorus following act 3 (3.15.23).

Despite the dearth of information, Michael Hattaway conjectures the appearance of Kyd's Revenge in considerable detail: "Revenge almost certainly wore an antic and spectacular costume of black, was probably clad in armour and bore a sword, and may even have brought in a blazing torch at his first entrance."[64] As we have seen, black would indeed be an appropriate color for a "sad" garment of the kind worn by Tamora, but Hattaway fails to explain why Revenge's costume should be "antic." Nor does he explain what an "antic costume" would look like.[65]

Hattaway bases his guess that Revenge wields sword and torch on another play, *The Lamentable Tragedy of Locrine*, probably written after *Titus*; *Locrine* was entered in the Stationers' Register on 20 July 1594 and printed the following year. This anonymous tragedy begins with a stage direction: "*Enter Ate with thunder and lightning, all in black, with a burning torch in one hand and a bloody sword in the other hand*" (1.1.0).[66] In 1609 Ben Jonson would also create a character of Ate in his *Masque of Queens*, where she becomes the chief witch: "This Dame I make to bear the person of Ate, or mischief (for so I interpret it) out of Homer's description of her, *Iliad* IX [505–12]."[67] Although this character may not wield a bloody sword, Jonson describes her in a way that suggests a somewhat more horrific version of the figure in *Locrine*: "*naked armed, barefooted, her frock tucked, her hair knotted and folded with vipers; in her hand a torch made of a dead man's arm, lighted; girded with a snake*" (lines 87–89). As the learned Jonson knew, Ate is the child of Eris (Strife) in classical myth and, although perhaps not precisely synonymous with Revenge, came to be associated with violence and vengeance.[68] Shakespeare captures this nexus in *King John*, performed by the Lord Chamberlain's Men c. 1595–96, when a character speaks of Ate as stirring someone "to blood and strife" (2.1.63). Similarly, Antony in *Julius Caesar*, performed in 1599, speaks of "Caesar's spirit, ranging for revenge, / With Ate by his side" (3.1.270–71).[69] Renaissance writers sometimes identify Ate with personified Revenge, as Thomas Heywood does in *Troia Britanica: or, Great Britaines Troy* (1609), when he calls Ate "goddess of revenge or strife."[70] If we imagine Ate as synonymous with Revenge and if we posit a connection between Tamora as Revenge in *Titus* and the character of Ate in *Locrine*, then Hattaway's conjecture about Revenge in *The Spanish Tragedy* may seem persuasive. But before we accept this cluster of assumptions, we need to consider more closely the meaning of revenge.

The sword that Hattaway assigns Revenge is commonly found in the hands of Justice, an abstraction with profoundly different implications. Whereas the phenomenon of justice ordinarily belongs to the state, revenge belongs to the individual or family – to the blood relatives of a victim.[71] Achieving justice is a matter of rationality, procedure, and law, while revenge satisfies the most primitive emotions. However harsh, justice has a goal and an end. Revenge knows not where to stop; it can sweep up the guilty and innocent alike. For Robert Dallington "revenge is the executioner of injustice."[72] In the words of Francis Bacon, "Revenge is a kinde of wilde justice."[73] Admittedly, theologians and poets frequently conflate the two when describing divinity. Richard Hooker, for example, speaks of tribulation as "Gods instrument of revenge and furie sometime, sometime as a rod of his just yeat moderate ire and displeasure."[74] In Shakespeare's *Richard II* (performed by the Lord Chamberlain's Men in 1595), John of Gaunt says that if the king has wronged anyone, "Let heaven revenge" (1.2.40).

Most often, however, justice is identified with the heavens, revenge with humankind. In *The Spanish Tragedy* when the body of Horatio is discovered, his mother says, "The heavens are just, murder cannot be hid, / Time is the author both of truth and right, / And time will bring this treachery to light" (2.5.57–59). In place of Isabella's confidence in heavenly justice, Horatio's father pledges personal retaliation: "Seest thou those wounds that yet are bleeding fresh? / I'll not entomb them till I have reveng'd: / Then will I joy amidst my discontent" (lines 53–55). To be sure, Hieronimo does not abandon his effort to obtain justice. He is, after all, knight marshal of Spain: he gathers evidence and takes it to higher authority in an effort to punish the malefactors. But pain and despair take their toll, and he comes to conflate justice and revenge: his sighs and passions "Beat at the windows of the brightest heavens, / Soliciting for justice and revenge" (3.7.13–14).

The distinction between justice and revenge becomes blurred in *Titus Andronicus* too, especially as Titus, like Hieronimo, begins to crack under the strain of grief and frustration.[75] But justice seems consistently associated with the heavens. Thus Titus says, "*Terras Astraea reliquit*" [Astraea (goddess of justice) has left the earth], and Publius adds that Justice is employed "with Jove in heaven" (4.3.4, 41). Titus must therefore seek Revenge, who is located elsewhere. "Which way shall I find Revenge's cave?" he asks when his severed hand is returned, along with the heads of his sons (3.1.270). In the scene wherein the crazed Titus seeks to shoot arrows at the heavens, he bids Publius and Sempronius to dig in the earth till they come to "Pluto's region" (4.3.13). Moments later Publius reports, "Pluto sends you word, / If you will have Revenge from hell, you shall" (4.3.38–39). Still later, Tamora, arriving at Titus' house, tells us what she will tell him – that she is "Revenge, sent from below" (5.2.3). Revenge, then, is associated with the underworld, or hell, as in *Julius Caesar* when Antony says that Caesar's spirit ranges "for revenge, / With Ate by his side come hot from hell" (3.1.270–71).[76]

If justice originates in heaven and is overseen by God/Jove, and if revenge originates in the underworld/hell and answers to Pluto, then it follows that the two abstractions should bear different implements when they are personified. Whereas the sword, used in public executions of malefactors, properly belongs to Justice, a dagger, used by individuals in pursuit of personal vengeance, is the appropriate weapon of Revenge.[77] Significantly, Revenge in *The Misfortunes of Arthur* carries a dagger, not a sword.[78] Almost certainly, then, Hattaway is mistaken in attributing a sword to Kyd's Revenge.[79] It is far more likely that both Kyd's Revenge and Shakespeare's Tamora, when masquerading as Revenge, are equipped with daggers. Interestingly, in *Titus*, the 1999 cinematic adaptation of the play by Julie Taymor, Tamora appears at Titus' door in black garb, her eyes covered by black gauze and her head covered by a leather helmet featuring a semicircular array of daggers, the blades pointing outward.[80]

Hattaway's contention that Kyd's Revenge carries a torch is certainly plausible since poets associate fire with revenge. In Shakespeare's *2 Henry VI*, for example, a character says that the house of York "Burns with revenging fire" (4.1.97). The Furies also carry torches and dwell in a place of flames. But there is a practical problem with assuming that Revenge brings a torch onstage in *The Spanish Tragedy*. The actor playing Revenge presumably cannot hold a torch for the entire running time of Kyd's long play. Indeed, at one point Revenge falls asleep. Revenge could conceivably affix a torch to some kind of holder, but the company of actors would then run the risk of having the torch flicker or even burn out as Hieronimo's revenge gathers momentum. In view of such practical difficulties, it seems unlikely that Kyd's Revenge brings a torch onstage.

Given the paucity of information available in plays where Revenge appears as a character,[81] the visual arts would seem to offer a surer means of discovering what Tamora-as-Revenge looked like. Unfortunately for our purpose, Revenge is one of the least common personifications, for people preferred images of the virtues on their overmantels, ceilings, walls, and embroidery. Hostile to the Christian ethos, Revenge is banished from Elizabethan interior design; instead, Justice and the other Cardinal Virtues predominate. One might expect to find Revenge in those prints personifying various vices, but the personification proves extremely rare even in woodcuts and engravings, perhaps because the abstraction lacks the canonical status of the Seven Deadly Sins.

When we do find Revenge in the pictorial arts, she is identifiable by an implement and by distinctive dress. A tapestry at Hampton Court, made in Brussels in the first half of the sixteenth century, features the image of Revenge on its border.[82] This female figure carries weaponry: a dagger in one hand, a bow in the other. The dagger would become the principal identifying mark of the personification for Shakespeare's contemporaries.

The tapestry also depicts Revenge wearing a helmet and armor on her upper torso; beneath the waist she wears a loose-fitting gown.

Personified Revenge also typically performs an action: in the arts she holds a finger to her mouth. The meaning of this distinctive gesture is not immediately apparent. Since ancient times, however, vengefulness has been associated with the mouth. Plutarch, for instance, writes: "When I looke unto Revenge, and the manner thereof, I finde for the most part, that if men proceede by way of choler, they misse of their purpose: for commonly all the heat & desire of revenge is spent in biting of lips, gnashing and grating of teeth, vaine running to and fro, in railing words with foolish threats and menaces."[83] Such facial expression becomes a staple of the Renaissance stage. In *The True Chronicle History of King Leir and His Three Daughters* (performed by the Queen's Men c. 1594), for example, a messenger describes Ragan's response to a letter that she reads:

See how her colour comes and goes agayne,
Now red as scarlet, now as pale as ash:
See how she knits her brow, and bytes her lips,
And stamps, and makes a dumbe shew of disdayne,
Mixt with revenge, and violent extreames.
                    (lines 1173–77)[84]

These lines amount to an extended stage direction, extraordinarily useful in helping us to imagine what the playgoers saw in performance. And to this description of lip biting we may add Cesare Ripa's account of Revenge as biting her finger.[85]

Although Revenge's index finger at her mouth may represent an involuntary action born of strong emotion, it may also signify a purposeful resolution on her part. Jan Muller's print of Horus (Greek Harpocrates), god of silence, depicts him with an index finger at his lips,[86] while Geoffrey Whitney's emblem of *Silentium* pictures a man at a desk, his index finger similarly placed.[87] (In ancient Rome, Angerona, goddess of silence, "was portrayed with a finger in front of her closed lips."[88]) Revengers, for their part, cloak their designs in secrecy when embarking on a vengeful and thus risky course of action.[89] When, for example, Strotzo in *Antonio's Revenge* agrees to become an accomplice in a revenge scheme, he assures the villainous duke, "a true rogue's lips are mute" (2.5.37); this stage direction follows: "*He lays finger on his mouth, and draws his dagger*" (2.5.39.s.d.). Similarly, when Hieronimo in *The Spanish Tragedy* determines to take matters into his own hands, he resolves to conceal what he knows:

> Hieronimo, thou must enjoin
> Thine eyes to observation, and thy tongue
> To milder speeches than thy spirit affords,
> Thy heart to patience, and thy hands to rest,
> Thy cap to courtesy, and thy knee to bow,
> Till to revenge thou know, when, where, and how.

(3.13.39–44)

The revenger keeps his counsel lest he alarm those he would entrap and dispatch. The gesture indicating silence, then, would seem to belong naturally to a man counseling himself to caution. And even after the execution of revenge, Hieronimo retreats further into silence when he bites out his tongue.

Revenge's gesture may, however, have yet another significance, as a prose narrative entitled *Historia septem infantium de Lara* suggests. Published in Antwerp in 1612, the book consists of forty plates illustrating a complicated story of violence and vengeance. Beneath each plate a sentence (or two) – in both Spanish and Latin – summarizes the action depicted above and identifies the symbolic personifications whom we see alongside the human personages. No fewer than nine of the etchings, made by Antonio Tempesta after designs by Otto van Veen, depict Revenge (Venganza/Vindicta).[90] In the pictures Revenge carries a weapon in her right hand and makes a gesture with her left: she wields a dagger and puts an index finger to her mouth. Looking more closely, we see that the tip of Revenge's finger is not just at her lips but actually in her mouth (fig. 11). Her gesture does not seem to be the common sign for silence, for she holds her finger at an angle, the palm of her hand away from her face. What, then, is she doing? In all likelihood, the gesture implies deliberation. Giovanni Pierio Valeriano Bolzani identifies a man with a finger at his lips as "Meditation, or Revenge" (fig. 12).[91] In the sixteenth century, as today, the gesture may designate thoughtfulness. Stephen Batman says that it shows "the heedefulnes that men ought to have, in speakinge."[92] Both Valeriano's and Tempesta's Revenge perform an action that today we easily recognize: that is, a person mulling over a question may touch the chin, lips, or even the teeth with an index finger.

What may we conclude about the costume, props, and gesture of Shakespeare's Tamora when she arrives at Titus' house? Her garment is either black, the color worn by the Furies, or red, the color associated with anger and violence; Giovanni Paolo Lomazzo observes that red "signifieth revenge."[93] The two colors could easily be conjoined if a black garment were flecked with red, the color of blood. Red spots mark her face: in

11 Revenge with a dagger (detail), by Antonio Tempesta (after a design by Otto van Veen), from *Historia septem infantium de Lara* (Antwerp, 1612)

12 Meditation, or Revenge, a woodcut from *Hieroglyphica sive de sacris aegyptiorum literis commentarii* (1556) by Giovanni Pierio Valeriano Bolzani

Chapman's *The Revenge of Bussy D'Ambois*, acted by the Queen's Revels Children c. 1610–11, a character expresses anxiety about returning to his wife, who has urged him to carry out a revenge; she expects to see the blood of the victim "freckling [his] hands and face" (1.1.118).[94] If Tamora resembles the personification in Tempesta's etchings and in the Hampton Court tapestry, she wears below the waist a long, billowing garment; her upper arms and torso are encased in armor; and on her head she wears a helmet from under which her tresses fall. Such attire would be in keeping with something Tamora says at the beginning of the scene: "in this strange and sad habiliment, / I will encounter with Andronicus" (5.2.1–2). According to the *OED*, a principal meaning of "habiliment" in its plural form is "personal accoutrements for war; armour, warlike apparel."

Revenge carries an unsheathed dagger in her right hand and makes a gesture with her left. A finger at her lips, while she turns toward her sons, may designate conspiratorial silence. If Tamora puts a finger at her mouth, as Tempesta's Revenge does, the gesture implies deliberation as she continues her campaign of vengeance against Titus. Although neither the etchings in *Historia septem infantium de Lara* nor the description by Cesare Ripa assigns a whip to Revenge, Tamora would evoke the Furies if she wears one in her belt. But she carries neither torch nor sword.[95] Significantly, the figure equipped with both torch and sword in plates 13 and 22 of Tempesta's illustrations is *Furor*, the male figure who accompanies Revenge.[96]

Murder

If imagining the appearance of Tamora as Revenge involves detective work, reconstructing her sons' appearance is even more problematic. All we know for certain is that Chiron and Demetrius are disguised when they arrive at Titus' house; the stage direction at the beginning of the scene is explicit. But some Shakespeareans incline to the view that the sons' symbolic identities are Titus' invention. In support of this notion, they point to the fact that Tamora does not initially call her sons by the names Rape and Murder. Instead, it is Titus who says to her: "Lo by thy side where Rape and Murder stands; / Now give some surance that thou art Revenge – " (5.2.45–46); and at the end of this speech, he refers to "Rapine and Murder there" (line 59). On the basis of these lines Harold F. Brooks argues that Titus invents symbolic names for Chiron and Demetrius: "He has recognized, not impersonations designed by Tamora, but the men themselves, and, under cover of his supposed madness, christens them after his knowledge of what they have done."[97] Persuaded by Brooks, Jonathan Bate suggests that Tamora actually resists the identification of her sons as Rape and Murder: "Tamora first tries to deny the identification, saying they are merely her *ministers* ["These are my ministers"], but when forced to name them plays along...."[98] It is only when Titus says, "Are they thy ministers? What are they call'd?" that Tamora replies, "Rape and Murder" (lines 61, 62).

Although the view of Brooks and Bate that Titus performs "a superb act of improvisation"[99] seems initially plausible, it overlooks the fact that Tamora, before Titus names any abstraction, has herself already spoken of Rape and Murder metaphorically: "There's not a hollow cave or lurking-place, / No vast obscurity or misty vale, / Where bloody murther or detested rape / Can couch [lie hidden] for fear, but I will find them out" (lines 35–38). Titus could be picking up this figurative language and expanding it into explicit personification. But it is equally likely that the "murder" and "rape" mentioned by Tamora are already personifications. Even Harold Brooks concedes that they are "half-personified."[100] Interestingly, Brooks and Bate, failing to connect the brothers' attire with the personifications named by Titus, say nothing of the costuming of Chiron and Demetrius. Yet we know that the brothers wear disguise. I should like to pursue the suggestion of Peter Daly that Tamora's sons, like their mother, "would have been appropriately clothed and provided with insignias to reveal their nature."[101] After all, if the garb and hand props of Chiron and Demetrius are not suggestive of personified identities (like those of Tamora), then why should the brothers be disguised upon their entry in this scene?

When Tamora calls her sons "ministers" (line 60), moreover, she is not denying the identification that Titus makes, as Brooks and Bate imagine. After all, rape and murder are crimes frequently committed as acts of revenge both in war and in domestic crises. In fact, the murder of Bassianus and the rape of Lavinia are explicitly such acts. Recall what Tamora tells her sons in an earlier scene: that Bassianus and Lavinia "call'd me foul adulteress, / Lascivious Goth, and all the bitterest terms / That ever ear did hear to such effect" (2.3.109–11). Therefore, she says, "Revenge it, as you love your mother's life, / Or be ye not henceforth call'd my children" (lines 114–15). Why should personified Rape and Murder not be the ministers, that is, the agents, of Revenge?

Long before Shakespeare wrote *Titus Andronicus*, Murder[102] had appeared as a character in Thomas Preston's *Cambises*, performed at a court or college c. 1558–69. We learn little about the appearance of this figure, who keeps company with Cruelty, except for a detail concerning his hands: "*Enter Crueltie and Murder with bloody hands*" (line 709.s.d.).[103] These two act as the agents of the tyrannical Cambises when they seize Smirdis. Murder explains to the doomed man, "King Cambises hath sent us unto thee, / Commaunding us straightly, with out mercy or favour: / Upon thee to bestow our behaviour" (lines 719–21). The two of them then "*Strike him in divers places*" (line 722.s.d.), spilling his blood: "*A little bladder of vineger prickt*" (line 726.s.d.). David Bevington sees a connection between Preston's Murder and Cruelty and "the familiar 'two Murderers' on the Elizabethan stage": for example, the unnamed murderers who slay Clarence at the behest of Richard of Gloucester in Shakespeare's *Richard III* and the murderers of Banquo in *Macbeth*.[104]

Whether Murder emerges as a character in *A Warning for Fair Women*, performed by an unknown company and then by the Lord Chamberlain's Men c. 1585–99 and perhaps antedating *Titus Andronicus*, is not entirely clear. In this play, which combines abstractions with historical personages, Thelma Greenfield suggests, "The dominating figure is Tragedy, who is almost completely identified with Murder."[105] At the beginning of the dramatic action, Tragedy enters, "*in her one hand a whip, in the other hand a knife*" (Induction.s.d.).[106] Like Preston's Murder, Tragedy is identified with blood: "*Enter Tragedie with a bowle of bloud in her hand*" (line 771.s.d.). Then, following the entry of the Furies, Tragedy declares, "Here enters Murther into al their hearts, / And doth possesse them with the hellish thirst / Of guiltlesse blood" (lines 840–42). It seems almost as though Tragedy, who is called "Murthers Beadle" (Induction, line 26), personifies Murder. Charles Cannon observes, "The bowl of blood, insofar as may be determined from the stage directions and the text, has been transferred from Tragedy's hands to those of Murther."[107] But since there are no other indications that a character named Murder actually appears onstage, we should probably interpret Tragedy's words as figurative: "Though Murther is mentioned as entering 'into al their hearts,' there is no provision for the physical entrance of Murther as a character."[108]

The character named Homicide in Robert Yarington's *Two Lamentable Tragedies*, performed at an undetermined venue c. 1594–95, is similarly identified with blood. At the beginning of the play Homicide complains that "I cannot glut my blood delighted eye" nor "bath my greedie handes in reeking blood."[109] Moments later he promises that if Avarice assists him, "I will quaffe thy health in bowles of blood," and afterward Avarice assures Homicide, "Let my confounding plots but goe before, / And thou shalt wade up to the chin in gore."[110] Still later Homicide, whose name has become Murder in the Quarto, says, "Now Avarice I have well satisfied, / My hungry thoughtes with blood and crueltie."[111] Shakespeare seems to remember such plays of the 1590s when he brings a murderer onstage in *Macbeth*: at the banquet Duncan's killer sees one of the murderers at the door and goes over to talk with him, observing, "There's blood upon thy face" (3.4.13).

Plays performed in the early 1590s strongly suggest that weaponry, in a particular context, could identify dramatic characters as murderers. In Robert Greene's *The Scottish History of James IV*, performed in the summer or fall of 1590 (possibly by the Queen's Men), the Scottish king seeks to have his wife killed, and Jaques eagerly undertakes the task. When the would-be murderer advances on Dorothea, the stage direction clearly indicates how the villain looks: "*Enter Jaques, his sword drawn*" (4.4.37.s.d.).[112] In the following scene King James urges Jaques to "sheathe thy murdering blade" (4.5.1). Similarly, in *The True Chronicle History of King Leir*, the murderous messenger hired by Ragan to kill her father envisions the manner of the crime as he exults in his opportunity for gain: "A purse of gold giv'n for a paltry stabbe!" (line 1226), and a later stage direction reveals his appearance as he advances on the sleeping Leir: "*Enter the messenger or murtherer with two daggers in his hands*" (lines 1453–54.s.d.).[113] When Leir awakes, he relates a dream filled with the symbolism of murder:

Me thought, my daughters, Gonorill & Ragan,
Stood both before me with such grim aspects,
Eche brandishing a faulchion in their hand,
Ready to lop a lymme off where it fell,
And in their other hands a naked poynyard,
Wherwith they stabd me in a hundred places.
(lines 1488–93)

In Shakespeare's version of the story, the playgoer is led to make a similar connection between the act of murder and a figure armed with an unsheathed dagger or sword or both. When in *King Lear* Kent and Oswald struggle, the latter cries, "Help, ho! murther, murther!" (2.2.43), and immediately the villainous Edmund appears. In the 1608 Quarto we find this stage direction: "*Enter Edmund the bastard with his rapier drawn*."[114] The juxtaposition of Oswald's words and Edmund's entry suggests that Edmund becomes, at least for a moment, an embodiment of murder.

Collectively, the evidence of plays by Shakespeare's contemporaries offers suggestive hints about the costuming of a character named Murder. To this we may add information provided by Cesare Ripa's *Iconologia*. Ripa

13 Homicide, a woodcut from Cesare Ripa's *Iconologia*, translated by Jean Baudoin and published as *Iconologie* (Paris, 1644)

intended his work, after all, not only as a guide for artists and sculptors but also for writers, as the title-page of his 1593 edition announces.[115] According to Ripa, Murder has, appropriately enough, a fierce countenance.[116] He wears a red mantle signifying the blood he spills; and he wears body armor, signifying his indomitable will. He carries an unsheathed sword in his right hand, and, in his left hand, he holds by the hair a severed head (fig. 13).[117] If personified Murder in *Titus* holds such a head, he calls to mind the

earlier scene when a messenger enters carrying the heads of Titus' sons
(3.1.233.s.d.); Titus subsequently turns to Marcus, saying, "Come, brother,
take a head, / And in this hand the other will I bear" (3.1.279–80). Murder
may also evoke the memory of a murderous Jack Cade, who watches with
approval as a comrade carries in the heads of Lord Say and Sir James Cromer
(*2 Henry VI*, 4.7.129.s.d.). If Murder holds no such head in *Titus*, he may
nevertheless have bloody hands like his counterpart in both *Cambises* and
Two Lamentable Tragedies and possibly a bloody face like the murderer
in *Macbeth*. Finally, a fierce dog may accompany Tamora's son, for when
in *Macbeth* Shakespeare personifies Murder, a wolf is called "his sentinel"
(2.1.53).[118]

Rape

Like Murder, Rape is rarely personified in the drama,[119] and the personification almost never appears in the visual arts.[120] Representations of Lust,
however, occasionally appear in sixteenth-century plays. For example, Lust
is a menacing figure in *A Warning for Fair Women*, arriving in the company of Furies and leading Mistress Sanders by the hand while Chastity
endeavors to pull her back (lines 803–15.s.d.).[121] Lust is, of course, not
synonymous with Rape, and today rape is seen as a crime of violence and
sadistic power rather than passion. But lust and rape converge in the minds
of Renaissance poets and playwrights. This is particularly true of perhaps
the most frequently depicted rape in European culture – that of Lucretia by
Sextus Tarquinius.[122] In Shakespeare's *Rape of Lucrece* (1594), for instance,
Tarquin is characterized as "Lust-breathed" (line 3). Lucrece herself speaks
of Tarquin's "scarlet lust" (line 1650). Similarly, in Thomas Heywood's *Rape
of Lucrece*, performed by Queen Anne's Men c. 1607, the rapist describes
himself as "lust-burnt" (line 1962).[123] In Thomas Middleton's *The Ghost of
Lucrece* (1600), Lucrece speaks of "Tarquin and Lust" coming to her home
(line 232).[124]

   The story of Tarquin and Lucrece has particular relevance for *Titus
Andronicus* since Shakespeare's poem and play were apparently written
about the same time, since the poem, like the play, evokes the classical
myth of Philomel, and since the raped Lavinia is explicitly compared with
Lucrece.[125] According to the poem, Tarquin bears a "falchion" (line 176),
a curved sword with which he threatens Lucrece; she later tells her family,
"against my heart he set his sword" (line 1640). Similarly, Middleton's

narrator in *The Ghost of Lucrece* speaks of a "lust-keen falchion" (line 21). Artistic treatments of the story mostly assign Tarquin a short sword or dagger, which functions both as means of intimidation and phallic symbol. For instance, in Titian's painting, c. 1570, the nude Lucrece in bed raises her arms in a protective gesture.[126] With one hand Tarquin grabs her arm; in his right hand he wields a dagger. Variations of this depiction are many, but in most Tarquin wears garb that is recognizably classical and has a knife or sword for a weapon.[127]

Although playwrights may not create a character named Rape, they do bring to the stage rapists and would-be rapists.[128] In Thomas Heywood's *The Rape of Lucrece*, we find this stage direction when the rapist advances on Lucrece: "*Enter Sextus* [Tarquin] *with his sword drawne and a taper light*" (lines 1915–16). Similarly, in *The Wonder of Women, or The Tragedy of Sophonisba*, acted by the Blackfriars Boys in 1606, Marston dramatizes another such figure in the character of Syphax,[129] who wields, at different points in the dramatic action, props that help identify his nature and purpose. This stage direction describes the scene where we first see Syphax doing violence to the newly married Sophonisba: "*Syphax, his dagger twon* [i.e., twined, wound] *about her hair, drags in Sophonisba in her nightgown petticoat*" (3.1.0.s.d.).[130] Later, in yet another attempt at sexual assault, Syphax sneaks up on the unsuspecting Sophonisba: "*Through the vault's mouth, in his nightgown, torch in his hand, Syphax enters just behind Sophonisba*" (4.1.42.s.d.); he announces to her, "This forest's deaf / As is my lust. Night and the god of silence / Swells my full pleasures" (lines 46–48). Only her swift action – "*Sophonisba snatcheth out her knife*" – and her determination to use it on herself prevents the rape. As the stage directions in these two plays suggest, dagger and torch are the visual symbols belonging to the would-be rapist. In *The Queen of Corinth* (acted by the King's Men c. 1616), moreover, the rapist of the virtuous Merione approaches her with drawn dagger (2.1.38).[131]

Although other plays are not especially useful in helping us determine what Tamora's son looks like, Cesare Ripa's *Iconologia* provides valuable hints.[132] According to Ripa, Rape has a military mien.[133] The personification wears a helmet featuring a predatory bird on top. Such a bird, with enveloping wings, captures the isolating, suffocating effects of the crime and perhaps evokes the story of Leda and the swan. Interestingly, Julie Taymor's cinematic adaptation of *Titus* seems inspired by Ripa: when Tamora's son shows up at Titus' door, Chiron has a (stuffed) bird perched on his head and a cloak covered with feathers.[134] Cesare Ripa's Rape also wears armor and carries a curved sword (like Tarquin in the Lucrece poems of both Shakespeare and Middleton); in his other hand he holds a shield. Painted on the shield is Pluto's rape of Proserpina.[135] Tamora's son in *Titus* may be equipped with both falchion and shield. Or perhaps he holds a falchion in one hand and a torch in the other, for a torch was "a traditional symbol of lust"[136] and, as we have seen, the would-be rapist in Marston's *Tragedy of Sophonisba* emerges from a vault and, with "*a torch in his hand*," advances upon Sophonisba (4.1.42.s.d.). The clothing of Tamora's son was almost certainly black, identified with lust since the Middle Ages.[137]

Rape, Murder, and Revenge

That Rape and Murder should appear together in *Titus Andronicus* is consonant with the nexus of these two elsewhere in the drama. In *A Warning for Fair Women*, Tragedy speaks of Lust and Murder, together with Gain, as having spurred on the villain (line 1254). In *The Tragical Reign of Selimus* (acted by the Queen's Men c. 1591–94), the queen chastises Selimus for surrounding himself with wicked guards, "Fleshing themselves in murther, lust, and rape" (line 2382).[138] In Dekker's *Lust's Dominion* (acted c. 1600) "Murder and Lust are twins" (1.1.94),[139] and in *The Honest Whore, Part 1* (acted by Prince Henry's Men c. 1604), "lust and murder" are again yoked together (2.1.350).[140] In Shakespeare's *Macbeth* (acted by the King's Men in 1606) the protagonist conjoins murder and rape when, immediately before the assassination, he describes personified Murder as moving "With Tarquin's ravishing strides" (2.1.55). In John Mason's *The Turk* (acted by the King's Revels Children c. 1607–8) a character speaks of having been "made a baud / To lust and murder" (lines 103–4).[141] In *Four Plays, or Moral Representations, in One* (acted by Lady Elizabeth's Men c. 1608–13), Murder and Lust – or at least their names – appear in the company of Revenge: four Furies enter bearing banners inscribed with the words *Murder, Lust, Revenge*, and *Drunkenness*.[142]

The combination of Murder and Lust/Rape together with Revenge has a compelling logic. Cesare Ripa observes in his description of Murder that homicide typically generates revenge.[143] The crime of rape, similarly, fuels a desire for vengeance. Shakespeare's Lucrece, for instance, says that she will report her rape to her husband "That he may vow, in that sad hour of mine, / Revenge on him that made me stop my breath" (lines 1179–80). Heywood's Lucrece makes this demand of her auditors: "Swear you'le revenge poor Lucrece on her foe" (line 2420). And the epilogue to Middleton's poem invokes "a chariot of Revenge" in which the ghost of Lucrece will "avenge / Her chaste untimely blood of flam'd desire" (lines 512, 514–15).

Because of their enormity, rape and murder, more than most crimes, demand retribution. The conjunction of Revenge, Murder, and Rape at Titus' door, then, must have seemed symbolically right to Shakespeare's playgoers. These three figures, dressed in armor and equipped with weaponry of sharp steel, would visually convey the implacability and menace of the forces they embody.

For Shakespeare's audience no English monarch was more renowned than Henry V. So successful had been his reign, and so disastrous his successor's, that Henry's life turned chroniclers into hagiographers. Holinshed writes that Henry "both lived & died a paterne in princehood, a lode-starre in honour, and mirrour of magnificence: the more highlie exalted in his life, the more deepelie lamented at his death, and famous to the world alwaie."[1] The very title of the chronicle play that helped to shape Shakespeare's Henriad supports the claim that Henry V was indeed "famous to the world alwaie": *The Famous Victories of Henry V*, acted by the Queen's Men in the 1580s. In view of this celebrated life no one in Shakespeare's audience would have been surprised to see and hear a personification of Fame at the beginning of *2 Henry IV*, acted by the Lord Chamberlain's Men in 1598. But the playwright chooses to open the play with Rumour instead. To the modern playgoer the choice may seem curious, since the words of Rumour identify this figure with the spurious and short-lived, whereas the play chronicles the accession of a man who goes on to win lasting acclaim. Shakespeare's choice of Rumour raises a series of questions: How exactly was the figure costumed and what hand prop was carried onto the stage? What do these iconographic features reveal about the meaning of the personified figure? And what is the significance of Rumour for the subsequent dramatic action of *2 Henry IV* and *Henry V*?[2]

By constructing a character named Rumour, Shakespeare makes new use of characters-as-symbols. In earlier plays actual personages adopt the guise of personifications. Dull and Jaquenetta, along with Tamora and her sons, double as personified figures. In *2 Henry IV*, by contrast, Rumour is a full-fledged personification with no other identity. Rumour, then, has an iconic status transcending, say, that of Spring and Winter in Shakespeare's early comedy. When Rumour steps onstage, it is as though a being from another world arrives in our own, commanding our attention in spectacular fashion and, in effect, claiming responsibility for everything we see and hear subsequently.

Tongues, wings, & trumpet: the affinity of Fame and Rumour

"*Enter Rumor painted full of tongues.*" This spare stage direction in the Quarto of 1600, repeated in the 1623 Folio, tells us all we know for certain about the physical appearance of the character in *2 Henry IV*; everything else is conjecture.[3] We do not even know the sex of Rumour. A recent editor suggests that Rumour is "the male negative incarnation of Fame"[4] (the word *rumor* is masculine in Latin while *fama* is feminine). Cesare Ripa's influential *Iconologia* presents Rumour as a man dressed in classical military garb and brandishing arrows.[5] Sixteenth-century stage history in England offers additional evidence. In the moral interlude *Clyomon and Clamydes* (written c. 1570, printed 1599) Clyomon applies masculine pronouns to Rumour, who appears as a character (line 1195).[6] And in Thomas Garter's *The Most Virtuous and Godly Susanna* (Stationers' Register 1569, printed 1578), Ill Report, perhaps synonymous with Rumour, is addressed as "boy" (line 72) and as "brother" (line 1257).[7] The martial metaphors of Shakespeare's Rumour also suggest masculinity. Harry Berger, Jr. reports that although he initially believed Rumour to be female, "I have been persuaded by my colleague John Lynch that several details in the speech make this far from certain, for example, the image of Rumor on horseback, the phrase '*my* household,' and the parade of phallic references between lines 8 and 15, suggesting that the ear-stuffing Rumor possibly fathered 'some other grief' on the big year and that the pipe (a Dionysian attachment?) may belong to the anatomy of 'My well-known body.'"[8] Berger refers especially to these lines of Rumour: "I speak of peace, while covert enmity / Under the smile of safety wounds the world; / And who but Rumor, who but only I, / Make fearful musters and prepar'd defense?" (lines 9–12). The literary evidence suggests that Shakespeare's Rumour may be male, but the issue is far from certain. Thomas Dekker's *Magnificent Entertainment*, honoring King James I in March 1604, describes Rumour as "comming all in a sweate to play the midwife" (lines 17–18).[9]

Although the 1600 Quarto leaves unspecified Rumour's iconographic features (apart from tongues), Shakespeare's personification may be winged, symbolic of the speed with which rumors travel.[10] In Chaucer's *House of Fame* tidings race from the dwelling of Rumour to that of Fame, where "Wynged wondres faste fleen, / Twenty thousand in a route" (lines 2118–19).[11] Wings also appear prominently in an October 1518 entertainment involving the imparting of news at Henry VIII's court. According to Edward Hall's account, "Then entred a person called Reaport, appareled in crymosyn satyn ful of tonges, sitting on a flyeng horse with wynges & fete of gold called, Pegasus."[12] Although there is no evidence that Shakespeare's personification is literally accompanied by such a horse, Rumour refers to the wind as "my post-horse" (line 4). Thomas Campion actually gives wings to Rumor's tongues in *The Somerset Masque*, presented at Whitehall in 1614: "*Rumor* [appeared] *in a skin coate* [a close-fitting leather jerkin or jacket] *full of winged tongues, and over it an antick robe; on his head a cap like a tongue, with a large paire of wings to it.*"[13] Although a modern audience may not bring a knowledge of such iconography to the theatre, we evoke those wings of Rumour when we say that rumors swirl, sweep, or fly.

Shakespeare's Rumour also probably carries a musical instrument, as this metaphor implies: "Rumor is a pipe / Blown by surmises, jealousies, conjectures" (lines 15–16). From these lines, Giorgio Melchiori infers a reference to a "recorder; a wooden instrument."[14] Rumour's characterization of the pipe may seem to confirm the inference: it is "of so easy and so plain a stop / That the blunt monster with uncounted heads, / The still-discordant wav'ring multitude, / Can play upon it" (lines 17–20). The playwright, however, may be referring to a metal horn, or trumpet, of the kind that Rumour sometimes carries: for example, in *The Comedy of Patient and Meek Grissell* (SR 1565) by John Phillip (lines 1672–77) and in *A New Tragical Comedy of Apius and Virginia* (SR 1567) by Richard Bower (lines 882–83).[15] The *OED*, moreover, records that a "pipe" can signify a metal organ pipe, and a poem by Michael Drayton, published in 1596, probably two years before the composition of *2 Henry IV*, specifically calls Fame's trumpet a "pipe." In Drayton's *débat* Fortune disparages Fame:

That trump thou saist, wakes dead men from theyr traunce
Is not of precious gold as some do deeme,
A brazen pipe, by which vaine fooles do daunce,
And but to sound so loude doth onely seeme.

          (lines 169–72)[16]

A "stop," moreover, need not refer to the finger hole in the tube of a wind instrument like a recorder; as the *OED* indicates, "stop" in a figurative sense is "sometimes vaguely used for 'note,' 'key,' 'tune.'" George Gascoigne in *The Steele Glas* so uses the word: "sweeter soundes, of concorde, peace, and love, / Are out of tune, and jarre in every stoppe" (lines 360–61).[17] Thus Shakespeare's Rumour may mean that the multitude plays an easy and plain tune on a trumpet.[18]

By appearing with tongues, wings, and trumpet, Shakespeare's Rumour would recall another personification, who shared the same features in plays and pageants, paintings and engravings – Fame.[19] Tongues like those that

14 Fame blows a trumpet; eyes and ears decorate the banner. Detail of an arch in the coronation procession of King James I. From Stephen Harrison's *The Arches of Triumph* (London, 1604), sig. F2. Engraving by William Kip

Shakespeare and Thomas Campion assign to Rumour belong to Fame in an arch erected for the coronation procession of King James I on 15 March 1604. In William Kip's engraving of the arch,[20] Fame blows a trumpet from which a banner hangs (fig. 14). On the banner appear eyes and ears, and, according to Thomas Dekker's account in *The Magnificent Entertainment*, Fame was also adorned with tongues: she stood "A woman in a watchet [light blue] roabe, thickly set with open eyes, and tongues" (lines 752–53). Similarly, tongues characterize Fame in *Sidero-thriambos*, a pageant designed by Anthony Munday for the lord mayor's show of 29 October 1618:

In the most eminent place sitteth Fame, seeming as if shee sounded her golden trumpet, the banner whereof, is plentifully powdred with tongues, eyes, and eares...(lines 139–41)[21]

Richard Linche, adapting Vincenzo Cartari's *Imagini de i dei de gli antichi*, cites Virgil's account of *Fama* in the *Aeneid* to explain the connection between tongues and the other organs of sense: "shee commonly seateth her selfe on the top of a high turret, where she uttereth and babbleth foorth all that either her eyes have seene, or her eares have heard."[22] Together, the descriptions of Linche, Munday, and Dekker suggest the extent to which Fame and Rumour overlap iconographically: the tongues, trumpet, and wings of the one are indistinguishable from those of the other.

   That the features of Rumour and Fame should be largely congruent seems apt, for the phenomena that each embodies are similar. The word *fama* in classical Latin can denote either rumor or fame. Virgil, whose *Aeneid* gave impetus to Renaissance portrayals of Fame, notes that *Fama* "sang alike of fact and falsehood" (4:190).[23] Ovid makes essentially the same observation by his description of *Fama*'s dwelling in his *Metamorphoses*: "Crowds fill the hall, shifting throngs come and go, and everywhere wander thousands of rumours, falsehoods mingled with the truth, and confused reports flit about" (12:53–55).[24] Chaucer in his *House of Fame* writes that in a valley near Fame's hilltop castle lies the dwelling of Rumour, perpetually moving, where tidings originate before they speed to Fame for dispersal (lines 2110–14). Thomas Dekker, describing Fame in James I's coronation procession, explains that her wings, trumpet, and "mantle of sundry cullours traversing her body" represent "the propertie of her swiftnesse, and aptnesse to disperse rumors" (*The Magnificent Entertainment*, lines 754–56). Fame has a similar function in Ben Jonson's *The Staple of News* (acted by the King's Men in 1626) where Register describes the news office:

     'Tis the house of fame, sir,
Where both the curious and the negligent,
The scrupulous and careless, wild and staid,
The idle and laborious: all do meet
To taste the *cornucopiae* of her rumours,
Which she, the mother of sport, pleaseth to scatter
Among the vulgar.   (3.2.115–21)[25]

And in Jonson's *The Masque of Queens*, performed at Whitehall on 2 February 1609, Fame "about her vaulted palace hurled / All rumors and reports, or true, or vain" (lines 367–68).[26]

Fame's role in hurling rumors and reports (whether accurate or erroneous) suggests that fame does not necessarily imply genuine accomplishment. Fame may have no more basis in fact than the wildest rumor. As sixteenth-century chroniclers knew, judgments tainted by self-interest and greed can result in fraudulent renown. In his chronicle of King Henry IV, for example, Edward Hall pauses to note how unscrupulous clerics embellished the reputations of those who rewarded their efforts:

> these monasticall persones, lerned and unliterate, better fed then taught, toke on them to write & regester in the boke of fame, the noble actes, the wise dooynges, and politike governances of kynges and princes, in whiche cronographie, if a kyng gave to them possessions or graunted them liberties or exalted them to honor & worldly dignitee, he was called a sainct, he was praised without any deserte above the moone, his genealogie was written, and not one jote that might exalt his fame, was ether forgotten or omitted. (1st year, fol. xir–v)

If fame may be fraudulent, rumor conversely may prove accurate. Someone who speaks of "rumor" may simply be expressing uncertainty about the veracity of something heard, as when a messenger in *King John* (acted by the Lord Chamberlain's Men c. 1595) tells the King:

> the first of April died
> Your noble mother; and as I hear, my lord,
> The Lady Constance in a frenzy died
> Three days before; but this from rumor's tongue
> I idly heard – if true or false I know not.
>   (4.2.120–24)[27]

Rumors can, of course, prove true. Thus in *Clyomon and Clamydes* what Rumour says proves accurate.[28] In Dekker's *The Honest Whore, Part 2* (acted by Prince Henry's Men, 1604–5), moreover, the duke tells Candido: "now our court / Shall be thy sphere, where from thy good report, / Rumours this truth unto the world shal sing, / A patient man's a patterne for a king" (5.2.494–97).[29] Near the beginning of his account of King James's coronation procession, Dekker explains what Rumour, mounted on horseback, announces: "this treasure of a kingdome (a man-ruler) hid so many yeares from us, was now brought to light, and at hand" (*The Magnificent Entertainment*, lines 19–20). And in a civic celebration marking the Prince of

Wales's arrival in Chester on 23 April 1610, Rumour recounts (accurately) Saint George's role as patron saint of England.[30] In each of these instances rumor and truth coincide.

An incident in *1 Henry VI* (acted by Lord Strange's Men in 1592) illustrates the affinity of rumor and fame. Entirely the playwright's invention, this episode involves the Countess of Auvergne, who has heard accounts of John Talbot: "Great is the rumor of this dreadful knight, / And his achievements of no less account" (2.3.7–8). As the word "rumor" suggests, she does not know whether to credit what she has heard, and so she seeks the corroboration of ocular evidence: "Fain would mine eyes be witness with mine ears / To give their censure of these rare reports" (lines 9–10). Whatever the outcome, the countess means to enhance her own stature by entrapping Talbot within her castle: "The plot is laid. If all things fall out right, / I shall as famous be by this exploit / As Scythian Tomyris by Cyrus' death" (lines 4–6). The moment of confrontation proves anti-climactic, however, for when she beholds Talbot face to face, she finds an unprepossessing figure: "Is this the Talbot, so much fear'd abroad / That with his name the mothers still their babes? / I see report is fabulous and false" (lines 16–18). She is compelled to revise her initial impression only when Talbot blows a horn summoning his men to his side. In this instance, the countess reflects, rumor and fame do indeed coincide: "Victorious Talbot, pardon my abuse. / I find thou art no less than fame hath bruited" (lines 67–68). The conflation of rumor and fame in this episode is epitomized by Talbot's horn, the most important accoutrement of both personifications.

This episode in *1 Henry VI* also suggests the dependence of fame upon rumor. That is, fame as a phenomenon does not enter into the world fully formed; it is generated by a process of accumulation. Especially in a culture where the spoken word has not yet lost its precedence to the written, fame begins with individual reports, with oral accounts, successively longer and more detailed. Shakespeare alludes to this process of becoming in *3 Henry VI* (acted by Lord Strange's Men in 1591), when Warwick tells Bona, daughter of the French king, that Edward, Duke of York, has directed him "To tell the passion of my sovereign's heart, / Where fame, late ent'ring at his heedful ears, / Hath plac'd thy beauty's image and thy virtue" (3.3.62–64). Whether "fame" here means "report" or "rumor" (as editors usually gloss the word), it is dependent on oral report. Presumably Bona's "fame" would transcend the status of rumor or report if it were amplified by other voices. Mere repetition can lead to the acceptance of rumor as fact: one report may constitute a rumor while many may be taken for corroboration.

Fame depends on a multitude of tongues. In Dekker's *Britannia's Honour*, celebrating the inauguration of Richard Deane as lord mayor of London in 1628, Fame declares that she possesses a "thousand tongues" (line 271).[31]

The phenomena of rumor and fame share something else, a certain tenuousness. If a rumor enjoys a precarious existence because always awaiting confirmation or refutation, fame may also prove unstable. Fame, after all, is vulnerable to declension, even oblivion, as Petrarch indicates by the design of his *Triumphs*, treating the victories seriatim of Love, Chastity, Death, Fame, Time, and Eternity.[32] Shakespeare explicitly alludes to this sequence in *Love's Labour's Lost* (acted by the Lord Chamberlain's Men c. 1594), when Navarre explains the purpose of his academy:

Let fame, that all hunt after in their lives,
Live regist'red upon our brazen tombs,
And then grace us in the disgrace of death;
When spite of cormorant devouring Time,
Th' endeavor of this present breath may buy
That honor which shall bate his scythe's keen edge,
And make us heirs of all eternity.   (1.1.1–7)

Although Navarre seems to envision his fame as triumphing over time, a contemporary of Shakespeare's, especially one who recognized the allusion to the *Triumphs*,[33] would be less sanguine, for Navarre reverses the Petrarchan pattern. *Love's Labour's Lost*, in the pageant of the Nine Worthies, provides dramatic evidence of time's destructive force. Honoring men deserving of fame, the entertainment degenerates into chaos when the courtly audience within the play rudely treats the amateur actors impersonating the heroes of the past. It is not just the actors who are diminished by the ridicule but also the famous heroes themselves.

An episode in *1 Henry VI*, Talbot's death scene, dramatizes the precarious quality that fame shares with rumor. When the beleaguered warrior realizes that fortune has turned against the English, he urges his son to flee. Young Talbot, however, sees in flight a threat to his reputation: "O, if you love my mother, / Dishonor not her honorable name / To make a bastard and a slave of me!" (4.5.13–15). In the following scene the father anticipates in his son's demise the loss of the family's name and fame:

In thee thy mother dies, our household's name,
My death's revenge, thy youth, and England's fame:
All these, and more, we hazard by thy stay;
All these are sav'd if thou wilt fly away.   (4.6.38–41)

Although young Talbot prevails, arguing that his flight would dishonor them both, no less than if his father fled the field, the older Talbot's apprehension is not misplaced. He knows that noble deeds do not guarantee fame. To attain renown, noble acts must be witnessed and reported. Unless given permanence by some means, fame will prove as fleeting as rumor.[34]

What rumor and fame share helps explain the playwright's choice of presenter in *2 Henry IV*. In particular, the precariousness inherent in both personifications enables Shakespeare to resolve a dramaturgical problem. In order to resuscitate the figures of Henry IV's reign, whose existence consisted chiefly of words on paper, and in order to engage a theatrical audience, Shakespeare needs to create the illusion that those personages inhabit a world of possibilities, not an unassailable record of accomplishment or failure. In the case of Prince Hal the problem is acute, since he was already fixed in the popular imagination as heroic; by the time Shakespeare wrote *Henry IV*, Hal had become a character in *The Famous Victories* (acted c. 1583–88). *Part 2* presents an especially formidable problem since the Hal of *Part 1* had already proved himself at Shrewsbury and seemed poised to claim his stature in history. The prince cannot step directly from the battlefield at the end of *Part 1* into the world of *Part 2* without seeming a static figure, marking time till his father dies and circumstance proves ripe for foreign adventure. His new status, won by martial valor and filial loyalty in *Part 1*, must be diminished, if not obscured. And so Shakespeare invites us to imagine Hal as he was when all that people knew of him was what they heard, when he had not yet taken up residence in the pages of history books.

How better to accomplish this than by making Hal the subject of errant rumor?

> My office is
> To noise abroad that Harry Monmouth fell
> Under the wrath of noble Hotspur's sword,
> And that the King before the Douglas' rage
> Stoop'd his anointed head as low as death.
>   (lines 28–32)

Rumour's speech generates an unsettled, problematic atmosphere, where knowledge is replaced by supposition or wishful thinking. A rumor, after all, expresses the speaker's uncertainty, as Philip the Bastard indicates in Shakespeare's earlier history, *King John*:

> as I travell'd hither through the land,
> I find the people strangely fantasied,
> Possess'd with rumors, full of idle dreams,
> Not knowing what they fear, but full of fear.
>
> (4.2.143–46)

By its inherent doubtfulness rumor is disturbing, whether a rumor later proves true or false. An angry Coriolanus evokes this aspect of rumor when he tells the citizens of Rome, "Let every feeble rumor shake your hearts!" (3.3.125), and it is this same quality that serves Shakespeare's purpose in *2 Henry IV*. The Hal of the history play is not yet the icon of the chroniclers but rather the man whose future lies unformed and whose past behavior occasions apprehension and dismay.

The presence of Rumour helps to turn back the clock to a time when Hal disappointed the righteous and encouraged the reprobate. The tongues that momentarily buoy the spirits of Northumberland at the beginning of *Part 2* also depress the reputation of Hal. The action that ensues is consonant with the impression that Hal has suffered a relapse. He still lives, or seems to, the life of indolence that marked his character throughout much of *Part 1*. His first words in *Part 2* – "Before God, I am exceeding weary" (2.2.1) – suggest physical and spiritual torpor, not the confidence of someone who has proved himself in battle. And he continues to consort with those who had been his companions in the tavern. To Poins, Hal concedes his still unsavory reputation: "thou thinkest me as far in the devil's book as thou and Falstaff, for obduracy and persistency" (lines 45–47). Not even Poins can guess what the word "thinkest" implies: that appearances may be illusory, that Hal's accession will lead him to redefine his relationship to everyone in his kingdom, friend and foe alike.

Winning fame: the virtuous pursuit

Like Chaucerians who have studied the subject of fame, Shakespeareans have tended to emphasize its Christian dimension – the accommodation of an ancient value within a theological framework subordinating the things of this world to those of the next. In their treatment of *Othello*, for instance, David L. Jeffrey and Patrick Grant write: "During the Middle Ages, fame is transformed (like fortune and Venus) into a theological symbol of some complexity. Primarily in the Christian symbol we must distinguish between earthly fame and heavenly fame, a contrast based on Scripture, where a distinction between earthly vanity and heavenly glory is often made."[35]

Because a Christian sees the fame achieved in this life as irrelevant to salvation, a seventeenth-century audience would presumably recognize the exaggeration, if not the blasphemy, in Michael Cassio's utterance: "Reputation, reputation, reputation! O, I have lost my reputation! I have lost the immortal part of myself, and what remains is bestial" (*Othello*, 2.3.262–64). Ironically, Iago's dismissive claim – "Reputation is an idle and most false imposition; oft got without merit, and lost without deserving" (lines 268–70) – is closer to the Christian view. (In *The House of Fame* Chaucer suggests the adventitious nature of fame by calling Fame the sister of Fortune [line 1547].) Owen Felltham undoubtedly articulates the attitude of many contemporaries when he writes, "It may seem strange, that the whole world of men, should be carried on with an earnest desire of a noble fame, and memory after their deaths: when yet we know it is not materiall to our well, or ill being, what censures passe upon us."[36] Felltham adds of the New Jerusalem, "Fame shall there be excluded, as a lying witnesse."[37] Even Francis Bacon, who never shared Felltham's religiosity, said, "Fame is like a river, that beareth up things light and swolne, and drownes things waighty and solide."[38] The priority for a Christian, therefore, is clear: Charles Gibson advises, "we must not labour or looke to eternize our names upon earth, but rather covet and crave that we may be in the nomber of those whose names are written in heaven."[39]

We need to beware, however, of imagining that a doctrinally Christian understanding colors fame throughout Renaissance culture. As any pragmatist can attest, fame has its claims. Presumably Shakespeare's audience could identify with Hamlet's dying words: "O God, Horatio, what a wounded name, / Things standing thus unknown, shall I leave behind me!" (5.2.344–45). Similarly that audience could understand the dread Coriolanus feels when his mother predicts, "if thou conquer Rome, the benefit / Which thou shalt thereby reap is such a name / Whose repetition will be dogg'd with curses" (5.3.142–44).[40] Behind these protagonists stands the long line of ghostly figures in the *Mirror for Magistrates*, who return to the world of the living in order to clarify their record in life, exculpate their misdeeds where possible, and underscore their achievements. The 1610 edition of the *Mirror* includes an Induction to one of its sections, identifying the personification of Fame with heaven: "I boldly looked round about, and loe, there stood in sight / True Fame, the trumpeter of heav'n that doth desire inflame / To glorious deeds, and by her power eternifies the name."[41]

In the pictorial arts of the sixteenth century we find personified Fame alongside various virtues. In Henry Peacham's *Minerva Britanna* (1612) an

15 Fame in the company of Temperance (with bridle) and Peace (with beehive).
Printer's device of Sigmund Feyerabend, engraved by Jost Amman

emblem dedicated to Sir Thomas Chaloner depicts Virtue handing a scroll
to Fame; another emblem in the same collection shows God's hand, extend-
ing out of a cloud, holding "the quill of Fame."[42] A mark of the Frankfurt
printer Sigmund Feyerabend, made by Jost Amman, depicts winged Fame
amid the clouds, blowing her trumpet while Peace rides a dolphin and
holds a sail.[43] In another of Feyerabend's devices Fame stands alongside
Temperance and Peace, forming a trio of virtues (fig. 15). And in still another device, Fame blows two trumpets simultaneously while sitting on a
globe representing the world (fig. 16). The image of God the Father, looking

16 Fame seated on a globe, God the Father above. Printer's device of Sigmund Feyerabend, engraved by Jost Amman

down benignly from heaven, suggests the congruity of Fame's activity with the divine will.

When he depicts Fame blowing a trumpet, Feyerabend gives vivid pictorial form to the pursuit of fame as an unalloyed good: in another printer's device Fame blows a trumpet while holding a second trumpet; below her a fashionably dressed man rides in a sled which is pulled by slow-moving lobsters, each headed in a different direction (fig. 17). With sly humor the printer records the difficulty and uncertainty of his own quest for fame. An object at the center of this device indicates that his effort is worthy of emulation: at the front of the sled is a statuette of Dame Fortune. She holds not the wheel that had been customary in medieval culture but rather a sail, suggesting her conflation with Occasion, or Opportunity, which became increasingly popular in the Renaissance.[44] The iconography suggests that in order to gain prosperity the aspirant must seize favorable wind and tide, that is, favorable circumstance. Wenceslaus Hollar's panorama of London,

17 Fame with trumpets, a sled below. Printer's device of Sigmund Feyerabend, engraved by Jost Amman

among the most accomplished etchings of the early seventeenth century, depicts Fame in a way that makes much the same point as Feyerabend, though on a grander scale. A personification appears on either side of the city's name in this exceptionally wide print. On the left is Mercury, the Roman deity with the winged cap, heavenly messenger and god of commerce. On the right flies winged Fame, identifiable by her trumpet (fig. 18). A close inspection of Fame's head reveals what is almost certainly a forelock – the same forelock that belongs to Opportunity in so many Renaissance representations. For Hollar, England's capital had actively sought and achieved a fame well worth celebrating.

18 Fame with forelock and trumpet. Detail from Wenceslaus Hollar's panoramic view of London

If England's capital attained fame, so did her monarchs. In fact, Queen Elizabeth's identification with Fame became a staple of both civic pageantry and praise in print. When she visited Norwich in 1578, she saw a gate of the city decorated with symbols of the houses of York and Lancaster; under red and white roses were her own coat of arms and verses calling her "The pearlesse prince of Fame."[45] At Elvetham in 1591 the queen listened to a song praising her as "dread Eliza, that faire name / Who filles the golden trump of Fame."[46] In Peele's *Arraignment of Paris*, performed at court by the Children of the Queen's Chapel in the early 1580s, the goddess Diana extravagantly praises Elizabeth, noting that "Her auncestors live in the house of fame" (5.1.1162).[47] A picture of Elizabeth ensconced in a chariot upon which Fame blows her horn decorates the title-page of Anthony Munday's *Zelauto, the Fountaine of Fame* (London, 1580).[48] Similarly, when a pamphlet chronicling Elizabeth's coronation procession was reprinted in 1604, the title-page was adorned with a woodcut of Fame blowing her trumpet.[49] Upon the death of Elizabeth, Thomas Newton composed a poem in which personified Fame addresses the queen: "Fame immortall is on earth, / As you in heaven, and will not lose her so: / You have her substance: I a God beneath, / Will keepe the substance of her life to shew."[50]

Perhaps the most interesting identification of the queen with Fame is the so-called Rainbow portrait (c. 1600), attributed to Marcus Gheeraerts the Younger and now in Hatfield House near London.[51] In the painting made just a few years before her death, Elizabeth wears an outer robe covered with eyes and ears. Frances Yates recognized the symbolism of the garment, observing that "The eyes, ears and mouths which are depicted all over the queen's cloak symbolize her Fame which is flying rapidly through the world, spoken of by many mouths, seen and heard by many eyes and ears."[52] Most recent viewers, however, resist the identification of Elizabeth with Fame. Roy Strong, for instance, who seems poised to acknowledge a connection between the robe and Fame in his book *Gloriana* (1987), draws back because he finds missing one element that Yates had specified: "A detailed examination of this garment shows no signs of the mouths read into it by scholars so that it could signify the Queen's fame."[53] More recently, Michael Neill, citing Strong, takes Yates to task for having identified the Rainbow portrait with Fame: "Yates's otherwise useful iconographic analysis of the painting mistakenly interprets folds on the garment as mouths and accordingly misreads its 'ears, eyes and tongues' as symbols of Fame."[54] Similarly, Daniel Fischlin says, "The eyes and ears evident in the 'Rainbow' portrait... do not signify fame, as Frances Yates has suggested in a reading discounted by Strong."[55]

Strong, Neill, and Fischlin are right in saying that mouths do not appear in the painting. Their doubt about the identification with Fame, however, is occasioned by a misconception – that Fame's form is normally decorated with mouths. In fact, Renaissance Fame is never decorated with mouths, only with eyes, ears, and, sometimes, tongues, as hundreds of prints and other representations demonstrate. Although Yates mistakenly imagined that she saw mouths in the Rainbow portrait, she was correct in identifying the eyes and ears on Elizabeth's garment with Fame. In that portrait the queen herself has indeed come to embody fame. Ironically, Roy Strong himself, whose work is cited by everyone who discusses the Rainbow portrait, acknowledged, almost twenty-five years before he published *Gloriana*, the connection with Fame, though he mistakenly thought that the presence of mouths would clinch the identification: "The cloak which encircles Elizabeth is covered with eyes and ears and is probably intended for Fame (although strictly speaking there should also be mouths)."[56]

Given the tradition of allying Queen Elizabeth herself with Fame, there was nothing necessarily suspect in the 1590s about Rumor/Fame presiding over a play dramatizing Prince Hal's accession, nothing pernicious in achieving the kind of fame that Hal as king would attain. Indeed, by adopting the course of action that will take him to France, Hal proves a devoted son. His father, a shrewd master of public relations, recommends in *2 Henry IV* a strategy that will culminate in Hal's achievement of fame: "Be it thy course to busy giddy minds / With foreign quarrels, that action, hence borne out, / May waste the memory of the former days" (4.5.213–15). By performing new actions – the martial exploits in France – the new king diminishes, if he does not altogether obliterate, the memory of his father's guilty legacy, acknowledged on the very eve of Agincourt in *Henry V*: "Not to-day, O Lord, / O, not to-day, think not upon the fault / My father made in compassing the crown!" (4.1.292–94).

For Shakespeare's contemporaries the most expeditious path to achieving fame was through martial valor. We have already noted how the career of Talbot, the celebrated warrior of *1 Henry VI*, is identified with fame. In *The Book of the Courtier*, moreover, Baldassare Castiglione writes: "You know that the true stimulus to great and daring deeds in war is glory [*la gloria*], and whosoever is moved thereto for gain or any other motive, apart from the fact that he never does anything good, deserves to be called not a gentleman, but a base merchant."[57] Machiavelli writes of Ferdinand of Aragon that "with fame and glory [*per fama e per gloria*] he has developed from a weak king to the foremost king of Christendom," by attacking Granada, strengthening his army, and driving the Moors from Spain.[58]

Renaissance entertainments honoring victory on the battlefield frequently personify Fame. For example, winged Fame, holding her trumpet, appears in the vehicle of Mars, god of war, in a 1579 celebration at the Pitti Palace, Florence (fig. 19). In the palace of Fame designed for *The Masque of Queens*, Inigo Jones chooses Achilles, Aeneas, Caesar, and other heroes to serve as the upper columns of the structure; the scenes depicted between the pillars, underneath, include land battles, sea fights, and triumphs.[59] Representations of Petrarch's triumph of Fame also customarily have a military complexion. In the engraving by Philips Galle after Maarten van Heemskerck, Fame's chariot is drawn by elephants, identified with the campaigns of Hannibal and, before him, of Alexander the Great when he invaded India (fig. 20).[60] Alongside the chariot, moreover, walk Alexander, Julius Caesar, and other warriors. These are among the Nine Worthies, subject of the pageant in *Love's Labour's Lost*. The nine figures – three pagans, three Jews, three Christians – are all warriors, and they appear elsewhere in Elizabethan design: for example, statues of the Worthies wearing classical military garb adorn the facade of Montacute House, Somerset, built in the 1590s.[61]

On the stage, too, Fame appears in a military context: she stands at the head of an army in John Pickering's *The Interlude of Vice (Horestes)* (acted by a boys' company and printed 1567).[62] Although she does not materialize

19 Fame atop the vehicle of Mars, a float in a 1579 celebration at the Pitti Palace,
Florence. From *Feste nelle nozze* (Florence, 1579) by Raffaello Gualterotti

as a personified character in *Tamburlaine the Great* (acted by the Admiral's
Men c. 1587), Theridimas describes Fame as though he sees and hears
her celebrating his general's life of conquest. Over the Scythian warrior,
Theridimas says, "Fame hovereth, sounding of her golden trump, / That
to the adverse poles of that straight line / Which measureth the glorious
frame of heaven / The name of mighty Tamburlaine is spread" (*Part 2*,
3.4.63–66).[63] And in *Edward III*, written at least in part by Shakespeare
and acted c. 1589–92 probably by Pembroke's or Strange's Men, a herald
salutes the king in terms recalling both ancient triumphal processions and
Petrarch's triumph of Fame: "Great servitor to bloody Mars in arms, / The
Frenchman's terror, and his country's fame, / Triumphant rideth like a
Roman peer" (5.1.178–80).[64]

Fame won on the battlefield inevitably comes at a price – the blood of
vanquished and victors alike. For Tamburlaine, no price is too great. For a
Christian, however, bloodshed may prompt introspection, even a twinge of
conscience. Describing Henry V's invasion of France, the chroniclers relate
a story of massive death caused by combat, disease, and weather. Raphael

20 The triumph of Fame, inspired by Petrarch's *Triumphs*, one of six engravings in a
series by Philips Galle after Maarten van Heemskerck

Holinshed represents Henry V on his deathbed, preoccupied with the issue
of self-aggrandizement, anticipating the verdict of history, and seemingly
apprehensive about the invasion's legitimacy. Addressing his retainers, "he
protested unto them, that neither the ambitious desire to inlarge his do-
minions, neither to purchase vaine renowme and worldlie fame, nor anie
other consideration had mooved him to take the warres in hand; but onelie
that in prosecuting his just title, he might in the end atteine to a perfect
peace, and come to enjoie those peeces of his inheritance, which to him of
right belonged" (583).

    Less defensive than Holinshed, Edward Hall represents Henry as moti-
vated by a desire for fame and concerned to perpetuate it once achieved;
Hall's deathbed scene has an entirely different tone than Holinshed's. Here
the king, seemingly unconcerned with the lives lost in his expedition, looks
forward to his demise because it precludes anything happening that might
detract from the fame won on the battlefield: "this short tyme and smal
tract of my mortal life, shal be a testimony of my strength, a declaracion of
my justice, and a settyng furth of all myne actes and procedynges, and shal
be the cause that I by death shal obteine fame, glorye and renoume, and

escape the reprehension of cowardnes, and the mote of all infamy, whiche I might have chaunsed to falle into if nature had lenger prolonged my life or daies" (10th year of Henry V, fol. lxxx). Shakespeare's Henry V seems much closer in spirit to Hall's king than to Holinshed's, for the theatrical character explicitly seeks fame by his invasion of France: "Either our history shall with full mouth / Speak freely of our acts, or else our grave, / Like Turkish mute, shall have a tongueless mouth, / Not worshipp'd with a waxen epitaph" (1.2.230–33). And addressing his men in the "Crispin Crispian" speech, Henry unashamedly expresses a concern with personal renown – theirs and his. At the site of his most important victory he rallies his outnumbered troops by anticipating what they will share if successful: "The fewer men, the greater share of honor" (4.3.22).[65] The consolation that Henry envisions for loss and even death is not the Christian salvation offered to medieval Crusaders but rather the secular glory that pagan warriors crave; the king proffers a future that Hector or Aeneas would instantly recognize and approve.

It seems fitting, then, that just before his first great military victory, at Shrewsbury in *1 Henry IV*, young Henry is presented in terms more classical than Christian. Sir Richard Vernon reports to Hotspur that he has seen the prince preparing for combat:

I saw young Harry with his beaver on,
His cushes on his thighs, gallantly arm'd,
Rise from the ground like feathered Mercury,
And vaulted with such ease into his seat
As if an angel dropp'd down from the clouds
To turn and wind a fiery Pegasus,
And witch the world with noble horsemanship.

(4.1.104–10)

Although we immediately apprehend the elaborate simile likening Prince Hal to Mercury wheeling about Pegasus, the modern audience may miss the more profound similitude. The lines identify a warrior on the brink of battle with a personification of the kind Cesare Ripa describes in his *Iconologia*: a figure who is himself winged and who guides a winged horse (fig. 21). The horseman is, of course, Mercury, symbolic of report and reputation; the horse is Pegasus, identified with fame since antiquity.[66] Ripa calls the composite symbol *Fama Chiara*, or Illustrious Fame.[67] By evoking this visual symbol, Shakespeare foreshadows the fame that Hal will win at Shrewsbury and, later, on a much grander scale at Agincourt: Hal is metamorphosing into Fame before our very eyes. Only the word

F A M A C H I A R A.

21 Fama Chiara (Illustrious Fame) represented by winged Mercury and Pegasus, from Cesare Ripa's *Iconologia* (Rome, 1603)

"angel" hints that he will transcend the status of his classical counterparts, that he will one day become what the chorus in *Henry V* calls "the mirror of all Christian kings" (act 2 chorus, line 6).

Perpetuating fame: written word vs. spoken word

Although the sword may win fame, weaponry is powerless to sustain it. Other means are required, and these depend not on steel or muscle, but on conceptual invention and verbal skill. For Shakespeare's culture, the surest way of perpetuating renown was through writing.[68] Jacques Amyot, in his address to the reader of Plutarch's *Lives*, argues that the written record "is a picture, which (as it were in a table) setteth before our eyes the things worthy of remembrance that have bene done in olde time by mighty nations, noble kings & princes, wise governors, valliant capteines, & persons renowmed for some notable quality."[69] Giorgio Vasari pauses in his life of Leon Battista Alberti to observe: "as far as fame and reputation [*quanto alla fama ed al nome*] are concerned the written word is more enduring and influential than anything else; for, provided they are honest and innocent of lies, books travel freely and are trusted wherever they go."[70] Even the ancients employed the written word to preserve reputation. Pliny in his *Natural History* records the practice not only of erecting statues of the honored dead but also "inscribing lists of honours on the bases to be read for all time, so that such records should not be read on their tombs only."[71] Writing also allows for the aggrandizement of reputation by the living. Julius Caesar, for example, ensured his renown not merely by his deeds on the battlefield but also by writing about his accomplishments: "Before Caesar, Suetonius tells us, no one making a report to the Senate had written in book form. Caesar was the first, as he was the first to write his war memoirs not as disconnected notes but as a narrative, a causal account of actions that implied logic beyond personal choice – where military strategy, the patterns of history, and the rhythms of Latin prose could meet."[72]

Edward Hall, in the dedication of his chronicle to Edward VI, notes what writing could accomplish: "[in antiquity] nothyng was set out to mennes knowledge ether how the world was made either howe man and beastes wer created, or how the worlde was destroyed by water, til father Moses had by devine inspiracion in the third age, invented letters, the treasure of memorie, and set furth five notable bokes, to the greate comfort of all people livyng at this daie" (sig. A2r); other classical societies also saw the merit of writing: "every nation was desirous to enhaunce lady Fame, and to suppresse that dedly beast Oblivion." To Hall, "Fame is the triumphe of glory, and memory by litterature is the verie dilator and setter furth of Fame." In the time of Hall and Vasari and Shakespeare, printing allowed fame to be achieved even more swiftly and on a grander scale than in antiquity.

Renaissance artists variously acknowledge the dependence of fame on the written word. In Gottfried Schalken's painting of Fame, now in the Pitti Palace, Florence, Fame has a trumpet in one hand, a book in the other.[73] The engraving of Fame's triumph, by Philips Galle after Maarten van Heemskerck, depicts Cato and Plato walking beside the triumphal car with books in their hands (fig. 20). In the House of Fame, created for Ben Jonson's *The Masque of Queens* in 1609, Inigo Jones represents the classical poets as structural supports upon whom rest the heroes above them: "for the lower columns, he [Jones] chose the statues of the most excellent poets, as Homer, Virgil, Lucan, etc., as being the substantial sup-porters of Fame" (lines 451–53). In Dekker's lord mayor's pageant, cele-brating the installation of John Swinerton in October 1612, Fame herself speaks of the worthies who "fill up Fames voluminous booke" (line 365).[74] According to John Taylor's account of a royal wedding in 1613, "like a scribe Fame waited to record" the nuptials.[75] And in Middleton's *The Tri-umphs of Love and Antiquity*, celebrating the installation of Sir William Cockaine as lord mayor in October 1619, the citizenry beheld a sanctu-ary of Fame where the names of mayors and benefactors of London were "enroll'd."[76]

Emblem books also demonstrate the dependence of fame upon writing. Geoffrey Whitney includes an emblem bearing the words "Scripta ma-nent" (writings remain) in *A Choice of Emblemes* (1586); the books in the foreground contrast with the crumbling architecture in the background, and the accompanying poem points the moral: "What thinges before three thousande yeares have paste, / What martiall knightes, have march'd up-pon this stage: / Whose actes, in bookes if writers did not save, / Their fame had ceaste, and gone with them to grave."[77] Another of Whitney's em-blems, a tribute to Sir Philip Sidney, depicts a quill pen slung from Fame's shoulder.[78] Thomas Goffe, in *The Courageous Turk*, acted by the students of Christ Church, Oxford, in 1619, provides the theatrical counterpart of such artistic renderings. The playwright brings Fame onstage to address the ghosts of Hector and Achilles and to explain how their reputation is preserved: "the gods awakt me Fame / From out the oblivious sepulcher of sleepe, / To drop that inke into old Homers pen, / Wherewith he curiously hath lin'd your names" (1.5.277–80).[79]

In *1 Henry VI* Shakespeare specifically addresses the issue of fame's sur-vival through writing, and he does so in the character of Talbot, whose own death will raise the issue again in a particularly poignant way. This warrior, saddened by the death of Salisbury, is determined to perpetuate his fallen comrade's fame:

And that hereafter ages may behold
What ruin happened in revenge of him,
Within their chiefest temple I'll erect
A tomb, wherein his corpse shall be interr'd;
Upon the which, that every one may read,
Shall be engrav'd the sack of Orleance,
The treacherous manner of his mournful death,
And what a terror he had been to France.

(2.2.10–17)

Without the tomb and its inscription, Talbot implies, Salisbury's fame might not survive, at least in France.

In view of the importance that inscriptions in stone and paper play in fostering fame, it may seem curious that Shakespeare's Henry V seems so indifferent to the creation of monuments bearing witness to his own deeds; nor does he anticipate his future in the pages of a chronicle as apparently the historical personage did. On the contrary, the theatrical hero expresses a distrust of written words. His metaphors involving writing invariably have a negative connotation: in *2 Henry IV*, as we have seen, the prince tells Poins, "thou thinkest me as far in the devil's book as thou and Falstaff" (2.2.45–46) – an "allusion to an old belief that the devil had a register of the men who were subject to him."[80] Hal knows by personal experience that what is written down may be untrue, and he takes pride in overturning his subjects' suppositions. As newly crowned king, Henry V says that he survives his father "To mock the expectation of the world, / To frustrate prophecies, and to rase out / Rotten opinion, who hath writ me down / After my seeming" (5.2.126–29). The relish he takes in surprising others does not betoken any reluctance on Henry's part to perpetuate the reputation he wins. Instead, his attitude suggests both an understanding of how fame is generated and a powerful desire to ensure future renown.

The impulse to construct memorials is informed by a barely subconscious sense of fame's fragility. As anyone who has ever visited an English or French graveyard knows, names and testaments inscribed on stone are as perishable as once they were handsome. Even a tomb within a church – like the one Talbot envisions for Salisbury – cannot escape the destructive effects of rising damp, the ravages of vandals, and the wholesale destruction of war – witness the depredations committed by Protestant reformers of the sixteenth century and by Cromwell's forces in the Civil War of the 1640s, not to mention the obliteration suffered by churches and their contents in Coventry, Normandy, and Germany in World War II. Contemporaries of Shakespeare were no less sensitive to this evanescence than we. In *The Triumphs of Honor and Industry*, celebrating the installation of the lord mayor on 29 October 1617, Thomas Middleton creates a Castle of Fame, but in the final speech of the pageant Honor reflects, "There is no human glory or renown, / But have their evening and their sure sun-setting."[81]

Although we seek to elevate the memory of a deed or a life above the transitory nature of human existence by inscribing it on a durable material, we also recognize that fame is inseparable from speech. An inscription is intended to inspire others to imagine the person no longer physically present and to give voice to what is remembered or evoked. Significantly, poets and mythographers who personify Fame and describe her abode emphasize the importance of sound. Ovid says that Fame's dwelling is constructed out of materials that amplify sound: "It is built all of echoing brass. The whole place resounds with confused noises, repeats all words and doubles what it hears. There is no quiet, no silence anywhere within" (*Metamorphoses*, 12:46–48). Chaucer's House of Fame is similarly noisy, filled with the din of musicians and petitioners to Lady Fame. According to Peter Pett, Fame in her hilltop palace has a trumpet of brass, and "Her trumpets sound was loud, and very shrill: / Reporting every matter very cleare; / Which when it once was sounded forth, did fill / The wood which to that hill adjoyned neare; / In which a thousand tatling ecchoes were, / That iterated every uttered sound."[82]

Cesare Ripa's description of *Fama Chiara* (Mercury and Pegasus) also emphasizes the importance of speech: "The bridle of this horse held by Mercury indicates that renown is transmitted by words and by speech, which resounds by force of the glorious deeds of men, and that such fame more or less reaches throughout the world as much as that of languages does, and by speaking of those men it is increased and spread."[83] Verses that Sir Thomas More wrote to accompany the painted cloths depicting Petrarch's *Triumphs*, designed by More himself for his father's house, also accentuate fame's dependence upon sound: "Fame I am called, marvayle you nothing, / Though I with tonges am compassed all rounde / For in voyce of people is my chiefe livyng."[84]

Because the dead depend on the living and, more specifically, on spoken words to guarantee fame, the effort to perpetuate fame by writing is ultimately doomed. Inscription merely postpones oblivion. The deliquesence of fame is poetically suggested by the loss of written words in Chaucer's House of Fame, where the names of the once famous, inscribed on frozen water, disappear when the sun melts the ice (lines 1136–47). Chaucer's metaphor suggests the inexorability of a natural process. Shakespeare, too, describes the loss of fame as the effacement of something written; for example, in *2 Henry VI* Gloucester complains of King Henry's intended marriage to Lady Margaret, telling the peers of England, "Fatal [is] this marriage, cancelling your fame, / Blotting your names from books of memory, / Rasing the characters of your renown, / Defacing monuments of conquer'd France" (1.1.99–102).

The written word cannot ensure the perpetuation of fame because the more time that passes, the less likely are records to prompt others, distant in time and place, to speak anew of the dead. Statues discolor and monuments crumble. Parchment grows brittle; books entomb the once famous in worm-eaten paper; memories decay. In the Royal Shakespeare Company production of *Love's Labour's Lost* in 1993/4, when Navarre spoke his opening lines about achieving fame, he held an open book in his hand and, finishing the lines, snapped it shut, releasing a cloud of dust, the harbinger of his own failure to achieve his goal through the written word.

Recognition of writing's vulnerability helps explain Hal's distrust of the written word. Although eager for fame, the king knows that it's not enough to have his deeds recorded on paper or stone. What he seeks, therefore, is not the written but the spoken word, and in *Henry V* he imagines that word as taking on a life of its own, repeated in such a way as to link present heroism with future fame:

Old men forget; yet all shall be forgot,
But he'll remember with advantages
What feats he did that day. Then shall our names,
Familiar in his mouth as household words,
Harry the King, Bedford and Exeter,
Warwick and Talbot, Salisbury and Gloucester,
Be in their flowing cups freshly rememb'red.
This story shall the good man teach his son;
And Crispin Crispian shall ne'er go by,
From this day to the ending of the world,
But we in it shall be remembered –
We few, we happy few, we band of brothers.

(4.3.49–60)

Their renown is assured not by tombs or monuments or chronicles but by living voices, as if these warriors could bypass the intermediary of written words, as if there existed an unbroken continuum of voices defying mutability and ratifying fame with all the warmth and feeling conveyed by speech.

Risking infamy: tongues of rumour and tongues of slander

Both before and after his success at Shrewsbury, Shakespeare's Hal adopts a strategy that may seem utterly contrary to his desire for fame: he encourages the widely held but mistaken judgment that he suffers from a weak character. This is a hazardous enterprise, for, so long as he lives, he runs the risk that infamy may replace the fame he has already earned. In fact, this eventuality is the very prospect that so preoccupies Henry V on his deathbed in Edward Hall's chronicle. There the king relishes the nearness of death because it precludes some future event in life that may compromise his reputation. The possibilities he envisions are sharply defined: either fame or infamy awaits.

The two trumpets conventionally held by personified Fame express those alternatives.[85] In Chaucer's *House of Fame* Aeolus, Fame's herald, carries a "trumpe of gold" (line 1678), called "Clere Laude" (line 1575), and a "blake trumpe of bras" (line 1637) called "Sklaundre" (line 1580). Renaissance artists, similarly, portray two trumpets symbolizing two possible outcomes.[86] In a design by Jan Vredeman de Vries, Fame holds in her right hand a trumpet from which a white banner hangs and out of which smoke rises, signifying fame (fig. 22). In her left hand she holds a second trumpet from which hangs a black banner; smoke emerges from the horn, curling downward to signify infamy. Sometimes these alternatives are represented by different figures. On the title-page of Sir Walter Ralegh's *History of the World* (1614), against a brightly lit background *Fama Bona* blows her trumpet while, opposite, against a dark background, *Fama Mala* (with mottled skin, wings, and garment) blows her trumpet of infamy.[87] And on the sixteenth-century stage both good fame and her dark counterpart appear with their corresponding trumpets. In Thomas Preston's *Cambises* (acted c. 1561, SR 1569) Shame enters "*with a trump black*" and announces of the Persian king, "As Fame dooth sound the royall trump of worthy men and trim: / So Shame dooth blowe with strained blast, the trump of shame on him" (4.351–52).[88] In Robert Wilson's *The Three Ladies of London* (acted c. 1581, perhaps by Leicester's Men), Fame plays a trumpet, presumably golden, as the dramatic action begins: "*Enter Fame sounding*" (line 2); although a trumpet of infamy does not take physical form, Fame anticipates the ignoble fate awaiting sinners: "you no doubt shall see, / Them plagued with painefull punishment for such their crueltie" (lines 25–26).[89]

Just as Renaissance artists personify Fame, so too they pictorialize detraction, especially that which springs from malice. Maarten van Heemskerck depicts Envy (*Invidia*) ensconced in a chariot and gnawing on a heart.[90] Spite (*Livor*), who actually drives the vehicle, holds reins attached to the horses, Detraction and Calumny, and all along the reins stretching from Spite's hands to Calumny's bridle, hang a row of tongues. By its grotesquerie the engraving accentuates the moral ugliness of detraction precipitated by envy. "Detraction's a bold monster," observes a character in Massinger and Field's *The Fatal Dowry* (acted by the King's Men, 1617–19), "and feares not / To wound the fame of princes" (3.1.178–79).[91] John Webster, lamenting

22 Fame with two trumpets, illustrating fame and infamy. An engraving by Jan
Vredeman de Vries

the death of Prince Henry, notes that Slander "hath a large and spacious
tongue, / Farre bigger then her mouth, to publish wrong."[92]

The historic Henry V, according to Holinshed, was the victim of mali-
cious detractors who sought to undermine his reputation. In the chronicle
Shakespeare read about a whispering campaign against the prince, begun
by the king's servants in 1411: "The prince sore offended with such persons, as by slanderous reports, [which] sought not onelie to spot his good

name abrode in the realme, but to sowe discord also betwixt him and his father, wrote his letters into everie part of the realme, to reproove all such slanderous devises of those that sought his discredit" (539). Although Hal in the two parts of *Henry IV* never embarks on any similar campaign to rescue his name, his failure to do so is purposeful; his inaction represents not only a recognition that disparagement and renown have an unusually close relationship but also a calculation that he can profit from that very nexus.

Since at least the time of Virgil, detraction and fame have been coupled. *Fama* possesses a potentially threatening aspect in the *Aeneid*; the Roman poet describes *Fama* as "a monster awful and huge" (4:181); this "foul goddess" (line 195) disseminates stories that undermine Aeneas' stature. The association of detraction and fame persists in Shakespeare's England. For example, in King James I's coronation procession, when Fame sounds her trumpet, Detraction and Oblivion throw off their slumber and seek "with clubs to beate downe" the fountain of virtue.[93] In *1 Henry IV* Falstaff, in his pragmatic fashion appreciates the vulnerability of fame: he asks of honor (meaning "fame"), "But will't not live with the living? No. Why? Detraction will not suffer it" (5.1.138–39). Shakespeare's Rumour in *2 Henry IV* himself acknowledges a kinship with detraction:

Upon my tongues continual slanders ride,
The which in every language I pronounce,
Stuffing the ears of men with false reports.
I speak of peace, while covert enmity
Under the smile of safety wounds the world.

(lines 6–10)

Adopting the metaphor of the "pipe," Rumour associates himself with "the blunt monster with uncounted heads" playing upon an instrument. Thomas Scot also aligns fame and slanderous rumor; he describes the House of Fame as inhabited by two pairs of sisters: True Fame and Good Fame, False Fame and Bad Fame. The latter two dwell in the lowest and darkest rooms: "There keepe they court, where Scandals, Libels, Lies, / Rumors, Reports, Suspicions, Calumnies, / Are favorites and governors of state."[94]

That the tongues responsible for rumor may be synonymous with the tongues of slander is theatrically appropriate to *Henry IV* since the prince has, in *Part 1*, been a target of deprecation by Hotspur, who envies Hal's status as heir apparent and who would seize the crown for himself. The tongues of rumor are also aptly evoked because Hal, even in *Part 2*, still suffers the ignominy of harsh judgments that he does little to set right. Alone among the figures dramatized in Shakespeare's histories, he cooperates with the deprecation of his character, actually encouraging the formation and dissemination of hostile opinions that disturb his father and generate unease among the people. The threat to social cohesion created by errant rumor is manifest in a welcoming reception for Queen Elizabeth at Bristol in 1574; there personified Dissension said: "A pestlens peall of rumour strang that flies through many a land, / The plain report whearof remains in me Dissenshons hand."[95]

With his first soliloquy of the Henriad, Prince Hal acknowledges his role in creating a disjunction between inner probity and outer disrepute:

So when this loose behavior I throw off
And pay the debt I never promised,
By how much better than my word I am,
By so much shall I falsify men's hopes,
And like bright metal on a sullen ground,
My reformation, glitt'ring o'er my fault,
Shall show more goodly and attract more eyes
Than that which hath no foil to set it off.

(1.2.208–15)

He would profit from the slander that attaches to his (misjudged) character, turning it to his advantage by heightening the contrast between a future anticipated with foreboding and a present worthy of celebration. In lending slander a popular credence, Hal rides a tiger, enacting, in effect, the advice of Francis Bacon, who writes of fame in its maleficent sense: "if a man can tame this monster, and bring her to feed at the hand, and govern her, and with her fly other ravening fowle, and kill them, it is somewhat worth."[96]

Eyes and ears: big brother vs. good government

To Hal's father, Warwick defends the prince's seemingly ignoble conduct by explaining that the prince, despite consorting with Falstaff and others in the world of the tavern, is not what he appears to be; Hal safeguards his essential integrity. Using a simile that acquires a special resonance when we remember Rumour "*painted full of tongues*" at the beginning of *Part 2*, Warwick later in this play justifies Hal's seemingly aberrant behavior:

The Prince but studies his companions
Like a strange tongue, wherein, to gain the language,
'Tis needful that the most immodest word
Be look'd upon and learnt, which once attain'd,
Your Highness knows, comes to no further use
But to be known and hated.   (4.4.68–73)

So Hal "learns" not in order to imitate or adopt but rather to inoculate himself against something potentially dangerous to his future kingship. Hal's knowledge of a tongue he does not speak will have an important function when he attains the crown, for as monarch he will be responsible for evaluating all that he hears and sees.

At the battle of Shrewsbury in *1 Henry IV* Hal makes an error when he misinterprets what he beholds: coming upon Falstaff "Breathless and bleeding on the ground," Hal assumes him dead. But seeing Falstaff hoist the dead Hotspur on his back, a surprised Hal tells his friend, "we will not trust our eyes / Without our ears: thou art not what thou seem'st" (5.4.136–37). The future will require even greater alertness on his part, for, as king, he will need to detect the false, the envious, and the merely flattering at court. In peacetime he must display the qualities so conspicuously lacking in Richard II, who piously assured Mowbray, "Impartial are our eyes and ears" (1.1.115), but who violated such assurances by his conduct. As king, Hal must be able to penetrate the accusation made out of selfishness or blandishment. He must test what is seen by what is heard and vice versa.

In the sixteenth century this requisite of good kingship was demonstrated by negative example. Writers and artists alike seized on an incident from the ancient world to exemplify the danger of slander. Mentioned by Vasari in his *Lives of the Artists*, the story of Apelles gained considerable popularity. According to Lucian's account, Apelles of Ephesus, an artist, was slandered by Antiphulus, who, envious of his rival's favor at court, claimed that Apelles had taken part in a conspiracy in Tyre. King Ptolemy, "who in general was not particularly sound of judgment, but had been brought up in the midst of courtly flattery" (1:363),[97] complacently credited the lie, and Apelles would have been executed had not one of the real conspirators, who knew the truth and felt sorry for the accused man, stepped forward to repudiate the false accusation and rescue Apelles' reputation. Although cleared of the charges, Apelles expressed his outrage through his art, completing a painting in which he depicted Slander as "a woman beautiful beyond measure," led by Envy and attended by Treachery and Deceit (1:365–67).[98]

Apelles makes visually arresting the credulity of Ptolemy by a detail of the king's appearance. Representing the moment when Slander recites the lie to the king, the artist portrays the listener as having "very large ears, almost like those of Midas" (1:365). Midas was of course the king who became identified with folly because, in being granted the wish that everything he touch turn to gold, he discovered that even the food from which he sought nourishment was similarly transformed. Dismayed by his predicament, he asked Dionysus to take back the gift. Midas' reputation for folly was also owing to his role as judge in a musical contest between Pan and Apollo. Choosing Pan, the impolitic Midas became the target of Apollo's ire; the god turned Midas' ears into those of an ass. The iconographic significance of those ears persisted in Shakespeare's time: in Jonson's *Volpone* (acted by the King's Men in 1606) a magistrate orders that Corvino be punished by wearing "a cap with fair long ass's ears" (5.12.137).[99]

In the Renaissance the elongated ears of Midas became identified with the sinister as well as the foolish, as we learn from Erasmus' commentary on the saying, "Midas has ass's ears": "Most . . . take the meaning of this allegory to be that Midas, being a despot, used to send out spies and eavesdroppers, whom he used as ears, to let him know whatever was being said or done all over the country."[100] Today Erasmus' comment in his *Adages* may well evoke the specter of a police state, the intrusion of totalitarian regimes into private lives, the apparatus of bugging and informants common to so many modern societies. The Orwellian words Big Brother conjure up a world where no secret is safe, where no one is secure. Of course, the scenario is not merely modern: Ben Jonson anticipates such a world in *Sejanus* (acted by the King's Men in 1603), where the virtuous Sabinus criticizes the emperor's favorite in remarks overheard by spies, who have hidden themselves between the roof and ceiling of his home.[101]

When, however, Erasmus, citing Lucian and others, says, "Many are the eyes and ears of kings, because they watch through their spies what each man says or does,"[102] he points to a different and more benign meaning: monarchs need the knowledge that only an intelligence network can provide; their own eyes and ears must be amplified by those of others. Recounting the second year of Henry V's reign, Hall represents the Earl of Westmorland giving advice to the king about a prospective military expedition in Scotland: "every persone entendyng a purposed enterprise . . . ought vigilantly to forsee with lincis iyes" potential problems (fol. xxxviii v). Hall's marginal notation reads: "Lynx is a beast like to a wolfe, whose sighte dooeth perce al thynges." It is this quality in a monarch that disturbs the rebel Worcester in *1 Henry IV*. At Shrewsbury he argues that his confederates should not accept the terms offered by the crown for resolving their dispute, that the king will forever suspect them: "Supposition all our lives shall be stuck full of eyes, / For treason is but trusted like the fox" (5.2.8–9).

Describing events in the twelfth year of Henry IV's reign, Hall explicitly aligns the sharp observations of a monarch with virtue: "princes sometime have Argus iyes and Midas eares" (fol. xxxi r). The marginal notation explains of Argus, "the poetes fain hym to have had an hundred iyes, sygnifiyng therby his wysedome and circumspeccion" (fol. xxxi v). As for Midas, "the poetes faine to have longe eares, signifiyng hereby that kynges heare farre of."

Cesare Ripa in his *Iconologia* creates *Ragione di stato*, a personification covered with eyes and ears.[103] Henry Peacham in *Minerva Britanna*, adopting the very same personification, explains its meaning:

He must be strongly arm'd against his foes
Without, within, with hidden patience:
Be serv'd with eies, and listening eares of those,
Who from all partes can give intelligence
  To gall his foe, or timely to prevent
  At home his malice, and intendiment.[104]

To be well informed, the ancients believed, was not only a requisite of good government, it was also a means of emulating the deity himself. The Lacedemonians, according to Vincenzo Cartari, fashioned representations of Jupiter to underscore this point: they "framed his picture with foure eares, as that Jupiter heareth and understandeth all things, alluded also to the wisdome of princes and magistrates, which ought to have information of every cause or matter throughly before they deliver out a definitive sentence or judgement: and likewise that they receive and admit intelligences and notices how their lawes, precepts, and edicts, are kept and observed among their subjects."[105] Similarly, Giovanni Paolo Lomazzo, in Richard Haydocke's translation, records that artists of earlier societies painted an upright judge "with 4 eares; warning us thereby, that with two hee shoulde heare the reasons of one side, and with the other two those on the other side."[106]

When Shakespeare's Henry V wraps himself in a borrowed cloak and goes out among his troops on the eve of Agincourt, he does so to gather intelligence; he plays the spy. Significantly, Jean Baudoin's translation of Ripa's *Iconologia* depicts a spy as a man with winged feet, who holds a lantern and draws a cloak across his face and body in order to conceal his identity; that cloak is covered with eyes and ears. Baudoin explains, "the eyes and ears signify that the business of such persons is to see all and to hear all, not only by day but also by night."[107] A modern audience may well view the disguised Henry V as overly devious, and even in Shakespeare's era spying could be seen as disreputable, for spies occupied a world of secrecy and supposition, a world where the line separating the true and the false was blurred. Thomas Heywood's account of Fame's palace envisions the inhabitants as spies, captive to the overheard word: "The courts are throng'd with multitudes of spies, / Light giddy people tatling what they please: / Who (in and out) through every chamber passe, / Whispering sometimes what is, and what neare was."[108]

Shakespeare's contemporaries, however, may well have seen the disguised Henry V as admirable. After all, to govern well and make wise decisions, Henry must possess accurate knowledge. His identity concealed by the cloak, he would gauge the morale of his men, learning their true sentiments about his campaign in France. To the extent that King Henry is interested in the opinions of his people and in their welfare, he displays qualities desirable in a monarch. And by listening to the criticism voiced by Williams, who worries that "if the cause be not good, the King himself hath a heavy reckoning to make" (4.1.134–35), the king has an opportunity to justify himself to his men – and to the audience – thus ensuring that his reputation will not be besmirched.

That Shakespeare's contemporaries identified a monarch's competence with knowledge of people's opinions is suggested by the Rainbow portrait of Queen Elizabeth, mentioned above. As we saw, the Queen wears an outer garment adorned with eyes and ears – not unlike the *Ragione di stato* of Ripa and the corresponding emblem of Peacham. Those eyes and ears not only celebrate Elizabeth's own fame but also demonstrate her virtue: she sees and hears all that is said or done in her kingdom and therefore is prepared to make prudent judgments.[109] She will not fall into the trap of the credulous King Ptolemy who, in ignorance, nearly put to death the innocent Apelles.

Rumour to Fame to Rumour: the Essex conspiracy

The fifth chorus of *Henry V*, recounting the triumphant return of the king to England, makes a double allusion, one classical, one contemporary:

> But now behold,
> In the quick forge and working-house of thought,
> How London doth pour out her citizens!
> The Mayor and all his brethren in best sort,

Like to the senators of th' antique Rome,
With the plebeians swarming at their heels,
Go forth and fetch their conqu'ring Caesar in;
As by a lower but by loving likelihood,
Were now the general of our gracious Empress,
As in good time he may, from Ireland coming,
Bringing rebellion broached on his sword,
How many would the peaceful city quit,
To welcome him!   (lines 22–34)

The "general" described as "from Ireland coming" is Robert Devereux, Earl of Essex, who departed England in March 1599 to subdue Tyrone and his Irish followers. When Shakespeare wrote the lines, presumably between 27 March 1599 and 28 September (when Essex returned), the playwright anticipated a welcome to London befitting a warrior who had already achieved conspicuous success and would undoubtedly distinguish himself once again. The homecoming, however, proved a debacle, one that illustrates both the evanescence of fame and, according to the earl's supporters, the wounding power of rumor.

Perhaps no contemporary of Shakespeare's sought fame more single-mindedly or succeeded more spectacularly than Essex. Although he could have settled for a comfortable, quiet life, he embarked on a series of military expeditions – to the Low Countries (1585–86), Portugal (1589), Rouen (1591), Cadiz (1596), the Azores (1597), and finally Ireland (1599). Each of these entailed considerable risk: in 1586 Sir Philip Sidney died in a campaign that saw Essex display conspicuous gallantry; Essex's own brother lost his life during the French expedition of 1591. Despite such exposure to jeopardy and death, Essex remained supremely self-confident. Consider his conduct at Lisbon: "the Earle of Essex (who preferring the honor of the cause, which was his countries, before his own safetie) sent a particuler cartell [i.e., written challenge], offering himselfe against any of theirs, if they had any of his qualitie: of, if they would not admit of that, sixe, eight, or tenne, or as many as they would appoynt, should meete so many of theirs in the head of our battaile to trie their fortunes with them."[110] So eager was Essex for combat that he sometimes dashed off to war without first securing his government's funding or even approval. Sir Henry Wotton notes that the Portuguese campaign could have ended badly for Essex: "all his hopes of advancement had like to bee strangled almost in the very cradle, by throwing himselfe into the Portugal voyage without the queenes consent, or so much as her knowledge."[111] Only the queen's affection for the charming, if temperamental, Essex saved him from his own indiscretions: "At his re-turne all was cleere, and this excursion was esteemed but a sally of youth: nay, he grew every day more and more in her gracious conceit."

The generation that came of age with Essex in the 1580s and 1590s was animated by what Anthony Esler calls "a Marlovian mood of high aspiration."[112] Sir Roger Williams, who served Essex in the field and ded-icated his *Brief Discourse of War* to the earl, observes that "no honorable mindes can bee free from honorable ambition."[113] Although Elizabethan culture was inclined to look with indulgence on those who embraced risk for the sake of winning renown, the intensity of Essex's quest often led to conflict with government ministers who had more complicated political objectives. On 13 September 1591, reacting to the queen's wish that he re-turn from France, Essex revealed to Lord Burghley an almost pathological fear of seeing his reputation besmirched: "If her majesty would now revoke me with disgrace, when Rouen were to be won, I would humbly beseech her that she would take from me my life, and not my poor reputation."[114] To the queen he wrote plaintively, "I am left alone of my poor house, to maintain the poor reputation that it hath hitherto lived in; your majesty in honour and justice will not force me to be the first that shall imbase it. Grief and unkindness confound my wits."[115]

The manic counterpart of this anxiety was his exultation in victory.[116] To Lord Burghley on 1 July 1596, Essex boasted of success at Calais and then Cadiz, envisioning himself as the beneficiary of Fame: "I shall not need to tell your l[ordship] that Cales [Calais] is won, and the King of Spain's great fleet at Cales defeated and destroyed. I shall less need to relate the particular circumstances of either; for as Fame itself will bring the first, so this gen-tleman that carries my letter will perform the second."[117] Essex knew that Ireland was likely to prove a more formidable challenge than any previous expedition. On 4 January 1599, before departing England, he wrote of his misgivings to Lord Willoughby: "Into Ireland I go. The queen hath irrevo-cably decreed it; the council do passionately urge it; and I am tied to my own reputation to use no tergiversation."[118] In this same letter Essex alludes to Elizabeth in what sounds like a premonition of his future relationship with her: "I am not ignorant what are the disadvantages of absence; the op-portunities of practising enemies when they are neither encountered nor overlooked: the constructions of princes under whom *magna fama* is more dangerous than *mala* and *successus minus quam nullus*."[119]

When the campaign in Ireland began to falter, when Elizabeth and her ministers chastised him for his decisions in the field, and when he sensed his authority in jeopardy, Essex embarked on a risky strategy to recoup his

fortunes by a single bold stroke: a return to London where he would per-
sonally appeal to the queen for understanding. Arriving at Nonsuch palace,
he made his way to the queen's bedchamber, where at first she received him
pleasantly, but soon after placed him under house arrest. Stung by the re-
proof, Essex chafed under the unprecedented restriction. What disturbed
him even more than the loss of his freedom was the realization that his
hard-won fame was melting away. Falling ill, he wrote the queen on 12 May
1600, imagining the demise of his good name as a living death: "[I] felt
the very pangs of death upon me, and saw that poor reputation, whatsoever it was that I enjoyed hitherto, not suffered to die with me, but buried,
and I alive."[120] Finding Elizabeth unmoved by his entreaties and forced to
endure a tribunal convened to examine his conduct in Ireland, Essex con-
sulted his supporters and came up with a desperate plan to capitalize on the
renown he still enjoyed: an armed assault on the court. Receiving a pledge
of support from a citizen supporter, he "began to discourse how much hee
was favored throughout the City, and perswaded himselfe by the former
acclamations of the people, and their hatefull murmurings against his adversaries, that very many were most devoted to his fame and fortune."[121]
His men prepared for the coup by hiring the Lord Chamberlain's men to
perform Shakespeare's *Richard II*, with its deposition scene, on 7 February
1601.[122] If Essex imagined that the performance of a play or the mere sight
of him advancing on the palace would rally people to his side, he suffered
a catastrophic disappointment. Far from rescuing his reputation, the enterprise ended in ignominy: on 8 February he was arrested, then tried for
high treason and subsequently executed.

Awaiting death on the morning of 25 February 1601, Essex sought to
make sense of his life, acknowledging a connection between the fame he
had for so long coveted and the calamity that so quickly overtook him:
"He thanked the queene that she had granted he should not be publikely
executed, lest his minde which was now setled might be disturbed with
the acclamations of the people, protesting that he had now learned how
vaine is the blast of popular favour."[123] Although he came to appreciate the
transience and instability of popular acclaim, Essex remained preoccupied
with how people would remember him: "I beseech you and the worlde to
holde a charitable opinion of me."[124] Even in his final moments Essex was
still trying to shape public opinion and thereby protect what remained of
his reputation.

After his death that task fell to his followers, none of whom was more
eloquent than Robert Pricket. His poem, *Honors Fame in Triumph Riding*,
printed in 1604, attributes Essex's demise not to his desire for fame but

rather to the ruinous effect of errant rumor. Describing the earl's military exploits, Pricket sees the fame Essex achieved as the just reward of valor in combat: "Brave troupes of horse he bravely led, / And thus at first his fame was spred " (sig. A4v).[125] The damage his standing suffered in Ireland, according to the poet, resulted from miscommunication and backbiting: "Some misse there was, directions all not kept, / Envie rous'd up, that winkt but never slept' (sig. Bv). As for the abortive rebellion in London, Pricket ascribes it to an effort to remove the earl's enemies at court: "forth he goes, / To raise a force so strong his part to take: / As that he might remove his setled foes, / And to his queene a quiet passage make" (sig. B4v). For Pricket, the earl's subsequent condemnation constitutes not punishment for treason but martyrdom occasioned by "monstrous mouthed lies" (sig. C2v).[126] Seen in the context of his career, the climb up the scaffold becomes one last effort to restore damaged renown: "See how he mounts with valiant courage bold, / in bloud to write the letters of his fame" (sig. Dr).

So long as Essex lived, he had the opportunity to set the record straight, so to speak. In death the word of mouth that had earlier shaped his reputation became a crescendo of hostile accusation and rumor: "Report doeth wound my soule: / So many treasons 'gainst that earle objected, / Who whilst he liv'd, could those reports controule" (sig. C2v). The poet seems to imagine that the relationship between rumor and fame remains fluid, that the process by which fame succumbed to rumor may be reversed and fame restored. Readers of the poem are enjoined to "Pluck from his hearse false rumors stayne" (sig. C2r).

When Shakespeare wrote the fifth chorus of *Henry V*, he could scarcely have guessed the fate that awaited Essex in Ireland or the aftermath that makes the comparison between triumphant king and disgraced earl seem so incongruous today. Yet the allusion to Essex, viewed in the light of subsequent history, has an important resonance for the play in which Rumour appears as a character as well as for the subsequent play chronicling King Henry's victories in France. The evocation of Essex reminds us of the nearly universal desire to convert momentary success into permanent renown, the dependence of fame on military valor, the tendency of fame to dissipate, sometimes quite suddenly, the vulnerability of fame to the envy of others, and the peculiarly intimate relationship of fame and rumor.

Because Hecate's presence in *Macbeth* is almost certainly owing to Thomas Middleton rather than Shakespeare, and because in classical antiquity she is a deity rather than an abstraction in the manner of Spring, Winter, or Revenge,[1] Hecate may seem a dubious choice for inclusion in this study. But although Middleton may be responsible for the character, Hecate had assumed a role in *Macbeth* even before the publication of the First Folio in 1623. Indeed, Hecate may have been a character in the play from the time that Middleton began writing for the King's Men, c. 1610, only a few years after the first performances. For nearly four hundred years, then, Hecate has belonged to Shakespeare's play.[2] Her inclusion here is based on a conviction that the deities in Shakespeare's plays, like those in his contemporaries' drama, function virtually as personifications. On the Renaissance stage deities represent a theatrical shorthand for certain worldly energies or human impulses.

In *Macbeth* Hecate functions as chief of the witches, and, like her, they constitute visual manifestations of evil. Interestingly, Ben Jonson conceives of the witches in his *Masque of Queens* as particular personifications. Describing the antimasque, which he calls "a spectacle of strangeness" (line 17), Jonson explains that he devised "twelve women in the habit of hags or witches, sustaining the persons of Ignorance, Suspicion, Credulity, etc." (lines 14–16).[3] Shakespeare is not so specific in his treatment of the witches, but they are threatening precisely because they possess powers conferred by supernatural beings. As such, the witches are not merely women; they represent unnamed forces of evil at large in the *Macbeth* world.

Hecate

With a long and rich history, Hecate accumulated an unusually wide array of associations in antiquity, and these provide perhaps the best avenue for understanding her appeal to a Jacobean playwright. Indeed, Ben Jonson's printed text of *The Masque of Queens*, with its evocation of Hecate, is filled with classical references.

In his *Theogony* Hesiod reports that Jupiter gave Hecate "splendid gifts."[4] Thus her realm is huge, encompassing "a share of the earth and the unfruitful sea." Accordingly, "whenever any one of men on earth offers rich sacrifices and prays for favour according to custom, he calls upon Hecate." To fisherman, for example, she "gives great catch"; to herdsmen she may "increase the stock."[5] In addition, she looks after competitors at games: "Good is she also when men contend at the games, for there too the goddess is with them and profits them." She extends her protection to warriors as well: "when men arm themselves for the battle that destroys men, then the goddess is at hand to give victory and grant glory readily to whom she will."

Hesiod's characterization suggests a deity whose identity has not entirely crystallized. Originating in southwestern Asia Minor, she assumed, among other roles, that of guardian of gateways into cities, sentry at the threshold in private homes, warding off "unhappy souls and other demonic creatures," protectress of children in general and of girls' transition to womanhood.[6] So blurred is her identity that Hecate frequently merges with other figures. Hesiod recounts that Hecate's father "made her a nurse of the young."[7] In this capacity Hecate becomes conflated with Diana (Greek Artemis), who similarly takes under her protection the young, both human and animal; at Ephesus, Hecate's statue actually stood inside Diana's sanctuary. Hecate also becomes linked with Luna, the planetary deity. In this capacity Hecate is identified with darkness and the activities that flourish there, including magic. Finally, Hecate belongs to the underworld as well. It is Hecate who comes to the aid of Ceres when Hades abducts her daughter. The Homeric Hymn "To Demeter" recounts that Hecate, having found Proserpina, becomes her "minister and companion"; relating this episode, the poet calls Hecate "tender-hearted."[8]

Because of the scope of Hecate's domain, which includes heaven, earth, and underworld, Virgil in his *Aeneid* calls her "threefold Hecate" (4: 511),[9] while Ovid in his *Metamorphoses* terms her "three-formed Hecate" (7:194).[10] For Horace, Hecate is "goddess of the triple form."[11] A fusion of Diana, Luna/Lucina, and Proserpina, Hecate in antiquity is sometimes represented by a statue of three connected bodies, each facing in a different direction.[12]

Although Hesiod imagines a benign figure who hears and acts upon prayers of petition, other Greek writers acknowledge a more disturbing deity. Diodorus of Sicily writes that Hecate "surpassed her father in boldness and lawlessness," and adds that Hecate exhibits a cruel streak: "she was also fond of hunting, and when she had no luck she would turn her arrows upon human beings instead of the beasts."[13] Even more troubling, she murders her father and founds a temple to Diana, "commanding that strangers who landed there should be sacrificed to the goddess." It is this malevolent figure who eventually comes to dominate ancient accounts of Hecate. Despite her occasional conflation with Luna and Diana, Hecate increasingly becomes identified with death and the afterlife, especially that part of the underworld occupied by the suffering dead, who linger "at the doorways, gates, and crossroads that she was asked to protect."[14] In a poem by Theocritus the speaker appeals to "that Hecat infernal who makes e'en the whelps to shiver on her goings to and fro where these tombs be and the red blood lies. All hail to thee, dread and awful Hecat!"[15] Hecate, who originally guarded against restless spirits, metamorphoses into a vengeful spirit herself.

Indicative of Hecate's dark side is her skill at preparing poisons; in fact, she kills her father by poison. Circe and Medea, called daughters of Hecate in some ancient accounts,[16] follow in their mother's footsteps. Thus, according to Diodorus, Circe "was taught by her mother Hecate about not a few drugs,"[17] and she discovers others on her own. With this knowledge Circe poisons her husband, king of the Sarmatians, and "committed many cruel and violent acts against her subjects."[18] In *The Odyssey* Circe proffers aid to the wandering Greeks, but "in the food she mixed evil drugs" (10:235)[19] and, striking them with her wand, transforms them into swine. Ovid in his *Metamorphoses* relates that Circe, angry at Glaucus for preferring Scylla to herself, "straightway bruised together uncanny herbs with juices of dreadful power, singing while she mixed them Hecate's own charms" (14:43–44). Circe then makes her way to Scylla's abode and "befouls and tinctures [the place] with her baleful poisons" (14:55–56). Scylla is transformed into "monster-shapes," Glaucus devastated.

Medea, at least initially, has a more benign nature than Circe. It is Medea who warns the Argonauts of peril and assists Jason in securing the Golden Fleece: her potion puts to sleep the dragon that guards the Fleece.[20] But when Jason later falls in love with Creusa, the jealous Medea embarks upon a campaign of horrific violence. In Seneca's version of the story, Medea's initial invocation of "three-formed Hecate" and the Furies presages her murderous acts. Directing that her sons bring to Jason's new bride a robe "anointed and imbued with baneful poisons" (line 576), she enjoins the goddess: "Give sting to my poisons, Hecate" (line 833).[21] To complete her revenge against Jason, Medea slays their own sons.

Because of her deeds and those of the daughters whom she instructs in death-dealing drugs, Hecate tends to be feared rather than loved. Virgil's description of a sacrifice in *The Aeneid* captures the anxiety over the goddess:

just before the rays and dawning of the early sun the ground rumbled underfoot, the wooded ridges began to quiver, and through the gloom dogs seemed to howl as the goddess drew nigh. (6:255–58)

At another point Virgil relates that Hecate's name is "wailed by night in city streets" (4:609), an allusion to the deity's traditional identification with places where roads cross and spirits gather.

   Mindful of Hecate's threefold aspect – celestial, terrestrial, and infernal – Shakespeare's contemporaries refer to her by various names. Thus Abraham Fraunce notes, "in heaven she is called Luna, in the woods Diana, under the earth Hecate, or Proserpina."[22] Ancient associations cling to Hecate. Shakespeare, for instance, recalls her identification with darkness when King Lear swears by "The mysteries of Hecat and the night" (1.1.110) and when Orlando in *As You Like It* invokes the "thrice-crowned queen of night" (3.2.2). In *Hamlet* Shakespeare recalls Hecate's proficiency with poison when, in the play-within-the-play, Lucianus addresses the concoction he pours into the ear of Hamlet's sleeping father: "Thou mixture rank, of midnight weeds collected, / With Hecat's ban [curse] thrice blasted, thrice infected" (3.2.257–58). Shakespeare also evokes Hecate's association with the moon and black magic when Macbeth says that "witchcraft celebrates / Pale Hecat's off'rings" (2.1.51–52). At night Milton's Comus, son of Circe and "skill'd in all his mother's witcheries," performs "abhorred rites to Hecate."[23] Evildoers of various kinds appeal to Hecate. In *The Faerie Queene* an agent of the sorcerer Archimago, invoking "the dreaded name / Of Hecate," inveigles Morpheus into conjuring a temptress in a false dream.[24] In Thomas Heywood's *The Brazen Age* (acted 1609–11) Medea, contemplating her "black arts," invokes "three-headed Hecate" and her "chariot drawne with winged snakes."[25] Typically Shakespeare's contemporaries couple Hecate with hell and with the spirits who dwell there. Michael Drayton, in *The Moon-Calfe*, although recalling that Hecate, when conflated with Luna/Lucina, benignly keeps watch over women in childbirth, also acknowledges that Hecate wields "power / Of all that keepe hels ugly balefull bower" (lines 110–11).[26]

   Unfortunately neither the speeches nor the stage directions in *Macbeth* provide very useful information about Hecate's appearance in the play.[27] Peter Thomson contends that Hecate is "presumably gorgeously costumed,"[28] but he does not venture an opinion about the nature of the costume. G. Wilson Knight, while not giving any particulars of attire, describes the onstage effect she creates: Hecate "does not appear as a very grim and portentous figure. She is fairy-like, ethereal, a delicate and, presumably,

palely beautiful goddess to be strongly contrasted with the bearded and
withered ugliness of the Weird Women."[29] Knight bases his surmise, in
part, on what Puck says at the end of *A Midsummer Night's Dream*: "we
fairies, that do run / By the triple Hecat's team / From the presence of the
sun, / Following darkness like a dream, / Now are frolic" (5.1.383–87). The
language of Hecate in *Macbeth*, however, seems at odds with whatever
"frolic" implies. Chastising the witches for daring "To trade and traffic
with Macbeth," Hecate calls herself "The close contriver of all harms," and
adds, "this night I'll spend / Unto a dismal and a fatal end" (3.5.7, 20–21).
To judge by her own words, this Hecate scarcely seems the "ethereal" and
"delicate" creature that Knight envisions. The context in which Hecate
appears, moreover, has little in common with that of the earlier comedy.
The nightmarish world of *Macbeth* contrasts markedly with the exuberance
and high spirits of *A Midsummer Night's Dream*, and that difference has
important implications for the presentation of Hecate.

We know that the most striking and peculiar aspect of Hecate's representation in the Renaissance concerns her head: she has three. The illustration
in Vincenzo Cartari's *Imagini* depicts her with a human torso but with the
heads of horse, dog, and boar.[30] Cartari explains the meaning by citing
her identification with crossroads: "Hecate the auncients worshipped and
adored, as she that had the guard and keeping of all crosse waies, and such
lanes as in the end concurred and conjoined themselves in one, and for
that cause they depictured her with three heads."[31] However arresting the
appearance of such a figure, Hecate on Shakespeare's stage almost certainly
did not wear those heads. They would, after all, have puzzled most playgoers, and even Shakespeare's contemporaries differed in their analysis of
this feature. Abraham Fraunce offers this explanation: "That of these three
faces, which was on the right side, was the face and head of a horse, figuring
the swiftnes of the moone in ending her revolution. The left was of a dogge,
noting that when she hideth her self from us she is then Proserpina with
her hellish hounde: the middle was of a boare, signifying her jurisdiction
in fields and forrests."[32] Stephen Batman, without referring specifically to
Hecate, attributes the triple heads to Diana, explaining the meaning as "the
change of every moone into Calends, Nones, & Ides."[33] Natale Conti reports that, instead of a boar, Hecate has, according to some sources, the
head of a man (along with horse and dog).[34]

Clearly, the multiple heads puzzled the mythographers, and the playwright would presumably not have wanted to bewilder playgoers.[35] It is
most likely, then, that the Hecate of the King's Men had a single head.
Hecate, however, may have had had three faces on that head. A bronze

23 In the center background, a statue of Hecate with three faces, holding a torch; Medea
in the foreground. Detail of an engraving by René Boyvin after Léonard Thiry, in *Livre
de la conqueste de la toison d'or, par le prince Jason de Tessalie: faict par figures avec
exposition d'icelles* (Paris, 1563).

statue attributed to Bartolomeo Bellano and dated c. 1480–90 depicts the
goddess as three-faced, each face representing a woman at a different stage
of life.[36] Such a representation might recall Hecate's triple identification
with heaven, earth, and hell without completely mystifying the audience.
Similarly, an engraving by René Boyvin after Léonard Thiry, in an illustrated narrative of Jason and the Golden Fleece,[37] depicts Medea dropping
objects into a cauldron, a statue of the three-faced Hecate, holding a torch,
nearby (fig. 23).

More helpful than the mythographers in estimating Hecate's appearance onstage is a play roughly contemporary with *Macbeth*: Middleton's
The Witch, performed by the King's Men c. 1613–16.[38] As a character,
Hecate has a disturbing appearance. Sebastian, who seeks out Hecate when
he returns from military service to discover his intended bride about to
marry another, wants the goddess to make his rival impotent. Sebastian is
so upset that he tells Hecate: "Whate'er thou art, I have no spare time to

fear thee, / My horrors are so strong and great already / That thou seemst nothing" (1.2.121–23).³⁹ The words "fear" and "horrors" are suggestive, indicating that what he sees must be troubling. Later in this same scene Sebastian says in an aside, "grant, you greater powers that dispose men, / That I may never need this hag again" (lines 179–80). Unspecific as the lines may be, they nevertheless suggest his feeling of repugnance. Hecate's own words and deeds support the impression. She hands a dead baby to a witch with these instructions: "Boil it well; preserve the fat" (1.2.19), an allusion to witches' use of such fat to enable their flight. Similarly, she evokes popular beliefs about witchcraft when, having been refused yeast, flour, and milk, she determines to exact revenge. "Is the heart of wax / Stuck full of magic needles?" she asks another witch, "And is the farmer's picture and his wife's / Laid down to th' fire yet?" (lines 46–47, 48–49). Her spiteful nature and casual cruelty suit a figure whose appearance instills fear in the observer, but the stage direction in the manuscript of *The Witch*, announcing the entry of Hecate, provides no specific information about costume or props: "*enter Heccat: & other witches: (with properties, and habbits fitting).*"⁴⁰

What complicates an estimate of Hecate's theatrical effect in *The Witch* and thus a reconstruction of her appearance is the play's obvious intent to provoke laughter. "The witch scenes tend to upstage the court scenes and mock them," comments Elizabeth Schafer, who contends that Middleton presents "a caricature of witches."⁴¹ Firestone, Hecate's son, seems chiefly designed for comedy (as his very name suggests). His characteristic stance is one of contempt, even for his mother: "How one villain smells out another straight! There's no knavery but is nosed like a dog and can smell out a dog's meaning" (1.2.91–93). Later, when the witches prepare for flight, he comments caustically, "They're all going a-birding tonight. They talk of fowls i'th' air that fly by day, I am sure they'll be a company of foul sluts there tonight" (3.3.15–17). Here he alludes to the sexual appetite of the witches,⁴² which Middleton emphasizes, perhaps for political purpose: "This focus enables him to turn the witch scenes into a grotesque shadow of corruption in high places, comparable to the use of pornography for political satire in the modern cinema."⁴³

What implications does such comedy have for the physical appearance of Hecate in *The Witch*? Would the Jacobean playgoer have been shocked or amused or both? A witch intended to produce a comic effect need not look very different from a witch intended to produce a more serious effect, for a witch can look frightening while being placed in a context that undercuts the fright. Jonson's description of the witches in *The Masque of Queens* sounds as though they were horrific in appearance, yet they may have been partly comic in performance.[44] A funny Hecate and a scary Hecate may look much the same. Still, if the primary purpose of Hecate were to evoke laughter, the costume and makeup of the actor might reflect this intent. That is, a certain exaggeration of body language and facial expression could prove risible, as could a wig worn askew or an oversize costume. Conversely, if the chief purpose were to evoke horror, the actor's costume and makeup might well reflect that intent. The black humor of *The Witch* indicates that Middleton has it both ways. The comedy arises, in part, from a disjunction between, on the one hand, what witches ordinarily represent and, on the other, what they actually say and do in this dramatic action.

Jonson's *Masque of Queens* suggests at least the aura that surrounds the goddess in *Macbeth*, if not details of her appearance, when the chief witch, whom Jonson calls "the Dame," invokes Hecate:

You that have oft been conscious of these sights,
And thou three-formèd star, that of these nights
Art only powerful, to whose triple name
Thus we incline, once, twice and thrice the same
If now with rites profane and foul enough
We do invoke thee, darken all this roof
With present fogs. Exhale earth's rott'nest vapors,
And strike a blindness through these blazing tapers.

(lines 221–28)

Although Hecate herself does not appear in *The Masque of Queens* (in his notes to the masque, Jonson identifies the speaker of these lines as Ate),[45] the Dame's allusion to "earth's rott'nest vapors" suggests that Hecate must embody the decay implied by "rot" and that her appearance is redolent of the underworld. Jonson's masque furnishes a clue to her appearance: the chief witch has hair "*knotted and folded with vipers*" (line 88).[46] This feature evokes the Furies of ancient Greece and Rome. Jonson tells us that his witches depend on "ancient and late writers" (line 34): he knows that the witch of Horace, Canidia, has "locks and dishevelled head entwined with short vipers,"[47] as does Lucan's Erictho (Jonson cites both authors in *The Masque of Queens*).[48] Natale Conti, moreover, says that "Hecate had tangles of hissing serpents and vipers that looked like intricately twisted knots, some of which encircled her neck and dropped down to her shoulders" (*Mythologies*, 143). Jonson's Dame also carries a torch, an implement customarily carried by the Furies, and she addresses "fiends and furies" (line 203). Hecate's domain, like that of Jonson's witches, is hellish, and as a formidable power in the underworld/hell, she keeps company with the Furies. Drayton in *The Moon-Calfe* relates that Hecate "Commands the Furies to step in and ayde her" (line 113).

In their performance of *Macbeth*, the King's Men could have used snakes in the costuming of Hecate, either by having her handle the reptiles or by giving her a Medusa-like wig. Those snakes would complement her traditional association with the Furies, who wield snakes and wear serpent-like hair. The other witches, appearing in scenes with Hecate, may have carried torches, a visual allusion to Hecate's abode in the underworld. Jonson's Dame refers to "these blazing tapers" (line 228),[49] and an illustration of a black sabbath in Francesco Mario Guazzo's *Compendium Maleficarum* (Milan, 1608) depicts several of the witches holding torches.[50] Finally, the entry of Hecate may have been accompanied by the noise of barking dogs, which, Natale Conti explains, signifies "the calamities and suffering destined to plague men constantly" (*Mythologies*, 148). Pierre Le Loyer, similarly, cites the Greek belief that Hecate "did use to send dogges unto men to feare and terrifie them."[51]

If Hecate in *Macbeth* were so costumed, the presentation would complement the associations that had accrued to the goddess in antiquity. Representative of ancient accounts is that by Apollonius of Rhodes, who describes Jason's sacrifice to the goddess. Separating himself from his men, Jason finds a deserted place, builds a fire, and sacrifices a sheep to Hecate, who hears him and soon arrives in full regalia: "round her horrible serpents twined themselves among the oak boughs; and there was a gleam of countless torches; and sharply howled around her the hounds of hell."[52] The chief elements of the description – snakes, torches, and hounds – produce a sense of shock in the observer: "All the meadows trembled at her step; and the nymphs that haunt the marsh and river shrieked." The overall effect of Hecate's appearance in *Macbeth* would similarly have induced fright, as we can surmise from a hyperbolic boast in another Jacobean play, *The Courageous Turk*: "I can looke more terrible, then night, / And command darknesse in the unwilling day: / Make Hecate start" (lines 1670–72).[53]

The three sisters of *Macbeth*

Our knowledge of the witches' appearance in *Macbeth* begins with Banquo's question when the warriors confront the three sisters:

> What are these
> So wither'd and so wild in their attire,
> That look not like th' inhabitants o' th' earth,
> And yet are on't?   (1.3.39–42)

These lines were probably inspired by Holinshed: "there met them three women in strange and wild apparell, resembling creatures of elder world."[54] Both chronicler and playwright use the same word, "wild," but without further elucidation, that word scarcely takes us very far in visualizing what Banquo and his companion see. An eyewitness description of a Jacobean performance seems to promise additional information. Simon Forman's account of seeing Macbeth at the Globe, 20 April 1611, begins: "ther was to be observed, firste, howe Mackbeth and Bancko, 2 noble men of Scotland, ridinge thorowe a wod, the <r> stode before them 3 women feiries or nimphes."[55] Alas, Forman's plot summary contains no other reference to the three sisters. What's more, his account sounds as though he were remembering Holinshed (according to "common opinion," the women may have been "some nymphs or feiries") rather than what the playgoer heard or saw at the Globe.[56]

Nicholas Brooke observes that "the words ["nymphs or feiries"] are not in the play, not likely ever to have been, and not likely to have occurred to anyone as a description of the Weïrd Sisters as played by male actors in 1611."[57] Do those words, however, tell us anything about the three sisters in *Macbeth*? The doublet "nymphs or feiries" may, for a modern reader, evoke benign creatures like Moth or Mustardseed in *A Midsummer Night's Dream*. But Willard Farnham cautions against any such notion. He points to Shakespeare's use of the word "fairies" in *Cymbeline*,[58] when Imogen beseeches the gods:

> To your protection I commend me, gods,
> From fairies and the tempters of the night
> Guard me, beseech ye.   (2.2.8–10)

In the early seventeenth century, moreover, "fairy" is often synonymous with "witch." In *Hamlet* Marcellus speaks of witches and fairies in the same breath, saying that at the season of our Savior's birth, "No fairy takes, nor witch hath power to charm" (1.1.163). Peter Heylen's account of Macbeth actually conflates the two terms: "[Macbeth and Banquo] travelling together through a forrest were mette by three fairies, or witches (weirds the Scots call them)."[59] As for "nymphs," when, in John Lyly's *Endymion*, a character sees fairies dancing around him, he cries out: "But what are these so fair fiends that cause my hairs to stand upright and spirits to fall down? Hags – out, alas! Nymphs, I crave pardon" (4.3.30–32).[60] Here the word "nymphs" amounts to a euphemism for "hags," or witches.[61]

That the three sisters of *Macbeth* are nothing like the devotees of Titania in *Dream* is clear from Banquo's address.[62]

> You seem to understand me,
> By each at once her choppy finger laying
> Upon her skinny lips. You should be women,
> And yet your beards forbid me to interpret
> That you are so.   (1.3.43–47)

The word "choppy," which means "full of clefts," indicates rough skin. Together with the words "skinny lips" and, a few lines earlier, "withered," Banquo's language at lines 44–45 suggests that the three women are old and lean and have the kind of bodies shaped by a hard life outdoors. Also distinguishing these three from the fairies of *Dream* is their sexual ambiguity: they have beards, a feature that would suit the adult male actors who presumably played their roles. Macbeth's later greeting, "How now, you secret, black, and midnight hags?" (4.1.48), seems to confirm Banquo's evocation of aged, unattractive women, though, according to the *OED*, the primary meanings of "hag" are "an evil spirit, daemon, or infernal being, in female form" and "a woman supposed to have dealings with Satan." The *OED* cites Macbeth's "midnight hags" as an instance of the second definition. It's likely, however, that "hag" has even here in Macbeth's line something of the meaning it conveys today. After all, in the eyes of Shakespeare's contemporaries, a witch was an "ugly, repulsive old woman" (*OED*). In *The Winter's Tale* Shakespeare seems to so use the word when the crazed Leontes terms Hermione "A gross hag!" (2.3.108).

In seeking to clarify the look of the three sisters, let us consider more closely Shakespeare's chief source, Holinshed's *Chronicle*, for the 1577 edition contains a number of woodcuts that purport to illustrate the narrative, and one of them actually depicts the encounter of Macbeth and Banquo with the three creatures. Far from resolving our questions, however, the chronicle presents a puzzle. Although it does picture the meeting on the heath, the three figures look nothing like the women wearing "wild" attire (1.3.40), who are evoked in the narrative. Instead, the woodcut depicts the three as young and attractive females, well coiffed and richly dressed.[63] In short, the picture seems to have little connection with Holinshed's written account, except that both represent Macbeth and Banquo on horseback. We know, of course, that a sixteenth-century book may use a single woodcut to illustrate different stories or different historical personages. But the woodcut depicting Macbeth's meeting appears only once in the 1577 Holinshed. Why such a disparity should exist between text and illustration remains a mystery.[64]

That mystery might be lightened if Holinshed conceived of the three sisters as shape-shifters. The illustration might then represent creatures who sometimes adopt strange and wild apparel and who, at other times, elect to appear in another guise altogether. Interestingly, Jacobean playwrights attribute just such powers to witches and evil spirits. In *Sophonisba* (acted by the Blackfriars Boys in 1606), for instance, John Marston creates a witch who deliberately alters her appearance: "*Enter Erictho in the shape of Sophonisba, her face veiled*" (4.1.211.s.d.).[65] And *The Witch of Edmonton* (acted by Prince Charles' Men in 1621) brings to the stage a spirit who possesses the ability to assume a pleasing shape: "*Enter a spirit in the shape of Katherine, vizarded, and takes it* [her mask] *off*" (3.1.74.s.d.).[66] Despite such stage directions, nothing in Holinshed's chronicle specifically attributes such power to the three sisters. Nor does the Folio text of *Macbeth*, though Marvin Rosenberg wonders: "might they change shape, color, image, from scene to scene?"[67]

Neither Shakespeare's play nor his narrative source provides more than a vague impression of what the three sisters look like. We need, therefore, to move beyond the play and consider other kinds of evidence, especially the witches described in witchcraft pamphlets and books, and the witches who appear elsewhere on the Jacobean stage.

The three sisters as witches

Before investigating these sources of information, we must ask a basic question: are the three sisters of *Macbeth* actually witches?[68] Critical opinion has been divided. Walter Clyde Curry believes that "the Weird Sisters are demons or devils in the form of witches."[69] For Willard Farnham, "the witches in Shakespeare's *Macbeth* are demons of the fairy order such as the Elizabethans also called hags or furies. They are fiends in the shape of old women."[70] But M. D. W. Jeffreys states flatly, "The three weird sisters are not witches."[71] Alan Brissenden offers a plethora of possibilities: "The weird sisters in *Macbeth* may be fairies, they may be some other kind of supernatural beings, they may be humans possessed of the devil."[72]

And Stephen Booth cites the nature of the witches as an instance of the "indefinition" he finds in tragedy: "What matters…is not hunting down an answer to the question 'What are the witches?' All the critical and theatrical efforts to answer that question demonstrate that the question cannot be answered."[73]

Shakespeareans who doubt that the three sisters are witches point out that neither Macbeth nor Banquo actually calls them witches. The word "witch" appears only twice in the dialogue: when one of the three sisters quotes a sailor's wife, "Aroint thee, witch!" (1.3.6), and when another of the three sisters describes the contents of the cauldron as containing "witch's mummy" (4.1.23). Nevertheless, the stage directions and speech headings characterize the three sisters as witches. We cannot, of course, be certain that Shakespeare was responsible for those directions and headings. But a survey of writings on witchcraft provides abundant evidence that the three sisters of *Macbeth* possess powers that Shakespeare's contemporaries ascribe to witches.

From the opening lines of *Macbeth* the three sisters are identified with phenomena of wind and storm: "When shall we three meet again?/In thunder, lightning, or in rain?" (1.1.1–2). Speaking of the sailor's ship in a later scene, one of the three tells another, "Though his bark cannot be lost,/Yet it shall be tempest-toss'd" (1.3.24–25). Such power to raise wind and storm belongs to witches. Jacobus Sprenger and Heinrich Kramer in *Malleus Maleficarum* relate that "devils and their disciples can by witchcraft cause lightnings and hailstorms and tempests."[74] King James, similarly, in his *Daemonologie* notes, "they can rayse stormes and tempestes in the aire, either upon sea or land."[75] Reginald Scot, while skeptical of witchcraft, acknowledges the common belief that hail, snow, thunder, lightning, and tempestuous winds "are raised by the cunning and power of witches and conjurers."[76] William Perkins testifies that witches "raise tempests by sea and by land,"[77] and, according to Alexander Roberts, witches "procure tempests, to stirre up thunder & lightning, move violent winds."[78] When, late in the play, Macbeth says that the three sisters "untie the winds, and let them fight/Against the churches; though the yesty waves/Confound and swallow navigation up" (4.1.52–54), the playwright grants them exactly those powers that his contemporaries assign to witches.[79]

Shakespeare's three sisters belong particularly to the air, which they manipulate, contaminate, and traverse. In the play's opening scene, they celebrate the peculiar atmosphere: "Fair is foul, and foul is fair, / Hover through the fog and filthy air" (1.1.11–12). The power to darken and disturb the air belongs to Satan and his agents. King James, for example, asks why the devil may not "thicken & obscure so the aire, that is next about them by contracting it strait together, that the beames of any other mans eyes, cannot pearce throw the same, to see them?"[80] Witches not only darken the air but also pollute it. Henry Holland reports that Satan "can infect and poyson the ayer and water with pestiferous exhalations."[81] And Alexander Roberts declares, "For the elements, it is an agreeing consent of all, that they [witches] can corrupt and infect them."[82] That same air provides a means of transport for witches, especially when they convene with Satan. Lambert Daneau explains, "he geveth them with a staffe, which they muste put between their legges, and at the saying of certen prayers in his name . . . they think straight that the staffe carieth them thither as they would goe, and so he perswadeth them that they be borne by the staffe, while he himselfe dothe carrie them."[83] Henry Boguet reports that a witch named Françoise Secretain went to Satan's sabbath "on a white staff which she placed between her legs."[84] Although Shakespeare's play offers no evidence that his witches possess such a staff, Macbeth suggests that they move through the air (presumably by some sort of flying machinery in the theatre): "Infected be the air whereon they ride" (4.1.138).[85]

Besides their power over meteorological phenomena and their capacity for flight, witches typically possess the power of prophecy.[86] George Gifford writes, "A witch is one that worketh by the devill, or by some devilish or curious art, either hurting or healing, revealing thinges secrete, or foretelling thinges to come, which the devil hath devised to entangle and snare mens souls."[87] Henry Holland says that witches are "cunning in praedictions" and possess "a great foresight in naturall events,"[88] while for William Perkins, "Divination is a part of witchcraft, whereby men reveale strange things, either past, present, or to come, by the assistance of the devill."[89] Shakespeare's Macbeth dramatizes such powers when the three sisters greet the Thane of Glamis as Thane of Cawdor (1.3.49), predict that he "shalt be King hereafter" (line 50), and when they reveal "A show of eight kings . . . and Banquo" (4.1.111.s.d.). Banquo himself has no hesitation about linking the prophecies with demonic forces. Learning that Macbeth has been named Thane of Cawdor, Banquo asks, "What, can the devil speak true?" (1.3.107). Moments later he adds, "The instruments of darkness tell us truths" (line 124).

The three sisters of Macbeth perform two other actions that Shakespeare's contemporaries associate with witches: they sing, according to the stage direction at 3.5.33 and again at the cauldron (4.1.43). The stage direction at 4.1.132, moreover, reveals that "The Witches dance."[90] Although the word "dance" does not appear in 1.3, the witches probably move rhythmically as they speak these lines: "The weird sisters, hand in hand, / Posters of the sea and land, / Thus do go, about, about, / Thrice to thine, and thrice to mine, / And thrice again, to make up nine" (1.3.32–36). Alan Brissenden observes that "Three and its square, nine, are odd numbers with ancient magical and cabbalistic significance, and are frequently used in ritual dance."[91]

We don't know whether the first performances of *Macbeth* at the Globe included such dancing. Today Shakespeareans are inclined to view the song and dance as the creation of Thomas Middleton, who began working for the King's Men c. 1610 and whose own play *The Witch* employs witches as characters. Shakespeare's company may have felt that the original version of *Macbeth* lacked sufficient theatrical appeal (there is no record of performance except for Simon Forman's account) and so decided to have Middleton enhance the role of the witches. Whenever the song and dance first entered *Macbeth*, these activities were certainly part of the play by the time the First Folio was published in 1623.

Although singing and dancing witches may seem incongruous to modern readers and playgoers, these activities would not have struck Shakespeare's audience as inconsistent with the dark purpose of witches.[92] European folklore had long imagined that those in league with Satan sang and danced when they met with him. Lambert Daneau, for instance, explains in bizarre detail the peculiar forms that witches' dance and songs take: "then fal they to dauncing, wherin he [Satan] leadeth the daunce, or els they hoppe and daunce merely about him, singing most filthy songes."[93] Boguet says, "they dance; and this they do in a ring back to back"; songs also become part of their ritual: "Most often Satan plays upon the flute, and at other times the witches are content to sing with their voices; but they sing at haphazard and in such confusion that one cannot hear the other."[94] In Ben Jonson's *Masque of Queens*, performed at Whitehall on 2 February 1609, we find this stage direction: "*These eleven witches . . . dance (which is an usual ceremony at their convents, or meetings)*" (lines 36–38). Later in the masque the witches again dance, Jonson describing the peculiar features of their motion: "*with a strange and sudden music they fell into a magical dance full of preposterous change and gesticulation, but most applying to their property, who at their meetings do all things contrary to the custom of men, dancing back to back and hip to hip, their hands joined, and making their circles backward, to the left hand, with strange fantastic motions of their heads and bodies*" (lines 327–32).

If books on witchcraft provide evidence that witches possess the traits we find in Shakespeare's weird sisters, those books fail to specify the kind of distinctive dress and physical characteristics that might immediately identify the three figures as witches in the theatre. This is not surprising since witches were notoriously difficult to detect by appearance alone. They could, people believed, be discovered by what they did. In addition to the actions described above, witches might hurt others by causing disease, sexual dysfunction, sterility, or death; sicken or kill livestock; take animal form; become invisible; create illusions; traffic with the devil, who might take the form of a cat, dog, or other common animal; celebrate a sabbath with Satan; allow the devil to suck their blood; kiss the devil obscenely; couple with each other or with the devil; make ointments with the fat of young children and use the ointment for flight; keep an evil spirit in a wicker bottle or leather bottle or woolpack. None of these activities, however, translates into a hypothesis about the costume for a witch in a play. Witches could also be identified by what they said. William Perkins claims that throughout Europe all witches, when questioned, "are of like cariage and behaviour in their examinations and convictions: they use the same answears, refuges, defenses, protestations."[95] Again, however, such alleged similarity fails to help us imagine the physical appearance of a witch onstage.

This is not to say that witches were without physical characteristics. In fact, people believed that when a person made a pact with the devil, he marked that individual bodily.[96] William Perkins, for example, says, "it is commonly thought, when the devill maketh his covenant with them, he alwaies leaveth his marke behind him, whereby he knowes them for his owne."[97] That mark represents a parody of Christian baptism. King James explains: "As none conveenes to the adoration and worshipping of God, except they be marked with his seale, the sacrament of Baptisme: so none serves Sathan, and conveenes to the adoring of him, that are not marked with that marke."[98] In *A Detection of damnable driftes*, we learn that Mother Osborne, accused of witchcraft, "hath a marke in the ende of one of her fingers like a pitt, and an other marke upon the outside of her right legge."[99] The difficulty for witch hunters was that Satan's mark might not readily be seen. Alexander Roberts reveals the cunning of the devil, who places his mark "in some part of the body, least either suspected or perceived by us (for hee is a cunning concealer) as under the eye-lids, or in the palat of the mouth, or other secret places."[100] Hence Lambert Daneau's advice to witch hunters: "when any of these [witches] shall be convented before them, [it is necessary] to poulle [cut off the hair] and shave them where occasion shall serve, al the body over, least haply the marke may lurke under the heare in any place."[101] Needless to say, such secret marks could not be made visible in the theatres of Jacobean England, no matter how close the groundlings may have been to the players.

The evidence of the witchcraft materials suggests that, despite secret marks, witches tended to look much like other women – except that they were old, poor, and generally unattractive.[102] In *The Wonderfull Discoverie of Witches*, Thomas Potts describes a witch named Elizabeth Sowtherns, alias Demdike, as "a very old woman, about the age of fourescore yeares, and had been a witch for fiftie yeares."[103] Of another witch named Anne Whittle, alias Chattox, Potts writes, "[she] was a very old withered, spent & decreped creature, her sight almost gone."[104] Similarly, Alexander Roberts refers to the common notion that witches are "melancholique, aged, and ignorant women."[105] For Samuel Harsnett a witch is "an olde weather-beaten croane, having her chinne, & her knees meeting for age, walking like a bow leaning on a shaft, hollow eyed, untoothed, furrowed on her face."[106] And Thomas Heywood observes of witches, "all such are for the most part stigmaticall and ouglie, in so much, that it is growne into a common adage, *Deformis ut saga, ... As deformed as a witch*."[107]

[margin note: Bill Harsnett, was a skeptic!]

The representation of Mother Sawyer, the witch of Edmonton, tallies with such characterizations. In the play by Rowley, Dekker, and Ford, acted in 1621, Elizabeth Sawyer complains that "an old woman / Ill-favoured grown with years, if she be poor / Must be called bawd or witch" (4.1.122–24).[108] She also describes herself as suffering from the kind of physical affliction brought on by advanced age: "I am poor, deformed and ignorant, / And like a bow buckled and bent together / By some more strong in mischiefs than myself" (2.1.3–5); and she has only one eye (2.1.89–90). Similarly, in Heywood and Brome's *The Late Lancashire Witches*, acted by the King's Men in August 1634,[109] one character denies being a witch, saying, "I am sure I look like no such ugly creature" and adds that nowadays witches "for the most part are ugly old beldams" (1.1.111–12, 119–20); in this same conversation another character refers to "an old wither'd witch" (line 124).[110]

The woodcuts in sixteenth- and seventeenth-century English books indicate that witches generally had no special physical characteristics that were readily apparent to the observer. For instance, the title-page of *The Apprehension and confession of three notorious Witches* (1589) depicts the bodies of three fully clothed women hanging from a gibbet; nothing in their appearance marks them as different from other women of their social class.[111] The four witches being examined by a magistrate in the frontispiece of *Newes from Scotland* (1591) wear ordinary garb and headgear.[112] A much later woodcut (1655) shows the bodies of four witches dangling from a gallows; again, we find nothing remarkable about the garb of the victims.[113] The 1658 quarto of *The Witch of Edmonton* features a woodcut with a picture of Mother Sawyer (along with the devil in the form of a dog and Cuddy Banks, the clown): she is fully dressed, wears a large hat, and carries a walking stick. It's difficult to know, however, whether this illustration tells us anything about the stage character in Jacobean London. R. A. Foakes doubts a connection: "there is no reason to think that the woodcut made for the title-page has any reference to the theatre."[114]

The Witch of Edmonton, despite its interest in the social conditions that produce witches, probably has little to tell us about the theatrical witches of *Macbeth*, for what sets the witch of Rowley, Dekker, and Ford apart from other Jacobean stage witches is the playwrights' essentially sympathetic attitude toward her.[115] When the dramatic action begins, Elizabeth Sawyer is *not* a witch. She is driven to witchcraft by her powerlessness in the face of persecution. "Why should the envious world / Throw all their scandalous malice upon me?" she asks in a soliloquy meant to engage the sympathy of the playgoer (2.1.1–2). The actor playing Elizabeth Sawyer may have the demeanor and carriage of an elderly person but would not seek to terrify.

The Late Lancashire Witches is scarcely more helpful. When a character tells her daughter, "I'le sing and be merry, weare as fine clothes, and as delicate dressings as thou wilt have me," the daughter replies: "you look like one o the Scottish wayward sisters" (1.1.441–43, 446–47). Although the mother speaks of "fine clothes," she apparently looks shabby to her daughter; hence the reference to "wayward sisters." The sense seems clear enough, but the comment is too general to clarify the character's appearance.[116] More useful is a passage to which A. R. Braunmuller draws attention in his edition of *Macbeth*; in *The Honestie of this Age* (1614) Barnaby Rich writes:

My Lady ... holdeth on her way, perhaps to the tyre makers shoppe, where shee shaketh out her crownes to bestowe upon some new fashioned atire, that if we may say, there be deformitie in art, upon such artificall deformed periwigs, that they were fitter to furnish a theater, or for her that in a stageplay, should represent some hagge of hell, then to bee used by a Christian woman ...[117]

The key word here would seem to be "deformitie." The precise shape such deformity took, however, remains a mystery. We might have better grounds for conjecture if the record in Henslowe's *Diary* of "a wiches gowne"[118] supplied a description, but the October 1602 entry tells us nothing about the garment; nor does it name the plays in which it was worn.

The witches of *Macbeth* would seem to be altogether different in their theatrical effect from those of *The Late Lancashire Witches* and *The Witch of Edmonton*. Shakespeare's witches are witches from the moment we first encounter them and they prove exceedingly dangerous, for their prophecies constitute a form of temptation to Macbeth and his wife, leading this couple to the most serious of political crimes, murder of a king. It seems logical to assume that the witches in *Macbeth* would physically embody that danger.[119] In a theatre where what is seen may be as important as what is heard, and in a tragedy rather than a tragicomedy, the playwrights would be missing a bet if they presented witches as unremarkable looking. Banquo's comments that they are "wild in their attire" and that they "look not like th' inhabitants o' th' earth" (1.3.40–41) confirm that the three figures are anything but conventional in appearance. The witches of *Macbeth* must be closer in costume and makeup to the witch of *Sophonisba* than to the unfortunate Elizabeth Sawyer in *The Witch of Edmonton*.

Marston and Jonson

Unlike *The Witch of Edmonton*, John Marston's *The Wonder of Women, or The Tragedy of Sophonisba*, represents a witch as truly fearsome. First staged in the late spring of 1606, perhaps just a few months before *Macbeth*, Marston's tragedy dramatizes a story of political intrigue, military conflict, and sexual obsession. The larger struggle pits Rome against Carthage, but the play focuses on the lust of Syphax, the Libyan king, for the virtuous Sophonisba. When his entreaties prove ineffectual, he seeks out a witch for help. The stage directions say nothing about the witch's appearance, but Syphax describes what he sees when he meets her:

A loathsome yellow leanness spreads her face
A heavy hell-like paleness loads her cheeks,
Unknown to a clear heaven.   (4.1.102–4)

Her hair is no more attractive than her skin: she "stalks out, heaves her proud head / With long unkempt hair" (lines 108–09). This description, which has no precedent in either of Marston's chief sources, Appian's *Roman History* and Livy's *History of Rome*, originates in Lucan's *Pharsalia*, where the author describes a witch: "A yellow leanenesse spreads her lothed face; / Her dreadfull lookes, knowne to no lightsome aire, / With heavy hell-like palenesse clogged are."[120] The decrepitude of Marston's witch matches her abode: she lives near a "once glorious temple," destroyed by "wrath and lust" (lines 144, 148). In creating a character out of Lucan's words, Marston departs from English stage precedent: Erictho has little in common with so-called "wise women" like Lyly's Mother Bombie in the 1580s.[121] Instead, Erictho is "a goetist with affinities to Ovid's and Seneca's Medea. As such, she appears to be the only fully-fledged example of her kind in Elizabethan drama."[122]

Marston's Erictho is described as lean and loathsome; she "revels in corruption and disgusting filth both physical and moral."[123] The impression she creates is unmistakable: Erictho inspires dread and repugnance in the beholder. Thus after their night together, when Erictho has assumed the form of the woman that Syphax lusts after,[124] he awakes and discovers the true identity of his sexual partner, crying out in horror, "Thou rotten scum of hell – / O my abhorrèd heart! O loathed delusion!" (5.1.2–3). But Marston, like Shakespeare, fails to offer anything more specific than this.

Ben Jonson's account of Maudlin, the witch in *The Sad Shepherd*, seems reminiscent of Marston's. Jonson's witch, who calls upon "Dame Hecat" (2.3.42), dwells "by the ruines of a shaken abbey" (2.8.17).[125] If Marston's witch devours bodily remains, Jonson's dwells "'Mongst graves, and grotts, neare an old charnell house" (line 19). When Maudlin leaves her abode, she carries about her an atmosphere of decay, journeying "in the foggs, / And rotten mistes" (lines 24–25). And she has expert knowledge of "The venom'd plants / Wherewith shee kills" (lines 42–43). All of this seems closer to Erictho than to the stereotypical village witch, who seeks vengeance against a neighbor when denied a cup of flour or pot of milk. But Jonson's unfinished play offers little detail about Maudlin's appearance. For additional hints about the witches of *Macbeth*, we need to turn once more to *The Masque of Queens*.

That there exists a connection between Jonson's 1609 masque and Shakespeare's play has long been a matter of speculation. Almost a century ago W. J. Lawrence suggested that Shakespeare's company, which was responsible for performing the antimasque of witches in *The Masque of Queens*, may have been led to embellish the original dramatization of the witches in *Macbeth* by the players' acquaintance with Jonson's work.[126] Shakespeareans today generally agree that the witch scenes in *Macbeth* were altered in the years following the first Jacobean performances of the play. Lawrence even speculates that "It was not even beyond the power of the players to obtain the use of the fantastically elaborate dresses originally worn" in the masque.[127]

We need to be cautious about insisting on a close connection between the witches of Jonson and Shakespeare, for the requirements of an aristocratic entertainment differ from those of a play at a public theatre. David Norbrook notes that "Shakespeare's treatment of the witches' language is strikingly different from the more orthodox strategy of Jonson's *Masque of Queens*."[128] Nevertheless, the conception of the witches created by Jonson seems in several respects very close to that of *Macbeth*.[129] Jonson's witches, for example, are physically unattractive, even repulsive. And what exactly do the figures in the masque look like? Jonson, who suggests the conventionality of a witch's costume when he describes the antimasque in *The Masque of Queens* ("twelve women in the habit of hags or witches"), provides something that neither Shakespeare nor Marston nor Middleton offers: details of costumes and props. Jonson accomplishes this because masquemakers typically pay close attention to costuming, and Jonson is among the most fastidious practitioners of the genre.

Jonson's witches are "*all differently attired: some with rats on their head, some on their shoulders; others with ointment pots at their girdles; all with spindles, timbrels, rattles, or other venefical* [i.e., pertaining to witchcraft] *instruments*" (lines 27–30). The author also reveals that, while Inigo Jones was responsible for constructing the costumes, Jonson himself created "*their properties of vipers, snakes, herbs, roots, and other ensigns of their magic*" (lines 32–33). The chief witch, whom Jonson calls the Dame, seems especially grotesque: she is "*naked armed, barefooted, her frock tucked, her hair knotted and folded with vipers; in her hand a torch made of a dead man's arm, lighted; girded with a snake*" (lines 87–89).

Although we don't know for certain that Shakespeare's witches carry such objects as vipers and herbs in their hands, the scene at the cauldron suggests that they do.[130] Certainly, the theatricality of the scene would be enhanced if, one by one, they toss into a pot the body parts they name:

Fillet of a fenny snake,
In the cauldron boil and bake;
Eye of newt and toe of frog,
Wool of bat and tongue of dog,
Adder's fork and blind-worm's sting,
Lizard's leg and howlet's wing.

(4.1.12–17)

And just as Jonson's witches handle herbs and roots, Shakespeare's witches toss into the cauldron "Root of hemlock" and "slips of yew" (lines 25, 27), both of which have lethal effects.

The makeup worn by the actors playing the witches probably made for a combination of facial pallor and yellowish hue: recall that "yellow leanness" and "hell-like paleness" characterize Marston's Erictho.[131] That makeup must have evoked putrefying flesh. Syphax calls Erictho "rotten scum," and Jonson's Maudlin, who lives near a charnel house, travels in "rotten mistes." The general effect is more horrific than comic: the witches evoke

24 A witch with matted hair and a snake on her lap sits beside a cauldron and receives
a visitor. Engraving from Jacob Cats, *'s Werelts begin, midden, eynde, besloten in den
trou-ringh* (Dordrecht, 1637)

disgust. Their facial expression, moreover, gives them a fierce look, sig-
nalling a malign intent. In Shakespeare's *1 Henry VI*, York, having captured
Joan la Pucelle, says, "See how the ugly witch doth bend her brows, / As
if, with Circe, she would change my shape!" (5.3.34–35). And a witch in
Macbeth calls attention to Hecate's scowl, saying, "how now, Hecat? you look
angerly" (3.5.1). Like Erictho, who has "long unkempt hair," the witches in
Macbeth are likely disheveled, and if their hair falls in matted strands (akin
to dreadlocks), it evokes the Furies of the underworld (fig. 24).

The clothing of Shakespeare's witches, while not described in the stage
directions, must be unusual. As we have seen, Banquo calls their garb "wild."
What it looks like may become apparent if we recall that the very essence
of witchcraft is inversion. In all they do, witches undermine expectation,

custom, hierarchy, and providential order: "Because their inspiration is demonic, their perception is overturned; they see and do everything the wrong way up."[132] If the ordinary dress of women is symmetrical, the costume of the witches must be the inverse – that is, irregularly shaped. If the ordinary dress of women is of a solid color (some shade of black, brown or gray), the costume of the witches must be irregularly colored, perhaps a patchwork of disparate colors. The costume's texture may also be unusual, evoking the skin of a snake: in *The Masque of Queens* one of the witches, Ignorance, is recognized by her "scaly vesture" (line 106). Whether Shakespeare's witches, like Jonson's, were also equipped with "venefical instruments" we shall never know.

Witches and fates

In most modern editions of Shakespeare's play, the three women whom Macbeth and Banquo meet are called "weird sisters" even though the word "weird" does not actually appear in the first printed edition. Instead, the 1623 Folio calls the sisters "weyward" three times, and another three times calls them "weyard." According to the *OED* "weyward" was "no doubt due to association with *wayward*, a word used many times by Shakespeare." "The question of what F[olio]'s compositors saw," A. R. Braunmuller observes, "and therefore what modern word or words F's 'weyward' and 'weyard' might represent cannot be decided."[133] Most editors, however, have accepted Lewis Theobald's 1733 emendation and changed both words in the Folio to "weird." This choice, concludes Braunmuller, "seems a plausible and metrically justifiable change."[134]

The word "weird" has encouraged Shakespeareans to conjecture a connection between the three sisters of the play and the three Fates of classical mythology, for the word "weird" sounds like Anglo-Saxon *wyrd*, which means "fate," and the *OED* defines "weird" as "claiming the supernatural power of dealing with fate or destiny." Precedent exists in historical narratives for conflating "weird" sisters and Fates: "From at least 1400, Scottish texts apply 'weird sister' to the three classical Fates, the Parcae."[135] Are there any implications for our understanding of the witches in *Macbeth*?

Henry N. Paul thinks not: "The effort of some scholars to liken the witches of the play to the Parcae of the Latins or to the Norns of Scandinavian mythology is without foundation in the play."[136] Yet Holinshed himself, recounting Macbeth's meeting with the three women, reports: "the common opinion was, that these women were either the weird sisters, that is (as

ye would say) *the goddesses of destinie*, or else some nymphs or feiries, in-
dued with knowledge of prophesie by their necromanticall science, bicause
everie thing came to passe as they had spoken."[137] Although the chronicler leaves the issue undecided, he entertains the possibility that the three
figures are the determiners of destiny, or fate.[138]

   Would the sight of the three witches have evoked the Fates for a playgoer
who may never have read the chronicler's history of Macbeth? I think it
likely, though we cannot say this with complete confidence. When Holinshed recounts that the three figures who confront Macbeth resemble "creatures of elder world," he apparently refers to Clotho, Lachesis, and Atropos
of the "ancient" world (*OED*). Playgoers, moreover, could have seen the
Fates elsewhere on the Renaissance stage. In Dekker's *Old Fortunatus*, acted
by the Admiral's Men in 1599, the stage direction indicates that "*three
Destinies enter working*" (2.2.213); "*working*" must mean handling the
thread of life, for moments later Fortune points to "This inckie thread"
(line 242).[139] In Fletcher and Field's *Four Plays, or Moral Representations,
in One*, acted by Lady Elizabeth's Men c. 1613–15, a stage direction indicates that the chariot of Death is "*drawn by the Destinies*" (third interlude,
line 11.s.d.).[140] The Fates appear in masques as well. In Thomas Campion's
Somerset Masque, performed 26 December 1613, spectators see "*the three
Destinies, in long robes of white taffata like aged women.*"[141] And in Jonson's
Lovers Made Men, performed 22 February 1617 in the home of Lord Hay,
the Fates sit by the bank of the river Lethe (lines 12–14); one holds a spindle;
another, shears.[142]

   The most interesting dramatization of the Fates occurs in *The Birth of
Merlin*, acted by Prince Charles' Men in 1622, where the three figures appear
in the company of Hecate. This "dreadful queen of night" (3.3.7) collab-
orates with the Fates, for she enters with them (probably through a trap
door) and exits with them too; the devil says, "Thanks Hecate, hail sister to
the gods, / There lies your way, haste with the Fates" (lines 15–16).[143] Similarly, in *The Sad Shepherd* Hecate is said to be present when Maudlin works
a spindle and a gypsy weaves the thread (2.3.39–50). Together these three,
Robert M. Adams observes, "suggest the ancient Fates or Norns, weaving
the magic threads of human life."[144] Ancient writers typically describe the
Fates as performing their work in the underworld: in Lucian, for instance,
we read that "the Fates and the Furies were there" [in Hades], along with
Aeacus and Charon.[145] Renaissance mythographers also locate the Fates
near the dwelling of Hecate. The 1627 French edition of Natale Conti's
mythology illustrates with a single engraving the contents of a chapter
dealing with "l'enfer": in a cartouche on the left stands Hecate (next to

Diana and Lucina).[146] Immediately to their right in another cartouche stand the three Furies, with their snakes and torches. Beneath them the three Fates spin, measure, and cut the thread of life. Similarly, in *Lovers Made Men*, as we have just seen, Jonson locates the Fates by the river Lethe in the underworld.

That the Fates should turn up in the company of Hecate is consistent with their similar function. What the original witches in *Macbeth* (before Middleton doubled them) have in common with the Fates is that they are three in number,[147] that they work in concert, that they inspire anxiety in humankind, that they act upon mortals in ways that often prove destructive, and that they may portend death. Significantly, the visual arts depict both Fates and witches in similar fashion. That is, artists often portray Fates and witches as nude, representing different stages of life, and cooperating in a common enterprise.[148] A chiaroscuro woodcut entitled *The Witches' Sabbath* by Hans Baldung Grien depicts three witches seated or kneeling on the ground by an urn;[149] one witch is young; another, middle-aged; and the other, elderly.[150] Another of this artist's woodcuts depicts the three Fates with the thread of life. Like his print of the witches, this woodcut depicts the Fates as nude and as representing various ages; Clotho is young and attractive; Lachesis, middle-aged and plump; Atropos, old and gnarled.[151] Baldung Grien's prints of Fates and witches are strikingly similar: his Fates, as Charles W. Talbot notes, are "indistinguishable" from the women he depicts in witches' sabbaths.[152] Given the resemblance of witches and Fates, conceptually and artistically, it is not surprising that Ben Jonson should assign to his witches an implement ordinarily handled by the Fates: in *The Masque of Queens* Jonson equips some of the witches "*with spindles*" (line 29), which he calls "*venefical instruments*" (lines 29–30).

Pierre Milan, in a print after Rosso Fiorentino, also suggests visually the connection between Fates and witches. Milan's Fates look not like the self-absorbed threesome in so many representations, who busily spin, measure, and cut the thread of life,[153] but rather like embodiments of menace. Both Atropos and Clotho hold bundles of wool or flax, and Atropos brandishes those bundles in arms that are raised aloft, as if in a threatening gesture.[154] In fact the position of her arms and the stylized material (to be spun) bring to mind images of an angry Jupiter, brandishing thunderbolts. For her part Clotho, who wears armor on her torso, stretches out the raw material with her hands so that it forms a jagged saw-like pattern. Lachesis, in the middle, holds a spindle and ball of thread.

These three figures are not only elaborately (and peculiarly) clothed[155] but also masked, and those masks conceal the eyes, creating a particularly

25 A gathering of masked witches, detail of an engraving by Jan Ziarnko, from Pierre de Lancre's *Tableau de l'inconstance des mauvais anges et demons* (Paris, 1613)

sinister effect. This print, which perhaps records a design for some sort of theatrical entertainment,[156] is germane to our consideration of *Macbeth* since masks commonly have a role in witchcraft.[157] "The wearing of masks," Stuart Clark writes, is a property of "the demonic" as well as the festive.[158] Specifically, masks help "transform women into witches."[159] Henry Boguet, for example, reports that when witches dance, they "mask themselves."[160] In his *Masque of Queens* Jonson observes that witches commonly attend "*convents, or meetings, where sometimes...they are vizarded and masked*" (lines 37–38). Jan Ziarnko's engraving of a witches' sabbath, in Pierre de Lancre's *Tableau de l'inconstance des mauvais anges et demons* (Paris, 1613), depicts a group of masked women (fig. 25).[161]

There is as well another connection between the weird sisters who confront Macbeth and the three Fates, and this involves an incident in the life of King James, shortly before the composition of Shakespeare's play. When the king visited Oxford on 29 August 1605, he witnessed an address of welcome, which Matthew Gwinn had designed: three sibyls greeted the king at the north gate of the city, near St. John's College. Sibyls were of course women of the ancient world, known for their powers of prophecy: people sought them out to discover what the future held.[162] It is this knowledge that the sibyls share with the Fates.[163] Indeed, saluting James as a descendant of Banquo, one of the sibyls refers to herself and the other two sibyls as *Fates*.

We can't say with certainty that Shakespeare knew of this little pageant, but Geoffrey Bullough, who includes it as an analogue of *Macbeth*, observes that the playwright "could have heard details of the Oxford visit," since "it was much discussed as a splendid occasion."[164]

When Matthew Gwinn created the greeting for King James, he must have known that witch-hunters linked the ancient sibyls with witchcraft. Johann Weyer, for instance, in 1563 wrote that "the several notorious Sibyls, [were] hired, as it were, by the evil spirit [Satan] to preserve and strengthen the reign which he had established among the human race."[165] In England William Perkins reported that "the ten Sibylles of Greece...were most famous witches, and did prophecie of many things to come."[166] The sibyls, then, who greeted King James in Oxford and who called themselves Fates, may well have brought to mind practitioners of witchcraft in antiquity. For anyone who had read Holinshed's account of Macbeth, Gwinn's three sibyls would almost certainly have recalled the weird sisters who prophesy to Macbeth and Banquo.

I am not arguing that the playgoer must see the three figures on Shakespeare's stage as arbiters of Macbeth's destiny. The playwright is too subtle to settle for anything so prescriptive. But Shakespearean tragedy invariably posits an intersection between, on the one hand, human agency and, on the other, external circumstance, whether the source of that circumstance is deemed fate, Fortune, nature, stars, gods, or God, and whether that effect is exerted through an individual or through the wider society. By bringing to the stage three witches whose precise identity remains mysterious, the playwright can hint at powerful forces impinging on Macbeth without cancelling the autonomy of this formidable warrior-king. In this sense Peter Stallybrass is surely right to say, "the last scene with the Witches [4.1] can be seen as the emblematic centre of the play, containing as it does both the vision of kings and the fullest display of the workings of the 'secret, black, and midnight hags.'"[167]

Early in Shakespeare's play, Timon of Athens presents a banquet followed by a masque. Although some indications of onstage movement are given, it is very difficult to know what the playgoers in Shakespeare's theatre saw. The Folio has this stage direction: "*Enter Cupid with the maske of ladies.*" Upon his entry Cupid addresses the host of the banquet:

Haile to thee worthy Timon and to all that of his
Bounties taste: the five best Sences acknowledge
thee their Patron, and come freely to gratulate
thy plentious bosome.
There tast, touch all pleas'd from thy table rise:
They onely now come but to Feast thine eies.[1]

The Folio text seems problematic here, for Cupid's speech begins in prose and then, for no apparent reason, shifts to poetry. H. J. Oliver comments, "There are signs that there was some dislocation here during the printing of the Folio."[2] But what form did that dislocation take? Does the Folio fail to reproduce accurately the script? Have words in the original script been omitted? Are some of the words the result of a compositor's error? Has Cupid's speech at some point been revised? Most editors (though not Oliver) believe that all of Cupid's speech must originally have been in verse; therefore they rearrange the first part so that it resembles iambic pentameter.[3] At the same time, most editors, following the lead of Warburton, emend "There" to "Th'ear." G. R. Hibbard explains: "since *The five best senses* have already been mentioned, and since the masquers come only to please the sight, it seems essential that the other four senses should be referred to here. 'There' for *Th'ear*, probably written as 'Th'ere' by Shakespeare, is an easy mistake to make."[4]

Let us suppose that editors are correct in emending the Folio's "There" to "Th'ear." What actually do the words of Cupid mean? To judge from the explanatory notes in modern editions, most Shakespeareans interpret Cupid's words metaphorically and suggest that the god of love refers to the senses of the banqueters. H. J. Oliver, for example, writes: "Cupid is saying that four senses have already been gratified at the banquet, and the masquers have come to gratify the fifth, i.e. sight."[5] This interpretation reads the verbs "acknowledge" and "gratulate" figuratively. Yet Cupid speaks of the ear, taste, and touch as having "come freely" and as "rising" from the table. He may therefore be speaking literally. We know that Jacobean and Caroline masques depend heavily upon personifications, including, in Thomas Carew's *Coelum Britannicum*, the Five Senses.[6] We also know that the Five Senses appear in early seventeenth-century civic pageantry and that they take pictorial form in prints and paintings. W. Moelwyn Merchant, who finds that *Timon of Athens* provides "the clearest evidence of Shakespeare's preoccupation with the visual arts," concludes that the text refers to a "dumb show of the five senses,"[7] followed by the dance of Amazons signaled in the Folio stage direction after Apemantus' speech: "*The Lords rise from table, with much adoring of Timon, and to shew their loves, each single out an Amazon, and all dance, men with women, a loftie straine or two to the hoboyes, and cease.*" Citing Merchant's suggestion, Catherine Shaw argues that playgoers must have witnessed "a dumb show of the senses who, during Cupid's prologue, acknowledge Timon as their patron and 'gratulate' his 'plenteous bosom.' "[8] Rolf Soellner also inclines to Merchant's view: "Perhaps this acknowledgment should be imagined as a dumb show in which Cupid leads the senses, with the sense of sight, the noblest, first, and with the other four bowing to it."[9]

We shall never know for certain whether personified Senses actually appeared onstage at Timon's banquet. Because the text of *Timon* is particularly uncertain here, almost any interpretation requires us to pile hypothesis upon hypothesis. Nevertheless, the views of Merchant, Shaw, and Soellner are plausible, perhaps even likely. I should therefore like to consider how the Five Senses might have looked on Shakespeare's stage. Pursuing Merchant's suggestion, moreover, that Cupid's masque "performs an essentially dramatic rather than a decorative function,"[10] I should like to explore the masque's purpose.

The Five Senses in the visual arts

Despite medieval antecedents,[11] representation of the Five Senses essentially begins, in the sixteenth century, with the engravings of Georg Pencz, a Nuremberg painter and portraitist, who may have trained with Albrecht Dürer. Giulia Bartrum observes of Pencz, "it is from his images that all later visual representations were to develop."[12] Between about 1539 and 1544, the artist made five designs of the Senses: each is represented by a nude woman performing a symbolic activity while seated indoors.[13] The artist also incorporates in each picture an animal, which had been associated with the particular Sense since the Middle Ages.[14] Later in the century the subject was enthusiastically taken up in the Netherlands. The most original Dutch artist was Frans Floris, a sculptor, architect, and designer of books of ornament. Floris represents each Sense as a woman in classical garb, performing a symbolic activity in an outdoor setting, and he includes one or more symbolic animals as well.[15] These designs were engraved by Cornelis Cort in 1561,[16] and they, in turn, prompted various other northern artists to represent the Five Senses.[17]

By the middle of Elizabeth's reign, representation of the Five Senses, based on Continental antecedents, had taken conventional form in England, as Richard Day's *A Booke of Christian Prayers* (1578) allows us to see. This book includes, in decorative borders, an extraordinary profusion of illustrative material, including New Testament narrative, the dance of Death, personifications of Virtues, and the Five Senses.[18] All of these take the form of woodcuts that appear in compartments located to one side of and below the text on each page; in other words, the illustrative material is L-shaped on verso pages (backward L on recto pages). To the other side of the text and above it are decorative panels, thus completely framing the text. Curiously, there exist no particular connections between the text on any given page and the illustrative border; indeed, the visual materials sometimes appear more than once and in very different contexts. Nonetheless, the Five Senses, each of whom is accompanied by a biblical citation, suggest how these personifications were popularly envisioned in England before Shakespeare and contemporary playwrights began their careers.

In Day's *Booke of Christian Prayers*, Sight is a classically attired woman who gazes into a mirror; at her feet is an eagle, renowned for its acute vision. In another compartment at the bottom of the page, an eagle stands at the edge of the sea and stares into the sun, evoking the belief that this bird had the ability to look directly at the sun.[19] Personified Hearing plays a lute; a horn and drum lie at her feet. In another panel a deer, known for its sensitive hearing, lies on the ground while surrounded by musical instruments and a book of music (fig. 26). The woman labeled "Smelling" holds a flower to her nose; in her other hand she grasps additional flowers. Next to her stands a dog, a creature with an especially keen sense of smell; in the lower compartment on the page, another dog sniffs a vase of flowers. Taste has a basket filled with fruit over her left wrist; with her right hand she raises a piece of fruit to her mouth. In the panel below, a chained monkey, with a bowl of food next to him, grasps a piece of fruit. "Touching" holds

26 Hearing and Sight, from Richard Day's *A Booke of Christian Prayers* (London, 1578)

a bird that pecks at her right hand; a turtle, which shrinks into its shell at the merest touch, crawls at her feet.[20] In a separate compartment we see a panorama: a boat with a fishing net in the water; in the background two other boats are under sail. On land in the foreground, we see a spider whose exceptional sense of touch is apparent in the web it navigates.[21]

Although none of these illustrations seems an exact copy of an earlier Continental engraving, all of them employ iconographic symbolism found in countless sixteenth-century engravings. To summarize briefly, an examination of several dozen Continental prints suggests the following: Sight is most often represented by a woman with a mirror, an eagle at her side; Hearing, by a woman playing a lute, a deer at her side; Smell, by a woman sniffing a flower, a dog at her side; Taste, by a woman eating a piece of fruit, a monkey nearby; and Touch, by a woman whose hand is pecked by a bird, a turtle at her feet; often a spider spins a web too. There are, of course, variations on such representations, but these are the most common.[22]

Such treatments of the Senses found their way into the decorative schemes of Elizabethan and Jacobean houses. For example, the Five Senses form the subject of an overmantel at Langleys, Great Waltham, Essex. These figures, rendered in plaster and executed c. 1621–28, have the characteristic activities and animals just described.[23] Interestingly, the artisan found the design in a Continental print. "Like most pieces of decoration in England which depend on a print," Anthony Wells-Cole points out, "this was copied absolutely faithfully from the source."[24] It is one of a multitude of decorative works that demonstrate beyond question the English knowledge of and dependence upon foreign prints.

The Senses in pageants and entertainments

The Senses who make their appearance in *Timon of Athens* form an ensemble, as they frequently do in the visual arts. A painting by Frans Francken the Younger, for instance, depicts all five around a circular table in a park-like setting; a great house is visible in the distance.[25] They could almost be a group of aristocratic women enjoying a meal *al fresco* except that each is engaged in a characteristic activity: Sight gazes at her face in a mirror; Hearing plays a lute while a book of music lies open on the table; Smell sniffs a flower; Taste raises food to her mouth; and Touch holds a bird that pecks her hand.

A print by Adriaen Collaert after Adam van Noort, probably made in the late 1580s, also combines all Five Senses in a single design (fig. 27). It has perhaps even more relevance for *Timon of Athens* because it depicts a wealthy man at table. In the background appears a magnificent house surrounded by a large garden; also visible is a fountain in which sculpted putti gambol. In the foreground the proprietor sits at a circular table, which is furnished with a platter of fruit, a knife, a plate, and additional pieces of fruit. Opposite him stands Sight, a nude woman holding a mirror in her left hand; beside her stands an eagle. Next to her sits Hearing, playing a lute; beside Hearing lies a deer. Opposite is Taste, holding a basket of fruit in her right hand and proffering a cup of wine to the host, who reaches out to receive it; behind her a monkey sits in a tree and eats a piece of fruit. Standing next to the host is Smell: she has flowers in her left hand and a wreath which she seems about to place on the man's head; next to her is a dog, whose nose is at table level. Finally, bare-breasted Touch sits beside the host, who has an arm around her shoulder; a bird pecks at her hand while a turtle lies on the ground by her foot. Anyone familiar with earlier representations of the

27 The Five Senses attend a man. A print, c. 1580s, by Adriaen Collaert after Adam van Noort

Senses will have no difficulty recognizing these personifications. But not everything in the print has an obvious precedent in sixteenth-century art, for the design includes something unusual: Sight holds in her right hand a torch, and at her feet lies a chest of coins; presumably gold, they would glisten attractively in the light.[26]

In reconstructing the appearance of Shakespeare's Senses, we can supplement the pictorial evidence provided by prints and paintings with the evidence afforded by civic pageantry in England near the time when *Timon of Athens* was first performed. Such entertainments must have been seen by many of the same people who frequented the London theatres. One pageant, designed by Anthony Munday for the lord mayor's installation of 29 October 1616, provides important clues to how the Senses may have looked in *Timon of Athens*, first staged perhaps ten years earlier (c. 1606–8?). *Chrysanaleia: The Golden Fishing: or, Honour of Fishmongers* describes a float that depicts a pelican feeding its young; Munday means to suggest that the mayor, John Leman, cares for his brethren with the same self-sacrifice as the bird believed to nourish its young with its own blood. Next to the pelican is a lemon

28 Sketch for a lord mayor's show, written by Anthony Munday in 1616

tree laden with fruit, an obvious reference to the name of the man being
honored. Under the tree sit the Five Senses. Munday explains: "because the
leman tree... both in fruite, flowers, rinde, pith, and juyce, are admirable
preservers of the sences in man, restoring, comforting, and relieving any the
least decay in them: wee seated the five Sences about the tree, in their best and
liveliest representations, as fitly jumping [agreeing] with our morall meth-
ode" (lines 126–33).[27] Although Munday fails to record any further information about the appearance of the personifications, John Gough Nichols
in the nineteenth century reproduced a surviving drawing of the float
(fig. 28), and it depicts the seated women with symbolic objects and animals.

Sight, accompanied by an eagle, gazes at her reflection in a mirror. Touch, accompanied by a turtle, holds a bird which pecks at her outstretched hand. Hearing plays a lute, but because she faces away from us we cannot see the instrument that probably accompanies her. The figure I interpret as Smell holds in her right hand a cornucopia of flowers. Taste holds a piece of fruit in her right hand (a lemon); other lemons litter the ground.[28]

Closer in time to Shakespeare's play is the coronation entertainment for King James I on 15 March 1604. The fourth triumphal arch in the procession, entitled *Nova Felix Arabia*, includes a fountain of Virtue surrounded by the Five Senses. The account by Thomas Dekker reveals that they are "Appareled in roabes of distinct cullours, proper to their natures; and holding scutchions in their handes: upon which were drawne herogliphicall bodyes, to express their qualities" (lines 765–67).[29] Dekker, however, is silent on the nature of the escutcheons with their hieroglyphic symbols. Fortunately, William Kip's engraving of this arch survives in Stephen Harrison's *The Arches of Triumph* (1604),[30] though the figures are so small that, unless one looks at an original Folio print, it is very difficult to see precisely what the personifications, seated in a semicircle, have in their hands (fig. 29). A careful inspection of the print reveals that Sight holds a mirror; Taste, a basket of food on her lap, fruit raised to her lips; Touch, a bird on her hand; Smell, a flower raised to her nose; and Hearing, a lute. The black and white engraving fails, of course, to supply information about the colors worn by the five figures. And not visible in the engraving, alas, are the escutcheons. If Dekker uses the word literally, small shields decorated with symbols must have been present. What did they look like?

Although we don't know with certainty their design, we can extrapolate from other representations of the Senses who bear such shields. The title-page of John Bulwer's *Philocophus: or, The Deafe and dumbe mans friend* (1648) depicts figures, dressed in classical Roman military garb, representing the Five Senses, and each of them carries a shield.[31] Sight holds peacock feathers; an eagle decorates the shield. Hearing, who holds a horn to his ear, carries a shield depicting an antlered deer. Smell carries a bouquet: the shield features a dog. Taste has a cornucopia in one hand, a shield decorated with a monkey in the other. And Touch holds hands with another figure; a spider and web adorn the shield. In all likelihood the shields held by the Senses on James I's triumphal arch depicted similar zoomorphic symbols, though we can be least certain about Touch, whose distinctive animal may be bird, turtle, or spider.

Even more useful than the title-page of Bulwer's book is *Lingua, or The Combat of the Tongue and the Five Senses for Superiority*, a play by Thomas

29 The Five Senses, a detail from William Kip's engraving in Stephen Harrison's *The Arches of Triumph* (London, 1604)

Tomkis which was performed at Trinity College, Cambridge, in the early years of the seventeenth century and first printed in 1607, near the time when *Timon of Athens* was first staged. In *Lingua*, which has been called "the most ambitious treatment of the theme of the Five Senses in English literature,"[32] Lingua (Tongue) creates a commotion by claiming that she should enjoy the same status as the Five Senses, each of whom becomes a character. Tomkis, who unlike most artists imagines the Senses as male (probably because his actors were male), provides what no other contemporary entertainment offers: a detailed description of the garments worn by the personifications. Auditus appears "*in a garland of bays intermingled with red and white roses upon a false hair, a cloth of silver mantle upon a pair of satin bases, wrought sleeves, buskins, gloves, &c.*" (337).[33] Tactus is dressed "*in a dark-coloured satin mantle over a pair of silk bases, a garland of bays, mixed with white and red roses, upon a black grogram* [coarse fabric], *a falchion* [sword], *wrought sleeves, buskins, &c*" (346). Olfactus has much the same headgear but a distinctive pattern on his sleeves. The stage direction describes him as dressed "*in a garland of bays intermingled with white and red roses upon a false hair, his sleeves wrought with flowers under a damask mantle, over a pair of silk bases; a pair of buskins drawn with ribbon, a flower in his hand*" (349). Olfactus is later accompanied by Tobacco, "*his neck bare, hung with Indian leaves, his face brown, painted with blue stripes, in his nose swines' teeth, on his head a painted wicker crown with tobacco-pipes set in it*" (420). Like the other Senses, Visus wears a chaplet of flowers, but his colors are different: "*in a garland of bays, mixed with white and red roses, a light-coloured taffeta mantle striped with silver, and fringed upon green silk bases, buskins, &c*" (353). Visus has a retinue of other figures, all connected with sight, including Lumen (with the sun painted on a shield), Coelum (a crown of stars on his head), and Color, "*clad in changeable silk, with a rainbow out of a cloud on her head*" (398). Gustus, dressed in the same fashion as Visus, differs "*only in colour*" (353). Later, Taste is accompanied by Bacchus, in a white suit, and Ceres, in a yellow silk robe (423). We cannot be sure that the colors worn by Tomkis' characters resembled those worn by the Senses in the coronation procession of King James, since the playwright does not explain the basis for assigning colors to particular Senses.

There is, however, a parallel between the play and the triumphal arch. Dekker specifies that in James's celebration the Senses hold "scutchions in their handes" (line 766), though, as we have seen, none appears in William Kip's engraving. The stage directions in *Lingua* not only assign escutcheons to the Five Senses but also describe them: for example, "*A page carrying a scutcheon argent, charged with an eagle displayed proper: then Visus, with a fan of peacock's feathers*" (398). Sight, then, is accompanied by a shield decorated with the animal traditionally associated with this sense; he carries, moreover, a fan made of feathers from a bird with especially brilliant plumage. Auditus is accompanied by a page "*bearing his target* [shield], *the field sable, a heart or*" (416). This shield has a golden hart, or deer, the traditional zoomorphic symbol. Olfactus has an escutcheon with his familiar animal and a retinue of figures connected with odor: "*Olfactus in a garment of several flowers, a page before him, bearing his target, his field vert, a hound argent, two boys with casting-bottles* [for sprinkling perfumed waters], *and two censers with incense, another with a velvet cushion stuck with flowers, another with a basket of herbs, another with a box of ointment*" (419). Personified Taste has its identifying animal and carries the cornucopia more commonly borne by Smell, though here presumably it carries fruit: "*a page with a shield argent, an ape proper with an apple; then Gustus with a cornucopia in his hand*" (423). Finally, a stage direction announces the entry of Tactus, "*a page before him bearing his scutcheon, a tortoise sable*" (425). A little later all Five Senses are described as themselves carrying their own identifying shields: "*Visus, Auditus, Tactus, Gustus, and Olfactus, every one with his shield upon his arm*" (428).

As the plot of *Lingua* unfolds and increasing contention develops among the contestants jostling for precedence and for the robe and golden coronet offered by Lingua,[34] the characters wield props that symbolically suggest their natures. One of these is quite unusual: Tactus enters "*with a great blackjack in his hand*" (439). According to the *OED* such a blackjack is a large leather jug for beer, coated externally with tar.[35] No artist or playwright, to my knowledge, assigns personified Touch such an object, though the blackjack would be especially appropriate if its surface were slightly sticky to the touch.[36] Gustus bears "*a voiding knife in his hand*" (447), and in sixteenth-century art personified Taste often carries a knife for paring fruit; a "voiding knife" was used in Shakespeare's time to clear away fragments of food from a table. We have already noted that Visus earlier appeared onstage with a fan made of peacock feathers not unlike those on the title-page of Bulwer's *Philocophus*.

The combined evidence provided by Anthony Munday's pageant for the lord mayor, the triumphal arch in James's coronation procession, and Thomas Tomkis' play suggests that, if indeed a dumb show of the Five Senses appeared in *Timon of Athens*, Sight held a mirror; Hearing, a lute; Smell, a flower; Taste, a piece of fruit; and Touch, a bird. We cannot rule out other possibilities of the sort that may be discovered in late sixteenth-century engravings. But for the Senses to be immediately recognizable to playgoers, those Senses would need to have been equipped with props clearly and unambiguously indicating their identities. Since symbolic animals were usually portrayed with the Senses, they may well have been present in some form.

Significantly, Thomas Middleton's *The Triumphs of Truth*, the lord mayor's show for 29 October 1613, identifies the Five Senses not by any objects held in the hand but only by symbolic animals: "upon the heighth of these five islands sit five persons, representing the Five Senses, – *Visus, Auditus, Tactus, Gustus, Olfactus*, or, Seeing, Hearing, Touching, Tasting, Smelling; at their feet their proper emblems, – *aquila, cervus, araneus, simia, canis*, an eagle, a hart, a spider, an ape, a dog."[37] (Here the spider takes the place of bird or turtle.) Such animals could have been depicted on the garments of the Senses in *Timon of Athens*. Alternatively, each Sense may have borne a small shield depicting the appropriate animal, as they do in *Lingua*.[38]

Shakespeare and Middleton

That Thomas Middleton employed the Five Senses in a 1613 pageant may have an even more direct connection with *Timon of Athens* than may initially appear, for he is almost certainly responsible for parts of the play, including act 1, scene 2, which contains the masquelike entry of Cupid.

For decades scholars have suspected the presence of two hands in *Timon of Athens*. William Wells's 1920 article argues, largely on the basis of diction, that the play's "second scene is undoubtedly non-Shakespearian," and that the style points to Middleton as the author.[39] Wells hypothesizes that *Timon of Athens* was originally written by Middleton and later revised by Shakespeare. In 1924 H. Dugdale Sykes subscribed to Wells's conclusion: *Timon* "is a play not originally written by Shakespeare but merely revised by him."[40] Sykes, who sees the hand of John Day in some of the play's speeches, finds "certain features of the text at large that are typical of Middleton."[41] Prompted by Wells's article, Sykes finds "abundant confirmatory evidence of Middleton's authorship of precisely those scenes which I could find no sufficient reason to connect either with Day or with Shakespeare." He cites three kinds of stylistic peculiarities, all characteristic of Middleton: abundance of rhyme; irregular, unscannable verse; and "frequent and aimless shifts from verse to prose."[42] Like Wells, Sykes concludes that act 1, scene 2 is not Shakespearean: "This long scene . . . is chiefly, if not wholly, Middleton's."[43]

Although scholars today are sometimes skeptical of demonstrating authorship entirely on stylistic grounds (witness the controversy over the putatively Shakespearean "A Funeral Elegy" by W. S.), the Middleton connection with *Timon of Athens* has, if anything, strengthened since the time of Wells and Sykes. David J. Lake, who raises the possibility that the author of act 1, scene 2, and certain other parts of the play previously attributed to Middleton was "Shakespeare writing in an unusually Middletonian manner," cautiously concludes that the available evidence "is strong enough to justify a strong suspicion of Middleton's presence, but no more."[44] At the same time, Lake clearly believes that someone other than Shakespeare was the original author of act 1, scene 2, and other sections of the play. Indeed, Lake observes that the imagery of the so-called Middleton sections of

Timon "is what one might expect if Shakespeare had read his predecessor's rough draft and adopted some useful ideas for his revision."[45] MacDonald P. Jackson adds weight to the argument for Middleton by focusing on the spelling of the exclamation *O/Oh* in Middleton's *Game at Chess* and in *Timon*. He concludes that this textual evidence "comes near to clinching the case for recognizing Middleton's presence in *Timon*."[46]

Stanley Wells and Gary Taylor, editors of *The Oxford Shakespeare*, accept the attribution of whole sections of *Timon* to Middleton. John Jowett, their collaborator, explains: "Lake, Jackson, and Holdsworth, developing a suggestion first made independently by Sykes and Wells, have shown, we believe conclusively, that parts of *Timon* were written by Thomas Middleton."[47] Those sections include the banquet scene of act 1, scene 2. And in a jointly written essay of 1993, Jowett and Taylor observe that "Lake, Jackson, and Holdsworth have recently provided compelling new evidence that, as earlier scholars had conjectured, about a third of the Folio text was written by Middleton."[48]

The consensus of scholarly opinion, then, holds that the banquet scene, especially the part featuring the arrival of Cupid, comes from Middleton's pen.[49] Stylistically, the shift from prose to verse in Cupid's speech is a feature associated with Middleton. The dramaturgy is also consistent with his other work. Middleton was fond of incorporating personifications and masquelike scenes on the stage: plays employing the device include *No Wit, No Help Like a Woman's* (the Four Elements and the Four Winds); *Michaelmas Term* (the Four [Law] Terms); *Women Beware Women* (Hymen, Ganymede, Hebe, Juno); *The World Tossed at Tennis* (Pallas, Jupiter, Nine Muses, Time); and *The Revenger's Tragedy* (a masque of revengers).[50] In *Hengist, King of Kent*, instrumental music accompanies an elaborate dumb show in which "*fortune is discovered uppon an alter, in her hand a golden round full of lotts*."[51] Middleton also includes Cupid as a character onstage. For example, in *The Nice Valor, or, The Passionate Madman*, a play apparently co-written with Francis Beaumont, "The Figure of Cupid, personated by a Lady," according to the *dramatis personae*, makes an appearance.[52] Middleton may not employ the Five Senses in any of these plays, but in *The World Tossed at Tennis*, he brings onstage characters who are described as "mocking the five senses": they are "*the Five Starches, White, Blue, Yellow, Green and Red, all properly habited to express their affected* [desired] *colours*."[53]

Let us assume that Middleton is indeed responsible for the masquelike episode of *Timon*. Why should he have deployed the Senses in the company of Cupid?[54]

The Five Senses appropriately belong with Cupid because of their role in amorous experience, something that devisers of emblems portray both visually and verbally. A case in point is the collection by Otto van Veen (Otho Vaenius), *Amorum Emblemata* (1608), published around the time that *Timon of Athens* was first staged. Cupid appears in all 124 emblems, many of which depict the deity having some particular sensuous experience. For example, while Cupid holds a mirror, the accompanying poem explains, "Even as the perfect glasse doth rightly shew the face, / The lover must appeer right as hee is in deed" (6).[55] Another design, labeled "Love often deaf," relates to hearing; opposite a picture of Cupid with his fingers in his ears, we read: "What ever fame brutes foorth which tendeth to disgrace, / Of loves deer prysed love; hee not endures to heare, / But makes himself bee deaf by stopping either eare, / To shew hee will not give to ill opinion place" (66). An emblem showing a woman picking flowers in a field involves the sense of smell: "Lyke to the wench that comes where fragrant flowers growes, / And still that flower plucks whereof first choise shee makes, / But it assoone forgets as shee another takes, / So doth the wavering mynd, for new choyce older lose" (212). The sense of taste is the subject of another emblem, which depicts a hungry Cupid helping himself to the contents of a pie: "The hungrie having meat can hardly it refrayn, / The thirstie at the well can il forbeare to drink, / The lover with his love tyme serving one would think, / For to enjoy her love as litle can abstayn" (84). The sense of touch finds expression in a picture of Cupid plucking a rose; the poem begins, "In plucking of the rose is pricking of the thorne" (160). The role of all these senses in lovemaking renders them appropriate to Cupid, the personification of love.

The love that is central to *Timon of Athens* is, admittedly, love of a less passionate kind, though the connection between the Senses and Cupid becomes clearer as we consider Ben Jonson's final Caroline entertainment, *Love's Welcome, The King and Queen's Entertainment at Bolsover, at the Earl of Newcastle's, the thirtieth of July, 1634.* In the opening song a tenor asks, "When were the senses in such order placed?" and another singer adds, "The sight, the hearing, smelling, touching, taste, / All at one banquet?" (lines 4–6).[56] Although the Senses were apparently not dramatized, the singers almost certainly refer to five paintings of the Senses, in lunettes, which decorate the pillared hall at Bolsover Castle, Derbyshire, where the entertainment was staged.[57] The paintings were installed sometime between 1620 and 1633, according to John P. Cutts, and so must have been visible during the king's reception in July 1634.[58] Those brilliantly colored panels are indebted to engravings by Cornelis Cort after Frans Floris, who, as we have seen, was instrumental in popularizing the personifications in the later sixteenth and early seventeenth centuries.

As the song of *Love's Welcome* continues, the bass voice sings that Love is responsible for the ordering of the Senses. Love, of course, is customarily represented by the figure of Cupid; and two Cupids make their appearance in Jonson's entertainment when, following the banquet, an address by Colonel Vitruvius (a satiric allusion to Inigo Jones), and a dance, they set down a second banquet before the royal guests.[59] The Cupids, winged and armed with bows and quivers, are named Eros (erotic love) and Anteros ("love in return").[60] Eros bears a palm branch, which Anteros tries to snatch from him. Van Veen, in his *Amorum Emblemata*, provides the pictorial counterpart of this contest: two winged Cupids, each equipped with a quiver of arrows, contend over a palm branch. The accompanying poem, under the title "Contending encreaseth love," explains,

Cupid and Anteros do stryve the palme to have,
Loving and beeing lovd together do contend,
The victorie doth moste on loving best depend,
Which either rightly deemes his truest love may crave.

(10)

In *Love's Welcome* Eros divides the palm, as Anteros indicates: "You are Love, / I, Love-again. In these two spheres we move, / Eros and Anteros" (lines 86–88). The resolution of the contest is amicable, Eros explaining, "We, either looking on each other, thrive" (line 104). The exchange expresses the solicitude of the host, William Cavendish, Earl of Newcastle, for king and queen and the expectation that the crown will suitably recompense him. It is through the delectation of the monarch's senses that Cavendish demonstrates both concern and affection.

The world of Jonson's courtly entertainment is utterly different from that of Shakespeare and Middleton's play: one is essentially light and celebratory, the other dark and bitter in tone. At issue in both, however, is love (especially in the sense of sympathetic concern and generosity of spirit) and, more specifically, love reciprocated. At Bolsover Castle, William Cavendish means to curry favor with the monarch and spares no expense in entertaining him: Margaret, Duchess of Newcastle, records that entertaining the king cost "in all between fourteen and fifteen thousand pounds."[61] In the play Timon treats his friends with magnanimity and expects to receive a similar bounty in return.[62] Later when they fail him, he recoils in dismay and misanthropy. These qualities manifest themselves at his mock banquet, the bleak counterpart of the earlier celebration over which Cupid presides. The god of love makes no appearance at the second fête in *Timon of Athens* because he is irrelevant: no one's action or speech involves real love. Nor do the Senses assume palpable form: no one's senses are gratified (the guests receive only dishes filled with water), and so there is no point in presenting the Senses as personifications.[63]

By the time the Barmecide feast in *Timon* breaks off, the playgoer recognizes that the personified Senses in the earlier masque with Cupid have all along had an admonitory force.[64] That is, the senses, which we instinctively seek to gratify, pose a potential risk to anyone who relies too heavily on their truth. Indeed, the senses may betray rather than serve us precisely because of their very immediacy: we tend to value sensory impressions, which, by their nature, are vivid and thus seemingly incontestable. We defer to their authority as we gain knowledge of the world. To judge by the senses alone, however, is to judge by appearances; it is to esteem the surfaces of life, prizing them uncritically. This is the very trap that Timon falls into when he takes at face value the sight and sound of bonhomie in those citizens of Athens who eventually prove fair-weather friends.

Significantly, the Five Senses had long been associated with human folly. They had, for instance, become part of illustrated editions of Sebastian Brant's *Ship of Fools*. A 1500 Paris supplement by Josse Bade (Badius) depicts the ship of Sight as a woman with a comb and mirror; the ship of Hearing as two women playing musical instruments (lute and harp); the ship of Smell as a woman with flowers in her hand; Taste as a group of fools eating and drinking; Touch as a woman in a fool's cap embracing a male fool.[65] Later editions continue to work variations on these illustrations, which conflate the Ship of Fools with the Five Senses.[66]

A series of prints by Adriaen Collaert after Maarten de Vos aligns several of the Senses with sinfulness. The artist makes this association by including in the background of each engraving biblical scenes from the Book of Genesis. Thus behind Taste, Adam and Eve eat the forbidden fruit; behind personified Hearing, God calls out to the fallen Adam and Eve; and behind Touch, Adam and Eve are driven out of the Garden of Eden. Although Netherlandish artists of the mid-sixteenth century seem to have originated the idea of introducing such background scenes as "moralizing exegesis,"[67] there was nothing new about imagining a connection between the Senses and moral peril.

Frank Kermode, who has traced the appearance of the Banquet of Sense in European literature and art, finds that it is inextricably linked with temptation and vice in both pagan and Christian contexts.[68] He cites, for instance, a speech in Jonson's *Poetaster*, when the character named Ovid holds a feast of the Senses during which two revelers, alternating verses, sing:

Here is beauty for the eye;
For the ear, sweet melody;
Ambrosiac odours for the smell;
Delicious nectar for the taste;
For the touch, a lady's waist;
Which doth all the rest excel!
                 (4.5.194–99)[69]

Despite the attractivenesss of the world evoked, the banquet, seen in dramatic context, is morally dubious. When the emperor arrives, he castigates the celebrants: "O who shall follow virtue and embrace her, / When her false bosom is found naught but air?" (4.6.38–39). Whether Jonson was chiefly inspired by a classical poet (Ovid, Homer), or by a contemporary (perhaps George Chapman), the playwright contrasts a life of sensual delight with one of prudence, temperance, and sexual restraint.[70]

The attitudes informing both Jonson's play and *The Ship of Fools* also find expression in Jan David's *Veridicus Christianus* (Antwerp, 1601). One illustration depicts a dwelling in the shape of a human head.[71] There are openings at the eyes, ears, nose, and mouth; these represent avenues of temptation and thus of potential vulnerability. Indeed, Death climbs a ladder to the window of an eye and, like a wily thief, seems about to creep inside. In the background we see instances of temptation: Eve with a piece of fruit in her hand; Bathsheba at her bath watched by David; and Lot's wife, who turned to a pillar of salt when she unwisely looked back at the city of Sodom.

A revised edition of Thomas Beard's *Theater of God's Judgments* makes a similar point by anecdotal rather than visual means. Thomas Taylor's addition to Beard's work, published in 1642, concludes with the description of a reprobate who inherits a large sum of money and promptly sets about squandering it to the peril of his soul: "He had a great longing to please all his five senses at once; nor could he bee at peace within himselfe till he had accomplish'd it; and allow'd to the delight of every sense a severall hundred pound; for which hee bespoke a curious faire roome, hung with the richest arras that could bee hir'd, and furnish'd with all the most exquisite pictures that might bee bought or borrowed, to please the eye."[72] To delight his hearing, the spendthrift hires musicians to play a variety of instruments; for olfactory pleasure he seeks out "aromaticks, and odoriferous perfumes"; he purchases "candies, preserves, all the junkets, even to the stretching of the apotecaries, or confectionaries art to palliate his taste"; and, finally, to delight his sense of touch, he hires "a beautifull and faire strumpet" to join him in a soft bed. The author relates that the man's friends would have helped pay his bills when he fell into debt, but they realize that he had learned nothing from his indulgence of the senses and subsequent financial ruin. Indeed, his unregenerate stance outrages his friends: "if I had, said hee, all the estate I before enjoyed, and ten times greater, I would spend it all to live one week like a god, though I were sure to be dam'd to hell the next day after."[73]

It was undoubtedly this jaundiced view of the senses that appealed to Middleton, a writer with a satiric streak, fond of dramatizing chicanery, trickery, and guile, vices that flourish when people fail to perceive the gulf separating reality from appearance. Middleton delights in depicting credulity, the nearly universal penchant for complacently trusting what our senses tell us, no matter what cautionary inhibition the intellect may urge. In particular, he targets the folly of those who allow themselves to be seduced by proffers of affection and solicitude. It is no accident that in *The Nice Valor*, a comedy jointly written by Middleton and Beaumont, Cupid appears in the company of fools: indeed, the god of love leads several fools in a dance (5.1.74–75.s.d.). And in *Your Five Gallants* Middleton presents the spectacle of five rogues trying to ingratiate themselves with a desirable young woman but, instead, finding themselves inveigled into performing a masque that, to the discerning viewer, reveals the very moral dangers they present. Like those five gallants performing the masque, the Five Senses in *Timon of Athens* exert an undeniable theatrical appeal, but they also dramatize the peril that threatens the unwary and the naive.

The appearance of deities in Shakespeare's late plays coincides with the flourishing of the Stuart masque, an art form paying homage to persons of social distinction through a fusion of music, dance, costume, scenery, and drama. Although masques had long been a feature of English court life, they enjoyed a rapid development in sophistication during the early years of the seventeenth century, thanks to a confluence of factors: the enthusiasm of King James and especially Queen Anne and their willingness to finance masque production lavishly;[1] a growing splendor in the design of costumes and special effects, partly an effort to rival Continental entertainments; the rise to prominence of Inigo Jones, who had first-hand knowledge of Italian *intermezzi* and who designed new illusionistic scenery; the talents of Ben Jonson and other writers who brought intellectual power, ingenuity, and learning to the grace and beauty inherent in the traditional masque.

Even before James became king, Shakespeare's company had enjoyed a fruitful association with the royal court: the Lord Chamberlain's Men performed plays on numerous occasions for Queen Elizabeth. When James succeeded her, he took Shakespeare's company under his personal protection, issuing letters patent on 19 May 1603, which granted

freely to use and exercise the art and faculty of playing comedies, tragedies, histories, interludes, morals, pastorals, stage plays, and such others like as they have already studied or hereafter shall use or study, as well for the recreation of our loving subjects as for our solace and pleasure when we shall think good to see them during our pleasure . . .[2]

This theatrical troupe performed frequently for King James, bringing to court drama that had proved successful at the Globe.[3] It is possible, even likely, that Shakespeare tailored such plays as *Measure for Measure* and *Macbeth* to appeal to the king's interests.[4] Certainly James delighted in performances by the King's Men: "No troupe acted more often before James than his own men. They played, according to one reckoning, 187 times between the issuance of the Patent and the year of Shakespeare's death."[5]

For the most pragmatic of reasons, Shakespeare's company took a direct hand in the production of certain Jacobean masques. Although courtiers participated in masques, they could not undertake roles that would compromise their stature. The antimasque, a rowdy and even grotesque counterpart of the larger stately dance, required professional actors in order to spare the dignity of courtly masquers, who would shrink from appearing as satyrs, witches, and the like. The King's Men thus, for example, furnished personnel for the antimasque of witches in *The Masque of Queens*, performed 2 February 1609, and for the antimasque of satyrs in *The Masque of Oberon*, performed 1 January 1611.

In response to their growing experience at court and to a shift in popular taste, the King's Men began to seek a somewhat different audience from that which frequented the Globe. The company leased the Blackfriars in 1608, adding a so-called private stage to their public venue in Southwark. What they gained thereby was a more select clientele – educated, sophisticated, monied, and socially distinguished (in comparison with crowds at the Globe). At the Blackfriars the King's Men were able to achieve a sense of intimacy that was all but impossible at the much larger and socially heterogeneous Globe, where groundlings surrounded the stage on three sides. The actors could now at least approximate the sense of occasion and atmosphere of a more courtly setting. Queen Anne herself attended performances at the Blackfriars, giving a special cachet to that theatre. On the indoor stage, moreover, the King's Men could expand their range of special effects, for they were able to control lighting by adjusting the number of candles, and they could make use of sound in ways impossible at an outdoor theatre. In general, then, they could achieve a greater subtlety of presentation.[6]

It can be no coincidence that, with their increased prominence at court and with the acquisition of the Blackfriars, Shakespeare's company began incorporating in their plays scenes drawing inspiration from the court masque. *Pericles*, for example, features episodes combining music, pageantry, and dance. F. D. Hoeniger comments on the visual at the expense of the dramatic: "The scene of the lists, where the various knights through their squires present their shields with devices and mottos to Thaisa and Simonides, is purely spectacular – a more undramatic episode is hard to imagine."[7] Similarly, the sword dance of armored knights at a banquet following the tournament is the kind of action that leads John Arthos to say that *Pericles* offers "pictures more than drama."[8] The long sheepshearing scene in *The Winter's Tale* includes dances of both shepherds and satyrs, who seem almost to have stepped out of a masque. In fact, Ben Jonson had created a dance of satyrs in *The Masque of Oberon*. Also manifesting an affinity with the masque is the spectacular appearance of Ceres, Juno, and Iris in *The Tempest*: this celebration of a betrothal resembles in some respects Jonson's *Hymenaei*, performed 5 and 6 January 1606, where Juno descends from the heavens to bless a marriage. And in *Henry VIII* Shakespeare, following the account in Holinshed, recreates the masque at Wolsey's palace where the king dances with Anne Boleyn. Later in this play Shakespeare creates another extraordinary spectacle when Queen Katharine has a vision of angels. On the basis of such scenes John D. Cox argues that *Henry VIII* constitutes "an experiment in adapting the principles of the court masque to the dramatic tradition of the public theatres."[9] Finally, *The Two Noble Kinsmen* not only borrows the second antimasque from Francis Beaumont's *Masque of the Inner Temple and Gray's Inn*, performed at Whitehall on 20 January 1613, but also contains a stately ceremony enacted before the altars of classical deities. Collectively, such scenes, occupying an increasingly important place in Shakespeare's tragicomic romances, perhaps justify Northrop Frye's view that Shakespeare "may have been temperamentally closer to the masque than Jonson was."[10]

Most masquelike scenes on the stage find their inspiration in the materials of Greek and Roman mythology. The ingenuity of the masquemakers lay in finding ways of using the creations of classical antiquity to achieve some local purpose. Graham Parry remarks on the way that masques evoke a world distant in time and place while offering contemporary compliment:

This emphasis on the antique, which was a feature of so many of the masques (expressed particularly through the architectural settings and the costumes) was a way of associating the principal figures in the action with the perfected civilisation of classical antiquity and its authoritative knowledge of the world; but it also acted as a form of flattery to the Court at large by implying that its members are all honorary citizens of sage heroic antiquity, an illusion reinforced by the fact that the fabulous beings on stage moved forward at the conclusion of the masque and drew everyone into the dance that took up the rest of the evening.[11]

By appropriating the deities of Mount Olympus, Shakespeare accomplishes what the makers of masques accomplished. That is, through theophanies in his late plays, he creates a sense of wonderment at the intervention of the divine in the realm of the human. Pericles, Posthumus, Ferdinand, Miranda, Palamon, Arcite, and Emilia all gain direct experience of the supernatural. In *Pericles*, *Cymbeline*, *The Winter's Tale*, *The Tempest*, and *The Two Noble Kinsmen*, as in Stuart masques, the divine is never far away.

The identity of the gods employed by Shakespeare varies from play to play depending on the requirements of the plot, for the deities embody forces, values, or institutions necessary to advance the dramatic action. In a sense, then, the deities – Jupiter, Diana, Ceres, Iris, Juno, Mars, Venus, and Hymen – objectify abstractions. They have a place, therefore, in this study of personifications. Reconstructing their appearance onstage, however, poses a challenge, for although these figures appear in numerous masques of the early seventeenth century, the design of costumes and the designation of props have been largely lost. We have printed versions of some scripts, but the only substantial collection of surviving costume designs is that by Inigo Jones, and some of his sketches have disappeared. In order to reconstruct the appearance of Shakespeare's deities, then, we need to look not only at extant masques and other literary evidence, including civic pageantry and contemporary drama, but also at the pictorial arts. This chapter, accordingly, supplements the verbal with the visual by examining woodcuts, engravings, etchings, and paintings, along with masques and plays.

By considering the iconography of Olympian deities, we may not only come to know how they looked to Jacobean playgoers but also better understand Shakespeare's purpose in bringing them onstage. Those deities are allusive, triggering in the minds of spectators similar images encountered in tapestries, painted cloths, statuary, and prints. All such representations are charged with meaning, as are, of course, deities on the stage. Far from being mere visual divertissements, the theophanies in Shakespeare's late plays are analogous to those in Jacobean masques: they challenge the spectators to understand the significance of what they see.

Cymbeline

"Shakespeare's most elaborate masque-like effect," according to Jean Jacquot, occurs in *Cymbeline*, when an imprisoned Posthumus, anticipating his own death, falls asleep and sees a vision of his dead relatives, who express bewilderment over his prolonged suffering.[12] "As in the Stuart court masques," writes Graham Holderness, "a group of characters appears to question, challenge or doubt the justice of existence, the equity of a sovereign's government, or the rationale of a divine providence."[13] In *Cymbeline*, "the most overtly theatrical of Shakespeare's plays,"[14] this function "is performed by a company of ghosts, those of Posthumus' father, mother and two brothers."[15] Those ghosts may even participate in a dance: they enter amid "*Solemn music*" and "*They circle Posthumus round as he lies sleeping*" (5.4.29.s.d.). Alan Brissenden observes, "Even though there is no specific direction that the ghosts dance around the sleeping prisoner it is clearly apparent that they circle him with regular motion, first, because of the music, then because of the pronounced rhythms of the prayer."[16]

The complaints of the ghosts trigger the most sensational moment of the scene: the descent from the heavens of Jupiter. His appearance is in keeping with the Roman culture that informs so much of *Cymbeline*, which "probably exceeds any other Shakespearian play in its fecundity of classical, and especially mythological, reference."[17] Quite literally a *deus ex machina*, Jupiter, like a god in a classical play, intervenes, moving the action away from suffering and toward respite and reconciliation. This deity is clearly meant to affect the theatrical audience as powerfully as Posthumus himself. But what exactly did Jacobean playgoers see when Jupiter appeared? Other plays and masques offer a clue.[18]

Jupiter

In *The Golden Age* (acted by Queen Anne's Men 1609–11), which has been called "a variation on the annual City pageants sponsored by the Mayor and guilds,"[19] Thomas Heywood dramatizes the moment when Jupiter, Neptune, and Pluto draw lots for their realms, and "*Jupiter drawes heaven*" (5.78).[20] From antiquity this deity was identified with phenomena of the sky, especially storms, thunder, and lightning. In John Heywood's *The Play of the Weather* (acted by a children's company in 1527), Jupiter mediates between quarrelling deities – Saturn, Phoebe, Phoebus, and Aeolus – who represent frost, rain, sun, and wind, respectively.[21] In *The Silver Age* (acted by the Queen's Men, 1609–11) Jupiter arrives from and returns to his home in the heavens: he "*discends in a cloude*" (2.98) and "*ascends in his cloud*" (4.155); for the Greeks he was "the cloud gatherer" (*Iliad*, 8:38).[22] Similarly, Marlowe in *Dido Queen of Carthage* (acted by the Children of the Queen's Chapel c. 1585–86) calls Jupiter "great master of the clouds" (4.2.4).[23]

Jupiter employs the most spectacular of meteorological phenomena as weaponry. According to Homer, "He thundered terribly and let fly his white lightning-bolt, and . . . he hurled it to earth; and a terrible flame arose of burning sulphur" (*Iliad*, 8:133–35). In *Fasti* Ovid explains that "Jupiter assumed the thunderbolts after the giants dared attempt to win the sky; at first he was unarmed." (3:439–40).[24] Giulio Romano, in the room of the giants at the Palazzo del Te, Mantua, depicts that struggle: Jupiter in the heavens hurls thunderbolts at the cringing giants below.[25]

On the Renaissance stage the thunderbolt is the most prominent of Jupiter's weapons. This stage direction in Ben Jonson's *Hymenaei*, celebrating the marriage of the Earl of Essex and Frances Howard, proves fruitfully expansive: "*Above her* [Juno] *the region of fire with a continual motion was seen to whirl circularly, and Jupiter standing in the top, figuring the heaven, brandishing his thunder*" (lines 201–03).[26] Similarly, Heywood in *The Silver Age* provides this stage direction for Jupiter's entrance: "*Thunder, lightnings, Jupiter descends in his majesty, his thunderbolt burning*" (4.154). The impression created by such staging is one of insurmountable power. Thomas Heywood's Jupiter describes himself as he who "with a powerfull nod / Shakes the heavens arches, ore the universe / Spreads dreads & awe" (4.150). John Lyly's Jupiter in *The Woman in the Moon* (acted at court c. 1591–95) calls himself "The king of gods, one of immortal race, / And he that with a beck controls the heavens."[27] In Jonson's *Masque of Augurs*, performed on Twelfth Night 1622 and again in early May, Jupiter declares his omnipotence:

Jove is that one whom first, midst, last, you call,
The power that governs and conserveth all;
Earth, sea and air are subject to our check,
And fate with heaven moving at our beck.
    Till Jove it ratify,
    It is no augury,
Though uttered by the mouth of Destiny.

(lines 380–86)

Spectators recognize Jupiter not only by his thunderbolt but also by his eagle, an association that goes back to Homer (*Odyssey*, 2:146–56).[28] Vincenzo Cartari points to the symbolism of the eagle: "as the eagle over all other birds whatsoever ruleth as cheef, so all the men in this world, and all other things inclosed within her spacious embracements, stand vassalized and subject to the all-commanding power of Jupiter" (sig. K2r–v).[29] In Heywood's *Golden Age* Jupiter, mustering forces to enlarge his dominion, takes the eagle as his symbol: "The eagle in our ensigne wee'l display" (5.73). When Jupiter appears in a chariot, an eagle typically draws the vehicle. Cartari notes, "There have beene few statues composed of Jupiter, to which hath not been annexed the shape of an eagle, which bird of all others the aunciens have most often appropriated unto him, by which (as it is poetised) his glorious charriot is swiftly drawne and conveied through the airie passages" (sig. K4r–v). Giorgio Vasari's Jupiter sits atop a four-wheeled vehicle, pulled by a single giant eagle.[30]

To signal his status as chief of the gods, Jupiter is customarily enthroned. In both *The Iliad* (8:443) and *The Aeneid* (10:116),[31] he sits upon a "throne of gold." In John Heywood's *Play of the Weather*, Jupiter is "presumably enthroned" at the beginning of the dramatic action; and at the end he declares that he will "ascende into our t[h]rone celestyall."[32] Cartari explains that in antiquity statues of Jupiter placed him "sitting upon a firme and irremovable seat, to signify that the vertue which governeth and preserveth the world, is firme, permanent, and continuing" (sig. K2r). Abraham Fraunce also sees Jupiter's posture as symbolically significant: "Jupiter is commonly pictured sitting, sith the eternall monarch of heaven, and earth, is alwaies immutable, one, and the same, and never subject to any alteration."[33] Jupiter's worldly dominion, however, may be suggested by a globe. A title-page for Ovid's *Metamorphoses* (Venice 1553) depicts Jupiter with his right foot and left knee resting upon a sphere, symbolic of the earth over which he presides.[34]

A crown also signals Jupiter's authority. In *The Golden Age* Thomas Heywood dramatizes Jupiter's war against his father Saturn; according to a stage direction, Jupiter "*drawes his sword, beates away Saturne, seiseth his crowne*" (4.53). Inigo Jones, in a sketch for *The Masque of Augurs*, depicts a crowned Jupiter flanked by other deities (O&S, 1:118).[35] Similarly, Jones's sketch of Jupiter for Aurelian Townsend's *Tempe Restored*, performed at the Whitehall Banqueting House on 14 February 1632, depicts the chief god wearing a crown (O&S, 2:218). Jupiter may carry a scepter as well.

Because of his supremacy Jupiter sometimes acts as an arbiter of disputes, a court of last resort. We have already noted his role as mediator between the elements in *The Play of the Weather*. He functions similarly in George Peele's *The Arraignment of Paris* (acted by the Children of the Queen's Chapel c. 1581–84), where three deities vie for the golden apple inscribed "to the fairest." Late in this play Jupiter approves the suggestion that Diana render the decision: "I can commend and well allow of it, / And so derive the matter from us all, / That Dian have the giving of the ball" (5.1.1073–75).[36] In *The Rare Triumphs of Love and Fortune* (acted at court in 1582) Jupiter tests the competing claims of Love and Fortune by directing them to exert their power over humankind. At the conclusion he orders them to cease their dispute: Mercury, his messenger, announces the decision, "Then thus our father Jupiter concludes / To stay the stroake of your unceasing strife" (lines 1564–65).[37] And in Robert Greene's *Comical History of Alphonsus, King of Aragon* (acted by the Queen's Men 1587–88), Venus, having sought to demonstrate her hegemony, finds herself restrained: "Venus is forst to trudge to heaven againe: / For Jupiter, that

God of peerles power, / Proclaimed hath a solemne festivall" (epilogue, lines 1917–19).[38]

When not listening to other deities, Jupiter may hear the pleas of his human subjects. Consider *The Triumph of Time*, part of Beaumont and Fletcher's *Four Plays, or Moral Representations, in One* (acted by Queen Elizabeth's Men c. 1613–15), "an attempt to fuse masque and drama."[39] When Anthropos prays to him, Jupiter directs Mercury, "Flee to Time, / And charge him presently release the bands / Of Poverty and Want this suiter sinks in" (scene 2, lines 12–14).[40] Later Time explains to Anthropos, "The god of riches / (Compell'd by him that saw thy miseries, / The ever just and wakeful Jove, at length) / Is come unto thee: use him as thine own" (scene 4, lines 27–30).

In keeping with his role as judge, Jupiter is invariably depicted as a mature man with a beard. Natale Conti observes of Jupiter, "The ancients contend that while he was not subject to death, he would grow to a great age, even to hoary old age."[41] Dekker in *London's Tempe*, the lord mayor's pageant for 29 October 1619, describes the deity's advanced age: "On the top [i.e. above a scene at Vulcan's forge] sits Jove, in a rich antique habite, a long white reverend hayre on his head, a beard long and curld: a mace of triple fire in his hand burning" (lines 197–99).[42] Abram Booth's sketch of this pageant survives; it shows an aged Jupiter who seems to have a mantle draped over his right shoulder.[43] Ordinarily this aged deity wears no garment above the waist. A design by Inigo Jones for *The Masque of Augurs*, for example, shows Jupiter sitting in the clouds, nude except for the fabric covering his lower body (O&S, 1:118). Vincenzo Cartari explains the significance of Jupiter's garb: "the upper parts of the picture appeare naked and unclothed, the lower parts covered and invested: dishadowing therby, that the mercie and compassion of the divine powers is alwaies manifest and apparent to those that are possessed with an understanding spirit: the lower parts being clothed, meaneth, that all the while that wee are here in the world delighted, and as it were rockt asleepe with the illecebrous [alluring] blandishments thereof, we cannot any way apprehend superior knowledges, but they are kept obscured, hid, and unrevealed from us" (sig. K2r).

Because the Christian God, listening to and acting upon prayers, functions much like Jupiter, it seems appropriate that representations of the classical deity and the Christian bear marked similarities. Thus when artists portray Christ in his role as judge, he bears a striking resemblance to Jupiter. Michelangelo's fresco of the Last Judgment in the Sistine Chapel depicts a seated Christ, his right arm raised as if to strike, his lower body covered with fabric, a white mantle draped over his shoulder.[44] In Maarten van

30 Jupiter, clutching thunderbolts and sitting upon his eagle, descends from the realm
of fire. Engraving by Dirk Barentsz

Heemskerck's print "The Triumph of Christ or Eternity," the risen Christ,
above the clouds, sits atop an eagle; this bearded figure is nude except for
the fabric draped over his right shoulder and covering his lower body.[45]

Given his representation in masques, plays, and pageants, Jupiter in
Cymbeline must have resembled a mature man with a beard, a gold crown,
and perhaps a scepter too, symbols of authority. If he wore any clothing, it
was merely a white cloth covering his lower body and perhaps draped over
one shoulder. Although we cannot be certain about the details of his physical appearance, we can be confident about the movement of Jupiter onstage.
Shakespeare's stage direction indicates that "*Jupiter descends in thunder and
lightning*" (5.4.92.s.d.), the aural and visual symbols of his majesty. The actor playing Jupiter is lowered to the stage by machinery, riding his sacred
bird: he descends "*sitting upon an eagle.*" Similar staging would later characterize Jupiter's appearance in Aurelian Townsend's *Tempe Restored* (O&S,
2:218). The deity in *Cymbeline* may have looked as he does in a print by Dirk
Barentsz: nude Jupiter sits astride his eagle and clutches thunderbolts in
both hands as he descends from the region of fire (fig. 30). If Shakespeare's

eagle rested upon simulated fire (as Barentsz's does) or upon simulated clouds (as Jones's does), the fire or clouds would have helped conceal the machinery.

clouds most likely,

The dramatic context explains Jupiter's presence in *Cymbeline*: the ghosts of Posthumus' relatives plead that his sufferings be intermitted at last. Sicilius says, "No more, thou Thunder-master, show / Thy spite on mortal flies" (5.4.30–31). Posthumus' mother asks, "Since, Jupiter, our son is good, / Take off his miseries" (lines 85–86). These and the appeals of the other Leonati prompt the descent of Jupiter, angry that his justice has been questioned: "*he throws a thunderbolt. The Ghosts fall on their knees*" (line 92.s.d.). Jupiter then upbraids them: "How dare you ghosts / Accuse the Thunderer, whose bolt, you know, / Sky-planted, batters all rebelling coasts?" (lines 94–96). Despite the chastisement, Jupiter's speech reassures his listeners that seeming happenstance is purposeful, that Posthumus' adversity is part of divine design:

Be not with mortal accidents oppress'd,
No care of yours it is, you know 'tis ours.
Whom best I love, I cross; to make my gift,
The more delay'd, delighted.

(lines 99–102)

Though a classical deity, Jupiter sounds not unlike the Christian god, who, similarly, provides personal assurance that divine providence overwatches humankind and guarantees ultimate justice, even if day-to-day experience fails to reveal the purpose of human adversity.

Shakespeare's concept of Jupiter is in keeping with the deity's presentation elsewhere in Elizabethan–Jacobean pageantry. For instance, at Norwich in 1578 the queen witnessed Henry Goldingham's masque in which Jupiter voiced his solicitude: "Feare not my power to overthrow thy wo, / I am the God that can eche misse amende."[46] In *Cymbeline*, as in masques and pageants, the eagle is the symbolic manifestation of that divine assurance. *London's Love to the Royal Prince Henry*, a pageant written by Anthony Munday in 1610, speaks of the prince's respect for the citizenry: the prince spreads "his gracious acceptaunce of their love and kindnes, like to the large extended winges of Joves birde the eagle, even over them all" (lines 177–79).[47]

Before he departs, Shakespeare's Jupiter leaves a tablet for Posthumus, the tangible evidence of divine solicitude: it contains a riddling prophecy that will assist the characters to make their way toward peace and reconciliation. Jupiter then orders, "Mount, eagle, to my palace crystalline"

(line 113). In what amounts to a stage direction Sicilius describes the deity's departure:

He came in thunder, his celestial breath
Was sulphurous to smell; the holy eagle
Stoop'd, as to foot us. His ascension is
More sweet than our blest fields. His royal bird
Prunes the immortal wing, and cloys his beak,
As when his god is pleas'd.   (lines 114–19)

The speech suggests that the eagle moves its body: it "stoop'd," that is, swooped. The eagle also preens and claws his beak, actions presumably controlled by the actor playing Jupiter.[48] Sicilius adds that both deity and bird disappear above: "The marble pavement closes" (line 120), he says, indicating the trap door in the underside of "the heavens" through which actor and eagle ascend, as earlier they had descended. With the trap door closed, spectators looking upward see only the "marble" heavens, that is, a simulated blue sky.

When earlier Shakespeareans discussed Jupiter's appearance in *Cymbeline*, they were inclined to ascribe the incident to a hand other than Shakespeare's: "The vision in *Cymbeline*... is almost certainly interpolated and spurious."[49] More recently, Shakespeareans respond to that vision with consternation, wry amusement, or even embarrassment. Joan Hartwig contends that the episode must be comic: "the self-consciousness of this artifice generates amazement of a sort that nullifies the wonder which a god's visitation should create within the illusion of the play."[50] A dubious Simon Palfrey remarks that "Jupiter's glittering, meretricious appearance is prone to accident or absurdity."[51] Such responses betray a distinctively modern sensibility, one that F. W. Brownlow describes: "We take the supernatural very seriously and, whether we believe in it or consider belief an offence against decency, the theatricality of Shakespeare's vision will probably strike us as frivolous."[52] The sense of wonderment created by Shakespeare's staging in the early seventeenth century, however, could scarcely have been less profound than the appearance of the ancient deity in a Stuart masque. Of Jupiter's descent in *Cymbeline* Catherine Shaw writes, "the concept is one comparable to the magnificence of the Jonsonian masques of the period."[53]

Our readiness to see humor in the prospect of an actor riding a giant eagle arises not only from our uneasiness with the supernatural but also from our supersophistication about special effects, largely the product of modern cinema, which becomes ever more skillful at dazzling the eyes of jaded moviegoers. Jacobean spectators had no such experience and therefore no such expectations. The contrivance that may seem faintly comic to a playgoer today need not have seemed so in 1610. The masque, after all, was the most artificial of entertainments; that was precisely its appeal. And the notion that divinity intervenes in human life was nothing less than an article of faith.

The Winter's Tale

The Winter's Tale celebrates not only nature in the form of Perdita, mistress of the sheepshearing festival, who distributes flowers to the revelers, but also art in the form of Hermione's statue, the pièce de résistance of Paulina's gallery. When she leads Leontes to view the objets d'art, the dialogue is filled with reference to artists' materials and craft: statue, stone, chisel, likeness, carver, image. The counterpart of the language is this dramatic action: "[Paulina draws a curtain, and discovers] Hermione [standing] like a statue" (5.3.20.s.d.). In the previous scene, where the statue is described, a gentleman attributes it to "that rare Italian master, Julio Romano" (5.2.97). The fact that we know Romano as a painter rather than a sculptor has occasioned ingenious speculation about Shakespeare's choice, the only contemporary artist named in any of his plays.[54] Perhaps the best explanation is the simplest: Romano was among the most renowned artists in Renaissance Europe; Paulina describes the statue as freshly painted – "The statue is but newly fix'd; the color's / Not dry" (5.3.47–48); and the English customarily painted statues, a practice to which Ben Jonson refers in The Magnetic Lady (5.7.90–93),[55] acted by the King's Men in 1632. Shakespeare's contemporaries, moreover, believed that Romano was a sculptor. As Stephen Orgel observes, Giorgio Vasari in his Lives of the Artists "quotes Giulio's epitaph, in which he is praised specifically for his skill at making lifelike sculpture."[56] Although Northrop Frye contends that since "in fact no statue has been made of Hermione…the entire reference to Romano seems pointless,"[57] the invocation of the artist's name underscores the problematic relationship between nature and art, subject of the colloquy between Perdita and Polixenes in the sheepshearing scene, and at issue again when the statue of Hermione is seemingly transformed from artifact to life.

The statue scene, by its treatment of artifice, its air of contrivance, and its sense of wonderment (5.3.22), evokes particular moments in Jacobean masques: the scene in The Lords' Masque by Thomas Campion when eight women, having been turned into statues by Jove, come to life; and the first antimasque in Beaumont's Masque of the Inner Temple and Gray's Inn wherein four statues return to life and dance. Both of these masques were performed in honor of the 1613 wedding of Princess Elizabeth to the Elector Palatine, Frederick, and so followed the writing of *The Winter's Tale*, which Simon Forman saw at the Globe on 15 May 1611.[58] Instead of adopting a masque convention, Shakespeare has dramatized an action so close in spirit to the masque that writers of those entertainments would imitate it.

Like the world of so many masques, that of *The Winter's Tale* belongs to classical antiquity: characters consult the oracle of Apollo; they invoke Jupiter, Mercury, Neptune, Dis, Juno, and Cytherea; at the sheepshearing festival Perdita is costumed as Flora, the Roman goddess of flowers; and Perdita alludes to the story of Proserpina, a myth that explains the cycle of seasons and that parallels too the death and resurrection of Hermione. Shakespeare evokes antiquity in another way as well, for he brings to the stage Time, a figure whom the playwright and his contemporaries believed to be the Kronos of ancient Greece.

Time was, of course, a popular personification in Elizabethan–Jacobean England, playing a role in royal receptions, civic pageants, drama, and masques. At the very beginning of Elizabeth's reign, for example, Father Time took part in the queen's coronation procession through London. Near the end of that reign, at Harefield place in 1602, the queen again witnessed a pageant featuring Time, who had "yeollow haire," wore a green robe,[59] and carried an hourglass (*Progresses of Elizabeth*, 3:588). The hourglass became Time's most prominent symbol, his most frequently employed prop onstage. In *The Thracian Wonder* (acted c. 1611 probably at the Red Bull), we find this stage direction, in all likelihood inspired by the chorus in *The Winter's Tale*: "*Enter Time with an hourglass, sets it down, and exit*" (1.3.15.s.d.).[60] And in Anthony Munday's *Chruso-thriambos, The Triumphs of Gold*, the lord mayor's pageant of 29 October 1611, Time, equipped with his hourglass, makes an appearance: "As thus I turne my glasse to times of old, / So tune thine eares to what must now be told" (lines 177–78).[61]

Makers of masques, with even greater resources at their command, created a visually striking figure. Francis Kynaston's *Corona Minervae*, a masque presented before Prince Charles on 27 February 1635, presents personified Time as a composite of day and night, with a distinctive wing for each side of his body: "*Time enters ... in a party coloured robe halfe white, halfe blacke, fringed with silver, with one wing of a swan, another of a batt.*"[62] Although the surviving stage directions of *The Winter's Tale* offer no evidence that Shakespeare's personification was so elaborately costumed, we nevertheless can conjecture with confidence Time's appearance.

Time

In Renaissance pageantry and art, personified Time is unremarkable: bald and bearded, he could be taken for almost any other aged man wearing classical robes. In some instances, however, he may have the legs of an animal. Misinterpreted today as the goat legs of a satyr,[63] they are actually those of a deer, renowned for its long life. Thomas Wilson explains, "the stagge... liveth (as Plinius dothe say) two hundreth yeares, and more."[64] Wilson apparently refers to a remark in *The Natural History*: "Stags admittedly have a long life, some having been caught a hundred years later with the gold necklaces that Alexander the Great had put on them already covered up by the hide in great folds of fat" (bk. 8, lines 119–22).[65] Horapollo too identified the stag with longevity, and, as Michael Bath observes, "Horapollo implies that the stag attains this hieroglyphic significance because it renews its antlers each year."[66] On the title-page of *Lapis Philosophicus* (1599), Father Time is depicted and described as "deer hoofed."[67] Those hooves are winged at the ankle, suggesting a connection between the fleet creature of the forest and the seeming speed of time. When Father Time appears in Petrarch's *Triumphs*, deer ordinarily draw his vehicle.[68]

The features belonging to Time are chiefly three, specified by Thomas Dekker in *Troia-Nova Triumphans, London Triumphing* (line 195), the lord mayor's pageant for 29 October 1612, and by Thomas Middleton's *The Triumphs of Truth*, the pageant for 29 October 1613, as scythe, hourglass, and wings.[69] The scythe represents the destructive effects of transience; the hourglass is the visual metaphor of time's passage; and the wings suggest our psychological sense of time's speed. Despite the near ubiquity of these three accoutrements in Elizabethan–Jacobean England, they constitute a marked departure from classical representations. In antiquity time was conceived as "the divine principle of eternal and inexhaustible creativeness," a concept symbolized by the ouroboros, a snake swallowing is tail.[70] This motif survives in some depictions of Petrarch's *Triumphs*, where the ouroboros[71] is held by Time, and in certain other pictures where it encircles Time's arm, as on the engraved title-page of Jean Chaumeau's *Histoire de Berry* (Lyons, 1566).[72] The ancients also conceived of time as *kairos*, "the brief, decisive moment which marks a turning-point in the life of human beings,"[73] and Lysippus represented this concept (in a now lost statue) by a winged youth holding a balance on the edge of a razor. Personified Time in the Renaissance conveys the same sense of opportunity when he wears a forelock, meant to be seized by the aspirant at an auspicious moment,[74] as he does on the title-page of *Lapis Philosophicus* (Oxford, 1599) by John

Case. Shakespeare evokes this sense of timeliness when Antonio, in *Much Ado about Nothing*, says, "he meant to take the present time by the top [i.e., the forelock]" (1.2.14–15).

As Erwin Panofsky has demonstrated, Time gained the hourglass, scythe (or sickle), and other symbols through a confusion: "the Greek expression for time, Chronos, was very similar to the name of Kronos (the Roman Saturn), oldest and most formidable of the gods."[75] Even in the ancient world the confusion is apparent. Cicero, for example, writes that "Saturn's Greek name is *Kronos*, which is the same as *chronos*, a space of time" (bk. 2, chap. 25).[76] An illustration in Vincenzo Cartari's *Le vere e nove imagini de gli dei delli antichi* (1615) demonstrates the conflation: Saturn and Father Time stand side by side, both old and bearded.[77] They could be identical twins except that Saturn holds a sickle (used to castrate his father) and a staff, while Time has wings and a winged crown. The confusion between these two is also manifest in Jonson's *Hymenaei*, where a marginal note claims that "Truth is feigned to be the daughter of Saturn, who indeed with the ancients was no other than Time, and so his name alludes, *Kronos*" (note to line 629).[78]

From this conflation Time became particularly identified with destruction and death. For instance, a character in *Respublica*, performed at the Christmas revels of 1553–54, calls Time "An auncient turner of houses upside downe, / and a comon consumer of cytie and towne" (lines 1301–2).[79] In Fulke Greville's *Mustapha*, Eternity tells personified Time: "your scithe mortall must to harme incline" (third act chorus, line 142).[80] Artists give powerful form to the concept. A painting by Frans Francken II depicts a group of men fighting two personifications: Death aims several arrows at the combatants while winged Time, hourglass atop his head, wields his scythe against them.[81]

More than any other single work, Petrarch's *Triumphs* gave impetus to the concept of Time as destroyer. Although Petrarch himself fails to describe Time in any detail, *The Triumph of Time* became a favorite of artists, who invariably represent Father Time in a triumphal procession. Personified in such a triumph, Time may possess a grotesque quality, as for example, in Philips Galle's print after Pieter Bruegel: Time rides in his vehicle while devouring a child,[82] a clear sign of the confusion with ancient Kronos, or Saturn, who ate his offspring in order to forestall a prophecy that his children would overthrow him. Shakespeare alludes to the destructive nature of Time in *Love's Labour's Lost* (acted by the Lord Chamberlain's Men c. 1594) when the prince speaks of "cormorant devouring Time" (1.1.4), and in *Measure for Measure* (acted by the King's Men c. 1604) when the duke cites "the tooth of time" (5.1.12). Time's formidable teeth are the subject of Henry Peacham's reminiscence: "I have seene time drawne by a painter standing upon an old ruine, winged, and with iron teeth."[83]

Depictions of Time exude a mood of melancholy, befitting a personification who presides over so much destruction and death. "How slowly does sad Time his feathers move!" writes Spenser in his *Epithalamion* (line 281).[84] In *Love Freed from Ignorance and Folly*, a masque performed 3 February 1611, Ben Jonson writes of "agèd Time" with "weary limbs" (lines 312–13). And in Middleton's *The World Tossed at Tennis*, apparently intended for performance as a masque then revised for performance at a Bankside playhouse in 1620, a character observes, "See, Time himself comes weeping." Time replies, "Who has more cause?" (line 309)[85] and he goes on to catalogue the toll of mutability.

Michiel Coxcie in a sixteenth-century print depicts Time sitting dejectedly amid the ruin of classical buildings: old and bearded, Time has an hourglass and a crutch.[86] Although never part of Time's iconography in antiquity, the crutch became common in the Renaissance due to the conflation of Time and ancient Saturn. Time may even have two crutches, as he does in some illustrations of Petrarch's *Triumphs*.[87] In all of these pictures the crutch symbolizes both advanced age and debility. A crutch may also, however, suggest Time's seeming slowness: in *Much Ado about Nothing* (acted by the Lord Chamberlain's Men in 1598) Claudio conveys his anxiety by saying, "Time goes on crutches till love have all his rites" (2.1.357–58).

In view of Time's identification with mutability and death, Shakespeare's personification in *The Winter's Tale* may, as Robert Adams suggests, enter "in toga and sandals, with the shaggy locks and fierce scythe that he inherited from his cannibalistic predecessor Saturn/Chronos."[88] And yet Shakespeare's Father Time makes no mention of a scythe. J. H. P. Pafford surmises that "as many emblematic figures of Time do not carry a scythe Shakespeare's Time may not have had one."[89] Given the dramatic context, however, there would be nothing inappropriate about Time's appearance with the implement for reaping.[90] After all, the playgoers have just witnessed Antigonus "*pursued by a bear*" (3.3.58.s.d.), and in the same scene the clown reports seeing the Sicilian ship go down at sea. Discovering the infant Perdita, the shepherd reflects on the conjunction of death and life when he tells the clown, "thou met'st with things dying, I with things new-born" (lines 113–14). With greater confidence we can say that Shakespeare's Time is old (4.1.10) and so probably bearded. His hair is gray: in *The Insatiate Countess*, performed by the King's Revels Children c. 1609, he is said to have "silver" locks (3.4.6); and he is partly bald: in the same play he is called "an old bald thing" (2.1.32–33).[91] Shakespeare's personification also has wings (line 4), symbolizing the swift passage of time.

Erwin Panofsky suggests that the words defining Father Time's chief function in Shakespeare's play are these: "I slide / O'er sixteen years" (lines 5–6). Panofsky comments: "Sometimes the figure of Father Time is used as a mere device to indicate the lapse of months, years, or centuries, as in Shakespeare's *Winter's Tale*."[92] Yet Shakespeareans have not been satisfied by this characterization of Time's role. Pafford, for instance, argues that Time has a significance that transcends the brief scene in which he addresses the playgoers: "Time's speech is not an interpolation but an integral part of the play."[93] If so, what does Time contribute? Pafford suggests that Time "gives information," and indeed he does. But this alone cannot account for Time's presence onstage, for as Nevill Coghill demonstrates, the points Time cites – that sixteen years have elapsed, that Leontes "shuts himself" away in penitence, and that we are about to see Perdita and Florizel – "are clearly made in the scene immediately following."[94] If conveying information were his sole *raison d'être*, Time would be unnecessary. Shakespeare could simply have moved from the scene of Perdita's discovery by the shepherd to the colloquy between Camillo and Polixenes about "the penitent King" (4.2.6–7) and "a daughter of most rare note" (lines 41–42).

In assessing Time's purpose, let us consider the one prop we are certain he carries – an hourglass: "I turn my glass, and give my scene such growing / As you had slept between" (4.1.16–17). By upending the device Father Time marks the chief division of the dramatic action: we are about to move from a world of anxiety, suffering, and death to one of exuberance, joy, and new life. Paradoxically, this sharp transition masks an underlying similarity between the two halves of the play. William Blissett, who notes that *The Winter's Tale* "is almost unique in the canon for its bilateral symmetry," enumerates some of the parallels:

in the first half Leontes offends and Polixenes is in a state of innocence, in the second Polixenes takes offense and Leontes is in a state of penitence; in the first, Camillo flees, Perdita is rejected, Paulina protests, and Hermione lies hidden as if in death; in the second, Camillo returns, Perdita is received, Paulina restores, and Hermione stands risen as if from death.[95]

Because the two halves of Time's hourglass look identical, Ernest Schanzer observes, "it may not be fanciful to think that this fact enhances our sense of the similarity of the shape and structure of the two halves of *The Winter's Tale*."[96]

The hourglass held in Father Time's hands has another and more specific implication – for the king who has so cruelly treated his family, precipitating the death of his son, the abandonment of his daughter, and the sequestration of his wife. By his behavior Leontes has violated humane impulses, codes of decorum, standards of civilized conduct. His is a display of imprudence and intemperance on an outrageous scale. In view of this excess, it is significant that the cardinal virtue of temperance was associated with devices for timekeeping in the late Middle Ages and in the Renaissance.[97] Lynn White points out, for instance, that manuscripts of *L'Epître d'Othéa* (c. 1400) are "embellished with pictures of Temperance adjusting a large mechanical clock" and that in a treatise of the Virtues c. 1470 personified Temperance has a clock on her head.[98] Similarly the mid-sixteenth-century tomb of François de Lannoy in Folleville, France, depicts Temperance with her familiar bridle in one hand and a clock in the other.[99] And a clock sits atop the head of Pieter Bruegel's personified Temperance.[100] The very word *temperance* seems to derive, ultimately, from the Latin *tempus*. Shakespeare makes the connection explicit when Hamlet defends himself against his mother's charge of "ecstasy" (madness): "Ecstasy? / My pulse as yours doth temperately keep time, / And makes as healthful music" (3.4.139–41). In another of his plays Shakespeare describes a character's intemperance by means of a clock. When King Richard II says, "now hath Time made me his numb'ring clock" (5.5.50), he is not only expressing his own sense of victimization but also, implicitly, conceding his past intemperance.

The association between temperance and time is not limited to mechanical clocks. Lynn White notes that a fresco, painted in the 1350s, in the Palazzo Pubblico, Siena, depicts Temperance with "our earliest picture anywhere of a sandglass."[101] Similarly, Cornelis Matsys in a mid-sixteenth-century print depicts personified Temperance holding an hourglass (fig. 31).[102] That device, in the hands of Shakespeare's Father Time, is a silent signal that, so far as Leontes is concerned, temperate behavior and sound judgment will characterize future action.

Inga-Stina Ewbank has suggested that Shakespeare's personified character may have been inspired by the prose romance on which he based his play, Robert Greene's *Pandosto The Triumph of Time* (1592), whose full title continues, *Wherein is discovered by a pleasant Historie, that although by the meanes of sinister fortune, Truth may be concealed, yet by Time in spight of fortune it is most manifestly revealed.*[103] A Latin tag follows: *Temporis filia veritas* (Truth is the daughter of Time).[104] That proverbial saying had a special resonance for an English audience, since Queen Mary had chosen it "for her personal device, for the legend on her crest, on the State seal of her

31 Temperance holds an hourglass. A print by Cornelis Matsys

reign, on her coins."[105] Given the queen's adoption of the adage, it seems
appropriate that in *Respublica*, written during the first year of Mary's reign,
Verity, called "the dawghter of Tyme" (line 1699), hands malefactors over to
Justice and Nemesis/Mary (lines 1798–1801). Queen Elizabeth, moreover,
witnessed an incident in her coronation procession (14 January 1559) that
gave a characteristically Protestant application to the dictum: from a hollow

place or cave "issued one personage whose name was Tyme, apparaylled as an olde man with a sythe in his hande, havynge wynges artificiallye made, leadinge a personage of lesser stature then himselfe, whiche was fynely and well apparaylled, all cladde in whyte silke, and directlye over her head was set her name and tytle in latin and Englyshe, *Temporis filia*, the daughter of Tyme."[106] As Elizabeth looked on, Truth delivered the book she held, the Bible in English. The young queen then demonstrated her Protestant allegiance by her handling of the book: "she as soone as she had received the booke, kyssed it, and with both her handes held up the same, and so laid it upon her brest, with great thankes to the citie."[107]

Thomas Dekker adopted this tableau in *The Whore of Babylon*, written in the early years of King James's reign (c. 1606) and acted by Prince Henry's Men. In a dumb show at the beginning of the play, Dekker dramatizes Time's role as revealer of truth: a curtain is drawn, "*discovering Truth in sad abiliments; uncrownd: her haire disheveld, and sleeping on a rock: Time (her father) attired likewise in black, and al his properties (as sithe, howreglasse and wings) of the same cullor, using all meanes to waken Truth, but not being able to doe it, he sits by her and mourns*" (lines 27–31).[108] There follows a funeral procession (for Queen Mary), consisting of counselors, pensioners, and ladies. With the beginning of Queen Elizabeth's reign, "*Trueth suddenly awakens, and beholding this sight, shews (with her father) arguments of joy, and Exeunt, returning presently: Time being shifted into light cullors, his properties likewise altred into silver, and Truth crowned*" (lines 34–37). In *The Winter's Tale* Time does not change costume, of course, nor does personified Truth make an onstage appearance. But the dramatic action involves the revelation of the true identity of a daughter, lost for many years to her father and mother. The dialogue too evokes the progression of truth through time. Near the end of the play, when a gentleman inquires, "Has the king found his heir?" another answers, "Most true, if ever truth were pregnant by circumstance" (5.2.29–31). Finally, in the last scene as she reveals to Leontes the statue of his wife and thus the truth about her fate, Paulina says, "'Tis time" (5.3.99).[109]

A corollary of truth's revelation is the righting of wrongs: ideally, justice may be achieved when the actual course of events becomes known. In *Respublica* the villainous Avarice reports of Time, "manie of my frendes hathe he brought to paine and smarte" (line 1304). In *The Trial of Treasure* (performed c. 1565), Time announces, "Time is the touchstone the just for to try."[110] In *As You Like It*, performed in 1599, Rosalind says, "Time is the old justice that examines all such offenders" (4.1.199–200). And in *The Rape of Lucrece* (1594) "Time's glory is . . . To unmask falsehood, and bring truth to light . . . To wrong the wronger till he render right" (lines 939–43). Time even holds the scales of justice in Gilles Corrozet's emblem book, *Hecatomgraphie* (1540).[111]

In keeping with his punitive role, Time may bear a whip of the kind that Hamlet cites (3.1.69). Such a whip takes visual form on the title-page of Giovanni Andrea Gilio's *Topica Poetica* (Venice, 1580).[112] In a print by Maarten van Heemskerck, Time is the charioteer who, whip in hand, drives the chariot of the world.[113] A mural by Paolo Veronese in the Villa Barbaro, Maser, puts a scourge in Time's hand.[114] And a stage direction in *The Sun's Darling* by Ford and Dekker, performed at the Phoenix theatre in 1624, represents Time wielding his instrument of correction: "*Enter Time with a whip, whipping Follie before him*" (1.1.85.s.d.).[115]

In *The Winter's Tale* much misdoing needs to be righted: Leontes must make amends for the ill treatment of his wife; his hostility toward Polixenes must be replaced by friendship forged anew; and, most important, he must welcome back and cherish the daughter he condemned to death. As the last act of the drama begins, it seems that all this is possible. After all, sixteen years earlier, when he learned of the deaths of wife and child, Leontes vowed to do penance: "Once a day I'll visit / The chapel where they lie, and tears shed there / Shall be my recreation" (3.2.238–40). Some things, though, can never be undone, however long the passage of time. Leontes' penitence cannot erase the sixteen years of suffering for a separated husband and wife; when they are reunited, Hermione's wrinkled face will epitomize their loss of precious time together. Nor can a guilty king's contrition restore to a father and mother those years when their daughter came of age in a foreign land. And Leontes' penitence cannot undo the death of Mamillius, who will never know rebirth in this world.

The Winter's Tale, then, dramatizes the double dimension of time, its capacity to chastise and destroy as well as reveal and restore. If Father Time's presence onstage signals the capacity of time to console the afflicted and to sort out the depredations of the past, he also symbolizes the destructive effects of transience. The self-description of Shakespeare's character is succinct: "I, that please some, try all, both joy and terror / Of good and bad, that makes and unfolds error" (4.1.1–2). This dual aspect is brilliantly realized in a print by Hieronymus Wierix (fig. 32). Father Time holds in his hands two objects with a melancholy significance: his scythe, symbolic of destruction and death, and a mirror, which he holds up to a couple who see the skeletal figure of Death reflected behind their images.[116] Something with a very different significance, however, decorates his form: in an evocation of the ancient Greek Kronos, who seems to have originated as an agricultural

32 Time, with fruit on his head, holds a scythe and mirror. Engraving by Hieronymus Wierix

deity, fruit literally adorns Time's head, symbolizing his capacity to bring events to benign fruition.

Shakespeare's Time accomplishes something else too, though this would have been more apparent in the early seventeenth century than today. According to Abraham Fraunce, "Tyme caused Desteny to write and lay downe al his decrees; comaunding foure other personages to put the same in execution, to weet, Spring, Summer, Autumne, Winter."[117] This role also finds expression in the Stuart masque: for example, in Francis Kynaston's *Corona Minervae*. Taking charge of a chaotic situation in which the Seasons of the year jostle for precedence, Time upbraids them: "Let Time then governe you, for order sake" (sig. B2v); and, replacing their confusion, he imposes a design. Henceforth they will follow a proper sequence: "thus I order yee, / Out of your discord to raise harmonie." Time's authority over the Seasons finds visual expression in a print by Philips Galle after Maarten van Heemskerck: Time, ensconced in a chariot drawn by deer, is accompanied by the Seasons, who walk beside the vehicle.[118] The action depicted in Galle's print and Kynaston's masque has implications for *The Winter's Tale*, for in Shakespeare's play Time heralds a change of seasons. We have witnessed the wintry half of the dramatic action; now we are about to see the spring and summer half. Who better to signal the procession than Father Time himself?

The Tempest

The least dramatic of Shakespeare's late plays, *The Tempest* cannot claim an especially compelling plot. Because Prospero so completely controls the other figures through his magic, there can be little suspense, few of the twists and turns that crowd the other late tragicomedies. Limited geographically to an isolated island and limited chronologically to a single day, *The Tempest* does not aspire to shift the action from one place to another or from one time to another as *Pericles* and *The Winter's Tale* do. In the theatre, however, *The Tempest* has long been a favorite, for it features a rich presentation of music, song, dance, costume, spectacle, and poetry, all combined in an atmosphere of enchantment.

The Tempest must have been particularly appealing at the indoor venue of the King's Men. Andrew Gurr writes that "*The Tempest* is the first of Shakespeare's plays definitely written for the Blackfriars."[119] Within the enclosed space of the private theatre, sound effects would have had greater impact than at the company's outdoor playhouse. Significantly, the first stage direction concerns what the audience hears: "*A tempestuous noise of thunder and lightning heard*" (1.1.0.s.d.). Later cues for instrumental music abound, a feature that Gurr traces to the theatre for which the play was written: "*The Tempest* is uniquely a musical play among Shakespeare's writings, and the consort of musicians at Blackfriars was justly famous."[120] No less important to the play in performance is spectacle, which takes the form of a storm at sea, a shipwreck, a banquet brought onstage by "strange shapes," a harpy who performs a vanishing trick, "divers spirits in shape of dogs and hounds," and dances of reapers and nymphs. Imaginary creatures require inventive costumes. Especially interesting must have been those of Ariel and Caliban, "fantastic creatures more at home in a masque than in a naturalistic world."[121]

Shakespeare's capacity for combining spectacle and music to induce a sense of wonderment reaches a culmination in the betrothal scene when classical deities celebrate the forthcoming wedding of Miranda and Ferdinand. In the glorification of marriage, the concern with illusion, the suddenness of revelation, Shakespeare approaches the realm of the Stuart masque. The play, writes Stephen Orgel, "is Shakespeare's most signifi-cant essay in this courtly genre."[122] Enid Welsford, who calls *The Tempest* "more masquelike than dramatic," suggests that the play was actually inspired by Jonsonian masques – *Hymenaei*, *Blackness*, and *Beauty*.[123] John Demaray, who believes that *The Tempest* was specifically written for performance at court, enumerates features that belong to the masque: "it is the play's dominating qualities of wonder and surprise and revelation – the hinging of action on unexpected magical events; the unanticipated 'discoveries' leading to the 'entry' of aristocratic characters into the drama's social world – that unmistakably associates *The Tempest* with the genre of court masques and spectacles."[124] Significantly, *The Tempest* enjoyed favor at a court delighting in masques; it was performed at Whitehall on 1 November (Hallowmas night) 1611 and again in 1613 as part of the entertainment celebrating the marriage of Princess Elizabeth to the Elector Palatine.

The scene that most vividly evokes the Stuart masque is, of course, the interlude of Ceres, Juno, and Iris, which Glynne Wickham has called "the theatrical climax of the whole play."[125] What mark Shakespeare's handling of masque materials here are consistency and fullness. R. C. Fulton distinguishes between the mythological creations of *The Tempest* and those of the earlier *Timon*: "The Olympian figures of Prospero's masque seem to arrive from a fully realized and vitally present mythical world, unlike the Cupid of *Timon of Athens*, who steps suddenly out of his past into Timon's house, bringing his properties with him, but little in the way of poetic allusiveness."[126] In *The Tempest*, Fulton adds, we find "clear evidence of a new concern for iconographic precision and amplitude of classical detail."

Ceres

Prospero marks the occasion of his daughter's betrothal by a masquelike presentation, which he initiates with an order to Ariel:

> Go bring the rabble
> (O'er whom I give thee pow'r) here to this place.
> Incite them to quick motion, for I must
> Bestow upon the eyes of this young couple
> Some vanity of mine art.   (4.1.37–41)

With those unnamed spirits, Ariel enacts the serene and stately pageant intended by Prospero, creating the effect typically achieved by masques. Ferdinand, who expresses his sense of wonderment – "This is a most majestic vision, and / Harmonious charmingly" – goes on to ask, "May I be bold / To think these spirits?" (lines 118–20), and Prospero acknowledges the exercise of his magic: "Sprits, which by mine art / I have from their confines call'd to enact / My present fancies" (lines 120–22).

Those spirits take the form of figures from classical mythology whose identities suit the occasion. Ceres befits the forthcoming marriage because she symbolizes the fertility and abundance of the earth. (In Renaissance depictions of the four elements, Ceres represents the earth.[127]) According to Cicero's *De Natura Deorum*, the name Ceres is "a corruption of 'Geres,' from *gero*, because she *bears* the crops; the same accidental change of the first letter is also seen in her Greek name *Demeter*, a corruption of *ge meter* ('mother earth')" (bk. 2, chap. 26). Natale Conti reports, "The Eleusinians celebrated in honor of Ceres the festival of the Thesmophoria, which were first instituted by Triptolemus in recompense for having been taught by Ceres how to plant seeds of grain and fruit" (*Mythologies*, 299). In Shakespeare's culture as in antiquity, Ceres seems to have played a role in fertility festivals. Paul Hentzner, visiting England in 1598, records what he saw in the fields near Windsor: "As we were returning to our inn, we happened to meet some country people celebrating their harvest-home; their last load of corn they crown with flowers, having besides an image richly dressed, by which perhaps they would signify Ceres."[128] What Hentzner detected, according to François Laroque, was the "parallel that existed between the amusements of the rustic festival and ancient myth."[129]

Because Ceres is credited with introducing grain to humankind, artists and sculptors adorn her with sheaves of wheat – in her garments, her hands, her hair. (That hair is blonde, or golden, the color of grain.[130]) Sometimes she holds a cornucopia filled with a combination of grain and fruit. Giulio Bonasone, for example, depicts Ceres with wheat in her hair, and a cornucopia in the crook of her right arm; with her left hand she receives additional sheaves of wheat from a putto.[131] In the tapestry of Summer, one of the Four Seasons at Hatfield House, Ceres' hair is crowned with wheat, while the ground in front of her is covered with fruit and vegetables.[132]

Sheaves of wheat became props in Renaissance entertainments representing Ceres. Queen Elizabeth, arriving at Kenilworth castle in 1575, crossed a bridge decorated with "sundrie presents" of various deities, including Ceres, whose gift was grain (*Progresses of Elizabeth*, 1:492). Similarly, at Bisham in 1592 Ceres, "having a crowne of wheat-ears," greeted Elizabeth.[133] On the stage, too, Ceres was synonymous with grain. In *The Cobbler's Prophecy* (acted c. 1589–93), Mercury addresses Ceres as "Plenties rich queene, cheerer of fainting souls, / Whose altars are adornde with ripend sheaves."[134] And in John Lyly's *Love's Metamorphosis* (acted c. 1589–90), the deity hands wheat to one of her nymphs: "Take thou these few eares of corn" (2.1.30).[135]

Although the stage directions in *The Tempest* do not specify wheat in Ceres' hands, Iris evokes the goddess' association with abundant grain, addressing her as "Ceres, most bounteous lady, thy rich leas / Of wheat, rye, barley, fetches, oats, and pease..." (4.1.60–61). Shakespeare's deity may also have flowers in her hand, as Ceres does in *Lingua*, a play of c. 1602–7 by Thomas Tomkis: "*Ceres* [enters] *with a crown of ears of corn, in a yellow silk robe, a bunch of poppy in her hand.*"[136] Vincenzo Cartari explains the flower's significance: in antiquity Ceres' "statue was framed to the assimilitude of an aged matron, having her head circumcinct and redemyted with eares of corne, holding in her hand the stalke of a poppie, in that this flower signifieth fertilitie and great encrease" (sig. N2r).

In addition to grain, Shakespeare's Ceres may hold a sickle. Hieronymus Cock, in an engraving after Frans Floris, depicts the deity with wheat in her hair and at her waist and on her lap, while her right hand holds the sickle used in the harvest (fig. 33). At the baptismal celebration for Prince Henry of Scotland in 1594 "dame Ceres [stood] with a sickle in her right hand, and a handfull of corne in the other" (*Progresses of Elizabeth*, 3:364). Similarly, Samuel Daniel in *The Vision of the Twelve Goddesses*, a masque performed on 8 January 1604 at Hampton Court, enlists Ceres as a personification of "plenty," and he gives her a sickle as prop: "Ceres, in straw colour and silver embroidery with ears of corn and a dressing of the same, presents a sickle" (lines 98–99).[137]

The cultivation of grain and other crops is of course seasonal, and for the ancients the story of Ceres explained why the land is fertile at some times of the year and not others. Hesiod recounts that Ceres' daughter Proserpina (Greek Persephone) was walking in a meadow picking flowers when suddenly the earth opened up beneath her and she was seized by Dis (Hades, Pluto), who carried her away to his kingdom in the underworld.[138] Unaware of what had happened, Ceres was mystified by her daughter's disappearance. Thomas Heywood, whose *Silver Age* dramatizes the myth, represents the distraught mother as finding only marks of a chariot in the field where Proserpina had vanished: "Behold the trace / Of some strange wagon, that hath scortch't the fields, / And sing'd the grasse" (3.137). Artists commonly depict the bereft mother with a torch in her hand, the emblem of her exhaustive search. Vincenzo Cartari explains: "Many also have de-pictured Ceres with many torches, lights, & firebrands in her hands...The reason was, as some hold, in that she had been so seene raging up and downe in the search and enquirie of her daughter Proserpina, ravished and stolne away by Pluto" (sig. N2r–v).

Shakespeare alludes to this myth when Ceres, referring to Venus and Cupid, tells Iris, "Since they did plot / The means that dusky Dis my daughter

33 Ceres with sheaves of wheat and a sickle. An engraving by Hieronymus Cock after Frans Floris

correct

got, / Her and her blind boy's scandall'd company / I have forsworn" (4.1.88–91). Shakespeare, however, probably gave no torch to Ceres in *The Tempest*, for that object would have evoked sadness, not joy. After all, during the period when Ceres searched for Proserpina, no plants grew and famine threatened the earth. Although Jupiter finally ordained that Ceres' daughter be returned, she was required to return to the underworld for a part of every year. Hence the winter months when the earth is unproductive. As Ovid relates, Jupiter "divides the revolving year into two equal parts. Now the goddess, the common divinity of two realms, spends half the months with her mother and with her husband, half" (*Metamorphoses*, 5:565–67).[139]

Shakespeare's Ceres, by contrast, knows no seasonal limitation. Indeed, the goddess envisions a future without winter at all:

Earth's increase, foison plenty,
Barns and garners never empty;
Vines with clust'ring bunches growing,
Plants with goodly burthen bowing;
Spring come to you at the farthest
In the very end of harvest!
Scarcity and want shall shun you,
Ceres' blessing so is on you.

(4.1.110–17)

Implicit in this vision is an evocation of the Golden Age when, according to Ovid, "the earth, untilled, brought forth her stores of grain, and the fields, though unfallowed, grew white with the heavy, bearded wheat" (*Metamorphoses*, 1:109–10). Following the Golden Age, cultivation was necessary to realize the potential abundance of the earth, and it was Ceres, Virgil relates, who "was the first to teach men to turn the earth with iron" (1:150–51).[140] As a mark of Ceres' importance to civilization, according to Pliny the Elder, "the first image of a god made of bronze at Rome was that dedicated to Ceres" (*Natural History*, bk. 34, chap. 9).

Agriculture can succeed only when a culture prizes the social conditions that make planting and harvesting possible, for these activities require not only planning and labor but also stability. Significantly, Pliny identifies Ceres with peace and law-giving (*Natural History*, bk. 7, chap. 56), while Ovid in his *Metamorphoses* records that Ceres "first gave laws" (5:343). In his *Fasti*, moreover, Ovid calls Ceres "the foster-child of Peace" (1:704). Perhaps inspired by such accounts, Cornelis Anthonisz represents Peace with sheaves of wheat in her hair, a branch laden with fruit in one hand, a cornucopia in the other.[141] This figure, labeled Pax, is virtually identical to representations of Ceres. A painting by Isaac Schwendtner, made for the Regensburg town hall in 1592, depicts Ceres shaking hands with Peace.[142] And in *The Allegory of the Tudor Succession* (c. 1572), a painting attributed to Lucas de Heere, the artist represents Queen Elizabeth leading by the hand personified Peace and Plenty (who holds a cornucopia).[143] Playwrights preserve the nexus: in *Histriomastix* Ceres appears in the company of other figures identified with abundant harvest and social stability: "*Enter Peace, Bacchus, Ceres, and Plenty, bearing the cornucopiæ.*"[144]

Conspicuous by her absence in Prospero's pageant is Venus, goddess of love. This may seem odd since fertility and passion are natural allies. In fact, Ceres and Venus often appear together in the arts. A painting by Peter Paul Rubens depicts Venus attended by Bacchus, who offers wine, and by Ceres, who wears a crown of wheat and holds a flower.[145] Such paintings have their inspiration in an ancient saying, cited by Cupid in Lyly's *Love's Metamorphosis* (5.1.46), – "Sine Cerere & Baccho friget Venus" (without Ceres and Bacchus Venus grows cold). Shakespeare, however, in *The Tempest* is less interested in the force of passion, intensified by food and drink, than in the establishment of a permanent relationship between Miranda and Ferdinand. When Ceres asks, "why hath thy Queen / Summon'd me hither?" Iris replies, "A contract of true love to celebrate, / And some donation freely to estate / On the bless'd lovers" (4.1.82–86).

What Prospero's masquelike program anticipates, then, is not sexual desire, which may or may not issue in the contract cited by Iris, but rather the stable marriage of Miranda and Ferdinand, with all of its blessings. Hence, Iris, referring to Venus and Cupid, tells Ceres:

> Here thought they to have done
> Some wanton charm upon this man and maid,
> Whose vows are, that no bed-right shall be paid
> Till Hymen's torch be lighted.   (4.1.94–97)

Because Shakespeare's – or Prospero's – emphasis falls on those vows, the goddess of love makes no appearance in *The Tempest*. The energetic dance of satyrs that marks the sheepshearing feast in Shakespeare's previous play has no counterpart here. Instead, we witness what Robert Ornstein calls "decorous country dances of reapers, but no antimasque of satyrs as graces the sheep-shearing feast in *The Winter's Tale*."[146]

Juno

If Ceres represents the earth and its plenty, Juno represents the air and, more specifically, the heavens, domain of divinity. In *De Natura Deorum* Cicero observes, "The air, lying between the sea and sky, is according to the Stoic theory deified under the name belonging to Juno, sister and wife of Jove, because it resembles and is closely connected with the aether" (bk. 2, chap. 26). Juno's identification with the air and the weather is manifest in

Ben Jonson's masque *Hymenaei*. In this collaborative work with Inigo Jones, Juno wears a veil "*bound with a fascia* [i.e., headband] *of several-colored silks*" (lines 197–98), signifying, according to Jonson, "the several mutations of the air, as showers, dews, serenity, force of winds, clouds, tempest, snow, hail, lightning, thunder" (note to line 197). Similarly, Samuel Daniel's Juno in *The Vision of the Twelve Goddesses* "Descends all clad in colours of the air, / Crown'd with bright stars, to signify her charge" (lines 291–92). In *The Tempest* Iris calls Juno "Queen o' th' sky" (4.1.70).

Shakespeare's stage direction at the entry of the deity, "*Juno descends*" (line 74.s.d.), indicates her abode in the heavens. Presumably, flying machinery was used to lower Juno to the stage; possibly she descended in a vehicle.[147] If so, it was drawn by two peacocks; Iris refers to the birds, saying, "Her peacocks fly amain" (line 74). It has even been suggested that Juno may "descend astride a single giant bird."[148] Sacred to Juno, the peacock acquired its magnificent tail when the goddess employed Argus, who had a hundred eyes, to spy on Io (transformed into a heifer), whom Juno suspected of a tryst with her husband. When Mercury, on Jupiter's command, subsequently slew Argus, Juno "took these eyes and set them on the feathers of her bird, filling his tail with star-like jewels" (*Metamorphoses*, 1:722–23).

Shakespeare's company need not have used a chariot for Juno's descent; the actor could have been lowered to the stage on a throne.[149] Indeed, Jones's design for *Hymenaei* so depicts the deity: "*in the top* [i.e., in the air] ... *was discovered Juno sitting in a throne*" (line 195). In the prologue to *Every Man In His Humor* (acted by the Lord Chamberlain's Men in 1598), Jonson alludes disparagingly to the practice of lowering gods to the stage: in his play no "creaking throne comes down, the boys to please" (line 16).[150] In whatever way the King's Men managed the descent of Juno, one or more peacocks would have signaled her identity. Jonson and Jones employ the bird in *Hymenaei*, where Juno sits on a throne supported by "*two beautiful peacocks*" (lines 195–96). In *The Vision of the Twelve Goddesses* Juno's sky-blue mantle is "figured with peacocks' feathers" (lines 60–61).

Prospero requires Juno's presence in his pageant because this deity presides over the institution of marriage: in *Pericles* Thaisa describes Juno as "queen of marriage" (2.3.30), and in *Hymenaei* Jonson calls her "governess of marriage" (line 206). There is no little irony in Juno's identity as deity of marriage, for her own marriage came about through the deceit of Jupiter: "being a sutor to Juno hee came in a forme most ignoble and base, an object full of contempt and scorne, resembling indeed a miserable cuckow, weather-beaten with raine & tempest, nummed, quaking, and halfe dead with coulde."[151] Disarmed by the bird's pitiful appearance, Juno "wraps it softly, till the storme was past, / In her warme skirt, when Jove within few houres / Takes hart, turnes god, and the faire queen deflours."[152] Henceforth the cuckoo came to signify lust and infidelity. Juno's role as marriage deity is also ironic because her husband is the least faithful of the Olympian gods, the lover of Semele, Danae, Alcmena, and Callisto, among others. Thomas Cooper records that Jupiter was "exceedingly geven to lechery, in deflouryng as wel maydens as wyves."[153] Queen Isabella in Marlowe's *Edward II* (acted by Pembroke's Men c. 1591–92), expresses her exasperation over the king's dalliance with Gaveston by alluding to the goddess: "Like frantic Juno will I fill the earth / With ghastly murmur of my sighs and cries" (1.4.178–79).[154] No such concern with marriage gone wrong is even hinted at in *The Tempest*.

For Shakespeare, Juno represents not only the institution of marriage but also the future prosperity of Miranda and Ferdinand. Christine de Pisan records that "Juno, upon the fables of poetis, is the goddes of riches."[155] Vincenzo Cartari also identifies the deity with material wealth: "Unto her also is dedicated among the auncients, the peacocke, as the bird cheefly appropriated unto her, as that men are so drawne and allured with the desire of riches to the possession and embracement thereof, as the diverse-coloured feathers of this bird, enticeth the beholders eyes more and more to view, & to gase upon them" (sig. L2v). Juno and riches were also associated in pageantry. At Norwich in 1578 Elizabeth saw a masque by Henry Goldingham in which Juno presented the queen with "a purse curiously wrought" (*Progresses of Elizabeth*, 2:160). Shakespeare explicitly evokes that association of Juno with prosperity when the goddess sings:

Honor, riches, marriage-blessing,
Long continuance, and increasing,
Hourly joys be still upon you!

(4.1.106–8)

The word "increasing" may refer, of course, both to their wealth and to the children they will have, for Juno is also a goddess of women, especially in childbirth. As she tells Ceres, "Go with me / To bless this twain, that they may prosperous be, / And honor'd in their issue" (lines 103–5).

What most clearly and economically identified Juno to Renaissance viewers, whether in the plastic arts or in masques and plays, was not only her peacock but also the symbols of her authority as queen of the gods. Hans Eworth, who painted Queen Elizabeth in the company of Minerva, Venus and Juno, gives the latter deity a crown; a scepter lies at Juno's feet, symbol of the power she cedes to Elizabeth.[156] In Jonson's *Hymenaei* Juno's attire

Iumon femme de Iupiter Repreſent
lair & Iris ſa meſſagere qui
eſt larc en Ciel.

34 Juno, holding a wand and the thunderbolt of her husband, is accompanied by Iris, who holds Juno's crown, a rainbow above. From Jean de Montlyard's translation of Natale Conti's *Mythologie* (Paris, 1627)

is described as "*rich and like a queen, a white diadem on her head … [and] in her right hand she held a scepter*" (lines 196–99). In a French translation of Natale Conti's *Mythologies*, Juno even wields the thunderbolt of her husband (fig. 34).[157] Samuel Daniel in his *Vision of the Twelve Goddesses* has Juno make a gift of her personal symbol: "*Juno, in a sky-colour mantle embroidered with gold and figured with peacocks' feathers, wearing a crown of gold on her head, presents a sceptre*" (lines 60–62). Juno's regal demeanor and emblems of office are similarly described in Peele's *Arraignment of Paris*: "stately Juno with her porte and grace, / Her roobes, her lawnes, her crounet and her mace" (1.3.104–5). Although stage directions in *The Tempest* specify neither diadem nor scepter, Iris calls Juno "Queen o' th' sky," and some symbol of rank is required to make her status visible to playgoers. Significantly, the costume designed by Inigo Jones for Juno in *Chloridia* depicts her as crowned and holding a scepter (O&S, 2:185).

Juno's emblems of power point toward a political significance. According to Cartari, she is "oftentimes pictured with a scepter in her hand, to shew

that shee hath the bestowing of governments, authorities, & kingdomes"
(sig. L2v). In the Judgment of Paris, a favorite topos of both antiquity and
the Renaissance, when Juno vied with Venus and Minerva for the golden
apple, "Juno promised him, if he should judge in her favor, that he would
rule over all the lands and be pre-eminent in wealth."[158] George Peele in
The Arraignment of Paris dramatizes Juno's offer by this show: "*Heereuppon
did rise a tree of gold laden with diadems and crownes of golde*" (2.2.456.s.d.).
In *The Vision of the Twelve Goddesses* Juno is called "the goddess of empire
and *regnorum praesidi* [i.e., the protectress of kingdoms]" (lines 25–26),
who bears "sceptre of command for kingdoms large" (line 290). When
in *The Tempest* Ceres greets Juno as "Highest Queen of state" (line 101),
Ceres not only acknowledges Juno's power but also alludes to the union of
two kingdoms through marriage – those of Milan (Miranda) and Naples
(Ferdinand).

Iris

In *The Tempest* Iris explains her role as intermediary between the heavens
and the earth. She speaks of Juno "Whose wat'ry arch and messenger am I"
(4.1.71), the word "wat'ry" recalling her ancestry. According to Abraham
Fraunce, Iris is the daughter of Thaumas and Electra, the one parent identified with the sea and the other with the sun.[159] Hence the chief characteristic
of Iris: the rainbow, created by a combination of moisture and light. In *All's
Well that Ends Well* (acted 1602–03), Shakespeare evokes this combination
when the countess sees tears in the eyes of Helena: "What's the matter, /
That this distempered messenger of wet, / The many-color'd Iris, rounds
thine eye?" (1.3.150–52). The very word *iridescence* has, of course, as its root
the name of Juno's messenger. Shakespeare again evokes the spectrum of
color produced by light through moisture when in *The Two Noble Kinsmen*
the Wooer describes the Jailer's Daughter, knee-deep in water:

> about her stuck
> Thousand fresh water-flowers of several colors,
> That methought she appear'd like the fair nymph
> That feeds the lake with waters, or as Iris
> Newly dropp'd down from heaven.   (4.1.84–88)

This speech, like Iris' self-description in *The Tempest*, points to the goddess's
special role as a link between the sky above and the world below.

Because of her colorful costume, Iris must have looked splendid when she appeared in Renaissance entertainments.[160] At Harefield Place in the summer of 1602, the queen witnessed a pageant presented by Lady Elizabeth Walsingham: Iris, who appeared wearing "her moist roabe of collers gay" (*Progresses of Elizabeth*, 3:592), presented a special robe to Elizabeth. Samuel Daniel's *Vision of the Twelve Goddesses* describes Iris as many-hued: "*Iris, the messenger of the goddesses descending from the mount where they were assembled (decked like the rainbow) spake…*" (lines 250–51). And in Beaumont's *Masque of the Inner Temple and Gray's Inn*, Iris is "*apparelled in a robe of discoloured* [i.e., many-colored] *taffeta, figured in variable colours, like the rainbow*" (lines 89–90).[161] Henry Peacham in *Graphice*, a book of instruction for artists, writes that Iris has "large wings dispred in the forme of a semi-circle, the feathers set in rancks of sundry colours, as purple, yellow, greene, redde, &c."[162] The range of color could be represented by flowers as well as fabric. Giovanni Lutero, the painter known as Dosso Dossi, depicts Iris with a garland of flowers on her head, another around her neck, and still others on her wrist.[163] John Lyly in *Love's Metamorphosis* refers to a "garland of flowers which hath all colours of the rainebowe" (4.1.27–28).

In classical myth as in *The Tempest*, Iris functions as a divine messenger. Homer calls her the "wind-footed" messenger of Zeus (*Iliad*, 2:788) and "the messenger of the gods" (15:146). In Roman culture Iris typically acts as the agent of Jupiter's wife. For instance, Ovid describes Iris as "messenger of Juno, clad in robes of many hues, [who] draws up water and feeds it to the clouds" (*Metamorphoses*, 1:270–71). Similarly, Renaissance authors describe Iris as the messenger of Juno whose company she keeps. In *The Silver Age* by Thomas Heywood, Juno and Iris together "*descend from the heavens*" (2.121). At Heidelberg in 1613 Princess Elizabeth was entertained by pageantry which included Juno in a chariot "drawne by peacockes, and driven by Iris."[164] A sketch by Inigo Jones for Jonson's *Chloridia* (1631) depicts Juno and Iris side by side (O&E 2:185).

As befits a messenger, Iris is extraordinarily swift and dressed accordingly, Cartari explaining, "shee is apparelled in loose vestures for the more nimblenesse and dispatch of the goddesses affaires and negotiations" (sig. L3r). Her passage through the skies is assisted by her route along the rainbow. Virgil speaks of Iris as "speeding her way along her thousand-hued rainbow" (*Aeneid*, 5:609), while Ovid describes her "gliding to earth along her rainbow arch" (*Metamorphoses*, 14:838). In an entertainment prepared for Queen Elizabeth at Kenilworth in 1575 (but not performed), "Iris commeth downe from the rainbowe, sent by Juno" (*Progresses of Elizabeth*, 1:503).

Wings signify the swiftness of Iris, as for example in the costumes that
Inigo Jones designed for *Chloridia* and *Hymenaei*. Hesiod calls those wings
"golden" (Hesiod 311), as does Homer (*The Iliad*, 8:398), while Virgil writes
that "Iris on dewy saffron wings flits down through the sky, trailing athwart
the sun a thousand shifting tints" (*Aeneid*, 4:700–1). Inigo Jones, however,
in *Hymenaei* may have given Iris blue wings and a similarly coloured gown,
according to Simpson and Bell, who assign an undescribed sketch to this
masque.[165] Orgel and Strong contest the suggestion, arguing that "Iris was a
painted rainbow and not an acting figure" (O&S, 1:description of 59). The
issue is a difficult one, for although Orgel and Strong may be right, Iris is,
in fact, customarily identified with the color blue.[166] The association of Iris
with this color seems logical since she speeds through the firmament and
since the rainbow is most frequently seen against the background of a blue
sky. In *Troilus and Cressida* (acted 1602–03), Ulysses describes her as "blue
Iris" (1.3.379); G. B. Evans observes in an explanatory note, "perhaps 'blue'
as associated with the sky; but cf. *Lucrece*, line 1587: 'Blue circles streamed,
like rainbows in the sky.'"[167] Whatever the color of her costume and wings
in *Hymenaei*, Shakespeare in *The Tempest* seems to have been guided by
classical precedent, for, as Ceres notes, Iris has "saffron wings" (4.1.78).

It is possible that Iris' costume included some kind of painted rainbow, which could have been attached to her torso or shoulders. A print by
Antonio Tempesta depicts Iris with what looks like a large rainbow behind
her.[168] A French translation of Conti's *Mythologies* places a rainbow just
above and behind her (fig. 34).[169] An itemized list of props and costumes in
Henslowe's *Diary* includes this entry: "Ierosses head, & raynbowe." Foakes
and Rickert speculate that the writer may mean "Iris's head."[170] Whether
or not they are right, the word "raynbowe" suggests either a prop or part of
a costume, perhaps a contrivance that could be attached to the body of the
actor playing Iris. We know that elsewhere the wings of Iris could be con-
figured in a semicircular shape. As we have seen, Henry Peacham describes
Iris as "a nymphe with large wings dispred in the forme of a semi-circle,
the feathers set in ranckes of sundry colours."[171]

Within Prospero's pageant, Ceres addresses Iris in a way that evokes at
once her identity as goddess of the rainbow, her wings, her association with
the color blue, and her role as divine messenger:

Hail, many-colored messenger, that ne'er
Dost disobey the wife of Jupiter;
Who with thy saffron wings upon my flow'rs
Diffusest honey-drops, refreshing show'rs,

And with each end of thy blue bow dost crown
My bosky acres and my unshrubb'd down,
Rich scarf to my proud earth.   (4.1.76–82)

These lines connect Juno's realm with that of Ceres, heaven and earth, the spiritual and the corporeal. The speech may even hint at the biblical significance of the rainbow. Following the great flood, Noah saw a rainbow, a sign of hope, symbol of reconciliation between God and humankind. As William Tyndale explains, "God ordeyned that the raynebowe shulde represent and signifie unto all men an othe that God sware to Noe and to all men after him that he wolde no more drownd the worlde thorow water."[172] In the Rainbow portrait of Queen Elizabeth, which hangs in Hatfield House outside London, the queen grasps a rainbow, symbol of her benign power and peaceful reign.[173] Henry Peacham in an emblem describes the rainbow in a way that points to a spiritual value: "The rainbowe, of his mercy, heere a signe."[174] Although it seems unwise to insist on a specifically Christian interpretation of Iris in *The Tempest*, Prospero's treatment of his enemies and his willingness to accept the son of an enemy as his own son-in-law suggest the value of reconciliation and forgiveness, peace after the turmoil at sea.

The Harpy

In Greek myth Iris has siblings named Aëllo, Ocypetes, and, sometimes, Celaeno. These sisters of Iris are known as harpies (literally "snatchers"). In *The Odyssey* Homer calls them storm-winds, who sweep people away to a most unpleasant fate; they seize the daughters of Pandareus: "the spirits of the storm snatched away the maidens and gave them to the hateful Erinyes to deal with" (20:77–78). Hesiod describes harpies as winged females with long hair (*Theogony*, line 266). For Apollonius of Rhodes they are bird-like creatures of the air and, on the orders of Zeus, they may snatch not a person but the food he would eat. Thus they afflict Phineus, a sooth-sayer who divulges a secret of the gods: "on a sudden, swooping through the clouds, the Harpies with their crooked beaks incessantly snatched the food away from his mouth and hands" (bk. 2, lines 187–88).[175] What the harpies don't snatch they despoil. Apollodorus writes, "what little they left stank so that nobody could touch it" (bk. 1, chap. 9).[176] In *The Aeneid* the harpies, who prevent Aeneas and his men from feasting on the cattle and goats they kill, are horrific: "No monster more baneful than these, no fiercer plague or wrath of the gods ever rose from the Stygian waves" (3:214–15). Virgil's harpies are a grotesque composite. They combine a female countenance with avian claws: "Maiden faces have these birds, foulest filth they drop, clawed hands are theirs, and faces ever gaunt with hunger" (*Aeneid*, 3:216–18).

Renaissance mythographers base their depictions of harpies on classical accounts, especially those in *The Aeneid*. Abraham Fraunce describes creatures that Virgil would recognize: harpies are "faced like virgins, winged like birdes, with pale and hungry visages, and crooked scraping clawes."[177] Citing Natale Conti, Fraunce recalls that their name signifies "the furious violence and rage of the windes"; he adds the Virgilian notion that they are "the most detestable monsters, that ever issued out of the Stygian lak."[178] Similarly, Stephen Batman calls harpies "moste ravening byrdes, faced with countenaunce lyke a mayde, crooked and bending clawes."[179] Less often harpies have lions' claws, probably the result of a conflation with the sphinx.[180] A fresco by Guercino, for instance, depicts a man seizing a harpy by her long hair; her bird-like appendages culminate in the paws of a lion.[181] In Thomas Carew's *Coelum Britannicum*, performed at the Whitehall banqueting house 18 February 1634, harpies are portrayed in much the same way. As the masque began, spectators saw "a large compartment composed of grotesque work, wherein were harpies with wings and lions' claws" (lines 4–5).[182]

Artists sometimes represent harpies with the serpent-like lower body described by Cesare Ripa. An illustration in Francesco Colonna's *Hypnerotomachia Poliphili* (1499) depicts several sculpted harpies on a fountain: they have the face and breasts of a woman, wings of a bird, and tail of a serpent.[183] Dirck Volkertsz Coornhert, in a print after Maarten van Heemskerck, represents three winged females who share a common female torso, the lower body terminating in the coils of a snake.[184] A design by Peter Paul Rubens for the entry of Ferdinand of Austria into Antwerp, 17 April 1635, depicts the creature in a scene illustrating the ferocity of war: a soldier and personified Pestilence attack a kneeling mother and child, while "Famine, in the form of a harpy with a dragon's tail, flies overhead."[185]

Neither the dialogue nor the stage directions of *The Tempest* provide much detail about Shakespeare's harpy. We know that Ariel, at the instruction of Prospero, performs the role of the harpy, and we know also that Ariel, in this capacity, has wings. Here our certitude ends. We may reasonably speculate, however, that Ariel as harpy has the female appearance depicted by artists.[186] It seems likely that Prospero's servant was played by a boy whose youthful countenance could seem feminine, especially if he were equipped with a wig supplying long hair; appropriate padding of the costume could readily suggest a female torso. The lower part of Ariel's garb may have culminated in the form of a serpent, but if the actor were required to move onstage under his own power, he would need sturdy limbs such as the bird-like legs represented in the 1542 Paris edition of Andrea Alciato's emblem book.[187]

The circumstances of the harpy's appearance in *The Tempest* evoke the world of masques. A dance of shapes accompanies the creation of the banquet: "*Solemn and strange music; and Prosper[o] on the top, invisible*" (3.3.17.s.d.). Following an exchange by Alonso and Gonzalo on the music, playgoers witness additional action:

Enter several strange Shapes, bringing in a banket; and dance about it with gentle actions of salutations; and inviting the King, etc., to eat, they depart. (line 19.s.d.)

As the courtiers begin their meal, another spectacle ensues:

Thunder and lightning. Enter Ariel, like a harpy, claps his wings upon the table, and with a quaint device the banquet vanishes. (line 52.s.d.)

Following Ariel's lengthy indictment of Alonso, Antonio, and Sebastian, the strange shapes return to remove the banquet table, now empty of food:

He vanishes in thunder; then, to soft music, enter the Shapes again, and dance, with mocks and mows, and carrying out the table. (line 82.s.d.)

Graham Holderness comments: "The stage directions governing the two dances irresistibly recall the procedures of the court masque: the first dance is an invitation or offering, the second a mocking and scurrilous anti-masque of ridicule and contempt."[188] The stage directions, moreover, by the reference to "a quaint device" suggest a delight in contrivance. Prospero expresses pleasure in the effect he has engineered: "Bravely the figure of this harpy hast thou / Perform'd, my Ariel" (3.3.83–84).

Like the actions of masques, the disappearing banquet staged by Prospero invites symbolic interpretation. Jacqueline Latham sees in the harpy a chastisement of those who have despoiled the rightful duke of Milan: Ariel as harpy is "an image of the greedy men of sin who have snatched, or tried to snatch, power and life from Prospero and later even from Alonso."[189] Donna Hamilton, too, sees a judicial significance. Noting Shakespeare's dependence on book 6 of *The Aeneid*, where Aeneas sees harpies at the gates of the underworld (6:286–89) and where Rhadamanthus judges the guilty, she writes: "The situation of Shakespeare's court party is similar. The three

35 A winged harpy, clutching a torch, confronts a man at table; instruments of punishment in the background. Detail from a panoramic print of the underworld by Mario Cartaro

men of sin have not yet faced their guilt; they are, says Ariel, 'unfit to live' and certainly ripe for punishment."[190]

All such interpretations find support in Ariel's speech. As harpy, he calls Alonso, Sabastian, and Antonio "men of sin" (3.3.53) and ascribes the shipwreck to their "foul deed" (line 72) in toppling Prospero from his Milanese dukedom. Motivated by ambition, these malefactors arrogated to themselves the power and position rightly belonging to another. The nature of their sin explains Ariel's costume: according to Thomas Cooper, harpies are "monstruous byrdes, having maidens vysages, & talons of a mervailous capacitie, wherfore men that be ravenous and great gatherers of goodes, be named sometyme *harpyiae*."[191] Natale Conti notes that "the ancients signified through this fable that avarice and a boundless desire for wealth are like a severe penalty imposed upon mortals by the decree of the gods" (*Mythologies*, 373). A sixteenth-century print by Mario Cartaro connects a particular kind of wrongdoing with the punishment administered by a harpy: within an enormous panorama of the underworld, a harpy grasps a torch and perches on a table where a man prepares to dine (fig. 35). The identifying label reads "Goloso" (greedy).

For all Prospero's concern with the reformation of those who have treated him so cruelly, he is no less concerned with regaining political power

himself. Ariel as harpy reminds his master's tormentors that "you three /
From Milan did supplant good Prospero" (3.3.70). Later when Prospero
identifies himself as "The wronged Duke of Milan" (5.1.107), the king of
Naples replies, "Thy dukedom I resign, and do entreat / Thou pardon me
my wrongs" (lines 118–19). Speaking to his brother, Prospero couples forgiveness with a demand:

> I do forgive
> Thy rankest fault – all of them; and require
> My dukedom of thee, which perforce, I know
> Thou must restore.   (5.1.131–34)

The harpy who initiates Prospero's revelation of identity and his effort to
regain power is a creature whose association with the vice of greed makes
this symbolic figure particularly apposite. After all, playwrights and poets
liken harpies to courtiers who seek the property of others. In *If This Be
Not a Good Play* (acted by the Queen's Men in 1611), Thomas Dekker
says that harpies' claws "being on courtiers lands / Once fastend, ne're let
loose" (1.1.116–17).[192] Similarly, Henry Peacham, in an emblem of a harpy
perched on a table, explains the significance of the monstrous creature:

> The courtes of kinges, are said to keepe a crew
> Of these still hungry for their private gaine:
> The first is he, that carries tales untrue,
> The second, whome base bribing doth maintaine,
>   The third and last, the parasite I find,
>   Who bites the worst, if princes will be blind.[193]

Peacham's emblem, which contains an allusion to the classical story of
Phineus, provides a specifically political context for the sin embodied by
the harpy. It was, of course, greedy ambition that led to the usurpation
of Prospero's dukedom in the first place and to his subsequent exile. The
harpy, then, confronts the malefactors with a symbol of their vice.

Prospero himself is not without blame for the fate that befell him. As
Peacham's last line suggests – "Who bites the worst, if princes will be blind" –
harpy-like courtiers prevail when the prince fails in his duties. But the
Prospero who presides over the vanishing banquet is presumably a different
Prospero: in control rather than detached, observant rather than inattentive
to the machinations of family and subjects. The staging of the banquet scene
points to his public responsibility: "throughout the scene we are aware of
the presence of Prospero '*on the top (invisible)*' – a presence which in the
context of hell suggests the judging power of a deity but in the context of

politics suggests the ruler's power and responsibility to be the chief judge in the land, as well as a model of moral rectitude."[194]

The Two Noble Kinsmen

From its opening moments *The Two Noble Kinsmen* signals its closeness to the masque. Of the first scene where Theseus and Hippolyta, en route to their wedding, are confronted by mourners, Theodore Spencer observes, "It is processional, static, dignified, in the manner of a masque: the exact opposite to the opening of *The Tempest*, where all is action and excitement."[195] What *Kinsmen* has in common with *The Tempest* is the extraordinary prominence accorded spectacle and music. "Whichever theatre it was designed for," writes N. W. Bawcutt, "the play required elaborate stage effects. There are repeated flourishes and fanfares for different instruments – horns, cornets, trumpets, and recorders," not to mention the accompaniment for song and dance later in the play.[196] Visual effects include the compelling opening where characters, bedecked in festive colors, meet the trio of queens in black; the entry of Theseus following his defeat of Creon, accompanied by Palamon and Arcite; the martial games at which the escaped Arcite distinguishes himself; the hunt, a solemn rite of May at which Palamon and Arcite fall to combat; and the Morris dance performed before Theseus and Hippolyta.

The prayer scene, thought to be Shakespeare's rather than Fletcher's,[197] represents the culmination of the play's emphasis on sight and sound. Palamon, Arcite, and Emilia seriatim propitiate deities at their respective altars and observe the divine response to their petitions. Despite the disparate interests of the votaries and the conflict inherent in the forces which Mars, Venus, and Diana personify, the playgoers witness no squabble among the gods in the manner of *The Rare Triumphs* or *Soliman and Perseda*. Instead, the scene proceeds by a series of tableaux in which each votary, attended by retainers, behaves with the decorum dictated by a ritualistic occasion. The petitioner enters, kneels, and prays aloud, then observes the visual and aural signs sent by the divinity.

Besides the sights and sounds stipulated in the stage directions, the playgoers and the characters within the play may have seen something else as well. Eugene Waith, in his edition of the play, records a suggestion made by R. A. Foakes: namely, that "the altar is ornamented in each case with some sign or symbol of the deity to whom it is dedicated."[198] We may reasonably go even further, I believe, and conjecture that the very image of each deity was present onstage. Indeed, Lois Potter, in her edition of *The Two Noble Kinsmen*, assumes just such staging when she refers to the possibility that "the statue of Mars extends a garland to Arcite."[199] Theatrically, such a representation of the god could lend greater impact to the spoken words. That is, the speeches of Palamon, Arcite, and Emilia would be all the more effective if directed to some tactile figure rather than to vacant space. The theatre, after all, demands that, so far as possible, ideas be made visual. What better way to individualize the petitioners and vivify their prayers than by placing a statue or painting of the deity upon an altar? Such staging would also be consistent with the tradition of masques wherein deities in all their regalia make themselves visible to humankind.[200] As a practical matter, the image of one deity could be changed to another by using the trap door in the floor of the stage or by using a curtain if the altar appears in the tiring-house wall.[201]

Mars

Hesiod's "Homeric Hymn to Ares" begins by saluting the god of war as "exceeding in strength, chariot-rider, golden-helmed, doughty in heart, shield-bearer, Saviour of cities, harnessed in bronze, strong of arm, unwearying, mighty with the spear" (Hesiod 433). Following this litany of praise, however, the speaker asks to be saved from his own warlike impulses, which are embodied in Ares (Roman Mars): "Restrain also the keen fury of my heart which provokes me to tread the ways of blood-curdling strife" (433–35). This short poem encapsulates the ambivalent feelings of a culture. To the extent that the deity externalizes behavior considered the epitome of aggressive masculinity, he warrants praise. But to the extent that he represents impulses leading to cruelty and wanton destruction, he occasions deep apprehension. In keeping with this divided attitude, *The Iliad* presents a mixed portrait of Ares, who embodies strength and resolution but suffers from a petulant nature. Even Zeus accuses him of bad temper, of spoiling for conflict: "Most hateful to me art thou of all gods that hold Olympus, for ever is strife dear to thee and wars and fightings" (*Iliad*, 5:889–90).

From the standpoint of a Christian ethos prizing forgiveness and mercy, Mars seems closer to the underworld than to Olympus. In his *Adages* Erasmus notes that "the poets of old time … recounted that war was a product of the infernal regions, by the agency of the Furies."[202] It was this aspect of Mars that colored representations of the deity from antiquity to the Renaissance. Alain de Lille, for instance, describes Mars in pejorative terms: "the blazing palace of Mars...knows only the rage and storm of fire"; the god "prepares arms for men, leads fanatics to entertain hopes, sows the seeds of insolence, fathers rage, weakens love. His very face shows what his heart is planning and by its redness proclaims the pestilential rage of internal fury."[203] In keeping with such a view, poets surround Mars with fearsome personifications. Whereas classical writers use a relatively simple formulation – Mars "bade Terror and Rout yoke his horses" (*Iliad*, 15:119) – later authors favor a more complicated iconographic program. Boccaccio in his *Teseida* recounts a prayer travelling to the palace of Mars and there seeing "mad Impulses coming forth proudly through the door; and Blind Sin and every Alas! appeared there too. Wrath, red as fire, and pale Fear were also to be seen in that place."[204] Similarly, Chaucer in *The Knight's Tale* describes the temple of Mars as containing Felonye, Ire, Drede, Contek [Strife], Deethe, Meschaunce, Woodnesse [Madness], Compleint, Outhees [Outcry], and Outrage (lines 1996–2012).[205] In *Histriomastix* personified War appears in the company of Ambition, Horror, Ruin, and Fury (5:284). Common to all of these descriptions is personified Anger or Fury, which any contemporary of Boccaccio, Chaucer, or Marston would recognize as one of the Seven Deadly Sins.

Mars, however, could be seen in a more positive light. Christine de Pisan writes, "every knyght that loveth and suweth armes and deedis of knyght-hode and hath a greet name of wurthynes may be callid sone of Mars."[206] In Shakespeare's *Richard II* (acted by the Lord Chamberlain's Men in 1595), York intends a compliment when he speaks of Edward the Black Prince as "that young Mars of men" (2.3.101); so too does Ben Jonson in *Prince Henry's Barriers* where the same historical figure is called "that Mars of men" (line 247).[207] Military valor merits such esteem when it accomplishes some worthy objective.[208] Thomas Heywood in *Londini Sinus Salutis, or, London's Harbour of Health, and Happinesse*, the lord mayor's pageant for 29 October 1635, envisions a Mars more protective than destructive:

Bellipotent Mars is from his spheare come downe,
To heighten these brave Triumphs of Renowne,
Seated in this mur'd citadel, defenc'd
With bullets wrapt in fire, and cloudes condenst.

(lines 261–64)[209]

Mars, however, is most frequently identified with bristling animosity. Of Shakespeare's characters Hotspur comes closest to typifying the spirit of the personification. In *1 Henry IV* (acted c. 1596–97), the king refers to

Hotspur as "Mars in swathling clothes" (3.2.112), and, before the battle of Shrewsbury, the rebel himself predicts that "The mailed Mars shall on his altar sit / Up to the ears in blood" (4.1.116–17). *Henry V*, a play acted in 1599 and chronicling the renown of the man who defeated Hotspur, suggests that Hal shares something in common with his bellicose adversary. The prologue asks a kingdom for a stage:

Then should the warlike Harry, like himself,
Assume the port of Mars, and at his heels
(Leash'd in, like hounds) should famine, sword, and fire
Crouch for employment.   (lines 5–8)

The king evoked in these lines is the man capable of slaughtering defenceless French prisoners, of threatening that unless Harfleur surrenders,

The gates of mercy shall be all shut up,
And the flesh'd soldier, rough and hard of heart,
In liberty of bloody hand, shall range,
With conscience wide as hell, mowing like grass
Your fresh fair virgins and your flow'ring infants.   (3.3.10–14)

Even Heywood's lord mayor's pageant concedes of Mars, "He is also cal'd *Ares* which signifieth Dammage or detriment, and *Mavors* quasi *Mares vorans*, of devouring of men" (lines 232–34).

In the pictorial arts Mars is typically fierce and sometimes accompanied by an array of other figures who help to define his nature. Maarten van Heemskerck depicts Mars sitting in a chariot while Fury holds the reins of horses named Destruction and Devastation; personified Cruelty brings along captives, while Famine, Blasphemy, and Strife accompany the vehicle.[210] In a print by Hendrik Goltzius the god of war rides in a chariot drawn by horses and riders whose names include Arrogance, Ambition, Injury, Rebellion, and Contempt; Cruelty and Pestilence, on foot, accompany the vehicle.[211] If such a complicated iconographic program belongs largely to the later Middle Ages and Renaissance, the artists acknowledge their dependence upon ancient representations by presenting Mars as a bearded man with classical gear; Homer tells us that Mars has a helm, shield, spear of bronze, and gleaming armor (*Iliad*, 15:125–28). Bernard Salomon depicts Mars wearing the greaves, breastplate, and plumed helmet of an ancient warrior, and wielding a long spear; he rides in a vehicle piled with classical weaponry and armor.[212] Salomon's Mars rides in a chariot drawn by wolves. This is a departure from Homer's description of Mars' "swift horses" (5:356), but congruent with Roman representations of Mars.[213]

d. IV

In addition to his metallic weaponry, Mars customarily carries a torch, symbolic of war's destruction and of the anger that fuels such mayhem. Shakespeare's Troilus speaks of "the hand of Mars / Beck'ning with fiery truncheon" (5.3.53). Heinrich Aldegrever's Mars carries a torch in one hand, a bow in the other; a dead body lies at his feet while a city burns in the background.[214] In a print ascribed to Hans Sebald Beham, Mars carries a torch in his right hand, a short sword in his left.[215] Even when Mars does not actually hold a torch, fire is likely to be a part of his representation. Thus Crispin van de Passe depicts Mars with sword and shield, while in the background an army maneuvers in the field and a city is put to the torch (fig. 36).

In *The Two Noble Kinsmen* Arcite stands before the altar of Mars, whom he calls "the god of our profession" (5.1.38), and he appeals for assistance in the forthcoming combat with Palamon: "Our intercession," he says, "Must be to him that makes the camp a cestron / Brimm'd with the blood of men" (lines 45–47). Arcite and his men advance to the altar of Mars and fall on their faces (line 48.s.d.). The knight's address envisions a personification of angry destruction:

Thou mighty one, that with thy power hast turn'd
Green Neptune into purple...
Comets forewarn, whose havoc in vast field
Unearthed skulls proclaim, whose breath blows down
The teeming Ceres' foison, who dost pluck
With hand armipotent from forth blue clouds
The mason'd turrets, that both mak'st and break'st
The stony girths of cities...   (lines 49–56)

The deity's response takes the form of menacing sound: "*Here they fall on their faces as formerly, and there is heard clanging of armor, with a short thunder, as the burst of a battle, whereupon they all rise and bow to the altar*" (line 61.s.d.) Arcite interprets the signs favorably, thanking the deity who "heal'st with blood / The earth when it is sick" (lines 64–65). The Mars he envisions is a deity of blood and death, not unlike that of Albrecht Altdorfer, who paints Mars with sword and torch, looking down on a world of choleric men engaging in a maelstrom of struggle.[216] A woodcut by Georg Pencz, similarly, depicts the planetary deity aloft, while below are frantic scenes of conflict and execution.[217]

From such evidence, pictorial and literary, we may reasonably conjecture that, if Mars appears on his altar in *The Two Noble Kinsmen*, he is attired in classical armor, wears a plumed helmet, and grasps a weapon (most likely

36 Mars with sword and shield. Engraving by Crispin van de Passe

a sword) in one hand, a torch in the other.[218] He wears a beard, and his hair is "a deepe yeallowe."[219] His expression is fierce; Chaucer says that Mars "looked grym as he were wood [mad]" (line 2042). His countenance is reddish, the color signifying "a warlike disposition."[220] The deity may stand, as he does in *The Knight's Tale*, rather than sit, suggestive of a choleric temperament and penchant for action. If he rides in a chariot, as Chaucer's deity does, the vehicle is drawn by either horses or wolves (Chaucer says, "A wolf ther stood biforn hym" [line 2047]). Suitably attired and weaponed, Mars incarnates ferocity and violent death.

Venus

If Mars is readily identified by his armor and weaponry, Venus lacks distinctive attire. In fact, artists usually portray her as nude or partially draped. Lucas Cranach, for instance, in several of his paintings depicts her wearing only an extraordinary hat.[221] Although nude, Venus wears jewelry, ordinarily a necklace and bracelet of gold or pearl. In Titian's *Venus with a Mirror* the blonde deity, who has a braided coiffure, is bedecked with a strand of pearls in her hair, pearl earrings, gold bracelets, and a ring on each hand.[222] The pearls recall Venus's origins in the sea: according to Hesiod, she was born of the foam created when the genitals of the castrated Uranus were thrown into the sea (Hesiod, 427); her Greek name Aphrodite derives from a word (*aphros*) meaning "foam."[223] The goddess may hold a seashell symbolic of her watery origins as she does in the bas-relief of the Tempio Malatestiano, Rimini.[224] The Homeric hymn "To Aphrodite" recounts her arrival on Cyprus, the island sacred to this deity: "the moist breath of the western wind wafted her over the waves of the loud-moaning sea in soft foam" (Hesiod, 427). Reaching land, she is welcomed by the Hours: "on her head they put a fine, well-wrought crown of gold, and in her pierced ears they hung ornaments of orichalc [ore or alloy of copper] and precious gold, and adorned her with golden necklaces." In George Peele's *Arraignment of Paris* Flora describes Venus, recounting "Her plumes, her pendants, bracelets and her ringes, / Her dayntie fan and twentie other thinges" (1.3.120–21).

Titian's *Venus of Urbino* presents a reclining nude bedecked with pearl earring, gold bracelet, and ring.[225] What identifies this figure as Venus is not the nudity – any classical deity, male or female, may be represented thus – but rather the roses she bears in her right hand.[226] In another of his paintings, *Venus and Cupid with a Partridge*, Titian depicts Venus with roses in her hand and, nearby, additional roses in a glass vase.[227] Since antiquity the goddess had been closely identified with flowers. Virgil in his *Dirae* refers to the "flowery garlands of Venus" (line 20).[228] In *The Aeneid* the poet speaks of her "roseate neck" and says, "From her head her ambrosial tresses breathed celestial fragrance" (1:403–4). Claudian writes, "Her chariot is heaped with flowers and the yoke thereof is fragrant with blossoms."[229] The rose in particular was sacred to Venus. In a poem credited to Ausonius, "Venus / is queen of both rose and morning star."[230] Ovid in his *Fasti* describes Venus' statue washed and decorated: "now give her other flowers, now give her the fresh-blown rose" (4:138).

Surveying depictions of Venus in antiquity, Vincenzo Cartari notes the symbolism of her flower: "The ancients used to dedicat unto this goddesse many plants & flowers, among the which, specially were the roses, whose fragrant and sweet odor is resembled unto the pleasing delights & outward faire shews and colours of love, & in that they are of that blushing and rubicund colour, and that they can hardly bee pluckt without their pricks, and molesting mens fingers: they are likened unto luxurious people" (sig. Cc3v).[231] The mythographer relates the distinctive color of the rose to the goddess' own history: "the poets do invent, that at the first they were of milke white colour, & grew verie pale and discoloured: until Venus on a certain time having intelligence that Mars . . . had complotted & determined a devise to have murdered her sweethart Adonis, and she in great hast and rage running to prevent & disanull the intended mischeef, greevously prickt hir foot on the stalks of these flowers, of which wound (sending forth abundance of bloud) they were presently turned into that fresh colour which now at this time they do retaine" (sig. Cc4r). George Peele, however, in *The Arraignment of Paris* offers an alternate explanation of the flower's color when Venus swears, "By this red rose, whose colour first began, / When erst my wanton boy (the more his blame) / Did drawe his bowe awry and hurt his dame" (5.1.1127–29).

Poets of the late Middle Ages and Renaissance make considerable use of the rose in portrayals of Venus and of amorous experience. Marlowe's "Passionate Shepherd to His Love" begins with the entreaty, "Come live with me, and be my love," and goes on to promise, "I will make thee beds of roses."[232] In Shakespeare's *Venus and Adonis* the goddess recalls that she led Mars a "prisoner in a red rose chain" (line 110). In Lyly's *Galatea* (acted 1584) Diana contends that "Venus's rods are made of roses" (3.4.89–90).[233] In *The Lord Hay's Masque*, performed 6 January 1607 to celebrate Hay's marriage to Honora Denny, Thomas Campion writes, "Roses, the garden's pride, / Are flowers for love" (lines 211–12).[234] And for Jonson's *Haddington Masque*, performed at court on 9 February 1608, Inigo Jones created a pilaster decorated with the spoils and trophies of Venus: depicted were "*old and young persons figured, bound with roses*" (lines 27–28).[235]

In addition to the rose, Venus is recognizable by two other accoutrements, both named by Thomas Heywood: "She goes armed with torches, and bound about with a marriage girdle."[236] Ben Jonson gives both to Venus in *Love's Triumph Through Callipolis*, a masque performed at court in 1631: "here I present am, / Both in my girdle and my flame" (lines 169–70).[237] The girdle is the classical *cestus*, which girds her torso under her breasts. Homer describes it in *The Iliad* (14:214), and it appears in numerous Renaissance prints and paintings, including *Venus with Ceres and Bacchus* by Hendrik Goltzius and a fresco at the Villa Barbaro, Maser, by Veronese.[238] Jonson's note in *Hymenaei* explains the significance of the *cestus*: it "was feigned to be variously wrought with the needle, and in it woven love, desire, sweetness, soft parley, gracefulness, persuasion and all the powers of Venus" (note to line 365).

The flame, while not especially common in Renaissance paintings and prints, has an obvious symbolic significance. In *The Aeneid* Venus speaks to Cupid about Dido: "I purpose to outwit the queen with guile and encircle her with love's flame" (1:673). Allan Gilbert comments on its appearance in Jonson's *Love's Triumph*: "The 'flame' is perhaps that of which Gyraldus... speaks, saying that among the Saxons there was a temple of Venus in which she was represented as standing naked in her chariot, her head wreathed with myrtle, a burning flame on her breast."[239] In *The Haddington Masque* a pilaster is decorated with trophies of Venus; these include "*hearts transfixed with arrows, others flaming*" (line 29). Hendrik Goltzius depicts Venus in a print with flaming arrows piercing hearts, which themselves burst into flame (fig. 37).

Although Venus is not consistently pictured with either special clothing or accoutrements (aside from those already mentioned), she is easily recognized by the animals that accompany her. Cartari reports: "Horace and Virgil affirme, that the chariot of Venus is drawn by two white swans, whereof Statius also maketh mention, saying, that those kind of birds are most mild, innocent, and harmless and therfore given unto Venus" (sig. Cc3r–v). Ovid, too, in his *Metamorphoses* mentions that Venus is "Borne through the middle air by flying swans on her light car" (10:717–18). A ceiling panel in the Villa Trento, Vicenza, depicts the goddess in a chariot drawn by four swans, while in a Schifanoia Palace mural two such birds pull her vehicle.[240]

Cartari records another tradition: "Pausanias saieth, that Venus is drawne in a coach through the airie passages, and two white doves (as Apuleius also affirmeth)... for it is writen indeed, that they are most abundantly inclined to procreation, & that almost at all times of the year, they ingender, increase, and bring forth their young" (sig. Cc3r). Four doves draw Venus' chariot in the Villa Farnesina, Rome.[241] Ben Jonson combines doves and swans in *The Haddington Masque*: "*with a solemn music, a bright sky breaking forth, there were discovered first two doves, then two swans with silver gears* [harnesses], *drawing forth a triumphant chariot in which Venus sat*" (lines 35–37). Sparrows, too, may accompany the goddess of love – Vulcan refers to his "wife's sparrows" in *Sappho and Phao* (4.4.39)[242] – for these birds were especially identified with lust. Flora's description of Venus in *The*

37 A reclining Venus holds a rose; Cupid wields an arrow. At their side are two doves, and, in the background, Venus' chariot is drawn by swans. Engraving by Hendrik Goltzius

Arraignment of Paris cites all three kinds of birds: "Faire Venus shee hath let her sparrowes flie, / To tende on her and make her melodie: / Her turtles [doves] and her swannes unyoked bee, / And flicker neere her side for companie" (1.3.144–47).

Although Palamon's prayer at the altar of Venus in *The Two Noble Kinsmen* evokes her customary association with passion, fertility, and love, that prayer has troubled some Shakespeareans, for it celebrates, with reference to her flame, the destructive effects of the deity, her penchant for inducing grotesque behavior in humankind:

> [Venus] canst make
> A cripple flourish with his crutch, and cure him
> Before Apollo; that mayst force the king
> To be his subject's vassal, and induce
> Stale gravity to dance; the poll'd bachelor,
> Whose youth, like wanton boys through bonfires,
> Have skipp'd thy flame, at seventy thou canst catch,
> And make him, to the scorn of his hoarse throat,
> Abuse young lays of love. What godlike power
> Hast thou not power upon?   (5.1.81–90)

Not a pretty picture, it is entirely in keeping with the power of Venus as set forth by mythographers, poets, and playwrights. Cartari, for example, records, "According...to the opinion of the poets, Venus was taken to be the goddesse of wantonnes & amorous delights, as that she inspired into the minds of men, libidinous desires, and lustfull appetites, & with whose power & assistance they attained the effect of their lose concupiscence" (sig. Cc2r). Similarly, Natale Conti writes, "the ancients fabled that Venus laughed at the perjuries of lovers because those who are roused by a kind of movement peculiar to their souls to broken vows are not in control of themselves but are carried away by this emotion through which the impulse drives them" (*Mythologies*, 236). Chaucer's *Knight's Tale*, the major inspiration for *Two Noble Kinsmen*, describes the walls of Venus' temple in terms that indicate her supremacy: "Thus may ye seen that wysdom ne richesse, / Beautee ne sleighte, strengthe ne hardynesse, / Ne may with Venus holde champartie [partnership in power], / For as hir list the world than may she gye" (lines 1947–50).

Long before the prayer scene of *The Two Noble Kinsmen*, English playwrights had dramatized the destructive force of Venus. In *The Rare Triumphs of Love and Fortune*, printed in 1589 but probably performed at Windsor Castle on 30 December 1582, Venus exults in her power:

> I torment the minde that never felt releefe;
> I plague the wretch that never thought on comfort in his greefe,
> That never had the hope of any happy chaunce,
> That never once so much as deem'd I would his state advance.[243]
>
>   (lines 113–16)

When this Venus boasts, "I make the noble love the bastarde in degree; / I tame and temper all the tunges that raile & scoffe at me" (lines 125–26), she sounds much like her counterpart in *The Two Noble Kinsmen*. Similarly, the goddess who constitutes part of the chorus in Kyd's *Soliman and Perseda* (acted c. 1588–91, perhaps at court) cares little about the feelings of her human prey. At one point she looks back over the action and tells Fortune and Death that it was she who "made great Soliman, sweete beauties thrall, / Humble himselfe at faire Persedas feete, / And made him praise love, and his captives beautie" (4.3.6–8).[244]

To represent her destructive power, the King's Men would almost certainly have depicted Venus together with Cupid. Mother and son commonly keep company: for example, Bernard Salomon's print has Venus ensconced in her chariot while Cupid, standing at the front, shoots arrows at winged hearts.[245] Venus and Cupid jointly hold a torch in an engraving by Marcantonio Raimondi.[246] Hans Eworth's painting of Queen Elizabeth in the company of three classical goddesses portrays Cupid clinging to Venus.[247] Cupid and Venus also appear side by side in "The Queen's Entertainment in Suffolk and Norfolk, 1578," where they are thrust out of heaven together (*Progresses of Elizabeth*, 2:189). Mother and son work in concert in Marlowe's *Dido Queen of Carthage* (2.1.304–33). In Hendrik Goltzius' depiction of Venus, the reclining deity has her arm around Cupid, who holds an arrow poised just above her heart (fig. 37).

By the time Shakespeare wrote *The Two Noble Kinsmen* he had already created a character of Cupid. In *Timon of Athens* the boy god presents an entertainment at a banquet: "*Enter Cupid with the masque of ladies*" (1.2.130.s.d.).[248] Unfortunately, neither the dialogue nor stage directions tell us anything about his costume. Other plays and entertainments, however, give us clues to his likely appearance in *Timon* and *Kinsmen*. In *Gismond of Salerne* (acted by the gentlemen of the Inner Temple 1567–68) where Cupid, personifying lust, especially in its sudden and heedless aspect, "*cometh downe from heaven*," the deity refers to his nudity and his wings:

Loe I, in shape that seme unto your sight
a naked boy, not clothed but with wing,
am that great god of love that with my might
do rule the world, and every living thing.

(1.1.1–4)[249]

Although nude, winged Cupid is armed, and his weaponry signals danger. In Beaumont and Fletcher's *A Wife for a Month* (acted by the King's Men in 1624), Cupid speaks of "My angry bow" (2.6.31).[250] Thomas Dekker in

London's Tempe, a pageant honoring the lord mayor in 1629, provides more detail about Cupid's arrows:

> Cupid sits in one place of this forge; on his head a curld yellow haire, his eyes hid in lawne, a bow and quiver, his armour: wings at his backe; his body in light colours, a changeable silke mantle crossing it: golden and silver arrowes, are ever and anon reached up to him, which hee shootes upward into the aire, and is still supplied with more from the forge. (lines 191–96)[251]

A golden arrow causes the victim to fall in love; a silver arrow causes aversion. As the words "eyes hid in lawn" indicate, Cupid wears a blindfold.[252] Consequently, his arrows may fall at random, engendering matches that are inappropriate, even grotesque. In Renaissance art Venus may herself handle the weaponry of Cupid, as she does in Bronzino's allegory, where the goddess carries a golden arrow in her right hand.[253] A woodcut by Georg Pencz depicts Venus the planetary deity in her chariot: she holds a giant arrow while, in front of her, Cupid aims an arrow at a heart.[254]

Cupid may also wield firebrands, as he does in Lyly's *Love's Metamorphosis* where a character inventories the god's appearance: "he should bee a god blind and naked, with wings, with bowe, with arrowes, with fire-brands" (2.1.51–52). The birth-to-death portrait of Sir Henry Unton, which illustrates a masque in progress, depicts ten Cupids, all of whom carry torches.[255] In Jonson's *Chloridia* (1631) Inigo Jones gives Cupid a crown of flames (O&S 2:172). And the Cupids who appear in Beaumont's *Masque of the Inner Temple and Gray's Inn* wear "flame-coloured taffeta" (lines 191–92).[256] When Cupid appears in Petrarch's *Triumphs*, he often stands on a vehicle out of which clouds of smoke billow from an unseen fire.[257]

Shakespeare's familiarity with ancient and contemporary depictions of Venus and Cupid can only be surmised. We know that he read Sir Thomas North's translation of Plutarch, who describes Cleopatra as resembling Venus. The account, alas, proves unhelpful: the Egyptian queen is "apparelled and attired like the goddesse Venus, commonly drawen in picture."[258] Shakespeare's own description of Cleopatra, spoken by the gruff soldier Enobarbus, is similarly lacking in specificity: she did lie

In her pavilion – cloth of gold, of tissue –
O'er-picturing that Venus where we see
The fancy outwork nature.

                    (2.2.198–201)

If Shakespeare's knowledge of ancient representations is unclear, we can nevertheless reconstruct from contemporary evidence what the playgoers would have seen if the goddess appeared on her altar in *The Two Noble Kinsmen.*

Whether in the form of a statue or painted image, her skin would appear exceptionally fair: Venus refers to the "ivory girdle of my armes" and to "my white fingers" in Heywood's *Brazen Age* (2.184). Her body would be nude or only partially draped; "The statue of Venus," says Chaucer, "Was naked, fletyunge in the large see" (lines 1955–56). The goddess of love would wear pearl and gold jewelry; her blonde hair would be adorned with roses. Chaucer says, "on hir heed, ful semely for to se, / A rose gerland, fressh and wel smellynge" (lines 1960–61). In his prayer Shakespeare's Palamon specifically refers to a floral wreath: "Take to thy grace / Me thy vow'd soldier, who do bear thy yoke / As 'twere a wreath of roses" (5.1.94–96). The account of an Italian entertainment contains an assemblage of features belonging to Venus: "at Milan in 1594 a commentator declares that she came on stage 'quite naked, very white, with a garland of roses in her golden hair.' "[259]

If Venus is conveyed in a chariot, doves draw the vehicle; Cartari notes that these birds are pleasing to the goddess because "they are most abundantly inclined to procreation" (sig. Cc3r). If Venus is not ensconced in a chariot, the birds may accompany her or decorate her veil or garment. In Daniel's *Vision of the Twelve Goddesses* Venus appears "in a mantle of dove-colour and silver embroidered with doves" (line 68). If she carries anything, it is likely to be fire or a flaming heart. In his prayer Palamon says, "To Phoebus thou / Add'st flames, hotter than his; the heavenly fires / Did scorch his mortal son, thine him" (5.1.90–92). Finally, Venus would probably be accompanied by a winged and blindfold Cupid, armed with quiver, bow, and arrows in the manner described by Chaucer: "Biforn hire stood hir sone Cupido; / Upon his shuldres wynges hadde he two, / And blynd he was, as it is often seene; / A bowe he bar and arwes brighte and kene" (lines 1963–66). The author of *Soliman and Perseda*, like many other playwrights and poets, describes those wings as golden (2.2.35). Together Venus and her son personify the awesome power of passion.

Diana

Informing most representations of Diana (Greek Artemis) is her identity as a huntress who dwells in the forest.[260] Her encounter with Actaeon, related by Ovid (*Metamorphoses*, 3:138–253), was a favorite of Shakespeare's era: the hunter stumbled across the goddess while she was bathing in a sylvan pool. Hyginus succinctly recounts the ensuing action: "He caught sight of the goddess, and to keep him from telling of it, she changed him into a stag. As a stag, then, he was mangled by his own hounds" (139). The myth, depicted by Rubens, Titian, and countless printmakers, as well as by the designer of a fountain at Nonsuch palace,[261] underscores Diana's destructive power, the danger signified by her weaponry. In Hesiod's "Homeric Hymn" Artemis/Diana possesses both a golden bow and golden arrows: "I sing of Artemis, whose shafts are of gold, who cheers on the hounds, the pure maiden, shooter of stags.... she draws her golden bow, rejoicing in the chase, and sends out grievous shafts" (Hesiod, 453). Inspired by the ancients, Renaissance artists and playwrights typically assign Diana a bow, quiver, and arrows, though she may also wield a spear. In *The Golden Age* by Heywood, Diana appears in the company of satyrs and nymphs, "*garlands on their heads, and javelings in their hands*" (2.27). In this play the goddess names another accoutrement of hunting too, a bugle, which she wears slung over her shoulder (2.30). As a huntress, Diana is often accompanied by hounds of the kind that chased down and killed Actaeon.

Diana proves most fierce in the defense of virginity. When her nymph Callisto is seduced by Jupiter and becomes pregnant, an angry Diana changes her into a bear (*Metamorphoses*, 2:401–507), and the goddess would have her nymph killed had not Jupiter intervened and taken her to the heavens where she becomes a star. (A dumb show in Heywood's *Golden Age* dramatizes Callisto's plight [3.35].) Queen Elizabeth's status as an unmarried woman made Diana a popular personification in the second half of the sixteenth century. Elizabeth herself witnessed an entertainment at Gray's Inn in March 1565 and, according to the Spanish ambassador, "The plot was founded on the question of marriage, discussed between Juno and Diana."[262] The purpose was clearly to exalt the married state, for Jupiter decided in favor of Juno. At that point, said the ambassador, "The queen turned to me and said, 'This is all against me.'" At Kenilworth in 1575, similarly, George Gascoigne wrote a play that urged the supremacy of Juno over Diana, but the entertainment was never performed, perhaps because the queen had become resentful of those urging her to marry and, implicitly, criticizing her virgin status.[263]

In the 1580s Diana figured prominently on the stage, especially in comedies where the virgin deity exercises hegemony. In John Lyly's *Galatea* Diana proudly describes herself as "goddess of chastity, whose thoughts are always answerable to her vows, whose eyes never glanced on desire, and whose heart abateth the point of Cupid's arrows" (3.4.32–35). George Peele in *The Arraignment of Paris* recasts the judgment of Paris so that it no longer celebrates the victory of Venus. Instead, Diana puts the golden apple into the hands of Queen Elizabeth at the play's conclusion (5.1.1240.s.d.). In an extravagant compliment Peele's Diana makes explicit the parallel between her realm and Elizabeth's: "The place Elizium hight, and of the place, / Her name that governes there Eliza is, / A kingdome that may well compare with mine" (5.1.1150–52). As it became less likely that Elizabeth would marry and bear children, playwrights increasingly argued the claims of Diana over those of Juno (or Venus).

Although a chaste goddess who surrounds herself with virgins, Diana may also be associated with women in childbirth. In the "Hymn to Artemis" by Callimachus, the goddess explains, "the cities of men I will visit only when women vexed by the sharp pangs of childbirth call me to their aid – even in the hour when I was born the Fates ordained that I should be their helper, forasmuch as my mother suffered no pain either when she gave me birth or when she carried me in her womb, but without travail put me from her body."[264] Cicero relates this protective aspect of the goddess to her identity as moon deity. In *De Natura Deorum* he writes of the Greeks, "Diana they identify with the moon"; and he goes on to say, "the name *luna* is derived from *lucere* 'to shine': for it is the same word as *Lucina*, and therefore in our country Juno Lucina is invoked in childbirth, as is Diana in her manifestation as Lucifera (the light-bringer) among the Greeks" (bk. 2, chap. 27). Chaucer preserves this identity in *The Knight's Tale* when he describes Diana's temple: "A womman travaillynge was hire biforn; / But for hir child so longe was unborn, / Ful pitously Lucyna gan she calle" (lines 2083–85). Shakespeare's Pericles, similarly, calls upon the goddess when his wife goes into labor:

Lucina, O!
Divinest patroness, and midwife gentle
To those that cry by night, convey thy Deity
Aboard our dancing boat, make swift the pangs
Of my queen's travails!   (3.1.10–14)

Later Diana appears to Pericles in a vision[265] and presides over the reunion with his wife at the deity's temple in Ephesus,[266] prompting Pericles to cry out, "Hail, Dian!" (5.3.1) and "Immortal Dian!" (line 36).[267]

Unlike Pericles, Emilia in *The Two Noble Kinsmen* envisions Diana in her capacity as protectress of virgins. At the deity's altar, the woman sought by both Palamon and Arcite asks that, if she is not to have the man who loves her best, then "grant / The file and quality I hold I may / Continue in thy band" (5.1.160–62). Relief would seem to be at hand for this young woman kneeling at the altar of the goddess who protects virgins: only moments earlier Emilia entered with her retinue, "*one before her carrying a silver hind, in which is convey'd incense and sweet odors, which being set upon the altar of Diana, her maids standing aloof, she sets fire to it; then they curtsy and kneel*" (5.1.136.s.d.). The atmosphere is quiet, dignified, serene. But the stillness conceals menace, a menace implicit in the very artifact that lies at the center of the ceremony – the silver hind. Deer, known for their skittishness, have good reason to be timid when they roam the forest: they are a favorite target of hunters, and no hunter is more formidable than Diana herself.

Even a deity accustomed to hearing entreaties of all sorts must find Emilia's prayer strange. To the single-minded goddess, Emilia presents a psyche too hopelessly irresolute to be truly conflicted:

I am bride-habited,
But maiden-hearted. A husband I have pointed,
But do not know him. Out of two I should
Choose one, and pray for his success, but I
Am guiltless of election. Of mine eyes
Were I to lose one, they are equal precious,
I could doom neither; that which perish'd should
Go to't unsentenc'd.   (5.1.150–57)

Given Emilia's predicament and her preference to continue in Diana's "band" only if she is fated *not* to marry the more deserving man, it is hardly surprising that the deity's answer to her prayer should be so peculiar. In Boccaccio's *Teseida*, which inspired Chaucer's *Knight's Tale*, in turn the inspiration for *The Two Noble Kinsmen*, the goddess responds variously. First, "the arrows of beautiful Diana's quiver resounded and her bow moved of its own accord."[268] Second, "The enkindled brands seemed like blood, and their spent heads wept such tears that they extinguished the coals." Presumably Shakespeare could not duplicate the latter action (also recounted by Chaucer) at either the Globe or the Blackfriars, for that special effect exceeded the resources of his stage; drops of blood at the end of brands would not likely have been visible to playgoers even if those drops could somehow have been produced. And in any event the significance of bloody brands weeping tears might well have remained as mysterious to Shakespeare's playgoers as they are to Boccaccio's Emilia, who "returned to her room as uncertain as she had been when she came out." Hence the playwright substitutes something else entirely – only a little less enigmatic – for Diana's response: "*Here the hind vanishes under the altar, and in the place ascends a rose tree, having one rose upon it*" (5.1.162.s.d.). Moments later,

"*Here is heard a sudden twang of instruments, and the rose falls from the tree, which vanishes under the altar*" (line 168.s.d.). Emilia describes what she sees: "The flow'r is fall'n, the tree descends" (line 169), presumably through the trap door in the floor of the stage.

The rose at Diana's altar has complicated iconographic implications. Although the flower was, as we have seen, associated with Venus from ancient times, it could have a very different significance in a Christian context. St. Elizabeth of Hungary, who left her family to become a nun, is identified with the flower.[269] For Christians the color of the rose can have a specific meaning, the red rose typically symbolizing martyrdom: "In the third century, Saint Cyprian exhorted Christians to die for their faith and win the 'red crown of roses.'"[270] The white rose is associated with purity, especially virginity: "The rose is a frequent symbol for the Virgin Mary, who is called a 'rose without thorns' since she was free of original sin. This may refer to St. Ambrose's legend that the rose grew, without thorns, in the Garden of Eden."[271] Painters sometimes depict the Virgin amid roses.[272] Thus in a German painting of the early fifteenth century, the Virgin Mary, seated in front of a trellis of roses, hands a white rose to her infant son.[273] Similarly, Domenico Veneziano, in the mid-fifteenth century, paints the Madonna and child in a bower of roses.[274]

Shakespeare in *A Midsummer Night's Dream* brings together the disparate symbolism of the flower when Duke Theseus advises a stubborn Hermia that marriage is preferable to a life of lonely solitude:

> examine well your blood,
> Whether (if you yield not to your father's choice)
> You can endure the livery of a nun,
> For aye to be in shady cloister mew'd,
> To live a barren sister all your life,
> Chaunting faint hymns to the cold fruitless moon.
> Thrice blessed they that master so their blood
> To undergo such maiden pilgrimage;
> But earthlier happy is the rose distill'd,
> Than that which withering on the virgin thorn
> Grows, lives, and dies in single blessedness.
>
> (1.1.68–78)

The mixed, even contradictory, symbolic heritage of the rose makes it particularly evocative of Emilia's plight in *The Two Noble Kinsmen*: she is a woman destined for marriage but seeking a future without a husband. As a symbol the rose evokes at once the passionate love she fears and the virginity she would preserve.

Appearing onstage in Shakespeare's *Pericles* or on the altar in *The Two Noble Kinsmen*, Diana would be youthful in appearance, her hair unbound in the manner of unmarried women. A painting of Diana by Frans Floris depicts the goddess in this fashion,[275] as does the rendering of a masque that forms part of the birth-to-death painting of Sir Henry Unton; here Diana's hair extends down to her waist.[276] Isaac Oliver's miniature painting of Diana also shows her tresses falling over her shoulders; that hair is decorated with a strand of pearls, which are draped over her forehead; she wears pearl earrings as well.[277]

Diana would be clad as a huntress, presumably in tunic and sandals or boots. Inigo Jones' sketch of Diana, probably for Jonson's *Time Vindicated to Himself and to His Honors*, depicts her with a long loose dress tucked under her breasts (O&S, 1:126). (Callimachus had said that Diana wears a "tunic with embroidered border reaching to the knee."[278]) Her clothing may be green, suggestive of her sylvan abode, as it is in *The Knight's Tale* (line 2079) and in Samuel Daniel's *Vision of the Twelve Goddesses* (line 75). During the masque in *Woodstock* (first performed c. 1594–95), moreover, Diana's knights are clad "*in green*" (4.2.124.s.d.).[279] And in *The Lord Hay's Masque* by Thomas Campion, performed Twelfth Night 1607, Diana turns into trees the knights of Apollo, who in their metamorphosed state wear robes "*of green taffeta cut into leaves*" (lines 413–14).[280] Speaking to the deity in *The Two Noble Kinsmen*, Emilia mentions the same color – "thy rare green eye" (5.1.144) – though this need not have any significance for Diana's dress.

It is equally likely that Diana's garments are silver, in keeping with her role as moon deity. At a courtly entertainment at Milan in 1594, Diana was "dressed in a silver skirt, tucked up"; and she wore "silver sandals."[281] In Shakespeare's *Pericles* she is called "Celestial Dian, goddess argentine" (5.1.250), and, addressing Pericles, Diana speaks of her "silver bow" (line 248). In *The Two Noble Kinsmen* Emilia evokes the same color when she calls Diana "sacred silver mistress" (5.1.146); and, as we have seen, an attendant carries a "*silver hind*" to the deity's altar. Henry Peacham indicates the symbolic significance of such objects when he writes that silver "signifieth purity, innocency, and chastity."[282] It is also possible that Diana's garments are white, the color traditionally associated with purity and virginity. Thomas Heywood in *Troia Britanica* writes that Diana's garments are "angell like, of virgin-white."[283] In Robert White's *Cupid's Banishment*, performed before Queen Anne on 4 May 1617, Diana is "attird all in white to shew the / purity of Chastity" (lines 150–51).[284] Later in this masque Diana observes that her nymphs, "retird from the leavy wods, / have left theire wonted habitts all of greene," and now "deckt all in virgins' hue they come to see / faire Albions queene" (lines 548–49, 553–54). In *The Two Noble Kinsmen* Emilia envisions the same color as she addresses Diana:

O sacred, shadowy, cold, and constant queen,
Abandoner of revels, mute, contemplative,
Sweet, solitary, white as chaste, and pure
As wind-fann'd snow, who to thy female knights
Allow'st no more blood than will make a blush.
                              (5.1.137–41)

Perhaps it is best to imagine Diana's garments as silvery white, for the *OED* gives as one meaning of *silver* "having the whiteness or lustre of silver." In John Lyly's *The Woman in the Moon*, a character is described as having a "forehead whiter than the silver moon's."[285] In Robert White's *Cupid's Banishment*, where Diana is attired "all in white," she has a "mantle / of silver tinsie [i.e., tinsel]" (lines 152–53). And in Beaumont and Fletcher's *Philaster*, acted by the King's Men c. 1609, a character refers to silver coins as "white money" (2.2.55).[286] Of course, Diana may wear a combination of colors – both silvery white and green; in *The Lord Hay's Masque* the transformed knights don a "habit" consisting of green leaves "*laid upon cloth of silver*" (line 414).

The costume of Shakespeare's Diana would also draw upon the goddess's identification with the moon in a more obvious way. (In her capacity as moon deity, Diana may be known as Phoebe or as Cynthia, from her birthplace on Mount Cynthus in the island of Delos.) In Agostino di Duccio's bas-relief at the Tempio Malatestiano, Rimini, Diana as planetary god holds a large crescent moon in her hands.[287] An engraving by Etienne de Laune depicts Diana holding a smaller crescent in her outstretched hand.[288] Usually, though, the crescent moon appears as a decoration in her hair, just above her forehead, as it does in *The Vision of the Twelve Goddesses* where crescents also appear on her garments: in Daniel's masque Diana's mantle is "embroidered with silver half moons and a croissant of pearl on her head" (lines 75–76). *The Two Noble Kinsmen* explicitly identifies Diana with the moon governing the tides when Emilia says, "See what our general of ebbs and flows / Out from the bowels of her holy altar / With sacred act advances" (5.1.163–65).

Shakespeare's Diana would also be equipped with weaponry: when in 1578 Queen Elizabeth visited Norwich she saw a masque by Henry Goldingham in which "Diana presented a bowe and arrowes nocked

38 Diana in hunting garb. Drawing with red and black
chalk, brown ink, and gray wash, by Abraham Bloemaert.
The Nelson–Atkins Museum of Art, Kansas City, Missouri
(Bequest of Milton McGreevy) 81–30/5.

[i.e., notched] and headed with silver" (*Progresses of Elizabeth*, 2:163). Inigo
Jones' design for the temple of Diana in *Florimène* (1635) gives the same implements to the goddess, who stands upon a pedestal (O&S, 2:328). Diana
may carry a javelin too. Antonio Tempesta depicts the deity in her temple:
seated, she holds a bow in her right hand and a boarspear in her left.[289] One
or more hunting dogs customarily accompany Diana as they do in Giulio
Bonasone's print, where the standing deity holds a bow in one hand, an
arrow in the other.[290] Diana wears a hunting horn too, as she does in the
plaster frieze of the High Great Chamber in Hardwick Hall, Derbyshire.[291]
Abraham Bloemaert, in a drawing contemporaneous with *Pericles* and *Two
Noble Kinsmen*, brings together the principal features of her iconography:
Diana holds the leash of a dog in her right hand, a bow in her left; she has a
hunting horn slung over her shoulder and a quiver on her back; a crescent
moon adorns her head (fig. 38).

Hymen

Of all the mythological figures whom Shakespeare brings to the stage, none is more rare in classical literature than Hymen, god of marriage. Catullus, who sets forth the deity's chief characteristics, calls him "Urania's son, thou who bearest away the tender maid to her bridegroom."[292] Catullus names several features that would mark Hymen from antiquity to the Renaissance: "Bind thy brows with the flowers of fragrant marjoram, put on the marriage veil, hither, hither merrily come, wearing on thy snow-white foot the yellow shoe." Hymen wears marjoram because it was used to make wedding wreaths and because it was a symbol of fertility.[293] The god also holds a pine torch, symbolizing passion; Catullus enjoins Hymen, "wakening on this joyful day, singing with resonant voice the nuptial songs, beat the ground with thy feet, shake with thy hand the pine torch."[294] Ovid too invokes Hymen, specifying the torch and adding an outer garment colored to match the yellow shoe: "through the boundless air Hymen, clad in a saffron mantle, departed" (*Metamorphoses*, 10:1–2). The color Hymen wears is traditionally identified with romantic love: Ptolemy tells us that yellow is the color of Venus the planetary god.[295] John Ferne, in *The Blazon of Gentrie* (1586), adds that yellow signifies the season of the year associated with generation: springtime.[296] And Giovanni Paolo Lomazzo, citing Virgil, reports that newly married women in ancient Rome, anxious to become pregnant, "used to adorn their heads with a vaile" of yellow.[297]

Although Hymen appears less often in Renaissance poetry than the more familiar deities of Olympus, poets invoke him when writing about marriage. In his *Epithalamion*, for instance, Spenser says, "Hymen is awake / And long since ready forth his masque to move, / With his bright tead [torch] that flames with many a flake" (lines 25–27).[298] On the stage too references to Hymen occur in the context of weddings. In *The Wonder of Women, or The Tragedy of Sophonisba*, as the newly married Sophonisba prepares to go to bed with her husband, he says, "*Io* to Hymen!" (1.2.42); this stage direction follows: "*Chorus with cornets, organ, and voices: Io to Hymen!*"[299] In *The Tempest* Prospero bids his future son-in-law, "take heed, / As Hymen's lamps shall light you" (4.1.22–23). Later in this scene Iris tells Ceres that Ferdinand and Miranda will not observe love's rites "Till Hymen's torch be lighted" (line 97). The Player King in *Hamlet* reports of his wife that "Hymen did our hands / Unite comutual in most sacred bands" (3.2.159–60). All such references are predicated on the social and moral significance of the marriage ceremony. As Claudian remarks of Hymen, "Without his sanction is no entry into wedlock nor is it lawful but with his leave to uplift the first wedding-torches."[300]

During the reign of Elizabeth, Hymen necessarily occupied an infrequent part in pageantry honoring the virgin queen, especially when it came to seem unlikely that Elizabeth would marry.[301] At her reception in Norwich, 1578, she witnessed "an excellent princely maske" by Henry Goldingham during which Hymen was invoked only to be rebuked: "Himineus denyeth his good-will, eyther in presence, or in person: notwithstanding, Diana has so countre-checked him therefore, as he shall ever hereafter be at your commaundement" (*Progresses of Elizabeth*, 2:160). The essential incompatibility of marriage god and virginity is apparent in Robert White's *Masque of Cupid's Banishment* (1617). In the preface to the printed masque, the author deems it necessary to answer in advance "some curious criticke" who would demand, "what should Hymen have to doe where Diana is?" (*Progresses of James*, 3:284). With the accession of King James, Hymen becomes much more prominent in courtly entertainments. The deity appeared, for example, at a masque on 27 December 1604 celebrating the wedding of Sir Philip Herbert and Lady Susan de Vere, daughter of the Earl of Oxford. Although no details of the god's appearance survive, a description by Sir Dudley Carleton reveals that Hymen played an important role: "Their conceit was a representation of Juno's temple at the lower end of the great hall, which was vaulted, and within it the maskers seated with store of lights about them, and it was no ill show; they were brought in by the four seasons of the yeare and *Hymeneus*, which for songs and speeches was as good as a play."[302]

Ben Jonson makes the god of marriage central to his early masque *Hymenaei*, celebrating the wedding of the Earl of Oxford and Lady Frances Howard, daughter of the Earl of Suffolk. John Porry's account to Sir Robert Cotton focuses on Hymen's role: "The conceite or soule of the mask was Hymen bringing in a bride and Juno pronuba's priest a bridegroom, proclaiming those two should be sacrificed to nuptial union."[303] Although the costume design by Inigo Jones does not survive, Jonson's printed text of the masque provides an unusually full description: "*entered Hymen, the god of marriage, in a saffron colored robe, his under vestures white, his socks yellow, a yellow veil of silk on his left arm, his head crowned with roses and marjoram, in his right hand a torch of pine tree*" (lines 42–45). Jonson adds several features to previous descriptions: a contrast in color between outer and undergarments; the rose,[304] a flower identified with the goddess of love; and the placement of the veil over the left arm. Hymen also appears in Jonson's *Haddington Masque*, though no new details are given: "*Here the musicians attired in yellow, with wreaths of marjoram, and veils like Hymen's priests*" (lines 290–91).

In *Hymen's Triumph*, performed by young women on 3 February 1614 at Denmark (Somerset) House, Hymen arrives in disguise and enumerates the paraphernalia that would ordinarily reveal his identity:

In this disguise and pastorall attire,
Without my saffron robe, without my torch,
Or other ensignes of my duty:
I Hymen am come hither secretly,
To make Arcadia see a worke of glory.[305]

Hymen also appears as part of a dumb show in *The Spanish Tragedy*, acted c. 1587. No stage directions describe the procession seen by playgoers, but Revenge summarizes the pantomime:

The two first, the nuptial torches bore,
As brightly burning as the mid-day's sun:
But after them doth Hymen hie as fast,
Clothed in sable, and a saffron robe,
And blows them out and quencheth them with blood,
As discontent that things continue so.

(3.15.30–35)[306]

Though unusual, the sable garment is, of course, appropriate to the denouement of this play, wherein the dynastic marriage of Bel-imperia and Balthazar will be prevented by their bloody deaths. More customary are Hymen's appearances as a masquer in Aston Cokayne's *Trappolin Creduto Principe* (written in 1632) and *The Obstinate Lady* (written c. 1629–31); in the latter Hymen is addressed: "thou fellow that always wear'st yellow, / Draw near in thy frock of saffron" (4.3.35–36).[307]

Inga-Stina Ewbank has written that "No device could better provide the sense of social occasion around a marriage than the masque, and any play which contains a wedding is almost bound to contain a marriage masque."[308] George Chapman in *The Widow's Tears* (acted c. 1605 by the Queen's Revels Children) brings to the stage a character who impersonates the god of marriage. Referring to a chorus of sylvans, one character says to another, "The device is rare; and there's your young nephew too, he hangs in the clouds deified with Hymen's shape" (3.2.13–15).[309] Although that "shape" is not further described, a stage direction specifies that "*Hymen descends*" (3.2.80.s.d.), indicating that, like other deities, he arrives from the heavens.[310] His entry, moreover, is accompanied by

six sylvans carrying torches (line 80.s.d.), and later in the scene Hymen
refers to having searched groves and thickets "With this clear-flamed and
good-aboding torch" (line 92).[311] A character also impersonates Hymen in
Thomas Middleton's *Women Beware Women* (acted in 1621 at an undetermined venue): "*Enter Hymen in yellow*" (5.2.50.s.d.).[312] We learn virtually
nothing of Hymen's appearance except that he bears a drinking vessel: "To
thee, fair bride, Hymen offers up / Of nuptial joys this the celestial cup"
(5.2.51–52). In defiance of expectation this cup contains a lethal potion
designed to effect a revenge.[313]

Perhaps because of such onstage impersonations by theatrical characters,
Shakespeareans sometimes doubt that the Hymen who appears at the close
of *As You Like It* is meant to be the deity himself: "It is left to the producer
to decide whether the masque shall be plainly a charade got up by Rosalind,
or whether it is pure magic, like the masque in *The Tempest*, in which the
actors were 'all spirits.'"[314] Agnes Latham notes that the role of Hymen "is
often given to Amiens, whose entrance is indicated in F[olio] but who has
nothing to say."[315] (Some productions omit Hymen entirely: "The final
scene has been criticized for clumsiness and cut about in performance,
with Hymen eliminated from several acting versions."[316]) However, as Alan
Brissenden points out, "the text does nothing to suggest that he is anything
other than a god: not Amiens, or another lord, or William, or anyone else,
dressed up"; he adds, "There is no reason why this should not be an early
theophany, a precursor of the appearances of Jupiter in *Cymbeline* and
Diana in *Pericles*."[317] Hymen, who has no precedent in Thomas Lodge's
Rosalynde, contributes to *As You Like It* a sense of ritual appropriate to a
momentous occasion: no fewer than four romantic relationships culminate
in marriage.

If the extant stage directions in *As You Like It* tell us nothing about how
the character looked in the theatre ("*Enter Hymen*" [5.4.107.s.d.]), those in
The Two Noble Kinsmen, where Hymen forms part of a marriage procession,
provide only a little more information: "*Enter Hymen with a torch burning;
a boy, in a white robe, before, singing and strewing flow'rs; after Hymen, a
nymph, encompass'd in her tresses, bearing a wheaten garland*" (1.1.0.s.d.).
Except for the marriage torch, no other details describe Hymen in this play,
otherwise so rich in stage directions.

The visual arts, however, can supplement the rather meager poetic and
dramatic evidence.[318] An illustration in Vincenzo Cartari's mythographic
work represents the god of marriage wearing a garland of flowers in his
hair, holding a torch in his right hand, and a veil in his left; he wears a short
tunic and a larger, loose outer garment.[319] Giulio Strozzi's *Erotilla* depicts

Hymen on the title-page of the 1615 (Rome) edition: although he has no flowers on his head, he stands in front of a rose bush, as does Juno opposite him. Like Cartari's deity, this Hymen wears a tunic along with a larger outer mantle, which is draped over his shoulders; he also wears sandals and has a torch in his right hand.

Occasionally, Hymen appears older than the figures portrayed by Cartari and Strozzi. For instance, Hymen is a mature, bearded man holding a torch in a pageant welcoming Charles IX to Paris in 1571 and celebrating his marriage to Princess Elizabeth; next to Hymen, atop a fountain, stands winged Cupid; at his feet lies a goat, symbolic of lust.[320] Similarly, a mural by Veronese at the Villa Barbaro, Maser, portrays Hymen as a young man with a short beard.[321] Usually, though, Hymen is quite youthful, even boyish. Rubens, who painted his *Allegory of Peace and War* (1629–30) when he was living in England, portrays Hymen as a child.[322] Mythographers comment on the features of a deity so young that he gives the impression of effeminacy. Although Alain de Lille describes Hymen as of indeterminate age, now youthful, now mature ("On his face there showed no signs of feminine softness; rather the authority of manly dignity alone held sway there"), he goes on to assert defensively the masculinity of the figure: "his hair lay in orderly fashion to prevent it from appearing to degenerate into feminine softness by the vagaries of devious arrangements."[323] Classical precedent exists for an almost child-like appearance. Claudian describes Hymen's "snowy white" cheeks, clothed "with scarce seen down of youth where ceased the ne'er cut hair" ("Epithalamium of Palladius and Celerina," 2:209). Inspired by such accounts, George Chapman, in his continuation of *Hero and Leander*, writes that Hymen "was a youth so sweet of face, / That many thought him of the femall race" (lines 93–94).[324] Phineas Fletcher characterizes Hymen's forehead as "almost maiden fair."[325]

Of unusual iconographic interest is a print by Jan van de Straeten (Stradanus): the youthful Hymen is elaborately dressed in vaguely classical fashion, wearing a long outer mantle, and inclining his head toward the torch he carries in his right hand (fig. 39). Beyond the torch are assembled the fruits of peace and civilization: chests overflowing with wealth, handsome plate and drinking vessels, splendid garments, a table set for a feast, and a large canopied bed; in the background people make their way to a church. On the other side of Hymen, a group of men are seated at table within the loggia of an imposing building; a troop of cavalry ride by; and a tournament is enacted before a large crowd. The creator of this composition clearly intends a parallel between the private and the public, between the marriage relationship and the other kinds of relationships that prevail

39 Hymen, his hair adorned with flowers, holds a torch. Engraving by Jan van de Straeten (Stradanus)

in a well-ordered society. The accompanying verses read, in part, "And just as concord secures tranquil peace among citizens / So no length of time will break a marriage contract." What the deity of marriage helps effect between husband and wife, the prince establishes within the body politic. The engraving, then, intends a political significance, one perhaps hinted at in *As You Like It*, when the couples joined in marriage prepare to leave the precincts of Arden and return to a court purged of its willful prince, and in *The Two Noble Kinsmen* when the prince, whose concern with ceremony and social obligation pervades the play, is led toward the temple by Hymen.

The Hymen of both *As You Like It* and *Two Noble Kinsmen* was almost certainly played by a boy, whose youth would suit the facial features and physique we see in most artistic representations; such a face and form signify innocence. Hymen's tunic would be white, the color of purity, while other articles of clothing – shoes, socks, and overmantle – would be yellow, a color associated with romantic love. Hymen's hair would be similarly colored: Thomas Heywood tells us that it is "golden."[326] Hymen would have flowers on his head (roses and marjoram), a veil over his left arm, and a torch in his right hand. Finally, his appearance would be accompanied by instrumental music: "still [i.e., soft] music" in *As You Like It* (5.4.107.s.d.), and music appropriate to the wedding procession in *The Two Noble Kinsmen*.

Epilogue

A paradox characterizes the appearance of deities in Shakespeare's late plays: that such momentous intervention in the dramatic action should be staged in ways that may seem contrived, conventional, or even archaic by the standards of Shakespeare's own day. Deities and personifications had long been a feature of English culture. Father Time, for example, had played a role in Elizabeth's coronation procession more than a half century before Shakespeare wrote *The Winter's Tale*, and even then Time would have looked thoroughly familiar to contemporaries of the young queen. Shakespeare makes no effort to soften the intrusion of such a figure into the fabric of the play; indeed, he does just the opposite. Like the various deities who populate the late plays, Father Time speaks in a way that sets him apart from the other characters. His is not supple blank verse but a stiffer poetry spoken in rhyme. So different is the speech of Time from that of the larger play that Shakespeareans, especially early in the twentieth century, supposed that a less accomplished collaborator must have been responsible for the lines.

If we are less likely than our forebears to find deities and personifications a blemish, it is because we have come to appreciate their theatrical contribution. The performance history of Shakespearean plays attests to the *coups de théâtre* possible when a deity descends from the heavens. A production of *As You Like It*, directed by Audrey Stanley, is illustrative. At the end of the play Hymen made a spectacular appearance. Playgoers witnessed "the descent from far above of a golden, eight-foot-tall figure of Hymen . . . who, backed with a golden sunburst, provided his benediction. The overall effect was highly moving and was best summed up by a five-year-old boy who, at the climax, asked: 'Oh, Mommy, can a god do that for us?' "[327] That child attests to the emotional power of a theophany, wherein the spectacle is inseparable from the meaning of the dramatic action.

Seeing *The Tempest* in a 1992 performance at London's Barbican Theatre convinced me that there is nothing naive about either the appearance or the action of deities in Shakespeare's late plays. Everything about this production was initially strange, for the actors, director, and set were all Japanese. Translated into that language, the play was adapted to an Asian setting. The locale became Sado, a bleak island in the Sea of Japan. Prospero became Neami, a founder of Noh theatre, banished to that island in 1434. The magician, then, combined the roles of exile and impresario. His betrothal pageant necessarily owed little to the iconography of classical Greece and Rome. No longer Roman gods, the deities wore the costume of Noh drama – kimonos and headdresses. Their entry was accompanied by a particularly haunting music, and they moved with the utmost formality. Far from evoking mirth, the combination of sight and sound created a genuine sense of wonderment. Never have I experienced a more sublime moment in the theatre. What Yukio Ninagawa, the director, achieved through the stylization of Prospero's pageant was much like the effect achieved by Jacobean masquemakers, who, preferring artifice to realism, brought the gods into the midst of people.

Conclusion

When his wife, Christina Muller, died, Bartholomeus Spranger, an artist born in Antwerp, memorialized her by turning to his craft: he made a drawing that Aegidius Sadeler II would convert into a print. The engraving, dated 1600, presents a sad-eyed Christina, her expression an intimation of calamity, as though she foresaw her own death (fig. 40). Her garb is that of a well-to-do woman in the prime of life, the ruff round her neck proclaiming her social status. The artist, however, has not sought to prettify his wife. She is no great beauty; she wears no visible jewelry; a nondescript cap mostly covers her hair. If we possessed a photo of Christina to place beside the print, we would discover, I believe, that Spranger has fashioned a remarkable likeness. He pays his wife the compliment of setting down her features with scrupulous accuracy.

The portrait of Christina appears within an oval frame that, in turn, rests upon a tomb. A memorial to a woman prematurely struck down, the print also conveys this woman's relationship to her husband and his feeling of loss. Balancing the portrait of Christina on the right side of the engraving, Spranger creates a self-portrait on the left. Like Christina, he looks out at the observer. His forehead is furrowed, his brows contracted in pain. And although he engages us with his eyes, he points a finger toward his wife as if to say: don't look at me, look at her.

If the print consisted only of the two portraits, we would know little about this couple except that they are husband and wife, the relationship made explicit by the inscription around the frame bordering Christina's image. The artist, however, wants us to understand their identities, and to accomplish this purpose he fills the design with a panoply of personifications. On one side of Christina's tomb, beneath the oval, sits Faith, a cross in one hand, an open book in the other. On the other side we see Wisdom represented by armed Minerva, her eyes downcast, a torch downturned. Between these two a putto gazes upward at Christina; an embodiment of Vanitas, he cradles a skull while treading on an hourglass. At his feet lie the tools of an artist and sculptor, an allusion to Spranger's profession. On the opposite side of the print, behind the artist, are three female figures who represent the Visual Arts. Above them flies winged Fame, an evocation of

40 Portrait of the artist and his wife. Engraving by Aegidius Sadeler II after Bartholomeus Spranger

Spranger's renown (he had worked for Cardinal Alessandro Farnese and Pope Pius V, and he had become court painter to Rudolf II in Prague). Together the various symbolic figures provide a context for reading the portraits: we know the salient features of Christina's character and mind, as well as her husband's occupation and accomplishments.

What separates the portraits and their respective clusters of personifications are two figures who quite literally come between husband and wife. Father Time, holding a huge scythe, stretches out a long arm toward Spranger while, below, Death wields his arrow. With a bony arm Death also grasps a rough block of stone, as if for use as a weapon. The line formed by Death's arm combines with the line of Time's torso to create a vertical demarcation between husband and wife. Time and Death provide the key to understanding what has happened: together they have effected a separation, consigning Christina and Bartholomeus to different realms. Time and Death also tell us the most important truth we need to know about the marriage of this man and woman – that theirs was a loving relationship. Death's arrow, we notice, is pointed not at Christina but at her husband's heart.

We can easily imagine a print consisting simply of the two portraits, and such a print could well make a claim on our emotions by the facial expressions of the deceased and the survivor. But Spranger has chosen not to offer the portraits alone. Instead, he fills the composition with no fewer than nine personifications, and he allows Time and Death to dominate by placing them at the very center. This artistic strategy makes for a powerfully engaging design. First, Spranger creates a sense of drama in what otherwise would be a static composition. Especially by giving Time and Death action to perform, he makes menace dynamic. Second, artist and wife become victims not of impersonal forces but of purposeful hostile intent. Formidable adversaries enhance the couple's stature. Third, Spranger connects his personal experience with that of the observer: the artist universalizes the particular pain of his grief. Every one of us, after all, feels the sharpness of Time's scythe and Death's arrow. Without those personified figures – stretching and threatening – Spranger's design would lose much of its capacity to compel and disturb.

The impulse toward both realistic rendering of the human form and the lively visualization of imagined abstractions animates English artifacts of the Renaissance as well. A particularly fine exemplar is to be found near a Jacobean house twenty miles from London. Beside Hatfield House stands the medieval church of St. Ethelreda. Like other churches of its time, it functions as a place both of worship and of burial, and by far the grandest of its funeral monuments belongs to Sir Robert Cecil, the first Lord Salisbury and the man responsible for building Hatfield House.[1] To the modern eye, the tomb may seem distinctly odd. On a black marble platform raised several feet above the floor lies Cecil's recumbent form, sculpted in stone and attired in full regalia as Lord Treasurer, complete with staff of office.[2] Below on a parallel platform lies an effigy of Cecil's decomposed body, shorn of worldly accoutrements, scarcely more than a skeleton.[3] Looking from one tier to the other, the observer stands poised between past and future, contemplating the grandeur of what was and the dissolution to come.

Designing the tomb about 1615, Maximilian Colt treats his subject with extraordinary fidelity.[4] No detail of Cecil's appearance, either in life or death, is overlooked. The effigy atop the tomb closely resembles Cecil's form at the time of burial. Similarly, the decayed corpse below seems based on a first-hand acquaintance with the fate of human flesh following death. A masterpiece of realistic portrayal, the tomb demonstrates the knowledge of anatomy and the capacity to create convincing illusion that we identify with Renaissance sculptors and artists.

The same exactitude extends to the figures who appear at the corners of the tomb and whose identities are revealed by the objects in their hands: Fortitude rests a hand on a broken column; Temperance pours the contents of one jug into another; Prudence looks into her mirror; and Justice, a sword in her right hand, holds scales in the left. The close observation of the four females ensures the tomb's overall stylistic coherence: the sculptor minutely renders every detail, from strands of hair to folds of drapery.[5] The Cardinal Virtues seem almost more real than Cecil himself, for they exhibit the plasticity and animation of the human body in motion. So carefully wrought are they that, one imagines, the sculptor must have used actual women as models.

However finely rendered, the four Virtues possess no naturalistic existence, of course. They never breathed the air that Cecil breathed – never breathed at all. Within the tomb, however, they share the same space, inhabit the same world. And despite their status as abstractions, they are an indispensable part of the ensemble. Bearing the upper platform on their shoulders, they not only link the contrasting images of Cecil's body but also give the monument its essential meaning. Embodying the qualities that marked Cecil's character in life, the Virtues constitute a visual shorthand for his temperament and spirit, decisions and deeds, that ensure his salvation after death.

Perhaps no written work better exemplifies the twin impulses informing both Robert Cecil's tomb and Spranger's memorial print than Henry Peacham's *The Art of Drawing*, initially published in 1606 and revised a few years later. A manual of instruction, the treatise assumes that the reader knows little or nothing of artistic technique. In considerable detail, therefore, Peacham explains how to represent the face, body, drapery, and the like. For example, he cautions the reader about exactitude: "be carefull to give as precise an evenesse to one side [of the face] as to the other; causing both your lines to meete at the tip of the chin."[6] Similarly, shadowing requires the utmost precision: "first a single shadowe in the temples, than a double shadow in the corner of the eies, a circular shadow down the cheek, under the neather lip, a little under the nosethril, from the side of the nose to the corner of the mouth."[7] Such recommendations spring from Peacham's own experience as an artist and from his perusal of Continental prints by such engravers as Hendrik Goltzius and Jan van de Straten (Stradanus).

In 1612 Peacham brought out a revised version of *The Art of Drawing*. Called *Graphice*,[8] the new work preserves the careful attention to rendering the countenance, body, and so forth of the earlier edition. *Graphice*, however, includes much new material: "The Second Book of Drawing and

Limning" treats personifications of many kinds. The first chapter of this new section teaches "how, according to truth to purtract [portray] and expresse, Eternitie, Hope, Victorie, Pietie, Providence, Vertue, Time, Peace, Concord, Fame, Common Safetie, Clemencie, Fate, &c. as they have been by antiquitie described either in Comes [Natale Conti], statues, or other the like publike monuments."[9] Peacham is just as detailed in his description of personifications as he was formerly in treating human flesh, and the personifications are no mere afterthought. The revised book is nearly double the size of the original, and much of the revision is devoted to those personifications, which are indebted to Cesare Ripa's *Iconologia*.[10]

What we do not find in the new section of *Graphice* is what the modern reader expects: a preface, introduction, or other preliminary statement explaining the rationale of the added material.[11] Instead, the description of personifications is simply appended to the existing manual. We look in vain for some acknowledgment that the revised work moves in new directions, that the 1612 *Graphice* includes very different subject matter from its 1606 predecessor, though the title-page, casting a wide net in anticipating the readership of the expanded book, advertises its appeal to *divers Tradesmen and Artificers, as namly Painters, Joyners, Free-masons, Cutters and Carvers, &c. for the farther gracing, beautifying, and garnishing of all their absolute and worthie peeces, either for Borders, Architecks, or Columnes, &c.*[12] What accounts for the omission of some explanation for the personifications within the work itself?

Nicholas Hilliard's *The Art of Limning*, composed c. 1600 though not published until the twentieth century, points to an answer. This treatise provides a detailed account of painting in miniature, what Hamlet calls "picture in little" (2.2.346). Like Peacham, Hilliard approaches his subject pragmatically.[13] In straightforward fashion he explains "the best way and means to practice and attain to skill in limning."[14] Scrupulous observation, he writes, should be foremost in the painter's method, and the creation of convincing illusion should be foremost among his goals. Looking at a miniature portrait, the beholder confronts, ideally, the very likeness of a living, breathing person. In his articulation of purpose and procedures, Hilliard sounds much like Peacham (it's entirely possible that Peacham had read Hilliard's work in manuscript).[15] Both share an indebtedness to Richard Haydocke's translation of Giovanni Paolo Lomazzo's *Trattato dell'arte della pittura*.[16] Both admire the same artists (Holbein, Dürer, Goltzius). Both affirm the value of art and celebrate the accomplishment of artists. Both emphasize the accurate rendering of what the artist sees. Both give considerable attention to the preparation of colors.

There can be no doubting Hilliard's (or Peacham's) dedication to verisimilitude. The master of miniature painting explains the principle of imitation, however, in a way that may initially baffle today's reader: "Now know that all painting imitateth nature, or the life; in everything, it resembleth so far forth as the painter's memory or skill can serve him to express, in all or any manner of story work [narrative painting], emblem, impresa, or other device whatsoever."[17] If we wonder how the first half of Hilliard's sentence relates to the second, it is because the list of instances seems askew. Having articulated the importance of imitation, Hilliard names artifacts based on sometimes arcane symbolism. Michael Leslie underscores the problem: "What is interesting here . . . is that these essentially non-naturalistic and non-realist works are precisely those chosen by Hilliard as examples of the imitation of nature or 'the life' in art."[18] The artist gives no indication that he sees any inconsistency between fidelity of representation and "story work, emblem, impresa, or other device." The naturalistic and the symbolic are not merely juxtaposed – they are indissoluble. The symbolic becomes the logical extension of an imitation of nature. Or, perhaps more accurately, the larger nature expresses itself in symbolic terms.

Given this conflation by Hilliard, Peacham's decision to add instruction on portraying personifications to his instruction on portraying the human face and form becomes explicable. The major sections of *Graphice*, in their different ways, serve the principle of imitation, broadly defined. Had Spranger and Colt produced treatises of their own, moreover, they would have embraced the attitudes of Hilliard and Peacham, for none of these artists finds any incongruity between, on the one hand, the depiction of individuals closely observed by the eye and, on the other, the depiction of concepts seen by the imagination. All of these men belong to an artistic era equally at home in the delineation of both recognizable historical figures and anthropomorphic constructions. Wherever we look in the arts of fifteenth-, sixteenth-, and seventeenth-century Europe, we find innumerable instances of both, whether the medium takes the form of paint, stone, plaster, bronze, ink, or words. So prevalent is the combination of realistic representation and conceptual abstraction that it may be considered nothing less than a defining characteristic of Renaissance culture.

Notes

Introduction

1. John Strype, *Annals of the Reformation and Establishment of Religion, and Other Various Occurrences in the Church of England; During the First Twelve Years of Queen Elizabeth's Happy Reign* (London, 1709), 239.

2. Ibid. Sergiusz Michalski, in *The Reformation and the Visual Arts: The Protestant Image Question in Western and Eastern Europe* (London and New York: Routledge, 1993), observes that Martin Luther suggested "putting inscriptions on the walls of churches, and he proposed placing around the representation of the Last Supper a golden inscription with a quotation from the Bible; but these were only casual utterances" (41).

3. Richard Haydocke, preface to *A Tracte Containing the Artes of curious Paintinge, Carvinge & Buildinge* (Oxford, 1598), sig. ¶5r–v. This book is a partial translation of Giovanni Paolo Lomazzo's *Trattato dell'arte de la pittura, scoltura ed architettura* (Milan, 1584). In quoting from early books such as this and modern original-spelling editions, I have made minor changes: *i/j*, *u/v*, and long *s* appear as they would in a modern text. Printers' abbreviations have been silently expanded. In most instances capital letters within sentences have been converted to lower-case.

4. Henry Peacham, *Graphice or The Most Auncient and Excellent Art of Drawing and Limming* (London, 1612), 8. Peacham's work was also issued with an alternate title: *The Gentleman's Exercise*.

5. Marguerite A. Tassi, "Lover, Poisoner, Counterfeiter: The Painter in Elizabethan Drama," *The Ben Jonson Journal* 7 (2000): 131.

6. Edward Norgate, *Miniatura or the Art of Limning*, ed. Jeffrey M. Muller and Jim Murrell (New Haven and London: Yale University Press for the Paul Mellon Centre for British Art, 1997), 105–06.

7. Translated from the original Latin by James Lees-Milne, *Tudor Renaissance* (London: B. T. Batsford, 1951), 48. The Latin is quoted by Reginald Blomfield, *A History of Renaissance Architecture in England, 1500–1800*, 2 vols. (London: George Bell and Sons, 1897), I: 17.

8. Lees-Milne, *Tudor Renaissance*, 48.

9. Roy Strong, *The English Icon: Elizabethan and Jacobean Portraiture* (London: The Paul Mellon Foundation for British Art [with Routledge & Kegan Paul]; New Haven: Yale University Press, 1969), 1. The only exceptions to this generalization,

according to Strong, were those artifacts "dictated by necessity such as the advent of an embassy, or by renewal on account of decay." Strong's argument would seem to apply more accurately to Tudor monarchs than to Stuart. After all, the accession of King James I initiated a period of building and collecting, especially among the nobility. See Linda Levy Peck, "Building, Buying, and Collecting in London, 1600–25," in *Material London, ca. 1600*, ed. Lena Cowen Orlin (Philadelphia: University of Pennsylvania Press, 2000), 268–89.

10. Margaret Aston, in *England's Iconoclasts*, vol. I: *Laws Against Images* (Oxford: Clarendon Press, 1988), notes that in the sixteenth century "idolatry became deeply engraved on the English conscience. The Reformation made it the deadliest of sins and it was one which no believer could be unaware of" (343). See also John Phillips, *The Reformation of Images: Destruction of Art in England, 1535–1660* (Berkeley, Los Angeles, London: University of California Press, 1973); and Paul Corby Finney, ed., *Seeing Beyond the Word: Visual Arts and the Calvinist Tradition* (Grand Rapids, MI: William B. Eerdmans, 1999).

11. Simon Schama, in *Rembrandt's Eyes* (New York: Alfred A. Knopf, 1999), says of Honthorst's commission, "The painting was such a tremendous success that the King redoubled his desperate attempts to have Honthorst remain in England, to no avail" (31).

12. Anthony Wells-Cole, *Art and Decoration in Elizabethan and Jacobean England: The Influence of Continental Prints, 1558–1625* (New Haven and London: Yale University Press for the Paul Mellon Centre for Studies in British Art, 1997).

13. Leonard Barkan, "Making Pictures Speak: Renaissance Art, Elizabethan Literature, Modern Scholarship," *Renaissance Quarterly* 48 (Summer 1995): 331.

14. Peacham, *Graphice*, sig. A2v.

15. "An Homyly agaynst perill of Idolatry and superfluous deckyng of Churches," in *The seconde Tome of Homelyes of such matters as were promised and Intituled in the former part of Homelyes, set out by the aucthoritie of the Queenes Majestie: And to be read in every paryshe Churche agreablye* (London, 1563), fol. 63r. This work is the second part of *Certaine Sermons appoynted by the Quenes Majesty, to be declared and read, by al Parsons, Vicars, & Curates, everi Sunday and holi day, in their Churches... Newely Imprinted in partes* (1563).

16. Lucy Gent, *Picture and Poetry 1560–1620: Relations between Literature and the Visual Arts in the English Renaissance* (Leamington Spa: James Hall, 1981), 16.

17. William Harrison, "The Description of Britaine," in Raphael Holinshed, *The Firste volume of the Chronicles of England, Scotlande, and Irelande* (London, 1577), fol. 85r.

18. Lisa Jardine, in *Worldly Goods* (London: Macmillan, 1996), observes that tapestries were far more expensive than paintings (26).

19. William Sheldon established his Barcheston workshop in the 1560s. Perhaps the most famous of the extant tapestries produced by Sheldon's workers are the Four Seasons, which today hang at Hatfield House, Hertfordshire. These tapestries are based on prints designed by Maarten de Vos. The season of Autumn is

reproduced in color by Gervase Jackson-Stops, ed., *The Treasure Houses of Britain: Five Hundred Years of Private Patronage and Art Collecting* (New Haven and London: Yale University Press; Washington, D.C.: the National Gallery of Art, 1985), 110–11. The Mortlake factory, a large operation established by James I in 1619, employed artisans from the Continent. Anthony Wells-Cole, in *Art and Decoration in Elizabethan and Jacobean England*, observes, "More than fifty weavers arrived secretly from the Netherlands under the leadership of Philip de Maecht: amongst them were weavers like Louis Dermoulen, who specialised in heads, and Pieter de Craigt, who specialised in flesh parts" (234).

20. *1 Henry IV*, in *The Riverside Shakespeare*, ed. G. Blakemore Evans et al., 2nd edn. (Boston and New York: Houghton Mifflin, 1997). All citations of Shakespeare in this book, unless otherwise indicated, are from this edition.

21. The paintings at Little Moreton Hall were not discovered until the late 1970s, when the National Trust removed oak paneling in the course of repair work. See E. Clive Rouse, "Elizabethan Wall Paintings at Little Moreton Hall," *National Trust Studies 1980* (London: Sotheby Parke Bernet, 1979): 112–18. Rouse observes, "The find is particularly important in that it has provided the Trust with its only extensive example (in a more modest property) of domestic wall decoration of late Elizabethan date" (113).

22. See Peter Thornton, *Seventeenth-Century Interior Decoration in England, France and Holland* (New Haven and London: Yale University Press for the Paul Mellon Centre for Studies in British Art, 1978), 110–11. Only in the homes of the very wealthy were carpets likely to cover floors. See Santina M. Levey, *Elizabethan Treasures: The Hardwick Hall Textiles* (New York: Harry N. Abrams, 1998), 26–28.

23. In Thomas Heywood's *A Woman Killed with Kindness*, ed. R. W. Van Fossen, The Revels Plays (1961; reprint, London: Methuen, 1970), the servants in John Frankford's household "*spread a carpet* [on a table], *set down lights and cards*" (8.123.s.d.), following a meal.

24. Peggy Muñoz Simonds, *Myth, Emblem, and Music in Shakespeare's "Cymbeline": An Iconographic Reconstruction* (Newark: University of Delaware Press; London and Toronto: Associated University Presses, 1992), 131. Simonds' discussion of Imogen's chamber is consistently fascinating. Martin White has suggested to me that Jachimo's remark about "designs of raised plaster" may refer to the actual ceiling above the Blackfriars stage.

25. Hugh Platt, "The Art of Molding and Casting," in *The Jewell House of Art and Nature* (London, 1594), bk. 4, 67.

26. John Ferne, *The Blazon of Gentrie: Devided into two parts* (London, 1586), pt. 1, 29. According to Ferne, the heraldry of Adam consists of ashes, dust, and earth.

27. Timothy Mowl, in *Elizabethan and Jacobean Style* (London: Phaidon, 1993), writes: "Audley End is obviously the key and archetypical Jacobean house" (140).

28. "The Diary of Horatio Busino, Chaplain of Pietro Contarini, Venetian Ambassador in England," in *The Journals of Two Travellers in Elizabethan and Early Stuart England*, ed. P. E. Razzell (London: Caliban Books, 1995), 160.

29. Many such implements are on view today at the Museum of London.

30. See, for example, the sixteenth-century painting of Margaret Wyatt, reproduced by Sophie McConnell and Alvin Grossman, *Metropolitan Jewelry* (New York: The Metropolitan Museum of Art; Boston: Little, Brown, 1991), 41.

31. Peacham, *Graphice*, 7.

32. Reproduced by G. Blakemore Evans, ed., *The Riverside Shakespeare*, pl. 4.

33. Christopher Marlowe, *Edward the Second*, ed. Charles R. Forker, The Revels Plays (Manchester: Manchester University Press; New York: St. Martin's Press, 1994).

34. Eric Mercer, "The Decoration of the Royal Palaces from 1553–1625," *The Archaeological Journal* 110 (1953): 152.

35. Malcolm Airs, in *The Tudor and Jacobean Country House: A Building History* (London: Sutton Publishing in association with The National Trust, 1995), observes: "Considerable amounts of re-used glass were employed by Henry VIII's Office of Works, and monastic glass was carefully salvaged after the dissolution" (129).

36. See Ruth Samson Luborsky and Elizabeth Morley Ingram, *A Guide to English Illustrated Books, 1536–1603*, 2 vols., Medieval and Renaissance Texts and Studies (Tempe: Arizona Center for Medieval and Renaissance Studies, 1998).

37. Reproduced by Susan Watkins, *In Public and in Private: Elizabeth I and Her World* (London: Thames and Hudson, 1998), 34.

38. Significantly, Peter Thornton's *Form and Decoration: Innovation in the Decorative Arts, 1470–1870* (London: Weidenfeld & Nicolson, 1998), which is arranged by city and period (beginning with Florence and Venice, 1470–1510), does not treat London until 1670–1730.

39. Mary E. Hazard, in *Elizabethan Silent Language* (Lincoln and London: University of Nebraska Press, 2000), writes: "One constant in Elizabethan style is manifest in every medium, the use of rich embellishment – whether in the golden flourish of Hilliard's inscriptions, the sugared conceit of the banquet subtlety, the curious fantasy of gold-threaded embroidery upon a lady's sleeve, the interplay of precious stones on a jeweled ornament, or the carved interstices of an architectural relief" (79).

40. For a description of furnishings and fittings in the houses of this era, see Lena Cowen Orlin, "'The Causes and Reasons of all Artificial Things' in the Elizabethan Domestic Environment," *Medieval and Renaissance Drama in England* 7 (1995): 19–75.

41. Harrison, "The Description of Britaine," in Holinshed, *The Firste volume*, fol. 85r.

42. Wendy Wall, *The Imprint of Gender: Authorship and Publication in the English Renaissance* (Ithaca, NY, and London: Cornell University Press, 1993), 190, n. 40.

43. Ben Jonson, *The Staple of News*, ed. Anthony Parr, The Revels Plays (Manchester: Manchester University Press; New York: St. Martin's Press, 1988), line 2 of the prologue for the stage. In the prologue for the court, Jonson makes a similar assertion: the play is "offered as a rite / To scholars, that can judge and fair report / The sense they hear, above the vulgar sort / Of nutcrackers, that only come for sight" (lines 5–8).

44. John Marston, *The Malcontent*, ed. George K. Hunter, The Revels Plays (London: Methuen, 1975), lines 34–37 of "To the Reader."

45. Andrew Gurr, *Playgoing in Shakespeare's London*, 2nd edn. (Cambridge: Cambridge University Press, 1996), 86. For a judicious assessment of the issue, see Gurr's section entitled "Audiences or Spectators," 86–98.

46. Huston Diehl, "Observing the Lord's Supper and the Lord Chamberlain's Men: The Visual Rhetoric of Ritual and Play in Early Modern England," *Renaissance Drama* n.s. 22 (1991): 167.

47. Stephen Gosson, *Playes Confuted in five Actions, Proving that they are not to be suffred in a Christian common weale* (London, 1582?), sig. Er.

48. Philip Stubbes, *The Anatomie of Abuses*, 4th edn. (London, 1595), 102.

49. T. W., *A Sermon preached at Pawles Crosse on Sunday the thirde of November 1577 in the time of the plague* (London, 1578), 46.

50. John Stockwood, *A Sermon Preached at Paules Crosse on Barthelmew day, being the 24 of August 1578* (London, [1578]), 134.

51. Quoted by Andrew Gurr, *The Shakespearean Stage, 1574–1642*, 3rd edn. (Cambridge: Cambridge University Press, 1992), 132. For the original Latin text, see E. K. Chambers, *The Elizabethan Stage*, 4 vols. (1923; reprint, Oxford: Clarendon Press, 1951), II: 361–62. De Witt notes that all four London amphitheatres – the Swan, Rose, Curtain, and Theatre – were "of notable beauty" (Gurr, *The Shakespeare Stage*, 132).

52. Chambers (3: 501) cites a letter dated 19 November 1602.

53. Reproduced by R. A. Foakes, *Illustrations of the English Stage, 1580–1642* (Stanford, CA: Stanford University Press, 1985), 73 (*Roxana*); 80 (*Messalina*). According to Chambers in *The Elizabethan Stage*, the picture of a stage on the title-page of *Roxana* "may be taken as representing a type of academic stage, as the play was at Trinity, Cambridge, *c.* 1592," while the stage depicted on the title page of *Messalina* is more likely to be the Salisbury Court theatre than the Fortune or Red Bull (II: 519).

54. Chambers, in *The Elizabethan Stage* (II: 437), quotes from the contract: "all the princypall and maine postes of the saide fframe and stadge forwarde shalbe square and wroughte palasterwise, with carved proporcions called satiers to be placed & sett on the topp of every of the same postes."

55. The drawings of the Cockpit in Drury Lane are reproduced by John Orrell, *The Theatres of Inigo Jones and John Webb* (Cambridge: Cambridge University Press, 1985), fig. 7. Worcester College, Oxford, owns the drawings, which have been dated c. 1616–18.

56. See John Ronayne, "Totus Mundus Agit Histrionem [The Whole World Moves the Actor]: The Interior Decorative Scheme of the Bankside Globe," in *Shakespeare's Globe Rebuilt*, ed. J. R. Mulryne and Margaret Shewring (Cambridge: Cambridge University Press, 1997), 121–46.

57. See Jean MacIntyre, *Costumes and Scripts in the Elizabethan Theatres* (Edmonton: University of Alberta Press, 1992). Although Stella Mary Newton, in *Renaissance Theatre Costume and the Sense of the Historic Past* (London: Rapp and Whiting, 1975), treats in detail costume in Continental entertainments, she declines to discuss English theatre: "documentary records of methods of production in the fifteenth and sixteenth centuries [in England] are scanty and pictorial representations seem to be even rarer" (23–24).

58. See the 5 February 1603 (new style) entry in *Henslowe's Diary*, ed. R. A. Foakes and R. T. Rickert (Cambridge: Cambridge University Press, 1961), which describes the purchase of "a womones gowne of black vellvett" (223).

59. Thomas Platter, in *The Journals of Two Travellers in Elizabethan and Early Stuart England*, 28.

60. See Ann Rosalind Jones and Peter Stallybrass, "The Circulation of Clothes and the Making of the English Theater," in *Renaissance Clothing and the Materials of Memory* (Cambridge: Cambridge University Press, 2000), 175–206.

61. Elaine Aston and George Savona, in *Theatre as Sign-System: A Semiotics of Text and Performance* (London and New York: Routledge, 1991), argue that "a compositional analogy is to be perceived between stage picture and painting, that stage pictures have been traditionally encoded in terms of the conventions of representation of realist art, and that the processes of decoding learnt for the purpose of 'reading' paintings are applicable equally to the stage picture" (156).

62. Strong, *The English Icon*, 30–31.

63. Gent, *Picture and Poetry*, 31. Gent goes on to observe that "the eyes of all but a very small handful of Elizabethans were uncultivated, in the sense that they were uneducated in looking at pictures" (33).

64. Huston Diehl, in *Staging Reform, Reforming the Stage: Protestantism and Popular Theater in Early Modern England* (Ithaca, NY, and London: Cornell University Press, 1997), traces the "intense interest in images and acts of seeing" on the Elizabethan and Jacobean stage to "the reformers' struggle to suppress a persistent iconophilia among the English people" (4).

65. One such print by Peter Flötner, c. 1525, depicts Justice, with her sword and scales, in stocks. Reproduced by Brian Gibbons, *Jacobean City Comedy* (Cambridge, MA: Harvard University Press, 1968), fig. 1. In *Youth*, performed during the Christmas season of 1513–14, Riot and Pride consign Charity to

the stocks. See T. W. Craik, *The Tudor Interlude: Stage, Costume, and Acting* (Leicester: Leicester University Press, 1962), for other such examples (94).

66. Scott McMillin and Sally-Beth MacLean, *The Queen's Men and Their Plays* (Cambridge: Cambridge University Press, 1998), 127.

67. See *An Edition of Robert Wilson's "Three Ladies of London" and "Three Lords and Three Ladies of London,"* ed. H. S. D. Mithal, The Renaissance Imagination 36 (New York and London: Garland, 1988). McMillin and MacLean, in *The Queen's Men*, offer valuable commentary on Wilson's dramaturgy (121–31).

68. Roelof van Straten provides a useful definition: "We can generally define a personification in the visual arts as a human or anthropomorphic figure who represents an abstract idea or concept, such as Prudence" (*An Introduction to Iconography*, trans. Patricia de Man, rev. English edn. [Yverdon, Switzerland, and Langhorne, PA: Gordon and Breach, 1994], 25).

69. Andrew Gurr and Mariko Ichikawa, in *Staging in Shakespeare's Theatres*, Oxford Shakespeare Topics (Oxford: Oxford University Press, 2000), observe: "Everything used to dress and equip the players on the early stages was symbolic" (53).

70. Alvin Kernan, "The Plays and the Playwrights," in *The Revels History of the Drama in English*, vol. III: *1576–1613* (London: Methuen, 1975), 399. Kernan writes, "One of the distinctive features of the Renaissance drama is its persistent, easy maintenance of a double focus."

71. George R. Kernodle, *From Art to Theatre: Form and Convention in the Renaissance* (1944; reprint. Chicago and London: University of Chicago Press, 1964), 2.

72. *Londons Jus Honorarium, Exprest in sundry triumphs, pagiants, and shews,* in *Thomas Heywood's Pageants: A Critical Edition*, ed. David M. Bergeron, The Renaissance Imagination 16 (New York and London: Garland, 1986), 25.

73. *The Magnificent Entertainment Given to King James*, in *The Dramatic Works of Thomas Dekker*, ed. Fredson Bowers, 4 vols. (Cambridge: Cambridge University Press, 1953–61), II: 295.

74. Jean MacIntyre and Garrett P. J. Epp, "'Cloathes worth all the rest': Costumes and Properties," in *A New History of Early English Drama*, ed. John D. Cox and David Scott Kastan (New York: Columbia University Press, 1997), 270. Similarly silent on the issue is the 600-page *A Companion to Renaissance Drama*, ed. Arthur F. Kinney (Oxford: Blackwell, 2002).

75. Henry Peacham, *The Compleat Gentleman* (London, 1634), 104. Peacham makes these remarks in a chapter entitled "Of Antiquities," which he added to this second and much enlarged edition of the work.

76. Ibid., 109.

77. Ibid.

78. Peacham's contemporaries could have known about ancient coins not only by handling the coins themselves but also by examining works that reproduced them. See, for example, *Deorum dearumque capita ex vetustis numismatibus*

in gratiam antiquitatis studiosorum effigiata et edita (Antwerp, 1573), a book of prints by Philips Galle. In addition to the depiction of various gods, the book contains such personifications as Justice, Liberty, Peace, Piety, Hope, and Virtue. Another edition of *Deorum dearumque capita* appeared in 1602; here commentaries in Latin accompany the pictures. See also A. R. Braunmuller, "Thomas Marsh, Henry Marsh, and the Roman Emperors," *The Library*, 6th Series, 6 (March 1984): 25–38.

79. Peacham may refer to *Antiquarum statuarum urbis Romae, quae in publicis privatisque locis visuntur, icones* (Rome, 1584). This book brings together some sixty-one woodcuts, most by Giovanni Battista Cavalieri; each is based on an ancient sculpture and identified by a brief label (e.g., "Bellona marmorea in hortis Cardinalis Ferrariæ"). Similar in format is *Icones statuarum antiquarum urbis Romae, Hieronymi Franzini bibliopolae ad signum fontis opera* (Rome, 1598), which contains woodcuts of Roman statues, historical personages, and various deities.

80. Although scholars have tended to neglect such pageants, seeing them merely as contributions to the evolution of the masque, David M. Bergeron, in *Practicing Renaissance Scholarship: Plays and Pageants, Patrons and Politics* (Pittsburgh, PA: Duquesne University Press, 2000), argues persuasively that civic pageants need to be seen as achievements in their own right (164–92).

81. See Marie Axton, *The Queen's Two Bodies: Drama and the Elizabethan Succession* (London: Royal Historical Society, 1977), 132.

82. For an account of Elizabeth's procession through London, especially in the context of medieval civic triumphs, see Gordon Kipling, *Enter the King: Theatre, Liturgy, and Ritual in the Medieval Civic Triumph* (Oxford: Clarendon Press, 1998), 125–29.

83. Henri Estienne, *The Art of Making Devises: Treating of Hieroglyphicks, Symboles, Emblemes, Ænigma's, Sentences, Parables, Reverses of Medalls, Armes, Blazons, Cimiers, Cyphres and Rebus*, trans. Thomas Blount (London, 1648), 15.

84. "The *impresa* has only two parts where the emblem has three" (Peter M. Daly, *Literature in the Light of the Emblem: Structural Parallels between the Emblem and Literature in the Sixteenth and Seventeenth Centuries*, 2nd edn. [Toronto, Buffalo, London: University of Toronto Press, 1998], 27).

85. At about the same time that the King's Men were performing *Pericles* at the Globe, c. 1608–09, the King's Revels Children were performing *The Insatiate Countess* at the Whitefriars. In this play originally drafted by John Marston and completed by William Barksted and Lewis Machin, masquers present "*shields to their several mistresses*" (2.1.48.s.d.); the Latin mottoes on the shields are read aloud and the symbolic pictures are then interpreted. See John Marston and others, *The Insatiate Countess*, ed. Giorgio Melchiori, The Revels Plays (Manchester and Dover, NH: Manchester University Press, 1984).

86. William Camden, *Remaines concerning Britaine*, 5th impression (London, 1636), 341.

87. Rosemary Freeman, *English Emblem Books* (London: Chatto and Windus, 1948), 15. Similarly, Dieter Mehl, in *The Elizabethan Dumb Show: The History of A Dramatic Convention* (London: Methuen, 1965), writes that the technique of emblems "is remarkably similar to that of the early dumb shows and reveals the same liking for puzzles and allegories as do the pantomimes and pageants" (13).

88. John Webster, *The White Devil*, ed. John Russell Brown, The Revels Plays (1960; reprint, London: Methuen, 1967).

89. Allardyce Nicoll, *Stuart Masques and the Renaissance Stage* (1938; reprint, New York: Benjamin Blom, 1968), 155.

90. For a survey of the European print, see David Landau and Peter Parshall, *The Renaissance Print, 1470–1550* (New Haven and London: Yale University Press, 1994).

91. Walter L. Strauss, *The Complete Drawings of Albrecht Dürer*, 6 vols. (New York: Abaris Books, 1974), II: 1074.

92. Evelyn Lincoln, in *The Invention of the Italian Renaissance Printmaker* (New Haven and London: Yale University Press, 2000), draws a useful contrast between printed words and printed pictures: "While the type set for printing a book had to be dismantled soon after the book was produced so that the letters would become available for the next project, an engraved plate or woodblock could be stored and reprinted in any amount at any time" (4).

93. Alan Young, *Tudor and Jacobean Tournaments* (London: George Philip, 1987), 123. See also Richard McCoy, *The Rites of Knighthood: The Literature and Politics of Elizabethan Chivalry* (Berkeley, Los Angeles, London: University of California Press, 1989).

94. Jerzy Limon, in *The Masque of Stuart Culture* (Newark: University of Delaware Press; London and Toronto: Associated University Presses, 1990), suggests that "many spectators did not understand the meaning of the stage design. This could be one of the reasons why the printed texts elucidate meaning that was not at all that clear during the performance" (38).

95. *The Masque of Queens*, in *Ben Jonson: The Complete Masques*, ed. Stephen Orgel, The Yale Ben Jonson (New Haven and London: Yale University Press, 1969), lines 92–97.

96. Stephen Orgel, "The Poetics of Spectacle," in Orgel and Roy Strong, *Inigo Jones: The Theatre of the Stuart Court*, 2 vols. (Berkeley: University of California Press; London: Sotheby Parke Bernet, 1973), I: 11.

97. Ferne, *The Blazon of Gentrie*, pt. 1, 148.

98. John Ford, *Love's Sacrifice*, ed. A. T. Moore, The Revels Plays (Manchester: Manchester University Press; New York: Palgrave, 2002); Ford's play was acted by the King's Men c. 1626–31. On the other hand, characters who are not aristocrats sometimes reveal an appreciation for symbolic designs. See Thomas Heywood, *A Critical Edition of "The Faire Maide of the Exchange,"* ed. Karl E. Snyder (New York and London: Garland, 1980), 2.2.255–71. Heywood's

play was acted (possibly by the Queen's Men) at an undetermined venue
c. 1603.

99. Philip Edwards, in his edition of *Hamlet* (Cambridge: Cambridge University
Press, 1985), notes of the word *inexplicable*, "Shakespeare does not use this
word elsewhere. The context suggests 'meaningless'" (153).

100. An incidental remark in Thomas Wright's *The Passions of the Minde* (London,
1601) suggests the importance of gesture without words: "The internall con-
ceites and affections of our minds, are not onely expressed with wordes, but
also declared with actions: as it appeareth in comedies, where dumbe shewes
often express the whole matter" (195–96).

101. Mehl, in *The Elizabethan Dumb Show*, suggests that "Ophelia's puzzled re-
action to the pantomime indicates that its significance was not immediately
obvious to an Elizabethan audience" (117). But Ophelia's question to Hamlet
about the meaning of the show serves the theatrical purpose of creating a
distinction between the rather formal style of the play-within-the-play and
the larger (more lifelike) drama. In addition, her inquiry and Hamlet's joking
reply anticipate the sexual banter between Ophelia and Hamlet later during
the entertainment.

102. Anthony Munday, *Sidero-thriambos, or Steele and Iron Triumphing*, in *Pageants
and Entertainments of Anthony Munday*, ed. David M. Bergeron, The Renaissance Imagination 11 (New York and London: Garland, 1985), 130.

103. For this reason complicated iconographic schemes were unsuitable for political propaganda. Theodore K. Rabb observes, "Buildings, collections, works
of art and cavalcades may have been choreographed to convey elaborate political meanings, but there is no evidence that their audience (except for a few
learned insiders) recognized, let alone understood, their intentions" ("Play,
not Politics: Who Really Understood the Symbolism of Renaissance Art?" *TLS*
November 10, 1995: 19).

104. See Leslie Thomson, ed., *Fortune: "All is but Fortune"* (Seattle and London:
University of Washington Press for the Folger Shakespeare Library, 2000).

105. Ilja M. Veldman, *Maarten van Heemskerck and Dutch Humanism in the
Sixteenth Century*, trans. Michael Hoyle (Maarssen: Gary Schwartz, 1977), 86.

106. In "Pieter Bruegel and *The Feast of Fools*," *Art Bulletin* 64 (December 1982):
640–46, Keith P. F. Moxey observes that "spectacles were a well-known symbol
of blindness and deception, while the action of selling spectacles was associated
with duplicity and fraud" (640).

107. Veldman, *Maarten van Heemskerck*, 86. Veldman translates the verses beneath
the print: "Blind Fortune, constant Toil and clever Industry pile up riches, as
does unceasing Frugality. The following bring forth riches in a very different
way: crafty Guile, merciless Violence, Theft, black Falsehood and Robbery"
(85).

108. Samuel Daniel, *The Worthy tract of Paulus Jovius, contayning a Discourse of rare
inventions, both Militarie and Amorous called Imprese* (London, 1585), sig. A7r.

109. Peacham, *The Compleat Gentleman* (1634), 110.

110. Ibid.

111. Immediately under the drawing of *Titus Andronicus* in performance are written passages from the first and last acts of Shakespeare's play; the page also contains Peacham's signature. However, June Schlueter, in "Rereading the Peacham Drawing," *Shakespeare Quarterly* 50 (Spring 1999): 171–84, proposes that the drawing represents "a sequence from a lost play," *Titus and Vespasian*, which, she believes, survives in a later German translation printed in 1620. Given the present state of our knowledge, this argument must of course remain highly speculative, and Schlueter does not dispute the key finding by G. Harold Metz that the paper on which the drawing was made dates from the last decade of the sixteenth century, when Shakespeare's play was written and performed (see Metz, "*Titus Andronicus*: A Watermark in the Longleat Manuscript," *Shakespeare Quarterly* 36 [Winter 1985]: 450–53).

112. Peacham, *Compleat Gentleman* (1634), 110.

113. Shakespeare's knowledge of the visual arts is the subject of an essay by Wylie Sypher, "Painting and Other Fine Arts," in *William Shakespeare: His World, His Work, His Influence*, ed. John F. Andrews, 3 vols. (New York: Charles Scribner's Sons, 1985), I: 241–56; and an essay by John Dixon Hunt, "The Visual Arts of Shakespeare's Day," in *Shakespeare: Pattern of Excelling Nature*, ed. David Bevington and Jay Halio (Newark: University of Delaware Press; London: Associated University Presses, 1978), 210–21. See also Arthur H. R. Fairchild, *Shakespeare and the Arts of Design (Architecture, Sculpture, and Painting)*, University of Missouri Studies 12 (Columbia: University of Missouri Press, 1937).

1 Spring and Winter in *Love's Labour's Lost*

1. John Kerrigan, ed., *Love's Labour's Lost*, New Penguin Shakespeare (Harmondsworth: Penguin, 1982), note to 5.2.874–75 (238).

2. G. R. Hibbard, ed., *Love's Labour's Lost*, New Oxford Shakespeare (Oxford: Clarendon Press, 1990), note to 5.2.872 (233).

3. H. R. Woudhuysen, ed., *Love's Labour's Lost*, Arden Shakespeare, 3rd Series (Walton-on-Thames: Thomas Nelson and Sons, 1998), note to 5.2.882–917 (294).

4. Hibbard, ed., *Love's Labour's Lost*, 10.

5. Personification of the seasons in England goes back to antiquity, though Shakespeare would almost certainly not have known this. At the Roman villa called Chedworth, archeologists have discovered mosaics of the four seasons: Winter is a man who wears a hooded cloak and carries a dead hare in one hand, a leafless branch in the other; Spring is a nude woman who carries a basket of flowers in her left hand, a bird perched on her right. See Roger Goodburn, *The*

Roman Villa: Chedworth (1979; reprint, London: The National Trust, 2000), plates 5.2 and 6.

6. See Miriam Gilbert, *Love's Labour's Lost*, Shakespeare in Performance (Manchester: Manchester University Press; New York: St. Martin's Press, 1993), 27–28.

7. Ibid., 33–34.

8. Reproduced by Kahren J. Hellerstedt and David G. Wilkins, *Netherlandish School: Pre-Rembrandt Etchers*, The Illustrated Bartsch 53 (New York: Abaris Books, 1985), 87.

9. Print Room of the British Museum, registration no. 1875.7.10.486.

10. Reproduced by Walter L. Strauss, *Netherlandish Artists: Matham, Saenredam, Muller*, The Illustrated Bartsch 4 (New York: Abaris Books, 1980), 435.

11. Reproduced by Ilja M. Veldman, "Seasons, Planets and Temperaments in the Work of Maarten van Heemskerck: Cosmo-astrological Allegory in Sixteenth-Century Netherlandish Prints," *Simiolus* 11, nos. 3/4 (1980): 158, fig. 10.

12. Reproduced by Leonard J. Slatkes, *Netherlandish Artists*, The Illustrated Bartsch 1 (New York: Abaris Books, 1978), 249.

13. Ibid., 283.

14. Reproduced by Strauss, *Netherlandish Artists: Matham, Saenredam, Muller*, 41.

15. Ibid., 130.

16. Spring, Winter, and the other Seasons appear in a variety of plays and civic pageants, but descriptions of these figures are almost wholly lacking. See, for example, *The Sun's Darling* (*The Dramatic Works of Thomas Dekker*, ed. Fredson Bowers, 4 vols. [Cambridge: Cambridge University Press, 1953–61], vol. IV): Spring enters at the beginning of act 2; Winter near the beginning of act 5. Dekker also makes characters out of the Seasons in *Britannia's Honor*, the lord mayor's show for 1628: about the Sun "are plac'd Spring, Summer, Autumne, and Winter, in proper habiliments" (*Dramatic Works*, vol. IV), lines 416–17. In Thomas Heywood's *The Brazen Age*, Aurora is attended by the Seasons, Days, and Hours (*The Dramatic Works of Thomas Heywood*, ed. R. H. Shepherd, 6 vols. [London: John Pearson, 1874], III: 228 (page number). Heywood also employs the Seasons in his lord mayor's pageant, *Londini Status Pacatus* (*Thomas Heywood's Pageants: A Critical Edition*, ed. David M. Bergeron, The Renaissance Imagination 16 [New York and London: Garland, 1986]): "Janus [is] plac'd upon an artificiall structure, built in a square modell, at the foure corners whereof sit foure persons representing the four seasons; Spring, Summer, Autume, Winter; every one habited agreeable to his propriety and condition" (lines 180–83).

17. Thomas Nabbes, *The Spring's Glory*, ed. John Russell Brown, in *A Book of Masques in Honour of Allardyce Nicoll*, ed. T. J. B. Spencer and Stanley W. Wells (Cambridge: Cambridge University Press, 1967).

18. Francis Kynaston, *Corona Minervae, or A Masque Presented before Prince Charles* (London, 1635), sig. Br.

19. *Chloridia*, in *Ben Jonson: The Complete Masques*, ed. Stephen Orgel, The Yale Ben Jonson (New Haven and London: Yale University Press, 1969). A pen and

ink sketch of the costume is reproduced by Stephen Orgel and Roy Strong, *Inigo Jones: The Theatre of the Stuart Court*, 2 vols. (Berkeley: University of California Press; London: Sotheby Parke Bernet, 1973), II: fig. 168.

20. Henry Peacham, *Graphice or The Most Auncient and Excellent Art of Drawing and Limming* (London, 1612), 133.

21. John Squire, *The Triumphs of Peace*, in *The Progresses, Processions, and Magnificent Festivities, of King James the First*, ed. John Nichols, 4 vols. (1828; reprint, New York: AMS Press, 1967), IV: 624.

22. Peacham, *Graphice*, 133.

23. *The Masque of Flowers*, ed. E. A. J. Honigmann, in *A Book of Masques*. The name of the masque's author is unknown.

24. Thomas Middleton, "At the House of the Right Honorable Sir Francis Jhones, L. Maior, For the solemne feast of Easter last [entertainment 8]," in *Honourable Entertainments by Thomas Middleton*, ed. R. C. Bald and F. P. Wilson, Malone Society Reprints (Oxford: Oxford University Press, 1953), sig. C2r.

25. Reproduced by Sebastian Buffa, *Antonio Tempesta, Italian Masters of the Sixteenth Century*, The Illustrated Bartsch 36 (New York: Abaris Books, 1983), 102. Spring's chariot is drawn by bulls, lambs, and swallows, all associated with fertility.

26. Reproduced by F. W. H. Hollstein, *Dutch and Flemish Etchings, Engravings and Woodcuts, ca. 1450–1700* (Amsterdam: Menno Hertzberger, 1949–), XIII: 13.

27. Print Room of the British Museum, reg. no. F.1.159.

28. Reproduced by Hellerstedt and Wilkins, *Netherlandish School: Pre-Rembrandt Etchers*, 90.

29. Print Room of the British Museum, reg. no. 1868.6.12.1559.

30. Reproduced by Slatkes, *Netherlandish Artists*, 284.

31. Print Room of the British Museum, reg. no. 1856.1.12.330.

32. Print Room of the British Museum, reg. no. 1909.6.12.141.

33. Reproduced by Arno Dolders, *Netherlandish Artists: Philips Galle*, The Illustrated Bartsch 56 (New York: Abaris Books, 1987), 332.

34. Print Room of the British Museum, reg. no. 1942.7.20.1/21.

35. See Richard Pennington, *A Descriptive Catalogue of the Etched Work of Wenceslaus Hollar, 1607–1677* (Cambridge: Cambridge University Press, 1982), 99–103.

36. Winter emphasizes his advanced years when he appears in *The Sun's Darling* (*The Dramatic Works of Thomas Dekker*, vol. IV): "as I am Winter, worne and spent / So farre with age, I am Tymes monument, / Antiquities example" (5.1.135–37). Similarly, the personification is called "old Hiems" in *A Midsummer Night's Dream* (2.1.109).

37. Reproduced by Strauss, *Netherlandish Artists: Matham, Saenredam, Muller*, 133.

38. See *Summer's Last Will and Testament*, in *Thomas Nashe*, ed. Stanley Wells, The Stratford-upon-Avon Library 1 (London: Edward Arnold, 1964), 89–139. Typical of the stage directions is this: "*Enter Summer leaning on Autumn's and*

Winter's shoulders..." (93). Despite his numerous speeches, Winter's appearance is not described.

39. Kynaston, *Corona Minervae*, sig. Br.

40. *The Masque of Beauty*, in *Ben Jonson: The Complete Masques*, ed. Orgel.

41. Squire, *The Triumphs of Peace*, in *The Progresses, Processions, and Magnificent Festivities, of King James the First*, IV: 624.

42. Ulpian Fulwell, *The Flower of Fame, Containing the bright Renowne, & moste fortunate raigne of King Henry the viii* (London, 1575), sig. B3v.

43. Peacham, *Graphice*, 136.

44. Bobbyann Roesen [Anne Barton], in "*Love's Labour's Lost*" (*Shakespeare Quarterly* 4 [October 1953]: 411–26), observes that Dull "sits mute and quiescent through all the arrangements for the pageant of the Nine Worthies, only at the very last, when roused by another character, entering the dialogue at all to offer us a personal performance upon the tabor, a talent as engaging and unexpected in Dull as song is in the Justice Silence of *2 Henry IV*" (416–17).

45. In the Royal Shakespeare Company production of 1993/4, directed by Ian Judge, Spring was represented by Jaquenetta, attired in a light green garment; her front was adorned with little flowers. Winter was represented by Dull, attired in a white garment, trimmed with white fur; icicles projected from his head and hands. Holofernes was costumed as the owl, Nathaniel as the cuckoo.

46. The stage direction following the King's remark, "Call them forth quickly, we will do so" (5.2.889), and Armado's "Holla! approach," reads "*Enter all*" in both the Quarto and Folio. Like so many other stage directions, this is tantalizing. I think it means what most directors have taken it to mean: that a number of people enter, not just two. Presumably other villagers accompany the personified figures. Armado's words, "This side is Hiems, Winter; this Ver, the Spring" (line 891), may indicate two groups rather than two individuals, as David Evett has suggested to me.

47. William C. Carroll, in *The Great Feast of Language in "Love's Labour's Lost"* (Princeton: Princeton University Press, 1976), observes that "The seasonal songs, above all, re-establish a sense of time as cyclical, not linear and therefore hopelessly irretrievable. Consider too the basic syntax of the songs. The 'when–then' construction assures us, in its logical format, that it is describing something 'natural' and inevitable" (214).

48. C. L. Barber, *Shakespeare's Festive Comedy: A Study of Dramatic Form and its Relation to Social Custom* (1959; reprint, Princeton: Princeton University Press, 1972), 118.

49. "The Owl," in *The Works of Michael Drayton*, ed. J. William Hebel, Kathleen Tillotson, and Bernard H. Newdigate, 5 vols. (Oxford: Blackwell, 1931–41), vol. II.

50. Hibbard, ed., *Love's Labour's Lost*, note to 5.2.880 (233–34).

51. Beryl Rowland, *Birds with Human Souls: A Guide to Bird Symbolism* (Knoxville: University of Tennessee Press, 1978), 41.

52. For the range of meanings associated with owls, see ibid., 115–20.

53. Catherine M. McLay, "The Dialogues of Spring and Winter: A Key to the Unity of *Love's Labour's Lost*," *Shakespeare Quarterly* 18 (Spring 1967): 125.

54. Keith P. F. Moxey, "Pieter Bruegel and *The Feast of Fools*," *Art Bulletin* 64 (December 1982): 643.

55. Peter Holland, ed., *Love's Labor's Lost*, Pelican Shakespeare (New York and London: Penguin, 2000), xxix.

56. For the identification of the owl with folly, see Gerta Calmann, "The Picture of Nobody: An Iconographical Study," *Journal of the Warburg and Courtauld Institutes* 23 (January–June 1960): 60–104, esp. 67–71.

57. Reproduced by Don Cameron Allen, ed., *The Owles Almanacke* (Baltimore, MD: Johns Hopkins University Press, 1943), opposite p. 25. Although this work has been attributed to Thomas Dekker, Allen writes, "The book is certainly not by Dekker" (6).

58. *The Masque of Owls*, in *Ben Jonson: The Complete Masques*, 425–32. Stephen Orgel notes that owls, "like gulls, [were] considered stupid birds by the Elizabethans" (425).

59. Reproduced in *Ausgewählte Werke* (Berlin: Kunstgewerbemuseum, 1963), fig. 69.

60. Paul Vandenbroeck, "Verbeeck's Peasant Weddings: A Study of Iconography and Social Function," *Simiolus* 14, no. 2 (1984): 105.

61. Here I take issue with Peter J. Seng, who, in *The Vocal Songs in the Plays of Shakespeare: A Critical History* (Cambridge, MA: Harvard University Press, 1967), says of the songs: "L. B. Wright seems to be correct in his view that they are largely extraneous. Shakespeare was merely giving his audience what would please it" (25).

62. Francis Berry, *The Shakespeare Inset: Word and Picture* (London: Routledge & Kegan Paul, 1965), 112.

2 Revenge, Murder, and Rape in *Titus Andronicus*

1. Jan Kott, "Shakespeare – Cruel and True [Peter Brook's *Titus*, 1955]," in *"Titus Andronicus": Critical Essays*, ed. Philip C. Kolin (New York and London: Garland, 1995), 395. See also William P. Shaw, "Text, Performance, and Perspective: Peter Brook's Landmark Production of *Titus Andronicus*, 1955," *Theatre History Studies* 10 (1990): 31–55.

2. Daniel Scuro, "*Titus Andronicus*: A Crimson-Flushed Stage! [*Titus* in 1955]," in *"Titus Andronicus": Critical Essays*, 406.

3. Kott, "Shakespeare – Cruel and True," in *"Titus Andronicus": Critical Essays*, 397.

4. Gerald Freedman, Introduction to *Titus Andronicus* (London: The Folio Society, 1970), 3.

5. Alan Hughes, ed., *Titus Andronicus*, New Cambridge Shakespeare (Cambridge: Cambridge University Press, 1994), 43.

6. Eugene M. Waith, ed., *Titus Andronicus*, New Oxford Shakespeare (Oxford: Clarendon Press, 1984), 55.

7. Ibid., 57.

8. Anthony Quayle, quoted by Hughes, ed., *Titus Andronicus*, 41.

9. Muriel St. Clare Byrne, quoted by Waith, ed., *Titus Andronicus*, 55.

10. Waith, ed., *Titus Andronicus* (quoting a review in the *New York Times*), 57.

11. Jonathan Bate comments on the importance of visual effect in Deborah Warner's RSC production of 1987–88, especially the sight of the ravished Lavinia by the astonished Marcus and by the playgoers: "This moment taught me more about that strange theatrical experience we call 'tragedy' than any theory has done." See "Staging the Unspeakable: Four Versions of *Titus Andronicus*," in *Shakespeare, from Text to Stage*, ed. Patricia Kennan and Mariangela Tempera, The Renaissance Revisited 1 (Bologna: Cooperativa Libraria Universitaria Editrice Bologna, 1992), 106.

12. Gustav Ungerer, "An Unrecorded Elizabethan Performance of *Titus Andronicus*," *Shakespeare Survey* 14 (1961): 102.

13. M. C. Bradbrook, "Moral Heraldry," in *Shakespeare and Elizabethan Poetry: A Study of His Earlier Work in Relation to the Poetry of the Time* (London: Chatto and Windus, 1951), 110.

14. Nicholas Brooke, *Shakespeare's Early Tragedies* (London: Methuen, 1968), 20.

15. Ann Haaker, "*Non sine causa*: The Use of Emblematic Method and Iconology in the Thematic Structure of *Titus Andronicus*," *Research Opportunities in Renaissance Drama* 13–14 (1970–71): 143. Haaker comments, "In no other play is symbolic spectacle so paramount" (144). She does not, however, discuss the costuming of Tamora and her sons at Titus' door.

16. Michael Hattaway, in "Playhouses and the Role of Drama," in *A Companion to English Renaissance Literature and Culture*, ed. Hattaway (Oxford: Blackwell, 2000), 136.

17. Lawrence Danson, *Tragic Alphabet: Shakespeare's Drama of Language* (New Haven and London: Yale University Press, 1974), 18.

18. Lukas Erne, in *Beyond "The Spanish Tragedy": A Study of the Works of Thomas Kyd*, The Revels Plays Companion Library (Manchester: Manchester University Press; New York: Palgrave, 2001), examines the play in great detail: he considers Revenge "as a supernatural exterior force (in Seneca's wake)" and "as an allegorical interior passion (in the tradition of the Morality plays)" (140), but he does not treat Revenge's costume or props.

19. Frances Teague, *Shakespeare's Speaking Properties* (Lewisburg, PA: Bucknell University Press; London: Associated University Presses, 1991), 89. Teague, while acknowledging Tamora's "special symbolic costume" (95), does not speculate about the nature of that costume.

20. Alan C. Dessen, *Titus Andronicus*, Shakespeare in Performance (Manchester: Manchester University Press; New York: St. Martin's Press, 1989), 79. In a review of Dessen's *Recovering Shakespeare's Theatrical Vocabulary* (Cambridge: Cambridge University Press, 1995), Grace Tiffany takes Dessen to task for suggesting that "*Titus Andronicus*' Tamora, disguised as Revenge, actually *does* represent Revenge for the Renaissance audience (why then does she mention her disguise?)." See her review in *Comparative Drama* 29 (Winter 1995–96): 532–34. The answer to Tiffany's question is that Renaissance dramatists virtually always identify symbolic characters through dialogue. The playwrights thereby ensure that every playgoer understands the visual symbolism.

21. Waith, ed., *Titus Andronicus*, note to 5.2.0 (176).

22. Jonathan Bate, ed., *Titus Andronicus*, Arden Shakespeare, 3rd Series (London and New York: Routledge, 1995), note to 5.2.47 (255). I do not dispute Bate's point that "Revenge traditionally rode in a chariot" – in *Antonio's Revenge* (ed. Reaveley Gair, The Revels Plays [Manchester: Manchester University Press; Baltimore: Johns Hopkins University Press, 1978]) the protagonist announces, "my soul's enthroned / In the triumphant chariot of revenge" (3.5.18–19) – but this is a comparatively rare motif (see Middleton's *The Ghost of Lucrece* below for another such instance), and I'm doubtful that we can just assume the playgoers' familiarity with this topos. Perhaps significantly, Bate does not cite a single example in Renaissance art or literature.

23. Waith, ed., *Titus Andronicus*, note to 5.2.0 (176).

24. For instances of stage chariots in other plays, see Alan C. Dessen and Leslie Thomson, *A Dictionary of Stage Directions in English Drama, 1580–1642* (Cambridge: Cambridge University Press, 1999), 47–48. Dessen and Thomson observe that a chariot is "a large property drawn onto the stage" (47).

25. Alison Findlay, *A Feminist Perspective on Renaissance Drama* (Oxford: Blackwell, 1999), 49, 51. Findlay's chapter on revenge tragedy is consistently insightful and fascinating. See also Gwynne Kennedy, *Just Anger: Representing Women's Anger in Early Modern England* (Carbondale and Edwardsville: Southern Illinois University Press, 2000); and M. L. Stapleton, *Fated Sky: The "Femina Furens" in Shakespeare* (Newark: University of Delaware Press; London: Associated University Presses, 2000).

26. Findlay, *A Feminist Perspective*, 53.

27. Juvenal, "Satire XIII," in *Juvenal and Persius*, trans. G. G. Ramsay, Loeb Classical Library (1918; reprint, New York: G. P. Putnam's Sons; London: William Heinemann, 1930), 261.

28. "*Respublica*," *An Interlude for Christmas 1553*, ed. W. W. Greg, EETS, no. 226 (London: Oxford University Press, 1952).

29. "*The Lamentable Tragedy of Locrine*": *A Critical Edition*, ed. Jane Lytton Gooch, Garland English Texts 7 (New York and London: Garland, 1981).

30. Vincenzo Cartari, *The Fountaine of Ancient Fiction, Wherein is lively depictured the Images and Statues of the gods of the Ancients, with their proper and perticular*

expositions, trans. Richard Linche (London, 1599), sig. Aa4v. This work is a partial translation of Cartari's *Imagini de i dei de gli antichi*.

31. Reproduced by Frederick Kiefer, *Fortune and Elizabethan Tragedy* (San Marino, CA: The Huntington Library, 1983), fig. 1.

32. Thomas Sackville, "Induction" to *A Mirror for Magistrates*, ed. Lily B. Campbell (1938; reprint, New York: Barnes and Noble, 1970), 306.

33. Cyril Tourneur [or Thomas Middleton], *The Revenger's Tragedy*, ed. R. A. Foakes, The Revels Plays (1966; reprint, London: Methuen, 1975).

34. *Histriomastix*, in *The Plays of John Marston*, ed. H. Harvey Wood, 3 vols. (Edinburgh and London: Oliver and Boyd, 1939), vol. III, act 5, pp. 287–88 (this edition lacks line numbers). Marston's authorship of the play is doubted today. Although *Histriomastix* has usually been dated c. 1598–99 and assigned to a boys' company, Roslyn Lander Knutson, in *Playing Companies and Commerce in Shakespeare's Time* (Cambridge: Cambridge University Press, 2001), makes a strong argument for an earlier date of composition: c. 1588–91 (93).

35. A ballad and a prose narrative, which relate the story of *Titus*, are both extant. G. Harold Metz, in *Shakespeare's Earliest Tragedy: Studies in "Titus Andronicus"* (Madison, Teaneck, NJ: Fairleigh Dickinson University Press; London: Associated University Presses, 1996), concludes that the ballad, which recounts the visit of the disguised Tamora to Titus, is indebted to the play (154). Metz, who observes that "There is no comparable incident in the *History*" (155), believes that the prose narrative preserves Shakespeare's source. For a different view of the tangled relationship between play, ballad, and narrative, see the review of Metz's book by MacD. P. Jackson in *The Papers of the Bibliographical Society of America* 92 (March 1998): 90–94.

36. "The Lamentable and Tragical History of Titus Andronicus," in Geoffrey Bullough, ed., *Narrative and Dramatic Sources of Shakespeare*, 8 vols. (London: Routledge & Kegan Paul; New York: Columbia University Press, 1957–75), VI: 47.

37. Apollodorus, *The Library*, trans. James George Frazer, Loeb Classical Library, 2 vols. (1921; reprint, London: William Heinemann; Cambridge, MA: Harvard University Press, 1939), I: 5.

38. Ovid, *Metamorphoses*, trans. Frank Justus Miller, 2nd edn., Loeb Classical Library, 2 vols. (1921; reprint, London: William Heinemann; Cambridge, MA: Harvard University Press, 1966–68), vol. I. Hereafter cited parenthetically by book and line number.

39. *Eumenides*, in *Aeschylus*, trans. Herbert Weir Smyth, ed. Hugh Lloyd-Jones, Loeb Classical Library, 2 vols. (1926; reprint, Cambridge, MA: Harvard University Press; London: William Heinemann, 1963), II: 279. (Apollo makes the remark.) "Eumenides," which signifies "the well meaning," is a euphemism for the creatures whom people feared to name.

40. Pierre Le Loyer, *A Treatise of Specters or straunge sights, visions and apparitions appearing sensibly unto men*, trans. Zachary Jones (London, 1605), fol. 15r.

41. *"The Tragedy of Tancred and Gismund," 1591–2*, ed. W. W. Greg, Malone Society Reprints (Oxford: Oxford University Press, 1915 [for 1914]). This play represents a revised version (by Robert Wilmot) of *Gismond of Salerne*.

42. Abraham Fraunce, *The Third part of the Countesse of Pembrokes Ivychurch, Entituled Amintas Dale* (London, 1592), fol. 28v.

43. For the use of torches on the stage, see Dessen and Thomson, *A Dictionary of Stage Directions*, 233–34.

44. Michael Drayton, *The Moon-Calfe*, in *The Works of Michael Drayton*, ed. J. William Hebel, Kathleen Tillotson, and Bernard Newdigate, 5 vols. (Oxford: Blackwell, 1931–41), III: 168.

45. Thomas Sackville and Thomas Norton, *Gorboduc*, in *Two Tudor Tragedies*, ed. William Tydeman (Harmondsworth: Penguin, 1992), 94.

46. George Peele, *The Battle of Alcazar*, ed. John Yoklavich, in *The Dramatic Works of George Peele*, in *The Life and Works of George Peele*, gen. ed. Charles Tyler Prouty, 3 vols. (New Haven and London: Yale University Press, 1952–70), vol. II.

47. Reproduced in *Inigo Jones: The Theatre of the Stuart Court*, ed. Stephen Orgel and Roy Strong, 2 vols. (Berkeley: University of California Press; London: Sotheby Parke Bernet, 1973), II: pl. 416.

48. Hughes, ed., *Titus Andronicus*, note to 5.2.82 (132).

49. Bate, ed., *Titus Andronicus*, note to 5.2.1 (252).

50. A. R. Braunmuller, in his New Cambridge edition of *Macbeth* (Cambridge: Cambridge University Press, 1997), observes that "such hair was a villain's mark" (note to 4.2.80); Braunmuller cites another such instance in *2 Henry VI* (1.2.13).

51. Thomas Hughes and others, *"The Misfortunes of Arthur": A Critical, Old-Spelling Edition*, ed. Brian Jay Corrigan (New York and London: Garland, 1992), dumb show preceding act 2, lines 8–9. Hughes and his colleagues must have known Kyd's play. As Corrigan observes, "No discussion of the representativeness of *The Misfortunes of Arthur* in its time could be complete without pointing out the striking similarities between it and Kyd's *The Spanish Tragedy*" (31).

52. Anthony Copley, *A Fig for Fortune* (London, 1596), 10.

53. Jonathan Bate suggests that, in giving Tamora a Fury-like identity, Shakespeare is indebted to Kyd. At one point Hieronimo "stares an old man in the face and assumes or pretends to assume that the Senex is an avenging fury sent from hell. Shakespeare picked up on this detail and decided to have a character actually impersonate a fury sent from hell." See "The Performance of Revenge: *Titus Andronicus* and *The Spanish Tragedy*," in *The Show Within: Dramatic and Other Insets, English Renaissance Drama (1550–1642)*, ed. François Laroque, Collection Astraea 4, 2 vols. (Montpellier: Centres d'Etudes et de Recherches Elisabethaines, Université Paul-Valéry, 1992), II: 271.

54. Philip Henslowe records a payment to Jonson, evidently for additions to *The Spanish Tragedy*, on 25 September 1601: "upon hn [*sic*] writting of his

adicians in geronymo." See *Henslowe's Diary*, ed. R. A. Foakes and R. T. Rickert (Cambridge: Cambridge University Press, 1961), 182.

55. Additional passage, probably by Ben Jonson, in Thomas Kyd, *The Spanish Tragedy*, ed. Philip Edwards, The Revels Plays (1959; reprint, London: Methuen, 1969), 126.

56. Otto van Veen, *Q[uinti] Horatii Flacci Emblemata* (Antwerp, 1607), 181; this same figure also shows up in another emblem (27). Van Veen's personification, carrying fasces, pruning hook, nails, and bridle, represents the punishment of God rather than the phenomenon of revenge. Battista Dossi's painting of Justice puts the fasces in her right hand; reproduced by Peter Humfrey and Mauro Lucco, *Dosso Dossi: Court Painter in Renaissance Ferrara*, ed. Andrea Bayer (New York: The Metropolitan Museum of Art, 1998), fig. 11.

57. Revenge appears briefly as a character in *The First Part of Jeronimo*, acted by an unidentified boys' company c. 1600–05, but neither costume nor prop is specified.

58. *The Interlude of Vice (Horestes)*, ed. Daniel Seltzer, Malone Society Reprints (Oxford: Oxford University Press, 1962). The title-page reads: *A Newe Enterlude of Vice Conteyninge, the Historye of Horestes with the cruell revengment of his Fathers death, upon his one naturall Mother.*

59. The exception to this generalization involves the disguise of Revenge as a beggar late in the action: *"Vyce entrith with a staffe & a bottell or dyshe and wallet"* (l2.1232.s.d.).

60. Hughes, ed., *Titus Andronicus*, 160.

61. Philip Edwards, "Thrusting Elysium into Hell: The Originality of *The Spanish Tragedy*," *The Elizabethan Theatre* 11 (1990): 127.

62. Justice, who is always represented in the arts as female, *"falls into a slumber"* in *"A Warning for Fair Women": A Critical Edition*, ed. Charles Dale Cannon (The Hague and Paris: Mouton, 1975), line 1800.s.d.

63. Findlay, in *A Feminist Perspective on Renaissance Drama*, says that Kyd creates "a male personification of Revenge" (52), but does not explain how she reached this conclusion.

64. Michael Hattaway, *Elizabethan Popular Theatre: Plays in Performance* (London: Routledge & Kegan Paul, 1982), 113.

65. For the range of meanings that "antic" may have on the stage, see Dessen and Thomson, *A Dictionary of Stage Directions*, 7–8.

66. *The Lamentable Tragedy of Locrine*, ed. Gooch, 43.

67. *The Masque of Queens*, in *Ben Jonson: The Complete Masques*, ed. Stephen Orgel, The Yale Ben Jonson (New Haven and London: Yale University Press, 1969), 530.

68. Thomas Cooper, in *Thesaurus Linguae Romanae & Britannicae* (London 1565), describes Ate as "the name of a hurtefull spirite, alwaye woorkynge ill to men" (sig. C6r of the *Dictionarium Historicum et Poeticum*). In *The Arraignment of Paris*, Ate, speaking the prologue, describes the forthcoming dramatic action as

representing a recompense for crime: "the fatall frute / Raught from the golden tree of Proserpine" (lines 6–7), i.e., the rape of Helen by the Trojans. See *The Arraignment of Paris*, ed. R. Mark Benbow, in *The Life and Dramatic Works of George Peele*, vol. III. In Peele's dramatization it is Ate rather than Eris who brings the golden apple into the midst of the goddesses.

69. Steve Sohmer, in *Shakespeare's Mystery Play: The Opening of the Globe Theatre 1599* (Manchester: Manchester University Press; New York: St. Martin's Press, 1999), notes that "Shakespeare's choice of Ate as Caesar's companion has never been satisfactorily explained." Sohmer writes that "Ate destroyed her victims by blinding them to the difference between right and wrong, and between 'advantageous and disadvantageous courses of action'. . . . At Sardis and Philippi, Shakespeare contrives for Antony's prophecy to be *literally* fulfilled," for both Brutus and Cassius complain of their vision (38). David Daniell, ed., *Julius Caesar*, Arden Shakespeare, 3rd Series (London: Thomas Nelson and Sons, 1998), identifies Ate as "Greek goddess of blind infatuation, daughter of Zeus in Homer, of Strife in Hesiod, and sister of lawlessness" (note to 3.1.271).

70. Thomas Heywood, *Troia Britanica: or, Great Britaines Troy* (London, 1609), sig. Bb6v (the pages are badly misnumbered).

71. Ronald Broude observes: "While revenge tragedy presents a highly formalized and rather idealized picture of divine justice, its portrayal of human vengeance tends to be more in keeping with the harsh realities of Renaissance life." See "Revenge and Revenge Tragedy in Renaissance England," *Renaissance Quarterly* 28 (Spring 1975): 57.

72. Robert Dallington, *Aphorismes Civill and Militarie: Amplified with Authorities, and exemplified with Historie, out of the first Quarterne of Fr. Guicciardine* (London, 1613), 13.

73. Francis Bacon, "Of Revenge," in *The Essayes or Counsels, Civill and Morall*, ed. Michael Kiernan (Oxford: Clarendon Press, 1985), 16.

74. Richard Hooker, *Of the Laws of Ecclesiastical Politie*, in *The Folger Library Edition of The Works of Richard Hooker*, ed. W. Speed Hill, 7 vols. (Cambridge, MA, and London: Belknap Press, 1977–98), II: 200.

75. Interestingly, Marcus contrasts justice and revenge when he says that Titus is "yet so just that he will not revenge" (4.1.128).

76. The association of Revenge with hell may be suggested visually in *Titus Andronicus*. David Willbern, in "Rape and Revenge in *Titus Andronicus*," *English Literary Renaissance* 8 (Spring 1978): 159–82, suggests: "It is plausible . . . that Tamora enters as Revenge through the trap-door in the stage. . . . Her invitations to Titus to 'Come down' (33, 43) would then be enticements into Hell itself" (177). Willbern credits this idea to Richard Hosley. Reprinted in *"Titus Andronicus": Critical Essays*, ed. Kolin, 171–94.

77. Dessen and Thomson, in *A Dictionary of Stage Directions*, list numerous instances of daggers appearing in stage directions (64).

78. Revenge has *"an Irish dagger by his side"* (*The Misfortunes of Arthur*, dumb show preceding act 2, lines 10–11). In a later play, *The Maid's Tragedy*, performed 1610–11 by the King's Men, Evadne, mistress of the king, exacts her revenge upon him with some kind of knife, possibly a dagger. See Beaumont and Fletcher, *The Maid's Tragedy*, ed. T. W. Craik, The Revels Plays (Manchester: Manchester University Press; New York: St. Martin's Press, 1988), note to 5.1.61.

79. It should be noted, however, that in a play written c. 1643–44 Revenge is said to enter *"with a sword in one hand, and a flaming torch in the other."* See Henry Burkhead, *A Tragedy of Cola's Furie, or Lirenda's Miserie* (Kilkenny, 1646), 46 (s.d. in act 4). There is no evidence that Burkhead's play, written nearly sixty years after *The Spanish Tragedy*, has any connection with Kyd's play or with *Locrine* or with *Titus*; nor is there any evidence that Burkhead's tragedy was ever performed. Patricia Coughlan, in "'Enter Revenge': Henry Burkhead and *Cola's Furie*," *Theatre Research International* 15 (Spring 1990): 1–17, observes that the play "does seem to be a closet drama" (3). Burkhead's play was printed in Ireland and must have had few English readers.

80. Illustrated by Julie Taymor, *Titus: The Illustrated Screenplay* (New York: Newmarket Press, 2000), 152–53. Taymor calls the headpiece "a crown of daggers" (154). The costume designer of this production was Milena Canonero.

81. A stage direction in Nathaniel Richards' *Messalina, The Roman Empress*, acted c. 1634–36, may suggest that Revenge appears as a character: "*Thunder. Enter angell, three murdered dames with revenge threatning*" (*Nathanael Richards' "Tragedy of Messallina, The Roman Emperesse,"* ed. A. R. Skemp, Materialien zur Kunde des älteren Englischen Dramas [1910; reprint, Nendeln, Liechtenstein: Kraus Reprint, 1970]), lines 2170–71. Skemp interprets the stage direction as meaning that the personification accompanies the three murdered women, for he cites Kyd's stage direction at the beginning of *The Spanish Tragedy*: "*Enter the Ghost of Andrea, and with him Revenge*" (note to line 2170). It is possible, of course, that the stage direction means that the three murdered women threaten revenge. In any case, there is no indication of costume or props for the figures whom Richards brings onstage.

82. Reproduced by H. C. Marillier, *The Tapestries at Hampton Court Palace*, rev. edn. (London: HMSO, 1962), pl. 1. The image of Revenge appears on the border of a tapestry depicting the return of Sarah by the Egyptians.

83. Plutarch, *The Philosophie, commonlie called, The Morals*, trans. Philemon Holland (London, 1603), 125.

84. *"The History of King Leir," 1605*, ed. W. W. Greg, Malone Society Reprints (1908 [for 1907]; reprint, Oxford: Oxford University Press, 1965).

85. Cesare Ripa, *Iconologia* (Rome, 1603), 494.

86. Reproduced by Walter L. Strauss, ed., *Netherlandish Artists: Matham, Saenredam, Muller*, The Illustrated Bartsch 4 (New York: Abaris Books, 1980), 454. Karen Pinkus, in *Picturing Silence: Emblem, Language, Counter-Reformation Materiality* (Ann Arbor: University of Michigan Press, 1996), notes

that this figure became in the Renaissance "an incorporation of prudence in the broadest sense" (11).

87. Reproduced by Pinkus, *Picturing Silence*, fig. 1.4. Whitney's collection of emblems, *A Choice of Emblemes*, was published in 1586.

88. Diane Apostolos-Cappadona, *Encyclopedia of Women in Religious Art* (New York: Continuum, 1996), 16.

89. In his study of silence in ancient Roman culture, Charles W. Hedrick, Jr. observes, "To keep silent is not only to refrain from speaking; to keep silent is to do something as well" (*History and Silence: Purge and Rehabilitation of Memory in Late Antiquity* [Austin: University of Texas Press, 2000], 125).

90. The plates are reproduced by Sebastian Buffa, ed., *Italian Masters of the Sixteenth Century: Antonio Tempesta*, The Illustrated Bartsch 37 (New York: Abaris Books, 1984), pls. 1388–1427.

91. Giovanni Pierio Valeriano Bolzani, *Hieroglyphica sive de sacris aegyptiorum literis commentarii* (Basel, 1556), "Meditatio vel ultio," fol. 259v.

92. Stephen Batman, *The Golden Booke of the Leaden Goddes* (London, 1577), sig. D3r (the pages are badly misnumbered). Batman makes the remark in a section on Harpocrates and Angerona.

93. Giovanni Paolo Lomazzo, *A Tracte Containing the Artes of curious Paintinge, Carvinge & Buildinge*, trans. Richard Haydocke (Oxford, 1598), bk. 3, 117.

94. *The Revenge of Bussy D'Ambois*, ed. Robert J. Lordi, in *The Plays of George Chapman: The Tragedies*, gen. ed. Allan Holaday, et al. (Cambridge: D. S. Brewer, 1987). Tamyra, in the next scene, says that Revenge "ever red sitt'st in the eyes / Of injur'd ladies" (1.2.1–2). She may, of course, be speaking metaphorically rather than literally.

95. Revengers may, of course, carry out their purposes by wielding swords. Here, though, I am concerned with the personification rather than with particular instances of revenge.

96. The second dumb show in *The Misfortunes of Arthur* conflates Revenge and Fury. Here Revenge is male rather than female and has "a threatning countenance" (lines 11–12): "The Irish man signified Revenge and Furie" (lines 16–17).

97. Harold F. Brooks, "Appendix" to *Titus Andronicus*, ed. J. C. Maxwell, Arden Shakespeare, 3rd edn. (1961; reprint, London: Methuen, 1963), 134.

98. Bate, ed., *Titus Andronicus*, note to 5.2.61 (256).

99. Ibid., 22.

100. Brooks, "Appendix" to *Titus Andronicus*, ed. Maxwell, 134.

101. Peter M. Daly, *Literature in the Light of the Emblem: Structural Parallels between the Emblem and Literature in the Sixteenth and Seventeenth Centuries*, 2nd edn. (Toronto, Buffalo, London: University of Toronto Press, 1998), 165. Daly, however, does not speculate about the costume and "insignias" of Chiron, Demetrius, or Tamora.

102. For a discussion of murderers in this and other plays, see Martin Wiggins, *Journeymen in Murder: The Assassin in English Renaissance Drama* (Oxford: Clarendon Press, 1991).

103. *A Critical Edition of Thomas Preston's "Cambises,"* ed. Robert Carl Johnson (Salzburg: Institut für Englische Sprache und Literatur, Universität Salzburg, 1975).

104. David Bevington, "'O Cruel, Irreligious Piety!': Stage Images of Civil Conflict in *Titus Andronicus*," in *"Titus Andronicus": Critical Essays*, ed. Kolin, 367.

105. Thelma N. Greenfield, *The Induction in Elizabethan Drama* (Eugene: University of Oregon Books, 1969), 46.

106. *"A Warning for Fair Women": A Critical Edition*, ed. Cannon.

107. Cannon, ed., *A Warning for Fair Women*, 18.

108. Ibid.

109. Robert Yarington, *Two Lamentable Tragedies* (London, 1601), sig. A2r. On the first page of the text, the play's title is given as *Two Tragedies in One*.

110. Ibid., sigs. A2v and C3r.

111. Ibid., sig. F3r.

112. Robert Greene, *The Scottish History of James the Fourth*, ed. Norman Sanders, The Revels Plays (London: Methuen, 1970).

113. *"The History of King Leir," 1605*, ed. Greg.

114. *The History of King Lear*, in *William Shakespeare: The Complete Works*, ed. Stanley Wells and Gary Taylor, with John Jowett and William Montgomery (Oxford: Clarendon Press, 1986), scene 7, line 40.

115. The title-page of Ripa's 1603 *Iconologia* advertises the book as necessary for "*Poeti, Pittori, Scultori, & altri.*"

116. Ripa, *Iconologia*, 201.

117. Although Ripa's 1603 edition fails to illustrate *Homicido*, the version translated into French by Jean Baudoin and entitled *Iconologie, ou explication nouvelle de plusieurs images, emblemes, et autres figures* (Paris, 1644) includes a small woodcut (pt. 2, 158), reproduced here as fig. 13.

118. Handling a fierce dog onstage carries certain risks, of course. But the company of actors may have been able to borrow a dog used for bearbaiting.

119. Ben Jonson, however, in *The Golden Age Restored*, a masque performed at court in 1615, has a character named Iron Age call forth "the evils." These include Rapine, along with Fraud, Slander, Pride, and others. Unfortunately for our purposes, these figures are not described. See *The Golden Age Restored* in *Ben Jonson: The Complete Masques*, line 46.

120. Although artists frequently depict combat and the despoliation of towns, scenes of rape are uncommon. John Hale notes that "rape, as opposed to abduction, is left to prose" ("Women and War in the Visual Arts of the Renaissance," in *War, Literature and the Arts in Sixteenth-Century Europe*, ed. J. R. Mulryne and Margaret Shewring [London: Macmillan, 1989], 48).

121. Lust also appears in an earlier play, *The Trial of Treasure* (acted c. 1565 possibly at a school or college), where we find this stage direction: "*Enter Lust, like a gallant.*" Another character tells him, "Mine apparel is not like unto thine / Disguised and jagged, of sundry fashion." It's difficult to know how much

significance this figure has for our purposes. Lust seems to have the meaning of "pleasure, delight" (*OED*) and is invoked in part to rhyme with the name of another character – "Just." See *The Trial of Treasure*, in *Anonymous Plays*, ed. John S. Farmer, 3rd Series (1906; reprint, New York: Barnes and Noble, 1966), [pp.] 207, 208. In the much later *The Traitor*, acted by Queen Henrietta's Men in 1631, Lust seems similarly attired: "*Enter Lust, richly apparelled*" (3.2.135). See *The Traitor*, in *The Dramatic Works and Poems of James Shirley*, ed. William Gifford and Alexander Dyce, 6 vols. (London: John Murray, 1833), vol. II. For these editions, which give act and scene numbers but not line numbers, the last numbers cited here represent page numbers.

122. The other famous classical rape is that of the Sabine women. For an analysis of artistic treatments of both Lucretia and the Sabines, see Norman Bryson, "Two Narratives of Rape in the Visual Arts: Lucretia and the Sabine Women," in *Rape*, ed. Sylvana Tomaselli and Roy Porter (Oxford: Blackwell, 1986), 152–73. Diane Wolfthal, in *Images of Rape: The "Heroic" Tradition and Its Alternatives* (Cambridge: Cambridge University Press, 1999), also discusses representations of the Sabine women. Heather James, in *Shakespeare's Troy: Drama, Politics, and the Translation of Empire* (Cambridge: Cambridge University Press, 1997), observes that "Rome was mythically founded on rape: the rape of the Sabine women, the rape of Lucrece, the rape of Ilia (raped by Mars, this vestal virgin bore Romulus and Remus), and Aeneas' dynastic marriage to Lavinia, which threatened to repeat the rape of Helen of Troy" (44). See also Stephanie H. Jed, *Chaste Thinking: The Rape of Lucretia and the Birth of Humanism* (Bloomington and Indianapolis: Indiana University Press, 1989).

123. Thomas Heywood, *The Rape of Lucrece*, ed. Allan Holaday, Illinois Studies in Language and Literature 34, no. 3 (Urbana: University of Illinois Press, 1950). Heywood's play must have been quite popular; Quartos were published in 1608, 1609, 1614, 1630, and 1638.

124. Thomas Middleton, *The Ghost of Lucrece*, ed. Joseph Quincy Adams (New York and London: Charles Scribner's Sons for the Trustees of Amherst College), 1937. Adams writes that Middleton "drew his inspiration from Shakespeare's popular *Lucrece*" (xviii).

125. When Marcus sees the raped and mutilated Lavinia, he says, "sure some Tereus hath deflow'red thee" (2.4.26); later, when Lavinia turns the leaves of Ovid's *Metamorphoses*, Titus says, "This is the tragic tale of Philomel" (4.1.47). There is an interesting connection between this myth and the Furies. The Furies attended the wedding of Tereus and Philomel and illuminated the ceremony with torches taken from a funeral. As for the connection between Shakespeare's Lavinia and Lucretia, when Lavinia reveals the identity of her attackers, Marcus alludes to "Lucrece' rape" (4.1.91).

126. Reproduced by Ian Donaldson, *The Rapes of Lucretia: A Myth and Its Transformations* (Oxford: Clarendon Press, 1982), pl. 1. See also A. Robin Bowers,

"Iconography and Rhetoric in Shakespeare's *Lucrece*," *Shakespeare Studies* 14 (1981): 1–21; and Bowers, "Emblem and Rape in Shakespeare's *Lucrece* and *Titus Andronicus*," *Studies in Iconography* 10 (1984–86): 79–96.

127. Paintings of the Sabine women also depict weaponry (swords or daggers) in the hands of the attackers. See, for example, Nicolas Poussin's version of the narrative (reproduced by Norman Bryson, in *Rape*, figs. 2 and 3).

128. Jocelyn Catty, in *Writing Rape, Writing Women in Early Modern England: Unbridled Speech* (London: Macmillan; New York: St. Martin's Press, 1999), includes a useful chapter called "'Some women love to struggle': Rape in Renaissance Drama" (91–118). She focuses, however, more closely on the victims of rape and their appearance than on the perpetrators of the crime.

129. "Lust is the moral disease of which Syphax is the hopeless victim," writes Michael Scott in *John Marston's Plays* (London: Macmillan, 1978), 82.

130. *The Tragedy of Sophonisba*, in *The Selected Plays of John Marston*, ed. MacDonald P. Jackson and Michael Neill (Cambridge: Cambridge University Press, 1986).

131. *The Queen of Corinth*, ed. Robert Kean Turner, in *The Dramatic Works in the Beaumont and Fletcher Canon*, gen. ed. Fredson Bowers, 10 vols. (Cambridge: Cambridge University Press, 1966–96), vol. VIII. The play was written by Fletcher, Massinger, and Field.

132. Diane Wolfthal, in *Images of Rape*, identifies a single instance of personified rape (fig. 12); the illustration depicts the rape of the Sabine women. Produced not in the Renaissance but in the eighteenth century, the personification appears in a German edition of Ripa's *Iconologia*, printed in 1758–60. Curiously, the figure is female rather than male: she wields a sword in one hand and carries a shield in the other; the "shield is adorned with an image of Proserpina struggling against her attacker, Jupiter" (27).

133. Ripa, *Iconologia*, 428–29.

134. Illustrated by Taymor, *Titus: The Illustrated Screenplay*, 155, 157. Taymor describes the bird as "an owl" with outstretched wings (154).

135. Ripa also assigns to Rape a wolf, which might be represented onstage by a fierce dog.

136. Ellen S. Jacobowitz and Stephanie Loeb Stepanek, *The Prints of Lucas van Leyden and His Contemporaries* (Washington, D.C.: National Gallery of Art, 1983), 66. The authors make this observation in their discussion of an engraving entitled *The Man with the Torch and a Woman followed by a Fool* (c. 1508).

137. See Dirk Bax, *Hieronymus Bosch: His Picture-Writing Deciphered*, trans. M. A. Bax-Botha (Rotterdam: A. A. Balkema, 1979), 94.

138. "*The Tragical Reign of Selimus*," *1594*, ed. W. Bang, Malone Society Reprints (1909 [for 1908]; reprint, Oxford: Oxford University Press, 1964).

139. *Lust's Dominion*, in *The Dramatic Works of Thomas Dekker*, ed. Fredson Bowers, 4 vols. (Cambridge: Cambridge University Press, 1953–61), vol. IV.

In its original form the play may have been performed in the early 1590s and then subsequently revised by Dekker, Haughton, Day, and Marston.

140. *The Honest Whore, Part 1*, in *The Dramatic Works of Thomas Dekker*, vol. II.

141. John Mason, *The Turk*, ed. Fernand Lagarde (Salzburg: Institut für Anglistik und Amerikanistik, Universität Salzburg, 1979).

142. *Four Plays, or Moral Representations, in One*, ed. Cyrus Hoy, in *The Dramatic Works in the Beaumont and Fletcher Canon*, vol. VIII, scene 6, interlude 3, lines 14–15.s.d.

143. Ripa, *Iconologia*, 201.

3 Rumour in *2 Henry IV*

1. Raphael Holinshed, *The Third volume of Chronicles . . . Now newlie recognised, augmented, and continued . . . to the yeare 1586* (London, 1587), 583. Hereafter cited parenthetically by page number.

2. Richard Abrams, in "Rumor's Reign in *2 Henry IV*: The Scope of a Person-ification," *English Literary Renaissance* 16 (Autumn 1986): 467–95, surveys critical opinion about this question.

3. Modern productions treat the figure of Rumour in a wide variety of ways. For some of these, see Barbara Hodgdon, *Henry IV, Part Two*, Shakespeare in Per-formance (Manchester: Manchester University Press; New York: St. Martin's Press, 1993), esp. 73 and 102.

4. Giorgio Melchiori, ed., *The Second Part of King Henry IV*, New Cambridge Shakespeare (Cambridge: Cambridge University Press, 1989), 59.

5. Cesare Ripa, *Iconologia overo descrittione di diverse imagini cavate dall'antichità, & di propria inventione* (Rome, 1603), 438. Ripa's picture (1630 edition) is reproduced by Leo Braudy, *The Frenzy of Renown: Fame and Its History* (New York and Oxford: Oxford University Press, 1986), fig. 4 of the illustrations entitled "The Faces of Fame." Thomas Wright, in *The Passions of the Minde* (1601), suggests the connection between arrows and a kind of speech: "rash men in speech have an arrow in their tongues" (171). Similarly, William Averell, in *A mervailous combat of contrarieties* (1588), writes that the hateful tongue is "more pearcing than an arrowe" (sig. C2v).

6. "*Clyomon and Clamydes*," *1599*, ed. W. W. Greg, Malone Society Reprints (Oxford: Oxford University Press, 1913). Greg observes, "The title-page states that the play had been performed by the Queen's players. This company acted regularly at court down to 1591" (v). Jean MacIntyre, in *Costumes and Scripts in the Elizabethan Theatres* (Edmonton: University of Alberta Press, 1992), discusses the doubling of roles required by the demands of the script and the size of the company of actors (38–39) but does not treat the costume of Rumour in *Clyomon*.

7. Thomas Garter, "*The Most Virtuous & Godly Susanna*," *1578*, ed. B. Ifor Evans and W. W. Greg, Malone Society Reprints (Oxford: Oxford University Press, 1937 [for 1936]).

8. Harry Berger, Jr., "Sneak's Noise or Rumor and Detextualization in *2 Henry IV*," *Kenyon Review* n.s. 6 (Fall 1984): 64.

9. *The Magnificent Entertainment*, in *The Dramatic Works of Thomas Dekker*, ed. Fredson Bowers, 4 vols. (Cambridge: Cambridge University Press, 1953–61), vol. II. Hereafter cited parenthetically by line number.

10. Henry Peacham in *Graphice or the Most Auncient and Excellent Art of Drawing and Limming* (London, 1612) notes that Fame's "thinne and light" garment permits swift movement: it is "open to the middle thigh that she might runne the faster" (113 [misnumbered as 117]).

11. *The House of Fame*, in *The Riverside Chaucer*, ed. Larry D. Benson, 3rd edn. (Boston: Houghton Mifflin, 1987).

12. Edward Hall, *The Union of the two noble and illustre famelies of Lancastre & Yorke* (London, 1548), 10th year of Henry VIII's reign, fol. lxvi r. (Hereafter cited parenthetically by year of reign and folio number.) Holinshed, in *The Third Volume of Chronicles*, repeats this sentence of Hall's verbatim (849). Prior to the entertainment at King Henry's court, Pegasus as a symbol of Fame had appeared at a pageant welcoming Philip of Austria to Paris in 1501 (Sydney Anglo, *Spectacle, Pageantry, and Early Tudor Policy* [Oxford: Clarendon Press, 1969], 134). See also W. R. Streitberger, *Court Revels, 1485–1559* (Toronto: University of Toronto Press, 1994), 99–100.

13. *The Somerset Masque*, in *The Works of Thomas Campion*, ed. Walter R. Davis (Garden City, NY: Doubleday, 1967), 271. The masque honored the marriage of the Earl of Somerset and Lady Frances Howard.

14. Melchiori, ed., *The Second Part of King Henry IV*, n. to line 15 of the Induction (60).

15. In *The Play of Patient Grissell*, ed. Ronald B. McKerrow and W. W. Greg, Malone Society Reprints (Oxford: Oxford University Press, 1909), Rumour enters "*blowyng & puffing*" and says, "And nowe have I occasion my troumpe to bloe" (line 1676). In *Apius and Virginia*, ed. Ronald B. McKerrow and W. W. Greg, Malone Society Reprints (Oxford: Oxford University Press, 1911), Rumour implies the presence of a trumpet by saying, "To skies I flie to blase abrode, / the trompe of depe defame" (lines 882–83).

16. *The Tragical Legend of Robert, Duke of Normandy*, in *The Works of Michael Drayton*, ed. J. William Hebel, Kathleen M. Tillotson, and Bernard H. Newdigate, 5 vols. (Oxford: Blackwell, 1931–41), vol. I. In Renaissance literature Fortune's relationship to Fame is frequently antagonistic. In *Soliman and Perseda*, for example, a character complains of "cursed Fortune, enemy to Fame" (1.4.48). See *"The Tragedye of Solyman and Perseda," Edited from the Original Texts with Introduction and Notes*, ed. John J. Murray (New York and London: Garland, 1991).

17. *George Gascoigne's "The Steele Glas" and "The Complainte of Phylomene": A Critical Edition*, ed. William L. Wallace (Salzburg: Institut für Englische Sprache und Literatur, Universität Salzburg, 1975).

18. If Rumour in *2 Henry IV* were referring to a recorder as opposed to a horn, Rumour would logically speak not of the "monster with uncounted heads" but rather the "monster with uncounted hands." For references to trumpets in the stage directions of Renaissance plays, see Alan Dessen and Leslie Thomson, *A Dictionary of Stage Directions in English Drama, 1580–1642* (Cambridge: Cambridge University Press, 1999), 237–38.

19. T. W. Craik, in *The Tudor Interlude: Stage, Costume, and Acting* (Leicester: Leicester University Press, 1962), observes that on the sixteenth-century stage Fame "is consistently referred to as feminine except in *Like Will to Like*, where her sex is unspecified" (65). Good Fame is a character in this play by Ulpian Fulwell (first printed in 1568). Unfortunately, the play tells us nothing about the character's costume. The actor who speaks the prologue to *The Travels of the Three English Brothers* (acted by Queen Anne's Men in 1607) by John Day, William Rowley, and George Wilkins is "attired like Fame," but the surviving text contains no description of costume; a feminine pronoun is the only indication of gender, and a reference to her "trump" is the only indication of a prop. See *The Travels* in *Three Renaissance Travel Plays*, ed. Anthony Parr, The Revels Plays Companion Library (Manchester: Manchester University Press; New York: St. Martin's Press, 1995), 59.

20. Reproduced by David M. Bergeron, *English Civic Pageantry, 1558–1642* (Columbia: University of South Carolina Press, 1971), fig. 5. Kip's engraving appears in Stephen Harrison's *Arches of Triumph Erected in honor of the High and Mighty Prince James the First* (London, 1604), sig. F2r.

21. *Sidero-thriambos, or Steele and Iron Triumphing*, in *Pageants and Entertainments of Anthony Munday: A Critical Edition*, ed. David M. Bergeron, The Renaissance Imagination 11 (New York and London: Garland, 1985).

22. Vincenzo Cartari, *The Fountaine of Ancient Fiction, Wherein is lively depictured the Images and Statues of the gods of the Ancients, with their proper and perticular expositions*, trans. Richard Linche (London, 1599), sig. V3v.

23. *Aeneid*, in *Virgil*, trans. H. Rushton Fairclough, rev. G. P. Goold, Loeb Classical Library, 2 vols. (1935; reprint, Cambridge, MA: Harvard University Press, 1999). Hereafter cited parenthetically by book and line numbers.

24. Ovid, *Metamorphoses*, trans. Frank Justus Miller, 2nd edn., Loeb Classical Library, 2 vols. (1921; reprint, Cambridge, MA: Harvard University Press, 1966–68), vol. II. Hereafter cited parenthetically by book and line numbers.

25. Ben Jonson, *The Staple of News*, ed. Anthony Parr, The Revels Plays (Manchester: Manchester University Press; New York: St. Martin's Press, 1988).

26. *The Masque of Queens*, in *Ben Jonson: The Complete Masques*, ed. Stephen Orgel, The Yale Ben Jonson (New Haven and London: Yale University Press, 1969).

27. Dermoth Cavanagh, in "'Possessed with Rumours': Popular Speech and *King John*," in *Shakespeare Yearbook* 6: *Shakespeare and History*, ed. Holger Klein and Rowland Wymer (Lewiston, NY, Queenston, Lampeter: Edwin Mellen Press, 1996), 171–94, assesses the significance of rumor in the world of this play.

28. "When Rumour enters at line 1196, his function is to fill in key elements of the romance which have been left undramatized" (Scott McMillin and Sally-Beth MacLean, *The Queen's Men and Their Plays* [Cambridge: Cambridge University Press, 1998], 150). McMillin and MacLean observe that Rumour, who tells the truth in *Clyomon*, is "very different" from Shakespeare's Rumor in *2 Henry IV* (223, n. 15).

29. *The Honest Whore, Part 2*, in *The Dramatic Works of Thomas Dekker*, vol. II.

30. *Chesters Triumph in Honor of Her Prince, As it was performed upon S. Georges Day 1610* (London, 1610), sig. Cr–v. Robert Amerie was apparently responsible for designing the ceremony of welcome.

31. *Britannia's Honor*, in *The Dramatic Works of Thomas Dekker*, vol. IV.

32. For a collection of essays exploring the significance of this work, see *Petrarch's "Triumphs": Allegory and Spectacle*, ed. Konrad Eisenbichler and Amilcare A. Iannucci, University of Toronto Italian Studies 4 (Ottawa: Dovehouse, 1990).

33. In the lines that follow, Navarre completes the Petrarchan allusion, saying of love and chastity, "brave conquerors – for so you are, / That war against your own affections / And the huge army of the world's desires – " (lines 8–10). Mary E. Hazard demonstrates the allusion to Petrarch, in "Shakespeare's 'Living Art': A Live Issue from *Love's Labour's Lost*," in *Shakespeare and the Arts: A Collection of Essays from the Ohio Shakespeare Conference*, ed. Cecile Williamson Cary and Henry S. Limouze (Washington, D. C.: University Press of America, 1982), 185–86.

34. Shakespeare provides the facetious counterpart of this realization in *Much Ado about Nothing*, when Benedick tells Beatrice, "If a man do not erect in this age his own tomb ere he dies, he shall live no longer in monument than the bell rings and the widow weeps" (5.2.77–80).

35. David L. Jeffrey and Patrick Grant, "Reputation in *Othello*," *Shakespeare Studies* 6 (1970): 197.

36. Owen Felltham, "Of Fame," in *Resolves, A Duple Century*, 3rd edn. (London, 1628), 45.

37. Ibid., 46.

38. Francis Bacon, "Of Praise," in *The Essayes or Counsels, Civill and Morall*, ed. Michael Kiernan (Oxford: Clarendon Press, 1985), 159.

39. Charles Gibson, *The Praise of a good Name, The reproch of an ill Name* (London, 1594), 50.

40. For a treatment of fame in this play, see D. J. Gordon, "Name and Fame: Shakespeare's Coriolanus," in *Papers Mainly Shakespearian*, ed. G. I. Duthie, Aberdeen University Studies 147 (Edinburgh: Oliver and Boyd, 1964), 40–57. Gordon discusses not only *Coriolanus* but also other Shakespearean plays, including *2 Henry IV*.

41. Richard Niccols, "A Winter Nights Vision: Being an Addition of Such Princes Especially Famous, who were exempted in the former Historie," in *A Mirror for Magistrates* (London, 1610), 558.

42. Henry Peacham, *Minerva Britanna or a Garden of Heroical Devises* (London, 1612), 35, 121.

43. For the full range of devices employing Fame and used by Feyerabend, see Ilse O'Dell, *Jost Ammans Buchschmuck-Holzschnitte für Sigmund Feyerabend* (Wiesbaden: Otto Harrassowitz, 1993), figs. f1–f55.

44. See Frederick Kiefer, *Fortune and Elizabethan Tragedy* (San Marino, CA: The Huntington Library, 1983), chap. 7.

45. *The Progresses and Public Processions of Queen Elizabeth*, ed. John Nichols, 3 vols. (1823; reprint, New York: Burt Franklin, [1966]), II: 143.

46. *Entertainments for Elizabeth I*, ed. Jean Wilson (Woodbridge: D. S. Brewer; Totowa, NJ: Rowman and Littlefield, 1980), 110.

47. *The Arraignment of Paris*, ed. R. Mark Benbow, in *The Dramatic Works of George Peele*, in *The Life and Works of George Peele*, gen. ed. Charles Tyler Prouty, 3 vols. (New Haven and London: Yale University Press, 1952–70), vol. III.

48. Reproduced by Edmund A. Bowles, *Musical Ensembles in Festival Books, 1500–1800: An Iconographical and Documentary Survey* (Ann Arbor, MI, and London: UMI Research Press, 1989), fig. 19.

49. *The Royall Passage of her Majesty from the Tower of London, to her Palace of White-hall, with all the Speaches and Devices, both of the Pageants and otherwise* (London, [1604]). The first edition (1558?) has no illustration on the title-page.

50. Thomas Newton, "The Death of Delia," in *The Progresses and Public Processions of Queen Elizabeth*, III: 635.

51. Reproduced by Erna Auerbach and C. Kingsley Adams, *Paintings and Sculpture at Hatfield House: A Catalogue* (London: Constable, 1971), color pl. 5.

52. Frances A. Yates, *Astraea: The Imperial Theme in the Sixteenth Century* (London and Boston: Routledge & Kegan Paul, 1975), 217.

53. Roy Strong, *Gloriana: the Portraits of Queen Elizabeth I* (London: Thames and Hudson, 1987), 158–59.

54. Michael Neill, "Broken English and Broken Irish: Nation, Language, and the Optic of Power in Shakespeare's Histories," *Shakespeare Quarterly* 45 (Spring 1994): 29, n. 98.

55. Daniel Fischlin, "Political Allegory, Absolutist Ideology, and the 'Rainbow Portrait' of Queen Elizabeth I," *Renaissance Quarterly* 50 (Spring 1997): 182.

56. Roy Strong, *Portraits of Queen Elizabeth* (Oxford: Clarendon Press, 1963), 86.

57. Baldassare Castiglione, *The Book of the Courtier*, trans. Charles S. Singleton (Garden City, NY: Doubleday, 1959), 69. The etching of Gloria by Domenico del Barbiere (c. 1506 – c. 1570) endows her with the same attributes that Fame sometimes possesses: the winged figure stands upon a globe and holds two trumpets.

58. Niccolò Machiavelli, *The Prince*, trans. James B. Atkinson, Library of Liberal Arts (Indianapolis: Bobbs–Merrill, 1976), 331.

59. *The Masque of Queens*, in *Ben Jonson: The Complete Masques*, lines 453–56.

60. Although some early manuscript illuminations depict Fame's chariot being drawn by white horses, later artists prefer elephants. Dorothy C. Shorr, in "Some Notes on the Iconography of Petrarch's Triumph of Fame," *Art Bulletin* 20 (March 1938): 100–07, observes that "according to Pliny, the first harnessed elephants seen at Rome were those that drew the chariot of Pompey at his triumph after the African war" (107). Lynn White, Jr., in "Indic Elements in the Iconography of Petrarch's *Trionfo della Morte*," *Speculum* 49 (April 1974): 201–21, sees a further significance in the elephants: "Following ancient tradition, the Middle Ages held that the elephant is the most intelligent of animals, and has by far the best memory" (209).

61. See Olive Cook, *The English Country House* (London: Thames and Hudson, 1974), fig. 71.

62. In *The Interlude of Vice (Horestes)*, ed. Daniel Seltzer et al., Malone Society Reprints (Oxford: Oxford University Press, 1962), this stage direction appears in the margin at line 1005: "*Enter in fame & let all the sodyers folow him in araye.*"

63. Christopher Marlowe, *Tamburlaine the Great*, ed. J. S. Cunningham, The Revels Plays (Manchester: Manchester University Press; Baltimore: The Johns Hopkins University Press, 1981).

64. *Edward III*, in *The Riverside Shakespeare*, ed. G. Blakemore Evans et al., 2nd edn. (Boston: Houghton Mifflin, 1997).

65. By "honor" the king designates fame earned by righteous action. As Robert Ashley observes in *Of Honour*, ed. Virgil B. Heltzel (San Marino, CA: The Huntington Library, 1947), "the name of renowne spreadeth yt self largely to all kind of fame, whether yt spring of good or come of dishonest causes; but honour we sett downe to arise only out of vertue" (37). In *Troia-Nova Triumphans*, personified Honor is called "eldest child of Fame" (*The Dramatic Works of Thomas Dekker*, III: 243). And in *The Memorable Masque* by George Chapman, performed 15 February 1613, the herald of Honor is "called Phemis, or Fame" (*Court Masques: Jacobean and Caroline Entertainments, 1605–1640*, ed. David Lindley [Oxford: Clarendon Press, 1995], 80).

66. In *Chaucer and the Imaginary World of Fame* (Totowa, NJ: Barnes & Noble, 1984), Piero Boitani observes that in antiquity Fulgentius "proclaims that Pegasus is to be taken 'in figura famae,' as a figure of fame" (43). In *The Mythologies* Fulgentius writes, "From her [the Gorgon's] blood Pegasus is said to have been born, shaped in the form of renown; whereby Pegasus is said to have wings, because fame is winged" (*Fulgentius the Mythographer*, trans. Leslie George Whitbread [Columbus: Ohio State University Press, 1971], 62).

67. In "Fame," in *Encyclopedia of Comparative Iconography: Themes Depicted in Works of Art*, ed. Helene E. Roberts, 2 vols. (Chicago and London: Fitzroy Dearborn, 1998), Liana De Girolami Cheney remarks on Ripa's account of Mercury: "This image refers to the ancient legend, Ripa states, that Jupiter honored Mercury with the task of being messenger of the gods by virtue of his

eloquent rhetoric and efficacious voice, which would expand and broadcast to all the good and heroic manifestations" (I: 312).

68. O. Elton, in "Literary Fame: a Renaissance Study," *Otia Merseiana* 4 (1904): 24–52, examining the significance of literature for fame's survival, sees Petrarch as especially influential in fashioning concepts of fame during the Renaissance.

69. Plutarch, *The Lives of the Noble Grecians and Romanes*, trans. Thomas North (London, 1579), sig. *3v–4r.

70. Giorgio Vasari, *Lives of the Artists*, trans. George Bull, 2 vols. (1965; reprint, London: Penguin, 1987), I: 208–9. Vasari himself painted Fame at several points in his career: at his house in Arezzo (1542); at the Palazzo della Cancelleria in Rome (1546); and at the Palazzo Vecchio in Florence (1560). See Cheney, "Fame," in *Encyclopedia of Comparative Iconography*, I: 307–13.

71. Pliny, *Natural History*, trans. H. Rackham et al., Loeb Classical Library, 10 vols. (Cambridge, MA: Harvard University Press, 1942–63), IX: 141 (bk. 34, chap. 9).

72. Braudy, *The Frenzy of Renown*, 85.

73. Although I have been unable to locate a good reproduction of the painting and although I did not see it on my last visit, it used to be located in the Sala della Fama, which is named for the ceiling fresco of Fame by Luigi Catani. See Claudio Pescio, *New Complete Guide of Pitti Palace*, trans. Rosalynd Pio (Florence: Bonechi, 1990), 104–05.

74. *Troia-Nova Triumphans, London Triumphing*, in *The Dramatic Works of Thomas Dekker*, vol. III.

75. John Taylor, *Heaven's Blessing, and Earths Joy, or A true relation of the supposed Sea-fights & Fire-workes, as were accomplished before the Royall Celebration, of the al-beloved Mariage, of the two peerlesse Paragons of Christendome, Fredericke & Elizabeth* (London, 1613), sig. D2v.

76. *The Triumphs of Love and Antiquity*, in *The Works of Thomas Middleton*, ed. A. H. Bullen, 8 vols. (London: J. C. Nimmo, 1885–86), VII: 322.

77. Geoffrey Whitney, *A Choice of Emblemes* (Leiden, 1586), 131.

78. Ibid., 196. A prefatory poem to part 2 of Whitney's *Emblemes* explains that Fame writes in "her goulden booke" (107).

79. Thomas Goffe, *The Couragious Turk*, ed. David Carnegie and Peter Davison, Malone Society Reprints (Oxford: Oxford University Press, 1974 [for 1968]).

80. James O. Halliwell, ed., *The Works of William Shakespeare*, 16 vols. (London: J. E. Adlard, 1853–65), X: 89.

81. *The Tryumphs of Honour and Industry*, in *The Works of Thomas Middleton*, VII: 306.

82. Peter Pett, *Times journey to seeke his Daughter Truth: and Truths Letter to Fame of Englands Excellencie* (London, 1599), sig. C2v.

83. "Il freno d'esso cavallo governato da Mercurio ci dinota, che la fama è portata dalle parole, & dalla voce, che suona dalle virtù degl'illustri fatti degl'huomini, & che tanto più, ò meno cotal fama perviene al mondo, quanto quella delle

lingue, & dal parlare del gl'huomini è accresciuta, & sparsa" (*Iconologia*, 143–44).

84. *The English Works of Sir Thomas More*, ed. W. E. Campbell et al., 2 vols. (London: Eyre and Spottiswoode; New York: Dial Press, 1931), I: 334.

85. Although *Fama* in the *Aeneid* "is assisted by Aeolus and his two trumpets," Alastair Fowler, in *Time's Purpled Masquers: Stars and the Afterlife in Renaissance English Literature* (Oxford: Clarendon Press, 1996), traces the two trumpets of Fame to Chrysostom. "Subsequent mythographic tradition tells of double trumpets, assigned by Gower to Renomee and Desfame" (90).

86. Although Fame's trumpet usually appears to be made of gold or brass in paintings, Thomas Middleton describes it differently in *The Triumphs of Truth*, celebrating the installation of the lord mayor on 29 October 1613: Fame has "on her head a crown of silver, and a silver trumpet in her hand, showing both her brightness and shrillness [piercingness]" (*The Triumphs of Truth*, in *Jacobean Civic Pageants*, ed. Richard Dutton, Ryburn Renaissance Texts and Studies [Keele: Keele University Press, 1995], 157). The silver contrasts with the gold that Middleton gives to Chastity, who has "in her hand a white silk banner, fill'd with stars of gold, expressing the eternity of her unspotted pureness."

87. Reproduced by Margery Corbett and Ronald Lightbown, *The Comely Frontispiece: The Emblematic Title-Page in England, 1550–1660* (London, Henley, and Boston: Routledge & Kegan Paul, 1979), 128.

88. *A Critical Edition of Thomas Preston's "Cambises,"* ed. Robert Carl Johnson (Salzburg: Institut für Englische Sprache und Literatur, Universität Salzburg, 1975).

89. *An Edition of Robert Wilson's "The Three Ladies of London" and "Three Lords and Three Ladies of London,"* ed. H. S. D. Mithal, The Renaissance Imagination 36 (New York and London: Garland, 1988). Although we learn that Wilson's Fame carries a trumpet, we discover no details about the costuming of this figure.

90. Reproduced by Ilja M. Veldman, *The New Hollstein: Dutch and Flemish Etchings, Engravings and Woodcuts, 1450–1700: Maarten van Heemskerck*, ed. Ger Luijten, 2 pts. (Roosendaal: Koninklijke van Poll, 1994), pt. 2, fig. 485/1.

91. Philip Massinger and Nathan Field, *The Fatal Dowry*, ed. T. A. Dunn, Fountainwell Drama Texts (Berkeley and Los Angeles: University of California Press, 1969).

92. John Webster, *A Monumental Columne, Erected to the living memory of the ever-glorious Henry, late Prince of Wales* (London, 1613), sig. B4v. Webster's poem also appeared in a made-up book, *Three Elegies on the most lamented Death of Prince Henrie* (London, 1613). Cyril Tourneur and Thomas Heywood wrote the other poems.

93. Harrison, *The Arches of Triumph*, sig. F1r.

94. Thomas Scot, *The Second Part of Philomythie, or Philomythologie* (London, 1625), sig. B2r.

95. *The Progresses and Public Processions of Queen Elizabeth*, I: 401.

96. Francis Bacon, "A Fragment of an Essay, Of Fame," in *The Essayes or Counsels*, 177. Michael Kiernan observes, "Having taken over Virgil's 'Parable' of Fame as a winged monster and established her horrific power … he turns to the control and profitable use of Fame's power, training the Virgilean monster into a Renaissance hunting hawk and using the specific stages of falconry" (xlv).

97. "Slander," in *Lucian*, trans. A. M. Harmon et al., Loeb Classical Library, 8 vols. (New York: G. P. Putnam's Sons, 1913–67), vol. I. Hereafter cited parenthetically by volume and page numbers.

98. Renaissance artists who treat this subject include Botticelli, Mantegna, Raphael, Federico Zuccaro, and Pieter Bruegel. See David Cast, *The Calumny of Apelles: A Study in the Humanist Tradition* (New Haven and London: Yale University Press, 1981).

99. Ben Jonson, *Volpone*, ed. R. B. Parker, The Revels Plays (Manchester: Manchester University Press, 1983).

100. *Adages*, trans. Margaret Mann Phillips, annotated by R. A. B. Mynors, in *The Collected Works of Erasmus* (Toronto, Buffalo, London: University of Toronto Press, 1974–), XXXI: 292.

101. Ben Jonson, *Sejanus His Fall*, ed. Philip Ayres, The Revels Plays (Manchester: Manchester University Press; New York: St. Martin's Press, 1990), act 4.

102. *The Collected Works of Erasmus*, XXXI: 147.

103. Ripa, *Iconologia*, 427. Fame appears on the title-page of Ripa's book (1603 edition): she is winged, holds a trumpet, and wears a garment covered with eyes and ears.

104. Peacham, *Minerva Britanna*, 22.

105. Cartari, *The Fountaine of Ancient Fiction*, trans. Linche, sig. K3r–v.

106. Giovanni Paolo Lomazzo, *A Tracte Containing the Artes of curious Paintinge, Carvinge & Buildinge*, trans. Richard Haydocke (Oxford, 1598), bk. 2, 30.

107. "Les yeux & les oreilles signifient, que le mestier de telles personnes est de tout voir, & de tout ouir, non pas seulement de jour, mais de nuit encore" (*Iconologie* [Paris, 1644], pt. 2, 153). As for the winged feet, Baudoin explains, "quelle leur adresse à flairer de loin les plus secrettes practiques" (such is their [spies'] skill at detecting from afar the most secret actions).

108. Thomas Heywood, *Troia Britanica: or, Great Britaines Troy* (London, 1609), sig. Aa2r (the pages are badly misnumbered).

109. Mary C. Erler, in "Sir John Davies and the Rainbow Portrait of Queen Elizabeth," *Modern Philology* 84 (May 1987): 359–71, notes the connection between the eyes and ears of the queen's garment and Sir Robert Cecil's role as "master of the queen's intelligence service" (370). Cecil is, of course, the man who built Hatfield House, where the Rainbow portrait hangs.

110. *A True Coppie of a Discourse written by a Gentleman, employed in the late voyage of Spaine and Portingale* (London, 1589), in *Occasional Issues of Unique or*

Very Rare Books, ed. Alexander B. Grosart, 17 (Manchester: privately printed, 1881), 84.

111. Sir Henry Wotton, *A Parallel betweene Robert late Earle of Essex, and George late Duke of Buckingham* (London, 1641), 3.

112. Anthony Esler, *The Aspiring Mind of the Elizabethan Younger Generation* (Durham, NC: Duke University Press, 1966), 79. Esler goes on to remark, "Essex seemed to imagine that war, like tilting or dueling, was essentially a sport in which the contestants won or lost honor, depending on their skill and courage" (94).

113. Sir Roger Williams, *A Briefe discourse of Warre* (London, 1590), sig. A3r.

114. In *Lives and Letters of the Devereux, Earls of Essex, in the Reigns of Elizabeth, James I, and Charles I, 1540–1646*, ed. Walter Bourchier Devereux, 2 vols. (London: John Murray, 1853), I: 240.

115. Ibid., I: 242.

116. In victory Essex made sure to advertise his achievements by commissioning portraits from the most acclaimed painters in England. Roy Strong, in *The English Renaissance Miniature* (London: Thames and Hudson, 1983), observes that Isaac Oliver painted Essex "bearded as he returned from the Cadiz expedition. Essex was very concerned with his own image. Up until the middle of the 1590s he had been faithful to Hilliard and to his follower in large, William Segar, but after 1596 he switched to a combination of Oliver for miniatures with the limner's future brother-in-law, Marcus Gheeraerts the Younger, for large-scale portraits" (161).

117. *Lives and Letters of the Devereux*, I: 372.

118. In *Calendar of the Manuscripts of the Most Hon. The Marquis of Salisbury... Preserved at Hatfield House, Hertfordshire*, 24 vols. (London: His Majesty's Stationery Office, 1883–1976:), pt. 9, 10.

119. Ibid.

120. *Lives and Letters of the Devereux*, II: 98.

121. William Camden, *The Historie of the Most Renowned and Victorious Princesse Elizabeth, Late Queene of England*, trans. R. N[orton] (London, 1630), 174.

122. Andrew Gurr, in *The Shakespearian Playing Companies* (Oxford: Clarendon Press, 1996), notes that "the players were unlikely to have known an armed insurrection was imminent" (289). In any event, "The players, who already had to remove their praise of Essex from the text of *Henry V* as soon as he returned disgraced and humiliated from Ireland in the early autumn of 1599, got away lightly."

123. Camden, *The Historie of... Princesse Elizabeth*, 187.

124. John Stowe, *The Annales of England, Faithfully collected out of the most autenticall Authors, Records, and other Monuments of Antiquitie* (London, 1605), 1407.

125. Robert Pricket, *Honors Fame in Triumph Riding, or, The Life and Death of the Late Honorable Earle of Essex* (London, 1604).

126. Anthony Miller, in *Roman Triumphs and Early Modern English Culture* (New York: Palgrave, 2001), observes that Pricket "takes specific aim at Essex's court rival, Sir Robert Cecil, representing him as an *arriviste* who belongs in the cart of baseness, not in the noble Essex's triumphal chariot" (81).

4 Hecate and the witches in *Macbeth*

1. H. A. Shapiro, in *Personifications in Greek Art: The Representation of Abstract Concepts, 600–400 B.C.* (Zurich: Akanthus, 1993), observes that "The Greeks of the fifth century B.C. did not have a word for personification, and they most likely conceived of personified abstractions in terms very different from our own" (12).
2. Even Shakespeareans interested in the staging of the play, however, sometimes decline to discuss Hecate on the grounds that her appearances in *Macbeth* are "spurious." See, for example, Ronald Watkins and Jeremy Lemmon, *Macbeth*, In Shakespeare's Playhouse Series (Totowa, NJ: Rowman and Littlefield, 1974), 22.
3. *The Masque of Queens*, in *Ben Jonson: The Complete Masques*, ed. Stephen Orgel, The Yale Ben Jonson (New Haven and London: Yale University Press, 1969). Jonson gives his witches the following names: Ignorance, Suspicion, Credulity, Falsehood, Murmur, Malice, Impudence, Slander, Execration, Bitterness, Fury, and Mischief (530, note to line 104).
4. *Theogony*, in *Hesiod: The Homeric Hymns and Homerica*, trans. Hugh G. Evelyn-White, Loeb Classical Library (Cambridge, MA: Harvard University Press; London: William Heinemann, 1977), 109.
5. Ibid., 111.
6. Sarah Iles Johnston, *Restless Dead: Encounters between the Living and the Dead in Ancient Greece* (Berkeley, Los Angeles, London: University of California Press, 1999), 209. In chap. 6, Johnston comprehensively examines Hecate's origins and history.
7. *Theogony*, in *Hesiod*, 113.
8. "To Demeter," in *Hesiod*, 291.
9. *The Aeneid*, in *Virgil*, trans. H. Rushton Fairclough, rev. G. P. Goold, Loeb Classical Library, 2 vols. (1935; reprint, Cambridge, MA: Harvard University Press, 1999). Hereafter cited parenthetically by book and line numbers.
10. Ovid, *Metamorphoses*, trans. Frank Justus Miller, 2nd edn., Loeb Classical Library, 2 vols. (1921; reprint, Cambridge, MA: Harvard University Press; London: William Heinemann, 1966–68). Hereafter cited parenthetically by book and line numbers.
11. "Ode 22," in *Horace: The Odes and Epodes*, trans. C. E. Bennett, rev. edn., Loeb Classical Library (1927; reprint, Cambridge, MA: Harvard University Press; London: William Heinemann, 1968), 249.

12. See, for example, the first-century A.D. statue reproduced by Irène Aghion, Claire Barbillon, and François Lissarrague, *Gods and Heroes of Classical Antiquity*, trans. Leonard N. Amico, Flammarion Iconographic Guides (Paris and New York: Flammarion, 1996), 143. Jeanne Addison Roberts, in "Shades of the Triple Hecate in Shakespeare," *Proceedings of the PMR Conference* 12/13 (1987–88): 47–66, argues that the triform goddess corresponds to the female categories of "Virgin, Whore, and Crone" (53).

13. *Diodorus of Sicily*, trans. C. H. Oldfather, Loeb Classical Library, 12 vols. (1935; reprint, Cambridge, MA: Harvard University Press; London: William Heinemann, 1967), 2: 483–85, (bk. 4, chap. 45).

14. Johnston, *Restless Dead*, 247.

15. Theocritus, "The Spell," in *The Greek Bucolic Poets*, trans. J. M. Edmonds, rev. edn., Loeb Classical Library (1928; reprint, Cambridge, MA: Harvard University Press; London: William Heinemann, 1970), 27.

16. Ancient accounts vary in their treatment of Hecate's relationship to Circe and Medea. Some represent Medea as a daughter of King Aeëtes and Eidyia, youngest of the Oceanides. Others report Medea's parents as Aeëtes and Hecate. Similarly, in some accounts Circe is the daughter of Helios and Perse rather than Hecate. See Edward Tripp, *The Meridian Handbook of Classical Mythology* (1970; reprint, New York: New American Library, 1974). See also the classical citations given by Jane Davidson Reid, *The Oxford Guide to Classical Mythology in the Arts, 1300–1990s*, 2 vols. (New York: Oxford University Press, 1993), I: 492.

17. *Diodorus of Sicily*, 485.

18. Ibid.

19. *Homer: The Odyssey*, trans. A. T. Murray, rev. George E. Dimock, 2nd edn., Loeb Classical Library (Cambridge, MA, and London: Harvard University Press; 1995). Hereafter cited parenthetically by book and line numbers.

20. Apollonius of Rhodes, *The Argonautica*, trans. R. C. Seaton, Loeb Classical Library (1912; reprint, Cambridge, MA: Harvard University Press; London: William Heinemann, 1980), bks. 3–4.

21. *Medea*, in *Seneca's Tragedies*, trans. Frank Justus Miller, Loeb Classical Library, 2 vols. (1929; reprint, London: William Heinemann; Cambridge, MA: Harvard University Press, 1968), vol. I.

22. Abraham Fraunce, *The Third part of the Countess of Pembrokes Ivychurch, Entituled Amintas Dale* (London, 1592), fol. 42v.

23. *Comus*, in *John Milton: Complete Poems and Major Prose*, ed. Merritt Y. Hughes (New York: Odyssey Press, 1957), lines 523, 535. In his poem "On the Death of the Bishop of Ely," Milton refers to "the triform goddess controlling her dragons with reins of gold" (lines 57–58).

24. Edmund Spenser, *The Faerie Queene*, ed. A. C. Hamilton (1977; reprint, London and New York: Longman, 1984), I.i.43.1–2.

25. Thomas Heywood, *The Brazen Age* (London, 1613), sig. Gv.

26. *The Moon-Calfe*, in *The Works of Michael Drayton*, ed. J. William Hebel, Kathleen M. Tillotson, and Bernard H. Newdigate, 5 vols. (Oxford: Blackwell, 1931–41), vol. III.

27. Bernice W. Kliman, in *Macbeth*, Shakespeare in Performance (Manchester: Manchester University Press; New York: St. Martin's Press, 1992), argues for the possibility that Restoration staging practices may "mirror to some extent Jacobean practices" (18) and reproduces the frontispiece to the edition of *Macbeth* included in Rowe's 1709 edition of Shakespeare's *Works* (23). She identifies as Hecate a figure "with flowing gown and hair," who holds up a hand, apparently in admonition (21). However, George Walton Williams, in an untitled note in *The Shakespeare Newsletter* 43 (1993): 3, argues persuasively that the figure identified as Hecate by Kliman is actually Banquo. John H. Astington, moreover, in "*Macbeth* and the Rowe Illustrations," *Shakespeare Quarterly* 49 (Spring 1998): 83–86, expresses doubt that the picture cited by Kliman mirrors stage practice. How likely is it that staging practices in the time of Nicholas Rowe, as Kliman contends, duplicated Jacobean practices? Although actors who had performed in the play before 1642 may still have been available to offer theatrical advice in the Restoration, the eighteen-year gap in performance history must have extinguished memories of most Jacobean staging. What's more, the gap between the addition of Hecate to *Macbeth* by the King's Men and the earliest Restoration revivals consisted of about fifty years. My own suspicion is that the Hecate who appeared in productions after 1660 may have had little connection with the production of *Macbeth* by the King's Men c. 1610.

28. Peter Thomson, *Shakespeare's Theatre*, 2nd edn. (London and New York: Routledge, 1992), 159.

29. G. Wilson Knight, "The 'Hecate' Scenes in *Macbeth*," in *The Shakespearian Tempest* (1932; reprint, London: Humphrey Milford; Oxford: Oxford University Press, 1940), 327.

30. Vincenzo Cartari, *Le imagini de i dei de gli antichi* (Venice, 1571), 117. Reproduced by Peter Mortenson, "*Friar Bacon and Friar Bungay*: Festive Comedy and 'Three-Form'd Luna,'" *English Literary Renaissance* 2 (Spring 1972): 194–207, illustration opposite 200.

31. Vincenzo Cartari, *The Fountaine of Ancient Fiction*, trans. Richard Linche (London, 1599), sig. H3^v. This work is a partial translation by Linche of Cartari's work.

32. Fraunce, *The Third part of the Countesse of Pembrokes Ivychurch*, fols. 42v–43r.

33. Stephen Batman, *The Golden Booke of the Leaden Goddes* (London, 1577), fol. 3v.

34. Natale Conti's *"Mythologies"*: *A Select Translation*, trans. Anthony DiMatteo, The Renaissance Imagination (New York and London: Garland, 1994), 145. Hereafter cited parenthetically.

35. Middleton and Shakespeare, like their contemporaries, understood that classical deities and abstractions could have a variety of meanings. Some playwrights

and masquemakers were concerned to limit the significance of a particular figure, lest the spectators become confused. For example, Samuel Daniel, in *The Vision of the Twelve Goddesses* (in *A Book of Masques in Honour of Allardyce Nicoll*, ed. T. J. B. Spencer and Stanley W. Wells [1967; reprint, Cambridge: Cambridge University Press, 1970]), writes: "though these images have often-times divers significations, yet it being not our purpose to represent them with all those curious and superfluous observations, we took them only to serve as hieroglyphics for our present intention, according to some one property that fitted our occasion, without observing other their mystical interpretations, wherein the authors themselves are so irregular and confused as the best mythologers, who will make somewhat to seem anything" (lines 31–37). Ben Jonson, by contrast, reveled in the multiplication of "significations." See John Peacock, "Ben Jonson's Masques and Italian Culture," in *Theatre of the English and Italian Renaissance*, ed. J. R. Mulryne and Margaret Shewring, Warwick Studies in the European Humanities (London: Macmillan, 1991), 73–94.

36. Reproduced by Kristen Lippincott, with Umberto Eco, E. H. Gombrich, and others, *The Story of Time* (London: Merrell Holberton in association with the National Maritime Museum, 2000), 185. Bellano's statue holds a flaming torch in her right hand; whatever she originally held in her left hand has been lost. The heart that she now holds in her left hand is thought to be a replacement for something that has disappeared.

37. *Livre de la conqueste de la toison d'or, par le Prince Jason de Tessalie: faict par figures avec exposition d'icelles*, ed. Jean de Mauregard (Paris, 1563). Jacques Gohory wrote the verses accompanying the illustrations. Hecate with three faces appears in illustration 20.

38. Although scholars, noting that the manuscript calls the play "ignorantly ill-fated," have assumed that *The Witch* was a failure onstage, Anne Lancashire, in "*The Witch*: Stage Flop or Political Mistake?" in *"Accompaninge the Players": Essays Celebrating Thomas Middleton, 1580–1980*, ed. Kenneth Friedenreich (New York: AMS Press, 1983), 161–81, argues that the play's brief theatrical run was the result of censorship.

39. Thomas Middleton, *The Witch*, in *Three Jacobean Witchcraft Plays*, ed. Peter Corbin and Douglas Sedge, The Revels Plays Companion Library (Manchester: Manchester University Press; New York: St. Martin's Press, 1986).

40. Thomas Middleton, *The Witch*, ed. W. W. Greg and F. P. Wilson, Malone Society Reprints (Oxford: Oxford University Press, 1950 [for 1948]), lines 181–82 (s.d. at the beginning of scene 2). Continental writers are similarly vague in describing the costume of witches. For example, in Leone di Somi's *Dialogues on Stage Affairs*, written c. 1565, a speaker observes that if a witch appears in a play, "we should have to dress her in fitting robes." See the Appendix in Allardyce Nicoll's *The Development of the Theatre: A Study of Theatrical Art from the Beginnings to the Present Day*, 5th edn. (New York: Harcourt Brace Jovanovich, 1966), 271.

41. Elizabeth Schafer, ed., *The Witch*, New Mermaids (New York: W. W. Norton; London: A. & C. Black, 1994), xxvi, xx. Similarly, Deborah Willis, in *Malevolent Nurture: Witch-Hunting and Maternal Power in Early Modern England* (Ithaca, NY, and London: Cornell University Press, 1995), says, "The scenes with Hecate are spectacular but not frightening. Primarily comic in effect, they travesty more than demonize her" (163).

42. Frances Dolan, in *Dangerous Familiars: Representations of Domestic Crime in England, 1550–1700* (Ithaca, NY, and London: Cornell University Press, 1994), observes that Hecate is "characterized by her roving, voracious sexual desire, which she satisfies with her son and with Almachildes, whom she enjoys as an incubus" (213).

43. Swapan Chakravorty, *Society and Politics in the Plays of Thomas Middleton* (Oxford: Clarendon Press, 1996), 111.

44. David Lindley, in *Court Masques: Jacobean and Caroline Entertainments, 1605–1640* (Oxford: Clarendon Press, 1995), writes of *The Masque of Queens*: "The witches may represent a demonized version of male fear of women, but it is perhaps equally possible that, though Jonson grounds his witch-lore firmly in scholarship, the performance might have emphasized the ridiculous self-delusions of witchcraft as much as its menace" (225).

45. J. M. Nosworthy, in *Shakespeare's Occasional Plays: Their Origin and Transmission* (London: Edward Arnold, 1965), identifies the speaker of these lines as Hecate: "Jonson's account of Hecate runs thus . . ." and he quotes Jonson's description of the Dame (41). But Jonson writes, "This Dame I make to bear the person of Ate, or mischief (for so I interpret it) out of Homer's description of her, *Iliad* IX.[505–12]" ("Appendix" to *The Masque of Queens*, ed. Orgel, 530).

46. Anthony Harris, in *Night's Black Agents: Witchcraft and Magic in Seventeenth-Century English Drama* (Manchester: Manchester University Press; Totowa, NJ: Rowman and Littlefield, 1980), suggests that a sketch by Inigo Jones of grotesque heads "may possibly be early drafts for the anti-masque [in *The Masque of Queens*], with the head-dresses being stylised representations of the 'ratts on they[r] heads' described by Jonson" (166–67). This speculation cannot be true if the witches, like their Dame, wear serpent-like hair. In any event, there is no evidence that the sketch has a connection with Jonson's masque.

47. "Epode 5," in *Horace: The Odes and Epodes*, 375.

48. Jonson, *The Masque of Queens*, in *The Complete Masques*, ed. Orgel, 530 (note to line 87). For the connection between witches and Furies, see the valuable article by Arthur R. McGee, "'Macbeth' and the Furies," *Shakespeare Survey* 19 (1966): 55–67.

49. Robert M. Adams, in *Ben Jonson's Plays and Masques* (New York and London: Norton, 1979), interprets "tapers" as "candles lighting the hall" where the masque is being presented (327.n.). But why should the witches not hold tapers in their hands? R. B. Graves, in *Lighting the Shakespearean Stage, 1567–1642*

(Carbondale and Edwardsville: Southern Illinois University Press, 1999), observes that "Tapers were employed indoors"; "smoked and stank"; and could be "placed in candlesticks" to be carried (22–23). Such smoky flames could effectively create an atmosphere appropriate to witches. Graves also points to the important association of tapers "with religious ceremony" (206).

50. Reproduced by Jeffrey B. Russell, *A History of Witchcraft: Sorcerers, Heretics, and Pagans* (1980; reprint, London: Thames and Hudson, 1987), 63.

51. Pierre Le Loyer, *A Treatise of Specters or straunge sights, visions and apparitions appearing sensibly unto men*, trans. Zachary Jones (London, 1605), fol. 11r.

52. Apollonius of Rhodes, *The Argonautica*, bk. 3, lines 1215–17.

53. Thomas Goffe, *The Couragious Turk*, ed. David Carnegie, Malone Society Reprints (Oxford: Oxford University Press, 1974 [for 1968]). This play was acted in February 1619 by students at Christ Church, Oxford.

54. Raphael Holinshed, *Chronicles of England, Scotland and Ireland*, 3 vols. in 2 (London, 1587), II: 170.

55. Simon Forman, *Booke of Plaies*, quoted by E. K. Chambers, *William Shakespeare: A Study of Facts and Problems*, 2 vols. (Oxford: Clarendon Press, 1930), II: 337.

56. Stephen Orgel notes that Simon Forman's account of the play presents a number of problems: "if we assume that Forman checked Holinshed to refresh his memory of the play, how can we explain his version of Macbeth's title, 'king of Codon,' which looks like an *auditory* error for Cawdor (Holinshed spells the name 'Cawder'), and the creation of Macbeth as Prince of Northumberland, where Holinshed, like the folio, has Malcolm created Prince of Cumberland?" See "Acting Scripts, Performing Texts," in *Crisis in Editing: Texts of the English Renaissance*, ed. Randall M. Leod [Randall McLeod] (New York: AMS Press, 1994), 270.

57. Nicholas Brooke, ed., *The Tragedy of Macbeth*, Oxford Shakespeare (Oxford: Clarendon Press, 1990), 234–35.

58. Willard Farnham, *Shakespeare's Tragic Frontier: The World of His Final Tragedies* (1950; reprint, Berkeley and Los Angeles: University of California Press, 1963), 94.

59. Peter Heylen, *Microcosmos, A Little Description of the Great World*, augmented and revised edn. (Oxford, 1625), 508.

60. John Lyly, *Endymion*, ed. David Bevington, The Revels Plays (Manchester: Manchester University Press; New York: St. Martin's Press, 1996).

61. Ibid., note to line 32. Bevington points out that calling the hags "nymphs" is akin to calling the Furies "Eumenides."

62. Although it is possible that the witches seen by Jacobean spectators of *Macbeth* may not have corresponded to Banquo's description, that description seems in keeping with the role of the witches in the dramatic action and with the overall tone of the play.

63. The 1577 woodcut is reproduced by John Doebler, *Shakespeare's Speaking Pictures: Studies in Iconic Imagery* (Albuquerque: University of New Mexico Press, 1974), pl. 24.

64. The account of Macbeth contained in Thomas Heywood's *The Hierarchie of the blessed Angells* (London, 1635) seems to suit the woodcut in the 1577 chronicle better than Holinshed's account. According to Heywood, who cites "Boëthius . . . In his Scotch historie," Macbeth and Banquo, "Riding alone, encountred on the way / (In a darke grove) three virgins wondrous faire, / As well in habit as in feature rare" (508).

65. John Marston, *The Tragedy of Sophonisba*, in *Three Jacobean Witchcraft Plays*, ed. Corbin and Sedge. Anthony Harris, in *Night's Black Agents*, observes that Erictho's "method of substituting herself for Sophonisba is not made entirely clear. The stage direction reads, 'Enter Erictho in the shape of Sophonisba,' which suggests that the witch has actually assumed the form of her rival. However, the direction adds that Erictho's face is veiled" and the sexual encounter occurs in the dark (66).

66. William Rowley, Thomas Dekker, and John Ford, *The Witch of Edmonton*, in *Three Jacobean Witchcraft Plays*, ed. Corbin and Sedge. Although first entered in the Stationers' Register in 1621, the play was apparently not printed until 1658.

67. Marvin Rosenberg, *The Masks of Macbeth* (Berkeley, Los Angeles, London: University of California Press, 1978), 9.

68. Diane Purkiss, in *The Witch in History: Early Modern and Twentieth-Century Representations* (London and New York: Routledge, 1996), contends that "the witches are *witches*, and not simply rather odd old women," and, as evidence, she points to their use of octosyllabic couplets: "Their speech is marked off from that of the other characters in a manner which insists on their iconic status and also on their difference from the human" (210). For most Shakespeareans, however, the octosyllabic couplets have not resolved the issue.

69. Walter Clyde Curry, *Shakespeare's Philosophical Patterns*, 2nd edn. (Baton Rouge: Louisiana State University Press, 1959), 60.

70. Farnham, *Shakespeare's Tragic Frontier*, 99.

71. M. D. W. Jeffreys, "The Weird sisters in *Macbeth*," *English Studies in Africa* 1 (March 1958): 53.

72. Alan Brissenden, *Shakespeare and the Dance* (London: Macmillan, 1981), 66.

73. Stephen Booth, *"King Lear," "Macbeth," Indefinition, and Tragedy* (New Haven: Yale University Press, 1983), 102. Booth continues: "What those frantic answers also demonstrate – and what matters – is the fact of the question. The play does not require that it be answered. Thinking about the play's action does."

74. Jacobus Sprenger and Heinrich Kramer, *Malleus Maleficarum: The Hammer of Witchcraft*, trans. Montague Summers, ed. Pennethorne Hughes (London: The Folio Society, 1968), 139.

75. King James, *Daemonologie, in Forme of a Dialogue* (Edinburgh, 1597), 46.

76. Reginald Scot, *The discoverie of witchcraft* (London, 1584), 2.

77. William Perkins, *A Discourse of the Damned Art of Witchcraft* (Cambridge, 1608), 174.

78. Alexander Roberts, *A Treatise of Witchcraft* (London, 1616), 19–20.

79. In *Dido Queen of Carthage* a character guesses that a suddenly overcast sky and storm are owing to a "fell enchantress," who can "dive into black tempests' treasury / When as she means to mask the world with clouds" (4.1.3, 5–6). See Christopher Marlowe, *"Dido Queen of Carthage" and "The Massacre at Paris,"* ed. H. J. Oliver, The Revels Plays (Cambridge, MA: Harvard University Press, 1968).

80. King James, *Daemonologie*, 39.

81. Henry Holland, *A Treatise against Witchcraft* (Cambridge, 1590), sig. G4r.

82. Roberts, *A Treatise of Witchcraft*, 19.

83. Lambert Daneau, *A Dialogue of Witches*, trans. Richard Watkins (London, 1575), sig. H2v.

84. Henry Boguet, *An Examen of Witches*, trans. E. Allen Ashwin, ed. Montague Summers (London: John Rodker, 1929), 5. Originally published as *Discours des sorciers*.

85. Glynne Wickham believes that, although the witches may not have flown in the first performances of *Macbeth*, the King's Men added a flying Hecate "some time between the first performance of *The Witch* and the publication of the first Folio in 1623." See "To Fly or Not to Fly?: The Problem of Hecate in Shakespeare's 'Macbeth,'" in *Essays on Drama and Theatre: Liber Amicorum Benjamin Hunningher* (Amsterdam: Moussault's; Antwerp: Standaard, 1973), 173.

86. A "witch" is defined by John Baret as "he that useth witchcraft, soothsaying…" See *An Alvearie or Triple Dictionarie, in Englishe, Latin, and French* (London, [1573]), sig. Kkk4v.

87. George Gifford, *A Discourse of the subtill Practises of Devilles by Witches and Sorcerers* (London, 1587), sig. B2r.

88. Holland, *A Treatise against Witchcraft*, sig. C3v.

89. Perkins, *A Discourse of the Damned Art of Witchcraft*, 56.

90. On the Renaissance stage, Furies, like witches, dance. For instance, in *Tancred and Gismund*, acted 1591, we find this stage direction at the beginning of act 4: "*Megæra riseth out of hell, with the other Furies, Alecto and Tysyphone, dauncing an hellish round*" (lines 855–57). See *"The Tragedy of Tancred and Gismund,"* *1591–2*, ed. W. W. Greg, Malone Society Reprints (Oxford: Oxford University Press, 1915 [for 1914]). Anthony Harris, in *Night's Black Agents*, suggests that the manner of the Furies' entry "may well mirror the first appearance of the Sisters" in *Macbeth* (161).

91. Brissenden, *Shakespeare and the Dance*, 66.

92. Readers of *Macbeth* today seem to feel that singing and dancing witches are somehow at odds with the notion that witches represent a real source of physical and moral danger. In *Faultlines: Cultural Materialism and the Politics of Dissident Reading* (Berkeley, Los Angeles, Oxford: University of California Press, 1992), Alan Sinfield writes: "For many members of Jacobean audiences, witches were a social and spiritual reality: they were as real as Edward the Confessor,

perhaps more so. As belief in the physical manifestation of supernatural powers, and especially demonic powers, weakened, the Witches were turned into an operatic display, with new scenes, singing and dancing, fine costumes, and flying machines" (105). Sinfield is not wrong, but his discussion of the play makes it sound as though singing and dancing witches, who flew about the stage, were invented by Sir William Davenant. In fact, those witches were part of the Jacobean *Macbeth*. Sinfield also fails to recognize that singing and dancing were activities that Shakespeare's contemporaries identified with witches.

93. Daneau, *A Dialogue of Witches*, sig. F7v.

94. Boguet, *An Examen of Witches*, 56.

95. Perkins, *A Discourse of the Damned Art of Witchcraft*, 192.

96. Deborah Willis, in *Malevolent Nurture*, observes that demonic imps were thought to be hungry for women's blood: "They would suck greedily from the witch's mark or teat – sometimes described in great detail as a nipplelike protuberance" (52). Willis relates this belief to "the centrality of the maternal breast in village constructions of the witch."

97. Perkins, *A Discourse of the Damned Art of Witchcraft*, 203.

98. King James, *Daemonologie*, 36.

99. *A Detection of damnable driftes, practized by three Witches arraigned at Chelmisford in Essex* (London, 1579), sig. Av.

100. Roberts, *A Treatise of Witchcraft*, 14–15.

101. Daneau, *A Dialogue of Witches*, sig. F5r.

102. The exception to this generalization concerns those representations of witches in Continental prints by Albrecht Dürer, Hans Baldung Grien, and Urs Graf. Their depiction of nude witches makes explicit what was always implicit: namely, that attitudes toward witchcraft invariably involve a society's attitude toward sexuality. There would, however, seem to be little direct relevance for our reconstruction of the witches in *Macbeth*, since the Jacobean actors would have been male and fully clothed. For artistic depictions of witches on the Continent, see Dale Hoak, "Witch-Hunting and Women in the Art of the Renaissance," *History Today* 31 (February 1981): 22–26; E. C. Erik Midelfort, "Heartland of the Witchcraze: Central and Northern Europe," *History Today* 31 (February 1981): 27–31; Charles Zika, "Fears of Flying: Representations of Witchcraft and Sexuality in Early Sixteenth-Century Germany," *Australian Journal of Art* 8 (1989–90): 19–47; Charles Zika, "She-Man: Visual Representations of Witchcraft and Sexuality in Sixteenth-Century Europe," in *Venus and Mars: Engendering Love and War in Medieval and Early Modern Europe*, ed. Andrew Lynch and Philippa Maddern (Nedlands: University of Australia Press, 1995), 147–90; Julia Nurse, "She-Devils, Harlots and Harridans in Northern Renaissance Prints," *History Today* 48 (July 1998): 41–48; Margaret A. Sullivan, "The Witches of Dürer and Hans Baldung Grien," *Renaissance Quarterly* 53 (Summer 2000): 332–401.

103. Thomas Potts, *The Wonderfull Discoverie of Witches* (London, 1613), sig. Bv.

104. Ibid., sig. D2r.

105. Roberts, *A Treatise of Witchcraft*, 4.

106. Samuel Harsnett, *A Declaration of egregious Popish Impostures* (London, 1603), 136.

107. Thomas Heywood, *Gunaikeion: or, Nine Bookes of Various History Concerninge Women* (London, 1624), 399.

108. The chief source of the play is a pamphlet by Henry Goodcole, entitled *The Wonderfull Discoverie of Elizabeth Sawyer, a witch, late of Edmonton* (1621). In their edition of the play, Corbin and Sedge demonstrate the playwrights' dependence on the pamphlet. See also Viviana Comensoli, "Witchcraft and Domestic Tragedy in *The Witch of Edmonton*," in *The Politics of Gender in Early Modern Europe*, ed. Jean R. Brink, Allison P. Coudert, and Maryanne C. Horowitz, Sixteenth Century Essays and Studies 12 (Kirksville, MO: Sixteenth Century Journal Publishers, 1989): 43–59.

109. The play is based on actual events. Andrew Gurr, in *The Shakespearian Playing Companies* (Oxford: Clarendon Press, 1996), notes: "The so-called witches had been charged in 1633 on the testimony of a young boy, Edmund Robinson, and his father. Twenty-one people from the Pendle area were tried, and twenty were found guilty of witchcraft at the Lancashire assizes in March 1634" (146–47). Eventually Robinson "confessed that the accusations were 'a meere fiction of his owne,' but no immediate judgement was made on the case. The six remained in custody in London from 16 July awaiting a Privy Council decision. It was that decision which Heywood and Brome's play was probably commissioned to influence" (147).

110. *An Edition of "The Late Lancashire Witches" by Thomas Heywood and Richard Brome*, ed. Laird H. Barber (New York and London: Garland, 1979).

111. Reproduced by Russell, *A History of Witchcraft: Sorcerers, Heretics, and Pagans*, 95.

112. Christina Larner, who reproduces the woodcut, points out that *Newes from Scotland* "provides us with the only contemporary representation of Scottish witches: woodcuts from an Englishman's imagination" ("Witch Beliefs and Witch-hunting in England and Scotland," *History Today* 31 [February 1981]: 32).

113. Ibid., 69. The woodcut appears in a work by Ralph Gardiner, *England's Grievance Discovered in Relation to the Coal Trade* (1655).

114. R. A. Foakes, *Illustrations of the English Stage, 1580–1642* (Stanford, CA: Stanford University Press, 1985), 144. Foakes reproduces the woodcut.

115. Also rather different from other theatrical treatments of the witch is Heywood's *The Wise Woman of Hogsdon*, acted c. 1603–05. Although the "wise woman" is called "the witch, the beldame, the hagge of Hogsdon" (1.2.379), and also an "enchantresse, sorceresse, shee-devill" (2.1.515), the playwright, as Michael H. Leonard notes, presents her "as a complete charlatan who gives the

pretense of having magical powers simply by outwitting her gullible clients" (*A Critical Edition of Thomas Heywood's "The Wise Woman of Hogsdon"* [New York and London: Garland, 1980], 30–31). At the end of the play one of the characters "gives her a benediction" (31). Jean E. Howard comments of Heywood's wise woman: "Only the stigmatised lower-class figure, the cunning woman, seems to have the power to right the social world threatened by gentlemanly profligacy and theatricality" ("Scripts and/versus Playhouses: Ideological Production and the Renaissance Public Stage," in *The Matter of Difference: Materialist Feminist Criticism of Shakespeare*, ed. Valerie Wayne [London and New York: Harvester Wheatsheaf, 1991], 231).

116. *The Late Lancashire Witches* must have been chiefly comic in performance. Herbert Berry cites an account of the original production by Nathaniel Tomkyns, who reports, "And though there be not in it (to my understanding) any poeticall genius, or art, or language, or judgement to state or tenet of witches (wch I expected,) or application to vertue but full of ribaldrie and of things improbable and impossible; yet in respect of the newnesse of ye subject (the witches being still visible and in prison here) and in regard it consisteth from the beginning to the ende of odd passages and fopperies to provoke laughter, and is mixed with divers songs and dances, it passeth for a merrie and ex^cellent new play." See Herbert Berry, "The Globe Bewitched and *El Hombre Fiel*," *Medieval and Renaissance Drama in England* 1 (1984): 212–13.

117. Barnaby Rich, *The Honestie of this Age* (London, 1614), 8–9. Braunmuller gives the citation in his edition of *Macbeth*, New Cambridge Shakespeare (Cambridge: Cambridge University Press, 1997), 239.

118. *Henslowe's Diary*, ed. R. A. Foakes and R. T. Rickert (Cambridge: Cambridge University Press, 1961), 218.

119. Janet Adelman, in "'Born of Woman': Fantasies of Maternal Power in *Macbeth*," in *Cannibals, Witches, and Divorce: Estranging the Renaissance*, ed. Marjorie Garber (Baltimore and London: Johns Hopkins University Press, 1987), 90–121, claims that Shakespeare's "witches would have been less frightening than their Continental sisters, their crimes less sensational" (99). Adelman reasons that "they are distinctly English witches; and most commentators on English witchcraft note how tame an affair it was in comparison with witchcraft belief on the Continent" (100). Any reading of contemporary pamphlets and books on the subject, however, reveals how menaced many people, including King James I, felt by the prospect of witchcraft in Jacobean England. Reginald Scot in *The discoverie of witchcraft* reports, "the name of a witch is so odious, and hir power so feared among the common people, that if the honestest bodie living chance to be arraigned therupon, she shall hardlie escape condemnation" (6). Surely, numbers of aged women, accused of witchcraft, would not have been put to death unless people felt genuinely threatened. Adelman's contention about English witches being "tame," in

contrast to their counterparts on the Continent, also seems at odds with German artists' depiction of witches as young and attractive rather than old and hostile.

120. *Lucan's Pharsalia: or The Civill Warres of Rome, betweene Pompey the great and Julius Caesar*, trans. Thomas May (London, 1627), sig. L2v.

121. Michael Pincombe, in *The Plays of John Lyly: Eros and Eliza*, The Revels Plays Companion Library (Manchester: Manchester University Press; New York: St. Martin's Press, 1996), observes, "Throughout the play, Mother Bombie is represented as a figure who may be misconstrued as a witch, but is actually a 'cunning woman' – a benevolent woman who uses her mysterious gifts of divination to help not harm" (159). Similarly, K. M. Briggs, in *Pale Hecate's Team* (London: Routledge & Kegan Paul, 1962), notes that Dipsas in Lyly's *Endimion* "is treated as a purely comical character for the greater part of the play" (62); at the close of the dramatic action, moreover, Dipsas expresses repentance for her deeds and is forgiven by Cynthia (65).

122. Peter Ure, "John Marston's *Sophonisba*: A Reconsideration," in *Elizabethan and Jacobean Drama: Critical Essays by Peter Ure*, ed. J. C. Maxwell (Liverpool: Liverpool University Press, 1974), 79. *Goety*, according to the *OED*, means "witchcraft or magic performed by the invocation and employment of evil spirits; necromancy." Ure calls Erictho "a witch of the most severely classical kind" (78). Corbin and Sedge, in *Three Jacobean Witchcraft Plays*, observe that Lucan's Erictho "is an arch-witch of terrifying power of whom even the Olympian gods are fearful" (6).

123. Geoffrey Bullough, ed., *Narrative and Dramatic Sources of Shakespeare*, 8 vols. (London: Routledge & Kegan Paul; New York: Columbia University Press, 1957–75), VII: 426.

124. Dolan, in *Dangerous Familiars*, notes what Marston's Erictho and Middleton's Hecate (in *The Witch*) have in common: "Witchcraft enables them to outwit the age and ugliness that are assumed to disqualify them from sexual congress" (213).

125. *The Sad Shepherd*, in *Ben Jonson*, ed. C. H. Herford and Percy and Evelyn Simpson, 11 vols. (Oxford: Clarendon Press, 1925–52), vol. VII.

126. W. J. Lawrence, "The Mystery of 'Macbeth': A Solution," *Fortnightly Review* n.s. 108 (November 1920): 777–83.

127. Ibid., 779.

128. David Norbrook, "*Macbeth* and the Politics of Historiography," in *Politics of Discourse: The Literature and History of Seventeenth-Century England*, ed. Kevin Sharpe and Steven N. Zwicker (Berkeley, Los Angeles, London: University of California Press, 1987), 108.

129. Harris, in *Night's Black Agents*, summarizes the resemblance between Jonson's witches and Shakespeare's (chaps. 5 and 6).

130. Soji Iwasaki, in "The Stage Tableau and Iconography of *Macbeth*," in *Japanese Studies in Shakespeare and His Contemporaries*, ed. Yoshiko Kawachi (Newark:

University of Delaware Press; London: Associated University Presses, 1998), discusses the iconographic properties of the cauldron (93–95).

131. Macbeth refers to "Pale Hecat's offerings" (2.1.52), possibly an allusion to facial pallor or to the moon or both. Macbeth does refer to "black Hecate's summons" (3.2.41), but the word *black* "suits both night and Macbeth's invocation of evil to come" (Braunmuller, ed., *Macbeth*, note to 3.2.41).

132. Stuart Clark, *Thinking with Demons: The Idea of Witchcraft in Early Modern Europe* (Oxford: Clarendon Press, 1997), 13. Of the vast literature on witchcraft, Clark's is by far the finest study I have come across.

133. Braunmuller, ed., *Macbeth*, 240.

134. Ibid.

135. Ibid.

136. Henry N. Paul, *The Royal Play of Macbeth* (1948; reprint, New York: Octagon Books, 1978), 193.

137. Holinshed, *The Chronicles*, II: 171.

138. K. M. Briggs, in *Pale Hecate's Team*, writes, "On the whole the witches, who are never so named, seem to have the ordinary witch characteristics; but something of the weird sisters clings to them; and they are even more like the supernatural hags of Scandinavian folklore" (78).

139. *Old Fortunatus*, in *The Dramatic Works of Thomas Dekker*, ed. Fredson Bowers, 4 vols. (Cambridge: Cambridge University Press, 1953–61), vol. 1.

140. *Four Plays, or Moral Representations, in One*, ed. Cyrus Hoy, in *The Dramatic Works in the Beaumont and Fletcher Canon*, gen. ed. Fredson Bowers, 10 vols. (Cambridge: Cambridge University Press, 1966–96), vol. VIII.

141. *The Somerset Masque*, in *The Works of Thomas Campion*, ed. Walter R. Davis (Garden City, NY: Doubleday, 1967), 272.

142. Jonson, *Lovers Made Men*, in *Ben Jonson: The Complete Masques*, ed. Orgel.

143. *A Critical Old-Spelling Edition of "The Birth of Merlin,"* ed. Joanna Udall (London: Modern Humanities Research Association, 1991). Although the 1662 quarto names Shakespeare on the title-page, along with William Rowley, the attribution to Shakespeare is erroneous. The play, licensed for acting in 1622, fails to describe how Hecate looked onstage.

144. Robert M. Adams, ed., *Ben Jonson's Plays and Masques*, A Norton Critical Edition (New York and London: W. W. Norton, 1979), 294.n.

145. "The Lover of Lies," in *Lucian*, trans. A. M. Harmon et al., 8 vols. Loeb Classical Library (London: William Heinemann; Cambridge, MA: Harvard University Press, 1913–67), III: 359.

146. Natale Conti, *Mythologie, ou explication des fables, edition nouvelle illustrée*, translated by Jean de Montlyard, revised and edited by Jean Baudoin (Paris, 1627), 176.

147. At 4.1.38 we find this stage direction: "*Enter Hecate, and the other three witches.*" Most editors posit a total of six witches. Nicholas Brooke, in his New Oxford Shakespeare edition, writes, "clearly other witches are required

as a singing and dancing chorus for Hecate (the Weïrd Sisters never do either)" (note to 4.1.38). A. R. Braunmuller, in his New Cambridge edition, comments: "Many editors delete these figures as superfluous, but they appropriately dignify Hecate's entrance and seem to be singers (unlike the witches of 1.1 and 1.3), needed for the song of 43 SD.1" (note to 4.1.38). Anthony Johnson, in "Number Symbolism in *Macbeth*," *Analysis: Quaderni di Anglistica* 4 (1986): 25–41, explores the significance of the number three in the play.

148. John Doebler believes that the 1577 Holinshed woodcut, depicting the meeting of Macbeth and the three sisters, "shows these three women as old, middle-aged and young" (*Shakespeare's Speaking Pictures*, 118). Although this is a tempting interpretation and would strengthen the association of the witches with the Fates, the three women of the woodcut all seem to be of approximately the same age. Jean MacIntyre, in *Costumes and Scripts in the Elizabethan Theatres* (Edmonton: University of Alberta Press, 1992), observes that "The three witches may be distinguishable to each other, but they seem to look alike to Macbeth and Banquo" (291).

149. The witches' urn may suggest Pandora's box. See the painting of *Eva Prima Pandora* by Jean Cousin the Elder for a similarly shaped urn. Reproduced by Bertrand Jestaz, *Art of the Renaissance*, trans. I. Mark Paris (New York: Harry N. Abrams, 1995), fig. 150.

150. Reproduced in *Hans Baldung Grien, Prints and Drawings*, ed. James H. Marrow and Alan Shestack (New Haven: Yale University Art Gallery, 1981), figs. 18A and 18B.

151. Reproduced by Charles W. Talbot, "Baldung and the Female Nude," in *Hans Baldung Grien, Prints and Drawings*, 19–37, fig. 31.

152. Talbot, "Baldung and the Female Nude," 36.

153. For the significance of spinning in ancient culture, see Elmer G. Suhr, *The Spinning Aphrodite* (New York: Helios Books, 1969).

154. Reproduced by Eugene A. Carroll, *Rosso Fiorentino: Drawings, Prints, and Decorative Arts* (Washington, D.C.: National Gallery of Art, 1987), 213. Interestingly, even though the figures are masked, they represent three stages of life, from youth (Clotho), to adulthood (Lachesis), to old age (Atropos). Like Ann Rosalind Jones and Peter Stallybrass, I interpret the figure on the left as Atropos and the figure on the right as Clotho. See *Renaissance Clothing and the Materials of Memory* (Cambridge: Cambridge University Press, 2000), 124.

155. Doebler, in *Shakespeare's Speaking Pictures*, finds that Milan's Fates are "dressed in a manner markedly similar to the three women illustrated by Holinshed" in his account of Macbeth (119). In my view the resemblance is very slight. Carroll, in *Rosso Fiorentino*, writes of Milan's print: "In spite of the subject there is nothing classical about the costumes of the Three Fates,

nothing, that is, that suggests antiquity. Nor do they look like modified contemporary dress. They are truly theatrical" (212).

156. "This is one of several engravings of masquerade costumes presumed to relate to the elaborate festivities staged at the royal court of Francis I" (David Acton, in *The French Renaissance in Prints from the Bibliothèque Nationale de France*, comp. Cynthia Burlingham, Marianne Grivel, and Henri Zerner [Los Angeles: Grunwald Center for the Graphic Arts, University of California, 1994], 298).

157. Some modern productions of *Macbeth* have presented the witches as masked. See, for example, H. R. Coursen, *"Macbeth": A Guide to the Play* (Westport, CT, and London: Greenwood Press, 1997), [140].

158. Clark, *Thinking with Demons*, 19.

159. Ibid.

160. Boguet, *An Examen of Witches*, 56.

161. Ziarnko, a Polish artist, lived in Paris from 1605 to 1629. See Margaret M. McGowan, "Pierre de Lancre's *Tableau de l'inconstance des mauvais anges et demons*: The Sabbat Sensationalised," in *The Damned Art: Essays in the Literature of Witchcraft*, ed. Sydney Anglo (London, Henley, Boston: Routledge & Kegan Paul, 1977), 182–201.

162. See H. W. Parke, *Sibyls and Sibylline Prophecy in Classical Antiquity*, ed. B. C. McClung (London and New York: Routledge, 1988). For an account of the ways in which medieval writers employed the sibyls, see William L. Kinter and Joseph R. Keller, *The Sibyl: Prophetess of Antiquity and Medieval Fay* (Philadelphia: Dorrance and Co., 1967). For the significance of sibyls to Catholic culture of the Renaissance, see Frederick Kiefer, *Writing on the Renaissance Stage: Written Words, Printed Pages, Metaphoric Books* (Newark: University of Delaware Press; London: Associated University Presses, 1996), 221–25.

163. In *Othello* the protagonist tells Desdemona that a sibyl "In her prophetic fury" sewed the handkerchief that she has lost (3.4.72). Bernard McElroy, in *Shakespeare's Mature Tragedies* (Princeton: Princeton University Press, 1973), cites this handkerchief in a compelling argument that Othello imagines "a malignant fate" as controlling his destiny (124).

164. Bullough, ed., *Narrative and Dramatic Sources of Shakespeare*, 7: 430. Bullough reproduces the ceremonial greeting, 470–72. The sibyl refers to the "fatal sisters" (*Fatidicas sorores*) in the first line of her speech, and to the Fates (*Fata*) at line 7. Bullough points out that "Since the Queen knew no Latin an English version was recited, but not published" (429.n.). Gwinn's Latin text was published in 1607.

165. *Witches, Devils, and Doctors in the Renaissance: Johann Weyer, "De praestigiis daemonum,"* ed. George Mora, trans. John Shea, Medieval and Renaissance Texts and Studies 73 (1991; reprint, Tempe: Arizona Center for Medieval and Renaissance Studies, 1998), 21. Weyer's book was popular

and influential. New editions appeared in 1564, 1566, 1568, 1577, and 1583.

166. Perkins, *A Discourse of the Damned Art of Witchcraft*, 123.
167. Peter Stallybrass, "*Macbeth* and Witchcraft," in *Focus on "Macbeth*," ed. John Russell Brown (London, Boston, Henley: Routledge & Kegan Paul, 1982), 200.

5 The Five Senses in *Timon of Athens*

1. *Timon of Athens*, in *The Norton Facsimile: The First Folio of Shakespeare*, ed. Charlton Hinman (New York: W. W. Norton, 1968), 697.
2. H. J. Oliver, ed., *Timon of Athens*, The Arden Shakespeare (Cambridge, MA: Harvard University Press, 1959), note to 1.2.118–21 (27). Oliver observes: "The exceptionally light mark after 'tast' is not a normal printing of the comma; the letters of 'tast' are out of alignment; in the earlier part of the speech the spacing is wrong, the 'a' of 'acknowledge' being separated from the rest of the word and attached to 'sences'; and in the first line of the following speech the letter 'l' is missing from 'welcome.' Apparently the type was dropped and not properly reset."
3. For example, G. Blakemore Evans in *The Riverside Shakespeare*, 2nd edn. (Boston: Houghton Mifflin, 1997), 1.2.122–27. Other editors who adopt the practice of rendering Cupid's speech entirely in poetry include Charlton Hinman, in *William Shakespeare: The Complete Works*, The Pelican Text Revised (Baltimore: Penguin, 1969); Maurice Charney, in *The Complete Signet Classic Shakespeare* (New York: Harcourt Brace Jovanovich, 1972); Stanley Wells and Gary Taylor, *William Shakespeare: The Complete Works* (Oxford: Clarendon Press, 1986); and David Bevington, *The Complete Works of Shakespeare*, updated 4th edn. (New York: Longman, 1997).
4. G. R. Hibbard, ed., *The Life of Timon of Athens*, New Penguin Shakespeare (1970; reprint, Harmondsworth: Penguin, 1981), note to 1.2.123–24 (164).
5. Oliver, ed., *Timon of Athens*, note to 1.2.118–21 (27). Oliver adds: "'Gratulate' elsewhere in Shakespeare means 'congratulate,' 'greet'; it could also mean 'gratify,' 'satisfy.' Perhaps it has both meanings here, where the presenter of the masque is using the stylized language of compliment."
6. A stage direction in Carew's masque, presented at the Whitehall Banqueting House on 18 February 1634, reads: "*They dance the seventh antimasque of the five senses.*" See *Coelum Britannicum*, in *Court Masques: Jacobean and Caroline Entertainments, 1605–1640*, ed. David Lindley (Oxford: Clarendon Press, 1995), line 758. A figure named Pleasure initiates the dance by saying, "Come forth, my subtle organs of delight, / With changing figures please the curious eye, / And charm the ear with moving harmony" (lines 755–57). Unfortunately the surviving text of the masque contains no specific description of the five figures.

7. W. Moelwyn Merchant, "*Timon of Athens* and the Visual Conceit," in *Shakespeare and the Artist* (London: Oxford University Press, 1959), 167–68, 169.

8. Catherine Shaw, "The Visual and the Symbolic in Shakespeare's Masques," in *Shakespeare and the Arts: A Collection of Essays from the Ohio Shakespeare Conference*, ed. Cecile Williamson Cary and Henry S. Limouze (Dayton, OH: University Press of America, 1982), 27.

9. Rolf Soellner, *"Timon of Athens": Shakespeare's Pessimistic Tragedy* (Columbus: Ohio State University Press, 1979), 70.

10. Merchant, "*Timon of Athens* and the Visual Conceit," in *Shakespeare and the Artist*, 168.

11. See Carl Nordenfalk, "Les Cinq Sens dans l'art du Moyen âge," *Revue de l'art* 34 (1976): 17–28.

12. Giulia Bartrum, *German Renaissance Prints, 1490–1550* (London: British Museum Press, 1995), 120.

13. Reproduced by Bartrum, figs. 111, a–e. The prints are also reproduced and discussed by David Landau, *Catalago completo dell'opera di Georg Pencz*, trans. Anthony Paul (Milan: Salamon e Agustoni, 1978), 64, figs. 104–08.

14. The animals that Pencz incorporates are lynx (sight), boar (hearing), vulture (smell), monkey (taste), and spider (touch).

15. The animals that Floris incorporates are eagle (sight), deer (hearing), dog (smell), monkey (taste), and a combination of bird, turtle, and spider (touch).

16. Reproduced in *Netherlandish Artists: Cornelis Cort*, ed. Walter L. Strauss and Tomoko Shimura, The Illustrated Bartsch 52 (New York: Abaris Books, 1986), figs. 231–35.

17. See Carl Nordenfalk, "The Five Senses in Late Medieval and Renaissance Art," *Journal of the Warburg and Courtauld Institutes* 48 (1985): 1–22.

18. See Samuel C. Chew, "The Iconography of *A Book of Christian Prayers* (1578) Illustrated," *Huntington Library Quarterly* 8 (May 1945): 293–305. This must have been a popular book, for there were new editions in 1581, 1590, and 1608.

19. See Peggy Muñoz Simonds, *Myth, Emblem, and Music in Shakespeare's "Cymbeline": An Iconographic Reconstruction* (Newark: University of Delaware Press; London and Toronto: Associated University Presses, 1992), 214.

20. Henry Peacham, in *Minerva Britanna or a Garden of Heroical Devises* (London, 1612), explains of the animal: "So quicke of sense as hath experience taught, / The tortoise lives within her armed shell, / That if wee lay the lightest straw aloft, / Or touch that castle wherein she doth dwell, / Shee feeles the same and quickly doth retire" (178). For a survey of how artists have depicted this sense, see Carl Nordenfalk, "The Sense of Touch in Art," in *The Verbal and the Visual: Essays in Honor of William Sebastian Heckscher*, ed. Karl-Ludwig Selig and Elizabeth Sears (New York: Italica Press, 1990), 109–32.

21. Sight is represented on sig. P3r; Hearing on sig. P3v; Taste on sig. P4r; Smelling on sig. P4v; and Touching on sig. Q1r in Richard Day's *A Booke of Christian*

Prayers, collected out of the auncient writers, and best learned in our tyme (London, 1578). The same designs appear later in the book on sigs. V3v–X1v.

22. For some of the variations in the form of prints, including work by Abraham de Bruyn, Raphael Sadeler after Maarten de Vos, Peter Cool after Maarten de Vos, Adriaen Collaert after Maarten de Vos, and Nicolas de Bruyn after Maarten de Vos, see Carl Nordenfalk, "The Five Senses in Flemish Art before 1600," in *Netherlandish Mannerism: Papers Given at a Symposium in Nationalmuseum Stockholm, September 21–22, 1984,* ed. Görel Cavalli-Björkman, Nationalmusei Skriftserie, n.s. 4 (Stockholm: Nationalmuseum, 1985), 135–54.

23. Reproduced by Anthony Wells-Cole, *Art and Decoration in Elizabethan and Jacobean England: The Influence of Continental Prints, 1558–1625* (New Haven and London: Yale University Press for the Paul Mellon Centre for Studies in British Art, 1997), fig. 272. Wells-Cole cites representations of the Senses, in either plaster or paint, at Boston Manor, Middlesex; Hilton Hall, Huntingdonshire; Burton Agnes Hall, Yorkshire; Chipchase Castle, Northumberland; Knole, Kent; and Blickling Hall, Norfolk. Other representations of the Five Senses, according to Margaret Jourdain, in *English Interior Decoration 1500 to 1830: A Study in the Development of Design* (London and New York: B. T. Batsford, 1950), include those "on the ceiling of the Queen's boudoir at Kew Palace (which was built by Samuel Fortrey in 1631); [and] on the upper stage of a chimney-piece in the assize courts, Bristol" (23).

24. Wells-Cole, *Art and Decoration,* 165.

25. Reproduced by Ursula Härting, *Frans Francken der Jüngere (1581–1642): Die Gemälde mit Kritischem Oeuvrekatalog,* Flämische Maler im Umkreis der grossen Meister 2 (Freren: Luca Verlag, 1989), fig. 393.

26. A chest of coins and jewelry, however, does appear in a painting of Sight in Bolsover Castle, Derbyshire. See the article by John P. Cutts, "When were the *Senses* in such order plac'd?" cited below. The Bolsover painting may be indebted to a painting entitled *Sight,* attributed to Jan Bruegel the Elder and Peter Paul Rubens: personified Sight sits at a round table that is covered with jewelry; a purse and coins lie at her feet. Reproduced by Matías Díaz Padrón and Mercedes Royo-Villanova, *David Teniers, Jan Brueghel y los gabinetes de pinturas* (Madrid: Museo del Prado, 1992), color plate 9 of the catalogue.

27. Anthony Munday, *Chrysanaleia: The Golden Fishing: or, Honour of Fishmongers,* in *Pageants and Entertainments of Anthony Munday: A Critical Edition,* ed. David M. Bergeron, The Renaissance Imagination 11 (New York and London: Garland, 1985). Bergeron, in *English Civic Pageantry, 1558–1642* (Columbia: University of South Carolina Press; London: Edward Arnold, 1971), points out that the drawings preserved by the Fishmongers' company constitute "the most extensive set of such drawings for any Lord Mayor's Show down to the closing of the theatres and comparable in value to the drawings of the 1604 royal entry" (155).

28. The design is not without anomalies. Although she holds a cornucopia of flowers, the figure I take to be Smell does not actually raise a flower to her nose,

and the dog we expect to see at her side is, instead, on the other side of the tree next to the figure holding the fruit. Since the only personification to hold fruit in depictions of the Senses is Taste, the woman next to the dog would seem to represent this sense. In her other hand, however, this figure with the lemon also appears to hold a small bouquet of flowers (lemon blossoms?); we look in vain for the monkey which normally accompanies personified Taste. The drawing raises as many questions as answers: Has the artist made mistakes in rendering the scene, somehow confusing Smell and Taste? Was the dog in fact beside the figure holding the cornucopia of flowers? Was there a monkey instead of a dog beside the woman holding the fruit? Did Taste really hold that bunch of flowers? Could the woman holding the cornucopia be meant to represent Taste? If so, why do we see flowers rather than fruit in the container? (I have found only one print in which Taste holds a cornucopia [by Adriaen Collaert after Maarten de Vos] and that container is clearly filled with fruit, not flowers.) If the woman with the lemon is meant to represent Taste, as I believe, then why does she fail to raise the fruit to her lips? The text of Munday's entertainment provides no answers.

29. *The Magnificent Entertainment*, in *The Dramatic Works of Thomas Dekker*, ed. Fredson Bowers, 4 vols. (Cambridge: Cambridge University Press, 1953–61), vol. II.

30. For a brief but useful discussion of Kip's engravings, see Antony Griffiths, *The Print in Stuart Britain, 1603–1689* (London: British Museum Press, 1998), 41–45. Griffiths notes Kip's connection with the Netherlands: the artist was born in Utrecht.

31. Reproduced by Margery Corbett and Ronald Lightbown, *The Comely Frontispiece: The Emblematic Title-Page in England, 1550–1660* (London, Henley, and Boston: Routledge & Kegan Paul, 1979), 210. Opposite the illustration in Bulwer's book are verses explaining that "Illustrious Nature heere descends / To dance the Senses masque" (ibid., 212).

32. Samuel C. Chew, *The Pilgrimage of Life* (1962; reprint, Port Washington, NY, and London: Kennikat Press, 1973), 195.

33. Thomas Tomkis, *Lingua*, in *A Select Collection of Old English Plays*, ed. W. Carew Hazlitt, 4th edn., 9 vols. (London: Reeves and Turner, 1874), vol. IX. Subsequent references within parentheses refer to page numbers in this edition.

34. The crown is inscribed with these words: "He of the five that proves himself the best, / Shall have his temples with this coronet blest" (359).

35. One such usage occurs in Richard Brome's *A Jovial Crew*, ed. Ann Haaker, Regents Renaissance Drama Series (Lincoln: University of Nebraska Press, 1968): "*Enter Randall and three or four servants with a great kettle, and black jacks*" (1.1.259.s.d.).

36. When Tactus appears holding the black jack, he and the other Senses have been drugged and set at odds by Lingua and have taken up household implements to use as weapons (437). Later Tactus "*pours the jack of beer upon Appetitus*" (441).

37. *The Triumphs of Truth*, in *The Works of Thomas Middleton*, ed. A. H. Bullen, 8 vols. (London: John C. Nimmo, 1885), 7: 246–47.

38. The Five Senses who appear in Thomas Nabbes' much later *Microcosmus, A Moral Mask* (performed 1637) would seem to have no direct connection with their counterparts in the pageants and entertainments described here: "*Seeing* a chambermaid. *Hearing* the usher of the hall. *Smelling* a huntsman or gardner. *Tasting* a cooke. *Touching* a gentleman-usher" (sig. Bv).

39. William Wells, "'Timon of Athens,'" *Notes and Queries* 6 (5 June 1920): 267.

40. H. Dugdale Sykes, "The Problem of 'Timon of Athens,'" in *Sidelights on Elizabethan Drama* (1924; reprint, London: Frank Cass, 1966), 12.

41. Ibid., 19.

42. Ibid., 22.

43. Ibid., 32.

44. David J. Lake, *The Canon of Thomas Middleton's Plays: Internal Evidence for the Major Problems of Authorship* (Cambridge: Cambridge University Press, 1975), 285.

45. Ibid., 286.

46. MacDonald P. Jackson, *Studies in Attribution: Middleton and Shakespeare*, Salzburg Studies in English Literature (Salzburg: Institut für Anglistik und Amerikanistik, Universität Salzburg, 1979), 214.

47. John Jowett, "*Timon of Athens*," in *William Shakespeare: A Textual Companion*, ed. Stanley Wells and Gary Taylor, with John Jowett and William Montgomery (Oxford: Clarendon Press, 1987), 501. Jowett refers to a forthcoming book by R. V. Holdsworth, *Middleton and Shakespeare: The Case for Middleton's Hand in "Timon of Athens."*

48. John Jowett and Gary Taylor, "'With New Additions': Theatrical Interpolation in *Measure for Measure*," in *Shakespeare Reshaped, 1606–1623* (Oxford: Clarendon Press, 1993), 214.

49. However, Karl Klein, in his New Cambridge *Timon of Athens* (Cambridge: Cambridge University Press, 2001), takes a somewhat more skeptical view of Middleton's contribution. Klein, who carefully summarizes the findings of Stanley Wells and Gary Taylor in *William Shakespeare: A Textual Companion*, writes: "The main ground for the Oxford editors' assertion that parts of *Timon* cannot have been written by Shakespeare is the function–words test. It is a computer-based frequency study of common words such as 'but,' 'not,' 'to,' etc.; these words occur with a determinable consistency in an author's work and thus provide evidence, should the statistical deviation either fall considerably below or above the standard deviation typical of an author. This method may serve to exclude a work from an author's canon, but cannot with any degree of conclusiveness attribute it to a specific canon" (65).

50. Thomas Middleton, *No Wit, No Help Like a Woman's*, ed. Lowell E. Johnson, Regents Renaissance Drama Series (Lincoln: University of Nebraska Press, 1976), 4.3.148.s.d.; *Michaelmas Term*, ed. Gail Kern Paster, The Revels Plays

(Manchester: Manchester University Press; New York: St. Martin's Press, 2000), Induction; *Women Beware Women*, ed. J. R. Mulryne, The Revels Plays (1975; reprint, Manchester: Manchester University Press, 1983), 5.2.50.s.d., 5.2.97.s.d.; *The World Tossed at Tennis*, in *The Works of Thomas Middleton*, vol. VII; *The Revenger's Tragedy*, ed. R. A. Foakes, The Revels Plays (1966; reprint, London: Methuen, 1975), 5.3.39.s.d.

51. *Hengist, King of Kent; or The Mayor of Queenborough*, ed. R. C. Bald (New York and London: Charles Scribner's Sons, 1938), lines 1–2 of the first dumb show.

52. In *The Nice Valour, or The Passionate Mad-man*, ed. George Walton Williams, in *The Dramatic Works in the Beaumont and Fletcher Canon*, gen. ed. Fredson Bowers, 10 vols. (Cambridge: Cambridge University Press, 1966–96), VII: 438. According to the stage directions, Cupid enters at 3.3.0.

53. *The World Tossed at Tennis*, in *The Works of Thomas Middleton*, 7: 168, 169. Ann Rosalind Jones and Peter Stallybrass, in *Renaissance Clothing and the Materials of Memory* (Cambridge: Cambridge University Press, 2000), explore Middleton's satiric purpose in making characters of the Five Starches (70ff.).

54. Catherine M. Shaw suggests: "Although Cupid may have been chosen as presenter because this figure was popular in court presentations, I think it likely that Shakespeare also saw the irony of using the allegorical personification of love and devotion in these circumstances" (*"Some Vanity of Mine Art": The Masque in English Renaissance Drama*, 2 vols. [Salzburg: Institut für Anglistik und Amerikanistik, Universität Salzburg, 1979], 2: 378–79). I think that Shaw is right to emphasize the irony of situation, as I shall go on to argue.

55. Otto van Veen, *Amorum Emblemata . . . Emblemes of Love, with verses in Latin, English, and Italian* (Antwerp, 1608). This emblem book, based chiefly on quotations from Ovid, is available in facsimile reprint (New York and London: Garland, 1979).

56. Ben Jonson, *Love's Welcome, The King and Queen's Entertainment at Bolsover*, in *Court Masques*, ed. Lindley. The entertainment was staged in what is called The Little Castle, a Jacobean structure at Bolsover. For a description, see P. A. Faulkner, *Bolsover Castle, Derbyshire* (1972; reprint, London: Her Majesty's Stationery Office, 1993). In recent years the building has been extensively restored. The paintings of the Senses are now in mint condition.

57. For the suggestion about the site of the entertainment, see Richard W. Goulding, *Bolsover Castle*, 5th edn. (Oxford: Oxford University Press, 1928), 30. However, Lisa Hopkins, in "Play Houses: Drama at Bolsover and Welbeck," *Early Theatre* 2 (1999): 25–44, suggests that the latter part of Jonson's entertainment may have been staged in the garden, perhaps at the fountain of Venus, rather than in the pillared hall. Cedric C. Brown, in "Courtesies of Place and Arts of Diplomacy in Ben Jonson's Last Two Entertainments for Royalty," *The Seventeenth Century* 9 (Autumn 1994): 147–71, offers yet another speculation: instead of the pillared hall, "it is more likely that a much larger room would have been needed for the 'banquet' and that would have meant using one of the new state rooms

probably just finished in what is now referred to as the Terrace Range" (160). Although we shall probably never know with certainty where Jonson's masque was performed, there could be no more appropriate venue than the hall that contained actual pictures of the Five Senses.

58. John P. Cutts, " 'When were the *Senses* in such order plac'd?' " *Comparative Drama* 4 (Spring 1970): 54.

59. For the topos of the two Cupids, see Theresa Tinkle, *Medieval Venuses and Cupids: Sexuality, Hermeneutics, and English Poetry* (Stanford: Stanford University Press, 1996); and Thomas Hyde, *The Poetic Theology of Love: Cupid in Renaissance Literature* (Newark: University of Delaware Press; London and Toronto: Associated University Presses, 1986).

60. Erwin Panofsky, in "Blind Cupid," in *Studies in Iconology: Humanistic Themes in the Art of the Renaissance* (New York: Oxford University Press, 1939), observes that the "function of the classical Anteros, who was considered the son either of Venus or Nemesis, had been to assure reciprocity in amorous relations," but Renaissance Neoplatonists were inclined to turn "the God of Mutual Love into a personification of virtuous purity" (126).

61. Margaret Cavendish, *The Life of the Thrice Noble, High and Puissant Prince William Cavendishe, Duke, Marquess, and Earl of Newcastle* (London, 1667), 140. Margaret Cavendish adds that by this extravagance her husband sought "to express his love and duty to his soveraign."

62. See Frederick Kiefer, *Fortune and Elizabethan Tragedy* (San Marino, CA: The Huntington Library, 1983), 312–18. More recently, Swapan Chakravorty, in *Society and Politics in the Plays of Thomas Middleton* (Oxford: Clarendon Press, 1996), suggests that *Timon of Athens* "may be read as an oblique text on the relationship of munificence and authority"; Timon's money "is revealed to be a token of bargain and exchange, a means of buying awe and subjection" (67).

63. Rolf Soellner, in *"Timon of Athens": Shakespeare's Pessimistic Tragedy*, remarks of the mock banquet: "The food does not flatter the senses now: the lukewarm water does not delight the taste; the smoke lacks the beguiling odor of delicate meats; the hardness of stones hurts the sense of touch. Nor are the eyes delighted by a masque; rather, the societal disorder is caricatured by the topsy-turvy flight of the guests" (77).

64. Robert C. Fulton, III, in "Timon, Cupid, and the Amazons" (*Shakespeare Studies* 9 [1976]: 283–99), writes: "the masque which the god of love presents is intended by its producer as a compliment for Timon, not as an admonition" (287). I agree completely. The admonition I see is not intended by the creator of the masque within the play but rather by Middleton. Timon, after all, would seem to be the inventor of Cupid's masque: Timon calls the entertainment "mine own device" (1.2.150). There would be no logic in Timon consciously warning himself.

65. Reproduced by Nordenfalk, "The Five Senses in Late Medieval and Renaissance Art," pl. 4, b–f.

66. See Chew, *The Pilgrimage of Life*, 192–93.

67. Nordenfalk, "The Five Senses in Flemish Art before 1600," 143. Nordenfalk reproduces the engravings as fig. 12, a–e. The artist also includes other biblical scenes, putting the Senses in a more benevolent light. For example, he depicts Mary Magdalene anointing Christ's feet in the representation of Smell; and Christ healing a blind man in Sight; Christ's apostles hauling in the miraculous catch of fish in Touch. Another artist who paints the Senses with admonitory force employs scenes derived from Ovid in the background: see Agnes Czobor, "'The Five Senses' by the Antwerp Artist Jacob de Backer," *Nederlands Kunsthistorisch Jaarboek* 23 (1972): 317–27.

68. See Frank Kermode, "The Banquet of Sense," in *Shakespeare, Spenser, Donne: Renaissance Essays* (New York: Viking Press, 1971), 84–115. Similarly, John Doebler, in *Shakespeare's Speaking Pictures: Studies in Iconic Imagery* (Albuquerque: University of New Mexico Press, 1974), sees in the Banquet of the Five Senses a variation on the Banquet of Sins (151). Robert S. Miola, in "Timon in Shakespeare's Athens," *Shakespeare Quarterly* 31 (Spring 1980): 21–30, observes that Timon's banquet "is a strikingly appropriate and resonant symbol of Athenian immorality" (25).

69. Ben Jonson, *Poetaster*, ed. Tom Cain, The Revels Plays (Manchester: Manchester University Press; New York: St. Martin's Press, 1995).

70. Tom Cain observes of *Poetaster*: "The banquet may be innocent and harmless in that it is not treasonable, but the licence is specifically sensual, condoning adultery" (ibid., 21).

71. The topos of the head or body as a dwelling or citadel has precedent in both ancient and medieval literature. See Louise Vinge, *The Five Senses: Studies in a Literary Tradition*, Publications of the Royal Society of Letters at Lund 72 (Lund: CWK Gleerup, 1975), especially chap. 2. Jan David's illustration of a house as a composite of the senses, pl. 66 in Jan David's *Veridicus Christianus*, is reproduced by John Harthan, *The History of the Illustrated Book: The Western Tradition* (London: Thames and Hudson, 1981), 107.

72. Thomas Taylor, *The Second Part of the Theatre of Gods Judgments, Collected out of the writings of sundry Ancient and Moderne Authors* (London, 1642), 110.

73. Ibid., 111.

6 Time and the deities in the late plays

1. Leeds Barroll, in *Anna of Denmark, Queen of England: A Cultural Biography* (Philadelphia: University of Pennsylvania Press, 2001), argues that the queen rather than the king was the moving force behind the production of masques.

2. Quoted by S. Schoenbaum, *William Shakespeare: A Compact Documentary Life* (New York and Oxford: Oxford University Press, 1977), 251.

3. In *Politics, Plague, and Shakespeare's Theater: The Stuart Years* (Ithaca, NY, and London: Cornell University Press, 1991), Leeds Barroll writes, "there is no suggestion in the comments of James's contemporaries that he had a special interest in drama" (69). Barroll does not, however, challenge the statistics collected by Schoenbaum concerning the number of performances by the King's Men at court.

4. In his New Cambridge edition of *Macbeth* (Cambridge: Cambridge University Press, 1997), A. R. Braunmuller writes: "When Scotland's King James became England's King James in March 1603, his accession made a Shakespearean Scottish play commercially viable and creatively attractive. King James and his Scottishness created an occasion, and at some point Shakespeare and the King's Men apparently seized the popular, commercial moment" (8).

5. Schoenbaum, *William Shakespeare: A Compact Documentary Life*, 252.

6. I am not arguing that the Blackfriars venue in itself prompted all the changes in Shakespeare's late plays. As Andrew Gurr observes, "*Pericles*, the first of the 'last plays,' made a hit at the Globe in 1607–8 well before the idea of using the two playhouses could have entered the minds of its leading sharers" (*The Shakespearian Playing Companies* [Oxford: Clarendon Press, 1996], 367). Nevertheless, the masquelike scenes of the late plays must have been more theatrically effective at the Blackfriars than at the Globe, and it is logical to assume that Shakespeare's dramaturgy would evolve to exploit the resources of a new theatre and the expectations of a somewhat different audience. Irwin Smith, in *Shakespeare's Blackfriars Playhouse: Its History and Its Design* (New York: New York University Press, 1964), points out that although Shakespeare had used masques in his earlier plays, "All were of the older and simpler form" and that "the incidence of masques in King's Men's plays increased markedly after the company occupied Blackfriars" (231–32).

7. F. D. Hoeniger, ed., *Pericles*, Arden Shakespeare (1963; reprint, London: Methuen, 1969), lxxvii.

8. John Arthos, "*Pericles, Prince of Tyre*: A Study in the Dramatic Use of Romantic Narrative," *Shakespeare Quarterly* 4 (July 1953): 265.

9. John D. Cox, "*Henry VIII* and the Masque," *ELH* 45 (Fall 1978): 391.

10. Northrop Frye, "Romance as Masque," in *Shakespeare's Romances Reconsidered*, ed. Carol McGinnis Kay and Henry E. Jacobs (Lincoln and London: University of Nebraska Press, 1978), 30.

11. Graham Parry, *The Golden Age Restor'd: The Culture of the Stuart Court, 1603–42* (Manchester: Manchester University Press, 1981), 48–49.

12. Jean Jacquot, "The Last Plays and the Masque," in *Shakespeare 1971: Proceedings of the World Shakespeare Congress, Vancouver, August 1971*, ed. Clifford Leech and J. M. R. Margeson (Toronto: University of Toronto Press, 1971), 166. The only exception Jacquot makes to this generalization is the betrothal celebration in *The Tempest*.

13. Graham Holderness, "Late Romances: Magic, Majesty and Masque," in *Shakespeare Out of Court: Dramatizations of Court Society* [with Nick Potter and John Turner] (London: Macmillan, 1990), 185.

14. Roger Warren, ed., *Cymbeline*, New Oxford Shakespeare (Oxford: Clarendon Press, 1998), 2.

15. Holderness, "Late Romances," 185.

16. Alan Brissenden, *Shakespeare and the Dance* (London: Macmillan, 1981), 85. Brissenden adds that "the masque qualities of the vision, its ritualised form, demand regular movement."

17. G. Wilson Knight, *The Crown of Life: Essays in Interpretation of Shakespeare's Final Plays* (London and New York: Oxford University Press, 1947), 183.

18. Anyone studying the iconography of the play will profit from the excellent book by Peggy Muñoz Simonds, *Myth, Emblem, and Music in Shakespeare's "Cymbeline": An Iconographic Reconstruction* (Newark: University of Delaware Press; London: Associated University Presses, 1992).

19. Andrew Gurr, *Playgoing in Shakespeare's London* (Cambridge: Cambridge University Press, 1987), 165.

20. Thomas Heywood, *The Golden Age: or the Lives of Jupiter and Saturne, with the deifying of the Heathen Gods*, in *The Dramatic Works of Thomas Heywood*, ed. R. H. Shepherd, 6 vols. (London: John Pearson, 1874), vol. III. Hereafter cited, along with Heywood's other *Ages* plays, parenthetically by act and page numbers. Roger Warren, in his edition of *Cymbeline*, argues that the descent of Jupiter in Heywood's play is indebted to Jupiter's descent in Shakespeare's (66–67).

21. John Heywood, *A Critical Edition of "The Play of the Wether,"* ed. Vicki Knudsen Robinson, The Renaissance Imagination 27 (New York and London: Garland, 1987), 116.

22. Homer, *The Iliad*, trans. A. T. Murray, Loeb Classical Library, 2 vols. (1924–25; reprint, Cambridge, MA: Harvard University Press; London: William Heinemann, 1971–76). Hereafter cited parenthetically by book and line numbers.

23. Christopher Marlowe, *Dido Queen of Carthage*, ed. H. J. Oliver, The Revels Plays (Cambridge, MA: Harvard University Press, 1968).

24. *Fasti*, in *Ovid*, trans. Sir James George Frazer, Loeb Classical Library, 6 vols. (1931; reprint, Cambridge, MA: Harvard University Press; London: William Heinemann, 1976), vol. V. Hereafter cited by book and line numbers.

25. Reproduced by Frederick Hartt, *Giulio Romano*, 2 vols. (New Haven: Yale University Press, 1958), II: figs. 337–47.

26. *Hymenaei*, in *Ben Jonson: The Complete Masques*, ed. Stephen Orgel, The Yale Ben Jonson (New Haven and London: Yale University Press, 1969). All citations of Jonson's masques are from this edition.

27. *The Woman in the Moon*, in *The Plays of John Lyly*, ed. Carter A. Daniel (Lewisburg, PA: Bucknell University Press; London and Toronto: Associated University Presses, 1988), act 2, p. 326.

28. Homer, *The Odyssey*, trans. A. T. Murray, 2nd edn., rev. George E. Dimock, Loeb Classical Library, 2 vols. (Cambridge, MA: Harvard University Press, 1995). Hereafter cited parenthetically by book and line numbers.

29. Vincenzo Cartari, *The Fountaine of Ancient Fiction, Wherein is lively depictured the Images and Statues of the gods of the Ancients, with their proper and perticular expositions*, trans. Richard Linche (London, 1599), sig. K2r–v. Hereafter cited parenthetically by signature numbers.

30. Reproduced by A. M. Nagler, *Theatre Festivals of the Medici, 1539–1637* (New Haven and London: Yale University Press, 1964), fig. 7.

31. *The Aeneid*, in *Virgil*, trans. H. Rushton Fairclough, rev. G. P. Goold, Loeb Classical Library, 2 vols. (1935; reprint, Cambridge, MA: Harvard University Press, 1999). Cited parenthetically by book and line numbers.

32. John Heywood, *"The Play of the Weather," 1533*, ed. T. N. S. Lennam, Malone Society Reprints (Oxford: Oxford University Press, 1977 [for 1971]), v.

33. Abraham Fraunce, *The Third part of the Countesse of Pembrokes Ivychurch, Entituled Amintas Dale* (London, 1592), fol. 13r.

34. Reproduced by J. Richard Judson and Carl van de Velde, *Book Illustrations and Title-Pages*, Corpus Rubenianum Ludwig Burchard 21, 2 vols. (London and Philadelphia: Harvey Miller-Heyden & Son, 1978), II: fig. 74.

35. Stephen Orgel and Roy Strong, *Inigo Jones: The Theatre of the Stuart Court*, 2 vols. (London: Sotheby Parke Bernet; Berkeley and Los Angeles: University of California Press, 1973). Hereafter cited parenthetically (O&S) by volume and catalogue number.

36. *The Arraignment of Paris*, ed. R. Mark Benbow, in *The Life and Works of George Peele*, gen. ed. Charles Tyler Prouty, 3 vols. (New Haven and London: Yale University Press, 1952–70), vol. III.

37. *An Edition of "The Rare Triumphs of Love and Fortune,"* ed. John Isaac Owen (New York and London: Garland, 1979). Roger Warren, in his edition of *Cymbeline*, notes that *The Rare Triumphs* "seems to have provided a specific stimulus for *Cymbeline*" (17).

38. *The Comical History of Alphonsus, King of Aragon*, in *The Plays & Poems of Robert Greene*, ed. J. Churton Collins, 2 vols. (Oxford: Clarendon Press, 1905), vol. I.

39. Suzanne Gossett, *The Influence of the Jacobean Masque on the Plays of Beaumont and Fletcher* (New York and London: Garland, 1988), 104.

40. *The Triumph of Time*, in *Four Plays in One*, ed. Cyrus Hoy, in *The Dramatic Works in the Beaumont and Fletcher Canon*, gen. ed. Fredson Bowers, 10 vols. (Cambridge: Cambridge University Press, 1966–96), vol. VIII.

41. *Natale Conti's "Mythologies," A Select Translation*, trans. Anthony DiMatteo, The Renaissance Imagination (New York and London: Garland, 1994), 41. Hereafter cited parenthetically by page number.

42. *London's Tempe*, in *The Dramatic Works of Thomas Dekker*, ed. Fredson Bowers, 4 vols. (Cambridge: Cambridge University Press, 1953–61), vol. IV.

43. Reproduced by Jean Robertson, "A Calendar of Dramatic Records in the Books of the London Clothworkers' Company," *Malone Society Collections* 5 (Oxford: Oxford University Press, 1960 [for 1959]), 4.

44. Reproduced by Frederick Hartt, *Michelangelo* (New York: Harry N. Abrams, 1984), frontispiece.

45. Reproduced by Ilja M. Veldman, *The New Hollstein: Dutch and Flemish Etchings, Engravings and Woodcuts, 1450–1700: Maarten van Heemskerck*, ed. Ger Luijten, 2 parts (Roosendaal: Koninklijke van Poll, 1994), pt. 2: fig. 496/1.

46. *The Progresses and Public Processions of Queen Elizabeth*, ed. John Nichols, 3 vols. (1823; reprint, New York: Burt Franklin, [1966]), II: 160. Hereafter cited parenthetically as *Progresses of Elizabeth*.

47. *Londons Love, to the Royal Prince Henrie*, in *Pageants and Entertainments of Anthony Munday: A Critical Edition*, ed. David M. Bergeron, The Renaissance Imagination 11 (New York and London: Garland, 1985).

48. Roger Warren, however, in his edition of *Cymbeline*, suggests that Jupiter descended in a chair: "perhaps the head, wings, and claws of the eagle were a façade fixed to the front of the chair" (note to 5.3.186.s.d.). Although Warren's suggestion represents a possibility of staging, the prospect of Jupiter arriving in a chair would be far less theatrically effective than Jupiter arriving on his eagle, and Warren himself notes how important is the entry of the god: "Unless Jupiter actually descends and makes a big, even sensational impact, this Act 5 sequence is deprived of its natural climax, and the rhythm of the whole play noticeably falters" (57).

49. Smith, *Shakespeare's Blackfriars Playhouse*, 232.

50. Joan Hartwig, *Shakespeare's Tragicomic Vision* (Baton Rouge: Louisiana State University Press, 1972), 97.

51. Simon Palfrey, *Late Shakespeare: A New World of Words* (Oxford: Clarendon Press, 1997), 244.

52. F. W. Brownlow, *Two Shakespearean Sequences* (Pittsburgh, PA: University of Pittsburgh Press, 1977), 148.

53. Catherine M. Shaw, *"Some Vanity of Mine Art": The Masque in English Renaissance Drama*, Salzburg Studies in English Literature, 2 vols. (Salzburg: Institut für Anglistik und Amerikanistik, Universität Salzburg, 1979), I: 158.

54. See, for example, Richard Studing, " 'That rare Italian Master' – Shakespeare's Julio Romano," *Humanities Association Bulletin* 23 (Summer 1971): 22–26. In his second note, Studing summarizes some dozen theories.

55. Ben Jonson, *The Magnetic Lady*, ed. Peter Happé, The Revels Plays (Manchester: Manchester University Press; New York: St. Martin's Press, 2000). Arthur H. R. Fairchild, in *Shakespeare and the Arts of Design (Architecture, Sculpture, and Painting)*, University of Missouri Studies 12:1 (Columbia: University of Missouri Press, 1937), comments on the practice of painting statues (58–59).

56. Stephen Orgel, ed., *The Winter's Tale*, The Oxford Shakespeare (Oxford: Clarendon Press, 1996), 56–57.

57. Northrop Frye, "Recognition in *The Winter's Tale*," *Essays in Shakespearean Criticism*, ed. James L. Calderwood and Harold E. Toliver (Englewood Cliffs, NJ: Prentice-Hall, 1970), 363.

58. In "The Restoration of Hermione in *The Winter's Tale*," in *Shakespeare's Romances Reconsidered*, ed. Kay and Jacobs, 125–33, David M. Bergeron proposes that the "renewal of Hermione was not in the earliest version of the play" (125). Bergeron bases his argument on Shakespeare's departure from his source, *Pandosto*, in which Hermione dies, and on Simon Forman's failure to recount the recovery of Hermione in his summary. If Bergeron's conjecture is correct, then Shakespeare's statue scene would follow the two masques cited above.

59. There is no obvious explanation for the green robe, nor does there seem to be any consistency in the color of Time's costume. In *Tom a Lincoln* (by Thomas Heywood?), performed c. 1611–16, Father Time, a choral figure perhaps influenced by Shakespeare's, remarks that he was "first clad in gowld, next silver, next that brasse, / And nowe in Iron." Here Time refers, of course, to the classical ages. See *Tom a Lincoln*, ed. Richard Proudfoot et al., Malone Society Reprints (Oxford: Oxford University Press, 1992), lines 128–29. Thomas Peyton, in *The Glasse of Time, in the second Age* (London, 1620), describes Time's garment as "azure blew" (63).

60. *"The Thracian Wonder," by William Rowley and Thomas Heywood: A Critical Edition*, ed. Michael Nolan, Salzburg Studies in English Literature 123 (Salzburg: Institut für Anglistik und Amerikanistik, Universität Salzburg, 1997). For evidence that Time in this play is indebted to Time in *The Winter's Tale*, see Charles Crupi, "*The Winter's Tale* and *The Thracian Wonder*," *Archiv für das Studium der Neueren Sprachen und Literaturen* 207 (January 1971): 341–47.

61. *Chruso-thriambos, The Triumphs of Gold*, in *Pageants and Entertainments of Anthony Munday*, ed. Bergeron.

62. Francis Kynaston, *Corona Minervae, or a Masque Presented before Prince Charles His Highnesse, The Duke of Yorke his Brother, and the Lady Mary his Sister* (London, 1635), sig. A3r.

63. Samuel C. Chew, in *The Pilgrimage of Life* (1962; reprint, Port Washington, NY, and London: Kennikat Press, 1973), refers to "Time's satyr-legs" (10). Similarly, Stephen Orgel, in "Textual Icons: Reading Early Modern Illustrations," in *The Renaissance Computer: Knowledge Technology in the First Age of Print*, ed. Neil Rhodes and Jonathan Sawday (London and New York: Routledge, 2000), 59–94, discussing personified Time on the title-page of William Cunningham's *The Cosmographical Glasse*, writes, "the goat legs have never been explained, and are apparently unparalleled" (61).

64. Thomas Wilson, *The Arte of Rhetorique* (n.p., 1553), fol. 45v.

65. Pliny, *Natural History*, trans. H. Rackham et al., Loeb Classical Library, 10 vols. (Cambridge, MA: Harvard University Press, 1938–62), vol. III. Hereafter cited parenthetically by book and line numbers.

66. Michael Bath, "The Iconography of Time," in *The Telling Image: Explorations in the Emblem*, ed. Ayers L. Bagley, Edward M. Griffin, and Austin J. McLean, AMS Studies in the Emblem 12 (New York: AMS Press, 1996), 31.

67. John Case, *Lapis Philosophicus* (Oxford, 1599), description of title-page as translated by S. K. Heninger, Jr., in *Touches of Sweet Harmony: Pythagorean Cosmology and Renaissance Poetics* (San Marino, CA: The Huntington Library, 1974), 219. Heninger reproduces the title-page [218]. The winged hooves suggest that the deer legs allude to the swiftness of time. Thomas Peyton, in *The Glasse of Time*, notes that Time is "More quick and nimble then the swift foote hinde" (63); Peyton also describes Time as "Gods speedy messenger" (68).

68. See, for example, a Flemish tapestry dating from the end of the fifteenth century: two deer with large antlers draw the four-wheeled vehicle. Reproduced by Mercedes Viale, *Tapestries from the Renaissance to the 19th Century*, trans. Hamish St Clair-Erskine and Anthony Rhodes (London: Cassell, 1988), fig. 21.

69. See *Troia-Nova Triumphans*, in *The Dramatic Works of Thomas Dekker*, vol. III; and Thomas Middleton, *The Triumphs of Truth*, in *Jacobean Civic Pageants*, ed. Richard Dutton, Ryburn Renaissance Texts and Studies (Keele: Keele University Press, 1995), 154.

70. Erwin Panofsky, "Father Time," in *Studies in Iconology: Humanistic Themes in the Art of the Renaissance* (New York: Oxford University Press, 1939), 72.

71. For the origins of the symbolic snake in antiquity, see Kristen Lippincott, with Umberto Eco, E. H. Gombrich, and others, *The Story of Time* (London: Merrell Holberton in association with the National Maritime Museum, 2000), 170–71.

72. Reproduced by Judson and van de Velde, *Book Illustrations and Title-Pages*, II: fig. 5.

73. Panofsky, *Studies in Iconology*, 71.

74. See Frederick Kiefer, *Fortune and Elizabethan Tragedy* (San Marino, CA: The Huntington Library, 1983), chap. 7 for a discussion of opportunity in Renaissance iconography and culture.

75. Panofsky, *Studies in Iconology*, 73. S. Cohen, in "The Early Renaissance Personification of Time and Changing Concepts of Temporality" (*Renaissance Studies* 14 [September 2000]: 301–28), discusses the concept of Time as destroyer, especially with reference to Petrarch. Cohen writes that his "findings contradict the assumptions that the *Trionfo del Tempo* illustrations portray 'the mighty relentless destroyer imagined by Petrarch,' . . . and that his image is based upon classical personifications of time, primarily on that of Kronos–Saturn" (304–05). An unwary reader might assume from this that Panofsky's essay is fundamentally flawed. Actually, Cohen's generalization is a good deal less sweeping than it initially appears to be, for he focuses narrowly on illustrations of Petrarch in the early Renaissance, whereas Panofsky ranges widely through Renaissance literature and art. If Panofsky's characterization of Petrarch's Time is not accurate in every particular, his overall discussion of the personification nevertheless remains the most important essay we have on the topic. Even Cohen concedes

"the relatively late synthesis of the already established personification of Time with the image of Saturn as a god of time" (325).

76. Cicero, *De Natura Deorum*, trans. H. Rackham, Loeb Classical Library (New York: G. P. Putnam's Sons; London: William Heinemann, 1933). Hereafter cited parenthetically by book and chapter numbers.

77. Reproduced in facsimile: Vincenzo Cartari, *Vere e nove imagini (Padua 1615)*, intro. Stephen Orgel, Philosophy of Images 12 (New York and London: Garland, 1979), 32.

78. Similarly, in *Time Vindicated to Himself and to His Honors*, a masque performed on Twelfth Night, 1623, Fame says, "he's Time itself, and his name Kronos" (line 15). See *Ben Jonson: The Complete Masques*.

79. *"Respublica": An Interlude for Christmas 1553*, ed. W. W. Greg, Early English Text Society 226 (London: Oxford University Press, 1952).

80. *Mustapha*, in *Poems and Dramas of Fulke Greville, First Lord Brooke*, ed. Geoffrey Bullough, 2 vols. (Edinburgh and London: Oliver and Boyd, 1939), vol. II. *Mustapha*, like Fulke Greville's other plays, is a closet drama. Bullough suggests that it "may have been first written by 1595" (58). Interestingly, Time in *Mustapha* is female: "Daughter of heaven am I" (3rd act chorus, line 25).

81. Reproduced by Ursula Härting, *Frans Francken der Jüngere (1581–1642): Die Gemälde mit kritischem Oeuvrekatalog*, Flämische Maler im Umkreis der grossen Meister 2 (Freren: Luca Verlag, 1989), fig. 32.

82. Reproduced by Arno Dolders, *Netherlandish Artists: Philips Galle*, The Illustrated Bartsch 56 (New York: Abaris Books, 1987), fig. 5601.081.

83. Henry Peacham, *Graphice or the Most Auncient and Excellent Art of Drawing and Limming* (London, 1612), 111. Such descriptions suggest the influence of Cesare Ripa. Alan R. Young, in *Henry Peacham* (New York: Twayne, 1979), observes that "even where he gives the impression of writing directly from experience," as when he describes the teeth of Time, Peacham's source for the description is Ripa's *Iconologia* (67).

84. *Epithalamion*, in *Edmund Spenser: Selected Shorter Poems*, ed. Douglas Brooks-Davies (London and New York: Longman, 1995).

85. *The World Tossed at Tennis*, in *The Works of Thomas Middleton*, ed. A. H. Bullen, 8 vols. (London: John C. Nimmo, 1885), vol. VII.

86. Reproduced by Teréz Gerszi, *Dessins hollandais et flamands*, 2nd edn., trans. Arlette Marinie (Paris: Editions Siloé, 1980), fig. 3.

87. See, for example, Maarten van Heemskerck's "The Triumph of Time," reproduced by Veldman, *The New Hollstein: Dutch and Flemish Etchings, Engravings and Woodcuts, 1450–1700: Maarten van Heemskerck*, II: fig. 495/1.

88. Robert M. Adams, *Shakespeare: The Four Romances* (New York and London: W. W. Norton, 1989), 113.

89. J. H. P. Pafford, ed., *The Winter's Tale*, Arden Shakespeare (London: Methuen; Cambridge, MA: Harvard University Press, 1963), 168.

90. As we have seen, the scythe is a common implement of Time's. Thomas Peyton, in *The Glasse of Time*, writes that Father Time stands with "a sharpe sith or sickle in his hand" (63).

91. John Marston and others, *The Insatiate Countess*, ed. Giorgio Melchiori, The Revels Plays (Manchester and Dover, NH: Manchester University Press, 1984.

92. Panofsky, *Studies in Iconology*, 81.

93. Pafford, ed., *The Winter's Tale*, 168.

94. Nevill Coghill, "Six Points of Stage-craft in *The Winter's Tale*," *Shakespeare Survey* 11 (1958): 35.

95. William Blissett, "This Wide Gap of Time: *The Winter's Tale*," *English Literary Renaissance* 1 (Winter 1971): 54.

96. Ernest Schanzer, ed., *The Winter's Tale*, New Penguin Shakespeare (1969; reprint, Harmondsworth: Penguin, 1981), 35.

97. Although she does not discuss the personification of Temperance, Lorna Hutson, in "Chivalry for Merchants; or, Knights of Temperance in the Realms of Gold," *Journal of Medieval and Early Modern Studies* 26 (Winter 1996): 29–59, observes that "There is good evidence to suggest that the conception of temperance as an art of timing was widely understood in the Renaissance" (47). Gordon McMullan, in the introduction to his edition of *King Henry VIII (All is True)*, Arden Shakespeare, 3rd Series (London: Thomson Learning, 2000), bases his treatment of "Truth and temperance" (85–93) on Hutson's work.

98. Lynn White, Jr., "The Iconography of *Temperantia* and the Virtuousness of Technology," in *Action and Conviction in Early Modern Europe: Essays in Memory of E. H. Harbison*, ed. Theodore K. Rabb and Jerrold E. Siegel (Princeton: Princeton University Press, 1969), 209, 214.

99. Reproduced by Helen F. North, *From Myth to Icon: Reflections of Greek Ethical Doctrine in Literature and Art* (Ithaca, NY, and London: Cornell University Press, 1979), pl. viii.

100. Reproduced by Dolders, *Netherlandish Artists: Philips Galle*, fig. 5601.070:7.

101. White, "The Iconography of *Temperantia*," 208.

102. The face between the breasts of Matsys' Temperance is a symbol belonging to virtue. Maarten van Heemskerck gives such a symbol to Fortitude in a drawing dated 1556; the photographic archive at the Warburg Institute, London, has a copy (Netherl. Art Inst. no. 2926). Similarly, Raphael places such a face on the chest of Prudence (reproduced by James Beck, *Raphael: The Stanza della Segnatura* [New York: George Braziller, 1993], 70). And Giorgio Vasari does the same with his painting of Justice (reproduced by Patricia Lee Rubin, *Giorgio Vasari: Art and History* [New Haven and London: Yale University Press, 1995], fig. 91). All such symbols probably derive from statues of Pallas Athena/Minerva in the ancient world.

103. Inga-Stina Ewbank, "The Triumph of Time in 'The Winter's Tale,'" *Review of English Literature* 5 (April 1964): 83–100.

104. Soji Iwasaki, in "*Veritas Filia Temporis* and Shakespeare," *English Literary Renaissance* 3 (Spring 1973): 249–63, explores the topos.

105. Fritz Saxl, "Veritas Filia Temporis," in *Philosophy and History: Essays Presented to Ernst Cassirer*, ed. Raymond Klibansky and H. J. Paton (1936; reprint, New York: Harper & Row, 1963), 207.

106. *The Quene's Majestie's passage through the citie of London to Westminster the daye before her coronacion*, in *Elizabethan Backgrounds: Historical Documents of the Age of Elizabeth I*, ed. Arthur F. Kinney (Hamden, CN: Archon Books, 1975), 28.

107. Ibid., 28–29.

108. *The Whore of Babylon*, in *The Dramatic Works of Thomas Dekker*, vol. II.

109. Plutarch, in *The Philosophie, commonlie called, The Morals*, trans. Philemon Holland (London, 1603), considers this question: "Why doe they repute Saturne the father of Trueth?" The answer aligns truth with time: "Is it for that (as some philosophers deeme) they are of opinion that Saturne is Time? And Time you know well findeth out and revealeth the Truth. Or, because as the poets fable, men lived under Saturnes reigne in the golden age: and if the life of man was then most just and righteous, it followeth consequently that there was much trueth in the world" (854).

110. *The Trial of Treasure*, in *Anonymous Plays*, ed. John S. Farmer, Early English Dramatists, 3rd series (1906; reprint, New York: Barnes and Noble, 1966), [p.] 245.

111. Reproduced in facsimile: Gilles Corrozet, *"Hecatomgraphie," 1540*, intro. Alison Saunders, Continental Emblem Books 6 (Ilkley, Yorkshire, and London: Scolar Press, 1974), sig. Niiv. The figure holding the scales is identified as *Le monde* in the 1540 edition, but as *Le temps* in the 1543 edition.

112. Reproduced by Chew, *The Pilgrimage of Life*, fig. 25. Gilio's Time also has an hourglass on his head.

113. Reproduced by Veldman, *The New Hollstein: Dutch and Flemish Etchings, Engravings and Woodcuts, 1450–1700: Maarten van Heemskerck*, II: fig. 482/1.

114. Reproduced by Terisio Pignatti, *Veronese*, 2 vols. (Venice: Alfieri, 1976), II: fig. 302.

115. *The Sun's Darling*, in *The Dramatic Works of Thomas Dekker*, vol. IV.

116. In "Time and His 'Glass' in *The Winter's Tale*," Raymond J. Rundus notes that "in some of the popular devices of the period Time had as an attribute a mirror in which Death was reflected, either behind a human figure or behind Time himself, indicating the relentless intrusion of the future and its attendant decay upon the vitality of the present" (*Shakespeare Quarterly* 25 [Winter 1974]: 124–25).

117. Fraunce, *The Third part of the Countesse of Pembrokes Ivychurch*, fol. 59r.

118. Reproduced by Veldman, *The New Hollstein: Dutch and Flemish Etchings, Engravings and Woodcuts, 1450–1700: Maarten van Heemskerck*, II: fig. 495/1.

119. Gurr, *The Shakespearian Playing Companies*, 367.

120. Gurr, "*The Tempest*'s Tempest at Blackfriars," *Shakespeare Survey* 41 (1988): 92.

121. Gossett, *The Influence of the Jacobean Masque on the Plays of Beaumont and Fletcher*, 84.

122. Stephen Orgel, ed., *The Tempest*, Oxford Shakespeare (Oxford: Clarendon Press, 1987), 44. Similarly, David Lindley, in his New Cambridge edition of *The Tempest* (Cambridge: Cambridge University Press, 2002), remarks that "the masque in *The Tempest* is more elaborate and more complex in its effect than any" of the masques incorporated in Shakespeare's earlier plays (18).

123. Enid Welsford, *The Court Masque: A Study in the Relationship between Poetry and the Revels* (1927; reprint. New York: Russell and Russell, 1962), 339, 336.

124. John G. Demaray, *Shakespeare and the Spectacles of Strangeness: "The Tempest" and the Transformation of Renaissance Theatrical Forms* (Pittsburgh, PA: Duquesne University Press, 1998), 46–47.

125. Glynne Wickham, "Masque and Anti-masque in 'The Tempest,'" *Essays and Studies* 28 (1975): 3.

126. R. C. Fulton, *Shakespeare and the Masque* (New York and London: Garland, 1988), 120.

127. See, for example, the title-page of George Sandys' *Ovid's Metamorphosis, Englished, Mythologiz'd, and Represented in Figures* (Oxford, 1632). Reproduced by S. K. Heninger, Jr., *The Cosmographical Glass: Renaissance Diagrams of the Universe* (San Marino, CA: The Huntington Library, 1977), fig. 103.

128. Paul Hentzner, *A Journey into England . . . in the Year MDXCVIII*, trans. R. Bentley, ed. Horace Walpole (Strawberry Hill, 1757), 79.

129. François Laroque, *Shakespeare's Festive World: Elizabethan Seasonal Entertainment and the Professional Stage*, trans. Janet Lloyd (Cambridge: Cambridge University Press, 1991), 221.

130. In *The Divine Weeks and Works of Guillaume de Saluste Sieur du Bartas, Translated by Josuah Sylvester*, ed. Susan Snyder, 2 vols. (Oxford: Clarendon Press, 1979), Summer crowns Ceres with "guilded eares, as yellow as her haire-is" (I: 225 [line 672]).

131. Reproduced by Suzanne Boorsch, ed., *Italian Masters of the Sixteenth Century*, The Illustrated Bartsch 29 (New York: Abaris Books, 1982), fig. 2 (174).

132. Reproduced by A. F. Kendrick, "The Hatfield Tapestries of the Seasons," *Annual Volume of the Walpole Society* 2 (1912–13; reprint, London: Wm. Dawson & Sons, 1969), pl. xlvi.

133. *The Entertainment at Bisham*, in *Entertainments for Elizabeth I*, ed. Jean Wilson (Woodbridge: D. S. Brewer; Totowa, NJ: Rowman & Littlefield, 1980), 46.

134. *"The Cobler's Prophecy" 1594*, ed. A. C. Wood and W. W. Greg, Malone Society Reprints (Oxford: Oxford University Press, 1914), sig. A3r.

135. John Lyly, *Love's Metamorphosis*, in *The Complete Works of John Lyly*, ed. R. Warwick Bond, 3 vols. (1902; reprint, Oxford: Clarendon Press, 1967), vol. III.

136. Thomas Tomkis, *Lingua*, in *A Select Collection of Old English Plays*, 4th edn., ed. W. Carew Hazlitt, 15 vols. (London: Reeves and Turner, 1874–76), IX: 423.

137. Samuel Daniel, *The Vision of the Twelve Goddesses*, ed. Joan Rees, in *A Book of Masques in Honour of Allardyce Nicoll*, ed. T. J. B. Spencer and Stanley W. Wells (1967; reprint, Cambridge: Cambridge University Press, 1970). Hereafter cited parenthetically by line number.

138. Hesiod, "To Demeter," in *The Homeric Hymns and Homerica*, trans. Hugh G. Evelyn-White, Loeb Classical Library (1914; reprint, Cambridge, MA: Harvard University Press; London William Heinemann, 1977), 289–91. Hereafter cited parenthetically by page number.

139. Ovid, *Metamorphoses*, trans. Frank Justus Miller, 2nd edn., Loeb Classical Library, 2 vols. (1921; reprint, Cambridge, MA: Harvard University Press, 1966–68), vol. I. Hereafter cited parenthetically by book and line numbers.

140. *The Georgics*, in *Virgil*, trans. Fairclough, vol. I. Cited parenthetically by book and line numbers.

141. Reproduced by Christine Megan Armstrong, *The Moralizing Prints of Cornelis Anthonisz* (Princeton: Princeton University Press, 1990), fig. 25a.

142. Reproduced by Kristin Eldyss Sorensen Zapalac, *"In His Image and Likeness": Political Iconography and Religious Change in Regensburg, 1500–1600* (Ithaca, NY, and London: Cornell University Press, 1990), fig. 3.

143. Reproduced by Margaret Aston, *The King's Bedpost: Reformation and Iconography in a Tudor Group Portrait* (Cambridge: Cambridge University Press, 1993), pl. vii. Twenty years later William Rogers made an engraving of the painting; here Plenty holds an enormous sheaf of wheat in her left arm, a cornucopia in her right (Aston, fig. 86).

144. *Histriomastix*, in *The Plays of John Marston*, ed. H. Harvey Wood, 3 vols. (Edinburgh and London: Oliver and Boyd, 1939), III: 300. Hereafter cited parenthetically by act and page numbers. Today scholars doubt the attribution of the play to Marston.

145. Reproduced by Kerry Downes, *Rubens* (London: Jupiter Books, 1980), pl. xi.

146. Robert Ornstein, *Shakespeare's Comedies: From Roman Farce to Romantic Mystery* (Newark: University of Delaware Press, 1986), 243.

147. Shaw, in *"Some Vanity of Mine Art,"* proposes that "Juno descended to the stage in a globe device from which she stepped to the acting area on cue" (1:163). Shaw bases this notion on a device in Jonson's *Hymenaei*: "a microcosm, or globe" (line 98), out of which step "the four humors and four affections" (line 100). But this globe in Jonson's masque seems to have no particular connection with Juno, who does not appear until line 195. Stephen Orgel, in his edition of *The Tempest*, believes that Juno arrives in a chariot, and this is not unlikely, for Iris says that she met Juno "Cutting the clouds towards Paphos; and her son / Dove-drawn with her" (4.1.93–94). The stage directions, however, fail to specify any vehicle, and Iris' remark about having met Juno

does not necessarily mean that the goddess actually descends in a chariot. Interestingly, Ceres explains how she recognizes Juno: "I know her by her gait" (line 102). Although this could possibly mean that Juno walks upon the stage, it may be a way of describing Juno more generally, as Orgel observes; according to the *OED*, *gait* signifies a "manner of walking or stepping, bearing or carriage while moving."

148. Virginia Mason Vaughan and Alden T. Vaughan, eds., *The Tempest*, Arden Shakespeare, 3rd Series (Walton-on-Thames: Thomas Nelson and Sons, 1999), note to 4.1.74 (248).

149. Jean MacIntyre, in *Costumes and Scripts in the Elizabethan Theatres* (Edmonton: University of Alberta Press, 1992), contends that the King's Men used a throne for the descent: "Juno's descent is managed like Jupiter's in *Cymbeline*, the throne this time 'costumed' as a chariot drawn by peacocks" (297). MacIntyre does not explain the conflation of throne and chariot. David Bevington, in "*The Tempest* and the Jacobean Court Masque," in *The Politics of the Stuart Court Masque*, ed. Bevington and Peter Holbrook (Cambridge: Cambridge University Press, 1998), 218–43, initially reports "Juno's descent in a chariot" (231), but later speaks of "the chariot by which Juno presumably descends from 'the heavens' to the main stage" (233); still later he becomes more tentative: "If she is provided with a chariot it is no doubt a handsome one" (233).

150. Ben Jonson, *Every Man In His Humour*, ed. Robert N. Watson, 2nd edn., New Mermaids (New York: W. W. Norton; London: A. & C. Black, 1998).

151. Francis Bacon, *The Wisedome of the Ancients*, trans. Arthur Gorges (London, 1619), 75.

152. Thomas Heywood, *Troia Britanica: or, Great Britaines Troy* (London, 1609), 83.

153. Thomas Cooper, *Thesaurus Linguae Romanae & Britannicae* (London, 1565), sig. K5v (of the *Dictionarium Historicum & Poeticum*).

154. Christopher Marlowe, *Edward the Second*, ed. Charles R. Forker, The Revels Plays (Manchester: Manchester University Press; New York: St. Martin's Press, 1994).

155. Christine de Pisan, *The Epistle of Othea*, trans. Stephen Scrope, ed. Curt F. Bühler, Early English Text Society 264 (London and New York: Oxford University Press, 1970), 61.

156. Reproduced by Michael Levey, *Painting at Court* (New York: New York University Press, 1971), fig. 79.

157. Natale Conti, *Mythologie, ou explication des fables, edition nouvelle illustrée*, translated by Jean de Montlyard, revised and edited by Jean Baudoin (Paris, 1627), 1040.

158. *The Myths of Hyginus*, trans. and ed. Mary Grant, University of Kansas Humanistic Studies 34 (Lawrence: University of Kansas Publications, 1960), 83. Hereafter cited parenthetically by page number.

159. Fraunce, *The Third part of the Countesse of Pembrokes Ivychurch*, fol. 16 [misnumbered as 15].

160. Demaray, in *Spectacles of Strangeness*, says that Queen Elizabeth wears the "costume of Iris" in the Rainbow portrait, now at Hatfield House, north of London (caption to fig. 2). But representations of Iris in the visual arts do not support this contention. In fact, there seems no specific connection between the Rainbow portrait of Elizabeth and the design for Iris made by Inigo Jones (reproduced by Demaray as fig. 3), except that the queen in the painting grasps a rainbow.

161. Francis Beaumont, *The Masque of the Inner Temple and Gray's Inn*, ed. Philip Edwards, in *A Book of Masques*.

162. Peacham, *Graphice*, 125 [misnumbered as 115].

163. Reproduced by Peter Humfrey and Mauro Lucco, *Dosso Dossi: Court Painter in Renaissance Ferrara*, ed. Andrea Bayer (New York: The Metropolitan Museum of Art, 1998), pl. 27. Although the identity of the figure with the wreaths of flowers has been disputed, the identification with Iris is argued by Giorgia Biasini, "Giove Pittore di Faffalle: un'ipotesi interpretativa del dipinto di Dosso Dossi," *Schifanoia* nos. 13–14 (1992): 2–29.

164. *The Progresses, Processions, and Magnificent Festivities, of King James the First*, ed. John Nichols, 4 vols. (1828; reprint, New York: AMS Press, 1967), II: 618. Hereafter cited parenthetically as *Progresses of James*. The actual design of Iris and the chariot is reproduced by J. R. Mulryne, "Marriage Entertainments in the Palatinate for Princess Elizabeth Stuart and the Elector Palatine," in *Italian Renaissance Festivals and Their European Influence*, ed. J. R. Mulryne and Margaret Shewring (Lewiston, NY: Edwin Mellen Press, 1992), pl. 52.

165. Percy Simpson and C. F. Bell, in *Designs by Inigo Jones for Masques and Plays at Court: A Descriptive Catalogue of Drawings for Scenery and Costumes* (Oxford: Walpole and Malone Societies, 1924), describe the unspecified costume, which they attribute to Iris in *Hymenaei*: "Small blue wings, like those of an insect, on shoulders. Low-breasted gown of shot blue and pink" (35).

166. See, for example, William Browne in *Britannia's Pastorals* (London, 1613–1616): "As in the rainbowes many coloured hewe / Here see we watchet deepned with a blewe" (part 2, 62). Similarly, in *The Philosophie, commonlie called, The Morals*, Plutarch writes of the rainbow: "Plato saith, that men derive the genealogie of it from Thaumas, as one would say, from wonder, because they marvelled much to see it: according as Homer sheweth in this verse: 'Like as when mightie Jupiter the purple rainbow bends...'" (828).

167. G. B. Evans, ed., *The Riverside Shakespeare*, 2nd edn. (Boston: Houghton Mifflin, 1997), note to 1.3.379 of *Troilus and Cressida*.

168. Antonio Tempesta, *Metamorphoseon sive transformationum Ovidianarum libri quindecim* (Antwerp, 1606), pl. 108.

169. Conti, *Mythologie*, (1627), trans. Montlyard, 1040.

170. *Henslowe's Diary*, ed. R. A. Foakes and R. T. Rickert (Cambridge: Cambridge University Press, 1961), 320 (line 70 and explanatory note).

171. Peacham, *Graphice*, 125 [misnumbered as 115]. Peacham also observes that "some give her wings to her feete" (ibid.).

172. William Tyndale, *The obedience of a Christen man* (Antwerp, 1528), fol. lxxxix r.

173. Of the painting Roy Strong writes, "The Rainbow is a traditional symbol of peace . . . but also carries within it an allusion to Elizabeth as the Sun" (*Portraits of Queen Elizabeth* [Oxford: Clarendon Press, 1963], 86).

174. Henry Peacham, *Minerva Britanna or a Garden of Heroical Devises* (London, 1612), 77.

175. Apollonius of Rhodes, *The Argonautica*, trans. R. C. Seaton, Loeb Classical Library (1912; reprint, Cambridge, MA: Harvard University Press, 1967).

176. Apollodorus, *The Library*, trans. Sir James George Frazer, Loeb Classical Library, 2 vols. (Cambridge, MA: Harvard University Press; London: William Heinemann, 1939), I: 105.

177. Fraunce, *The Third part of the Countesse of Pembrokes Ivychurch*, fol. 28v.

178. Ibid.

179. Stephen Batman, *The Doome warning all men to the Judgemente* (London? 1581), 25. Although this book is lavishly illustrated with woodcuts, Batman provides no picture of a harpy.

180. In Montlyard's translation of Conti, *Mythologie, ou explication des fables* (Paris, 1627), an illustration depicts "Sfinx" with a woman's face, wings, breasts, and a lion's paws (952).

181. Reproduced by Luigi Salerno, *I dipinti del Guercino* (Rome: Ugo Bozzi Editore, 1988), fig. 7c.

182. Thomas Carew, *Coelum Britannicum*, in *Court Masques*, ed. Lindley.

183. Reproduced in facsimile: Francesco Colonna, *"Hypnerotomachia Poliphili,"* Venice, 1499, The Renaissance and the Gods 1, intro. Stephen Orgel (New York and London: Garland, 1976), sig. fv. The same illustration appears in the English translation by R. D., *Hypnerotomachia: The Strife of Love in a Dreame* (London, 1592), fol. 47v. Reproduced in facsimile: *Hypnerotomachia: The Strife of Love in a Dreame*, intro. Lucy Gent (Delmar, NY: Scholars' Facsimiles and Reprints, 1973). The translation specifies "foure perfect harpies" (fol. 48r).

184. Reproduced by Ilja M. Veldman, *Dirck Volkertsz. Coornhert*, The Illustrated Bartsch 55 (Supplement) (New York: Abaris Books, 1991), fig. 5501.009.12. This print is one of a series known as *Twelve Patriarchs*.

185. John Rupert Martin, *The Decorations for the Pompa Introitus Ferdinandi*, Corpus Rubenianum Ludwig Burchard 16 (London and New York: Phaidon, 1972), 171; reproduced as fig. 82. Theodoor van Thulden etched this design, based on the oil sketch by Rubens (fig. 83). The scene forms a compartment in *The Temple of Janus*.

186. C. Walter Hodges, in *Enter the Whole Army: A Pictorial Study of Shakespearean Staging, 1576–1616* (Cambridge: Cambridge University Press, 1999), provides a conjectural rendering of Ariel as harpy: the physique is masculine and Ariel wears bat wings (fig. 47). Hodges, in the same figure, suggests the means whereby the banquet vanishes: the food and dishware are attached to the surface of a table; Ariel then turns upside down the table top, which is hinged in the middle at both ends. This suggestion about the vanishing trick is quite plausible, but Hodges offers no justification for the bat wings.

187. Reproduced by Peter Daly, Virginia W. Callahan, and Simon Cuttler, *Andreas Alciatus*, Index Emblematicus, 2 vols. (Toronto, Buffalo, London: University of Toronto Press, 1985), II: emblem 32 (Paris, 1542).

188. Holderness, *Shakespeare Out of Court*, 187.

189. Jacqueline E. M. Latham, "The Magic Banquet in *The Tempest*," *Shakespeare Studies* 12 (1979): 224.

190. Donna B. Hamilton, *Virgil and "The Tempest": The Politics of Imitation* (Columbus: Ohio State University Press, 1990), 76.

191. Cooper, *Thesaurus Linguae Romanae & Britannicae*, sig. J3v (of the *Dictionarium*).

192. *If This Be Not a Good Play*, in *The Dramatic Works of Thomas Dekker*, vol. III.

193. Peacham, *Minerva Britanna*, 115. The emblem is reproduced by Lindley, ed., *The Tempest*, 27.

194. Hamilton, *Virgil and "The Tempest*," 77.

195. Theodore Spencer, "*The Two Noble Kinsmen*," *Modern Philology* 36 (February 1939): 258.

196. N. W. Bawcutt, ed., *The Two Noble Kinsmen*, New Penguin Shakespeare (1977; reprint, Harmondsworth: Penguin, 1987), 11.

197. For a survey of the authorship question, see G. Harold Metz, ed., *Sources of Four Plays Ascribed to Shakespeare* (Columbia: University of Missouri Press, 1989), 373–435.

198. Eugene M. Waith, ed., *The Two Noble Kinsmen*, Oxford Shakespeare (Oxford: Clarendon Press, 1989), note to 5.1 (185).

199. Lois Potter, ed., *The Two Noble Kinsmen*, Arden Shakespeare, 3rd Series (Walton-on Thames: Thomas Nelson and Sons, 1997), note to 5.1.61 (291).

200. Jean MacIntyre, in *Costumes and Scripts in the Elizabethan Theatres*, observes that "the tripartite scene at the three altars, though recognizably 'religious' in the play's terms since characters bow and pray, is 'realistic' only according to masque ritual" (314).

201. It is not clear whether Shakespeare's company used one altar for all three deities or three altars. In her edition of the play, Potter observes: "The central door could have concealed an elaborate altar, or (with the curtains opening and closing between visits) a series of altars to the different gods addressed in 5.1. Alternatively, three different altars might have been used, since that of Diana requires a trap door, more likely to have been positioned in front of the tiring house than within it" (63).

202. *The "Adages" of Erasmus: A Study with Translations*, trans. Margaret Mann Phillips (Cambridge: Cambridge University Press, 1964), 314.

203. Alain de Lille, *Anticlaudianus or The Good and Perfect Man*, trans. James J. Sheridan (Toronto: Pontifical Institute of Mediaeval Studies, 1973), 133.

204. Giovanni Boccaccio, *The Book of Theseus: Teseida delle Nozze d'Emilia*, trans. Bernadette Marie McCoy (New York: Medieval Text Association, 1974), 173.

205. *The Knight's Tale*, in *The Riverside Chaucer*, ed. Larry D. Benson, 3rd edn. (Boston: Houghton Mifflin, 1987).

206. Christine de Pisan, *The Epistle of Othea*, 21.

207. *Prince Henry's Barriers*, in *Ben Jonson: The Complete Masques*.

208. Clayton G. MacKenzie, in *Emblems of Mortality: Iconographic Experiments in Shakespeare's Theatre* (Lanham, MD, New York, and Oxford: University Press of America, 2000), frames the divided identity of the god in these terms: "This native English Mars had a split personality. At home, he was the preserver of peace, the protector of the English realm; abroad he was the irresistible warrior" (50).

209. *Londini Sinus Salutis*, in *Thomas Heywood's Pageants: A Critical Edition*, ed. David M. Bergeron, The Renaissance Imagination 10 (New York and London: Garland, 1986).

210. Reproduced by Veldman, *The New Hollstein: Dutch and Flemish Etchings, Engravings and Woodcuts, 1450–1700: Maarten van Heemskerck*, II: fig. 486/1.

211. Reproduced by Walter L. Strauss, ed., *Netherlandish Artists: Hendrik Goltzius*, The Illustrated Bartsch 3, part 2 (New York: Abaris Books, 1982), fig. 0301.108.S3.

212. Bernard Salomon, "Mars," Print Room of the British Museum, reg. no. 1903.4.8.35 (33).

213. In *Londini Sinus Salutis*, Thomas Heywood records that in front of Mars "was portraied a wolfe devouring a lambe, the wolfe being the beast particularly offered upon his shrine, and because the two Romane twinnes the first founders of Rome, Romulus and Remus, were fained to be the sonnes of Mars (of which the one slewe the other) therefore Romulus is figured upon his chariot as the unnaturall survivor" (lines 240–43). See *Thomas Heywood's Pageants: A Critical Edition*.

214. Reproduced by Robert A. Koch, *Early German Masters: Jacob Bink, Georg Pencz, Heinrich Aldegrever*, The Illustrated Bartsch 16 (New York: Abaris Books, 1980), fig. 82 (390).

215. Reproduced by Robert A. Koch, *Early German Masters: Barthel Beham, Hans Sebald Beham*, The Illustrated Bartsch 15 (New York: Abaris Books, 1978), 131, App. 5[c] (230). This print was "probably engraved by Theodore de Bry" (131).

216. Reproduced by Colin Eisler, *Paintings from the Samuel H. Kress Collection* (Oxford: Phaidon Press, 1977), fig. 30. Eisler attributes the painting to the "circle of" Altdorfer.

217. Reproduced by Giulia Bartrum, *German Renaissance Prints, 1490–1550* (London: British Museum Press, 1995), fig. 109b.

218. In *Selimus*, a play performed by the Queen's Men c. 1591–94, Mars is described as wearing an "adamantine coate" (line 2489); and he is "Mounted upon his firie-shining waine" (line 2490). See *"The Tragical Reign of Selimus" 1594*, ed. W. Bang, Malone Society Reprints (1908; reprint, Oxford: Oxford University Press, 1964).

219. Giovanni Paolo Lomazzo, *A Tracte Containing the Artes of curious Paintinge, Carvinge & Buildinge written first in Italian by Io: Paul Lomatius painter of Milan*, trans. Richard Haydocke (Oxford, 1598), bk. 2, 19.

220. Peacham, *Graphice*, 151. Peacham remarks of the color: "Red is named in armory geules, it signifieth a warlike disposition, a haughtie courage, dreadlesse of dangers among planets it is attributed to Mars, among stones to the rubie."

221. See Katharine Baetjer, *European Paintings in the Metropolitan Museum of Art by Artists Born in or before 1865: A Summary Catalogue*, 2 vols. (New York: The Metropolitan Museum of Art, 1980), II: 296; and Max J. Friedländer and Jakob Rosenberg, *The Paintings of Lucas Cranach*, rev. edn. (Ithaca, NY: Cornell University Press, 1978), figs. 242–49.

222. Reproduced by Harold E. Wethey, *The Paintings of Titian: Complete Edition*, 3 vols. (London: Phaidon, 1969–75), III: fig. 127.

223. The ancients differ in their accounts of the generation following castration. Although the Orphic Rhapsodies, for instance, relate the birth of Aphrodite to the genitals of Uranos, Apollodorus says that the Erinyes are born from the blood of the castrated Uranos. See M. L. West, *The Orphic Poems* (Oxford: Clarendon Press, 1983), 122.

224. This sculpture in the Tempio, perhaps the work of Matteo de' Pasti, is reproduced by John Pope-Hennessy, *Italian Renaissance Sculpture*, 3rd edn., 3 parts (London and New York: Phaidon, 1985), pl. 101.

225. Reproduced by Wethey, *The Paintings of Titian*, III: fig. 73.

226. For the symbolism of the rose in antiquity, see Geoffrey Grigson, *The Goddess of Love: The Birth, Triumph, Death and Return of Aphrodite* (London: Constable, 1976), 190–94. Grigson also discusses the significance of myrtle for the goddess (194–96).

227. Wethey, *The Paintings of Titian*, III: fig. 107.

228. *Dirae*, in *Virgil*, vol. III.

229. *Claudian*, trans. Maurice Platnauer, Loeb Classical Library, 2 vols. (New York: G. P. Putnam's Sons; London: William Heinemann, 1922), II: 213 (lines 103–04).

230. "On the Freshly Blooming Roses," in *The Last Poets of Imperial Rome*, trans. Harold Isbell (Baltimore: Penguin, 1971), 70.

231. Cartari's treatment of Venus is the subject of John Mulryan's "Venus, Cupid and the Italian Mythographers," *Humanistica Lovaniensia* 23 (1974): 31–41. This article evaluates the presentation of Venus by Cartari, Boccaccio, Lilio Gregorio Giraldi, and Natale Conti.

232. "The Passionate Shepherd to His Love," in *Christopher Marlowe: The Poems*, ed. Millar Maclure, The Revels Plays (London: Methuen, 1968), 257.

233. John Lyly, *Galatea*, ed. G. K. Hunter, The Revels Plays (Manchester: Manchester University Press; New York: St. Martin's Press, 2000).

234. Thomas Campion, *The Lord Hay's Masque*, in *Court Masques*, ed. Lindley.

235. *The Haddington Masque*, in *Ben Jonson: The Complete Masques*.

236. Thomas Heywood, *Gunaikeion: or, Nine Bookes of Various History, Concerninge Women* (London, 1624), 8.

237. *Love's Triumph Through Callipolis*, in *Ben Jonson: The Complete Masques*.

238. Reproduced by Walter S. Melion, "Karel van Mander's 'Life of Goltzius,'" in *Cultural Differentiation and Cultural Identity in the Visual Arts*, ed. Susan J. Barnes and Walter S. Melion, Studies in the History of Art 27 (Washington, D.C.: National Gallery of Art [distributed by the University Press of New England], 1989), fig. 10; Pignatti, *Veronese*, II: fig. 248.

239. Allan H. Gilbert, *The Symbolic Persons in the Masques of Ben Jonson* (Durham, NC: Duke University Press, 1948), 247. Mirella Levi d'Ancona, in *The Garden of the Renaissance: Botanical Symbolism in Italian Painting*, Arte e Archeologia, Studi e Documenti 10 (Florence: Leo S. Olschki, 1972), explains that "the myrtle was held sacred to Venus, both because it grew near the seashore and because it was said by legend to have been used by Venus to cover her nakedness when she was born from the sea" (238).

240. Reproduced by Gert van der Sman, "L'Eolia di Villa Trento," *Arte Veneta* 42 (1988), fig. 2; Paolo d'Ancona, *The Schifanoia Months at Ferrara*, trans. Lucia Krasnik (Milan: Edizioni del Milone, 1954), pl. 13.

241. Reproduced by Hartt, *Giulio Romano*, II: fig. 41.

242. John Lyly, *Sappho and Phao*, ed. David Bevington, The Revels Plays (Manchester: Manchester University Press; New York: St. Martin's Press, 1991).

243. *An Edition of "The Rare Triumphs of Love and Fortune,"* ed. Owen.

244. *The Tragedye of Solyman and Perseda*, ed. John J. Murray (New York and London: Garland, 1991).

245. Bernard Salomon, "Venus and Cupid in Chariot," Print Room of the British Museum, reg. no. 1903.4.8.35 (30).

246. Reproduced by Marcia B. Hall, *After Raphael: Painting in Central Italy in the Sixteenth Century* (Cambridge: Cambridge University Press, 1999), fig. 31.

247. Reproduced by Levey, *Painting at Court*, fig. 79.

248. Fulton, in *Shakespeare and the Masque*, has an extended discussion of Cupid at Timon's banquet (83–114); he points out that, in Renaissance iconography, Cupid may be either sinister or benign.

249. Robert Wilmot and others, *Gismond of Salerne*, in *Early English Classical Tragedies*, ed. John W. Cunliffe (Oxford: Clarendon Press, 1912).

250. *A Wife for a Month*, ed. Robert Kean Turner, in *The Dramatic Works in the Beaumont and Fletcher Canon*, vol. VI.

251. *London's Tempe*, in *The Dramatic Works of Thomas Dekker*, vol. IV.

252. See Erwin Panofsky's seminal essay, "Blind Cupid," in *Studies in Iconology*, 95–128.

253. Reproduced by Jean-Pierre Maquerlot, *Shakespeare and the Mannerist Tradition* (Cambridge: Cambridge University Press, 1995), pl. viii.

254. Reproduced by Bartrum, *German Renaissance Prints*, fig. 109c.

255. Reproduced by *The Riverside Shakespeare*, pl. 4.

256. Beaumont, *Masque of the Inner Temple and Gray's Inn*, in *A Book of Masques*. Similarly, Cupid appears "in a flame colour'd habite" in Thomas Nabbes' *Microcosmus, A Morall Maske* (London, 1637), sig. Bv.

257. See, for example, the engraving by Philips Galle after Maarten van Heemskerck. Reproduced by Dolders, *Netherlandish Artists: Philips Galle*, fig. 5601.077:1.

258. *Plutarch's Lives of the Noble Grecians and Romanes*, in *Narrative and Dramatic Sources of Shakespeare*, ed. Geoffrey Bullough, 8 vols. (New York: Columbia University Press, 1957–75), V: 274.

259. Allardyce Nicoll, *Stuart Masques and the Renaissance Stage* (1938; reprint. New York: Arno Press, 1980), 174.

260. Thomas Cooper suggests that her characteristic activity of hunting is related to her virginity: "The daughter of Jupiter, whiche fleeing the company of menne, to the intent that she would not be moved with carnall lustes, did continually exercise hirselfe in huntinge wylde beastes" (*Thesaurus Linguae Romanae & Britannicae*, sig. G6v [of the *Dictionarium*]).

261. See Roy Strong, *The Renaissance Garden in England* (London: Thames and Hudson, 1979), 66–69.

262. Quoted by Marie Axton, *The Queen's Two Bodies: Drama and the Elizabethan Succession* (London: Royal Historical Society, 1977), 49.

263. Jean Wilson, in *Entertainments for Elizabeth I*, comments of the Kenilworth pageantry, "Elizabeth had in fact been greatly displeased by the tenor of the entertainment, and was with difficulty persuaded not to terminate her visit earlier than intended" (122).

264. *Callimachus: Hymns and Epigrams*, trans. A. W. Mair, Loeb Classical Library (1921; reprint, Cambridge, MA: Harvard University Press, 1955), 63.

265. Hodges, in *Enter the Whole Army*, offers a conjectural rendering of Diana's appearance to Pericles: Hodges depicts a seated Diana, holding a bow, encircled by clouds, a crescent moon above her (fig. 45). Hodges writes: "The clouds themselves in this drawing are suggested in English scenic practice by the designs of Inigo Jones for court masques, devised by Ben Jonson and others – admittedly of a later date..." (131).

266. Bruce R. Smith, in "Pageants into Play: Shakespeare's Three Perspectives on Idea and Image," in *Pageantry in the Shakespearean Theater*, ed. David M. Bergeron (Athens: University of Georgia Press, 1985), 220–46, speculates about Diana's presence in the final scene of *Pericles*: "If Glynne Wickham is right that the King's Men, especially after they took over the Blackfriars

Theatre, had available the same kind of props that are inventoried for court productions, we may imagine a statue of Diana in a 'temple' stage mansion as the focal point of this summary pageant moment in *Pericles*" (236). The extant stage directions, however, say nothing of a "stage mansion."

267. See Frederick Kiefer, *Writing on the Renaissance Stage: Written Words, Printed Pages, Metaphoric Books* (Newark: University of Delaware Press, 1996), 209–11.

268. Boccaccio, *The Book of Theseus*, 183–84.

269. Diane Apostolos-Cappadona, in *Encyclopedia of Women in Religious Art* (New York: Continuum, 1996), observes that Elizabeth of Hungary, unhappy in her marriage, "turned to religion, devoting her time to charitable activities, especially feeding the hungry. Once, when she was smuggling bread in her apron, her suspicious husband confronted her only to find her apron filled with roses" (120).

270. Margaret B. Freeman, *The Unicorn Tapestries* (1976; reprint, New York: The Metropolitan Museum of Art, 1983), 121.

271. Gertrude Grace Sill, *A Handbook of Symbols in Christian Art* (New York: Macmillan, 1975), 52.

272. See Levi d'Ancona, *The Garden of the Renaissance: Botanical Symbolism in Italian Painting*, 332–40.

273. Reproduced by Freeman, *The Unicorn Tapestries*, fig. 146.

274. Reproduced by Bertrand Jestaz, *Art of the Renaissance*, trans. I. Mark Paris (New York: Harry N. Abrams, 1995), fig. 327. Although the attribution to Veneziano is not certain, Jestaz writes, "His manner is so distinctive that he must be credited with the lovely *Madonna and Child in a Rose Bower*" (55).

275. Reproduced by Philippa Berry, *Of Chastity and Power: Elizabethan Literature and the Unmarried Queen* (London and New York: Routledge, 1989), pl. 2. Dora Zuntz, in "A Painting of Diana by Frans Floris: A Discovery at Hatfield House," *Apollo* 68 (November 1958): 154–55, demonstrates that the painting does not represent Queen Elizabeth as Diana, as had previously been believed. Instead, the painting "was produced in the years between 1558 and 1560 as a full length figure of *Diana Enthroned* with the dog by her side, under trees, in the studio of Frans Floris in Antwerp" (155). See also Erna Auerbach and C. Kingsley Adams, *Paintings and Sculpture at Hatfield House: A Catalogue* (London: Constable, 1971), 92–93.

276. Reproduced in *The Riverside Shakespeare*, pl. 4.

277. Reproduced by Roy Strong, *The English Renaissance Miniature* (London: Thames and Hudson, 1983), fig. 229.

278. "To Artemis," in *Callimachus: Hymns and Epigrams*, 61.

279. *Woodstock: A Moral History*, ed. A. P. Rossiter (London: Chatto and Windus, 1946).

280. *The Lord Hay's Masque*, in *Court Masques*, ed. Lindley.

281. Nicholl, *Stuart Masques*, 175.

282. Peacham, *Graphice*, 145.

283. Heywood, *Troia Britanica*, 41.

284. Robert White, *Cupid's Banishment*, ed. C. E. McGee, in *Renaissance Drama* 19 (1988). Hereafter cited parenthetically by line numbers.

285. *The Woman in the Moon*, in *The Plays of John Lyly*, ed. Daniel, act 1, p. 322.

286. Francis Beaumont and John Fletcher, *Philaster or Love Lies-a-Bleeding*, ed. Andrew Gurr, The Revels Plays (London: Methuen, 1969).

287. Reproduced by Cesare Brandi, *Il Tempio Malatestiano* (Rimini: Edizioni Radio Italiana, 1956), 97.

288. Reproduced by Jean-Jacques Lévêque, *L'Ecole de Fontainebleau* (Neuchatel: Editions Ides et Calendes, 1984), 16.

289. Tempesta, *Metamorphoseon sive transformationum Ovidianarum libri quin-decim*, 61.

290. Reproduced by Suzanne Boorsch and John Spike, ed., *Italian Masters of the Sixteenth Century*, The Illustrated Bartsch 28 (New York: Abaris Books, 1985), fig. 141 (148).

291. Reproduced by Mark Girouard, *Hardwick Hall* (1989; reprint, London: The National Trust, 1994), 56. Girouard calls the plasterwork, which was probably modeled by Abraham Smith and colored by John Ballechouse, "crude but immensely evocative." Much of the original color has, of course, faded.

292. *Catullus*, trans. Francis Warre Cornish, 2nd edn., rev. G. P. Goold, Loeb Classical Library (Cambridge, MA: Harvard University Press; London: William Heinemann, 1988), 69.

293. Levi d'Ancona, *The Garden of the Renaissance*, 228.

294. *Catullus*, 69.

295. Ptolemy, *Tetrabiblos*, ed. and trans. F. E. Robbins, Loeb Classical Library (1940; reprint, Cambridge, MA: Harvard University Press; London: William Heinemann, 1971), 193 (bk. 2, chap. 9).

296. John Ferne, *The Blazon of Gentrie: Devided into two parts* (London, 1586), pt. 1, 169.

297. Lomazzo, *A Tracte Containing the Artes of curious Paintinge, Carvinge & Buildinge*, trans. Haydocke, bk. 3, 120.

298. *Epithalmion*, in *Edmund Spenser: Selected Shorter Poems*, ed. Brooks-Davies.

299. *The Wonder of Women, or The Tragedy of Sophonisba*, in *The Selected Plays of John Marston*, ed. MacDonald P. Jackson and Michael Neill (Cambridge: Cambridge University Press, 1986). *Io* is a "Greek and Latin shout of triumph" (note to 1.2.42).

300. "Epithalmium of Palladius and Celerina," in *Claudian*, trans. Platnauer, 2: 207 (lines 32–33).

301. In "Juno versus Diana: The Treatment of Elizabeth I's Marriage in Plays and Entertainments, 1561–1581" (*The Historical Journal* 38 [June 1995]: 257–74), Susan Doran observes that "many masques and plays in the 1560s...should

be viewed as part of the general pressure on the queen to marry"; "the iconography of Astraea or the Virgin Queen" appeared later as Elizabeth's intention to remain unmarried became clear (265).

302. *Dudley Carleton to John Chamberlain, 1603–1624, Jacobean Letters*, ed. Maurice Lee, Jr. (New Brunswick, NJ: Rutgers University Press, 1972), 67.

303. Quoted by E. K. Chambers, *The Elizabethan Stage*, 4 vols. (Oxford: Clarendon Press, 1923), III: 379.

304. Classical precedent exists for the rose as an accoutrement of Hymen. In *Medea* Seneca's chorus, addressing Hymen, describes his adornment with the flower: "hither come, reeling with drunken footstep, binding thy temples with garlands of roses" (lines 69–70). See *Seneca's Tragedies*, trans. Frank Justus Miller, Loeb Classical Library, 2 vols. (1929; reprint, Cambridge, MA: Harvard University Press; London: William Heinemann, 1968), vol. I.

305. *Hymen's Triumph*, in *The Complete Works in Verse and Prose of Samuel Daniel*, ed. Alexander B. Grosart, 7 vols. (1885–96; reprint, New York: Russell & Russell, 1963), III: 331. The prologue is not present in the surviving manuscript (ed. John Pitcher, Malone Society Reprint [Oxford: Oxford University Press, 1994]); it appears in the 1615 (printed) edition.

306. Thomas Kyd, *The Spanish Tragedy*, ed. Philip Edwards, The Revels Plays (1959; reprint, London: Methuen, 1969).

307. Aston Cokayne, *The Obstinate Lady*, ed. Catherine M. Shaw, The Renaissance Imagination 17 (New York and London: Garland, 1986). Although there is no record of performance, the play was written for production, probably at the Blackfriars or Salisbury Court; the prologue addresses "gallants" in a theatre.

308. Inga-Stina Ewbank, "'These Pretty Devices': A Study of Masques in Plays," in *A Book of Masques*, 414.

309. George Chapman, *The Widow's Tears*, ed. Akihiro Yamada, The Revels Plays (London: Methuen, 1975).

310. In Shakespeare's *As You Like It*, Hymen may also descend: if the play "was first performed at the Globe, the god may have descended in a throne from the 'cover' over the stage as does Jupiter in *Cym.* 5.5.186, or appeared on the upper level with music played in the adjacent music rooms" (Michael Hattaway, ed., New Cambridge *As You Like It* [Cambridge: Cambridge University Press, 2000], n. to 5.4.92.s.d.1 [192]). Hattaway does not indicate why he thinks the god may have appeared "in a throne."

311. "The symbolic torch of Hymen, god of marriage, was supposed to promise happiness if it burned with a clear flame, the opposite if it smoked" (*The Riverside Shakespeare*, note to 4.1.23 of *The Tempest*).

312. Thomas Middleton, *Women Beware Women*, ed. J. R. Mulryne, The Revels Plays (1975; reprint, London: Methuen, 1983).

313. Similarly, Isabella in Marlowe's *Edward II* evokes the same kind of drinking vessel when she looks back ruefully on her wedding day and wishes that "The cup of Hymen had been full of poison" (1.4.174). Charles Forker, in his edition

of Marlowe's play, observes that Marlowe's speech for Isabella superimposes the image of Hymen upon Ovid's description of Circe "skimming along the surface of the sea as she sets out to transform Scylla into a monster by poisoning her bathing pool" (note to 4.1.172).

314. Agnes Latham, ed., *As You Like It*, The Arden Shakespeare (London: Methuen, 1975), note to 5.4.106.s.d. (126).

315. Ibid.

316. Alan Brissenden, ed., *As You Like It*, Oxford Shakespeare (Oxford: Clarendon Press, 1993), note to 5.4.0.s.d. (217).

317. Ibid., 19.

318. Walter Friedlaender, in "Hymenaea," in *Essays in Honor of Erwin Panofsky*, ed. Millard Meiss, 2 vols., De Artibus Opuscula 40 (New York: New York University Press, 1961), I: 153–56, devotes an article to the god of marriage. But because Friedlaender focuses on the mid-seventeenth-century paintings of Nicolas Poussin, this article is not very useful for our purposes.

319. Vincenzo Cartari, *Le imagini de i dei de gli antichi* (Venice, 1571), 199. Reproduced by Gilbert, *The Symbolic Persons in the Masques of Ben Jonson*, fig. 52.

320. Reproduced by Lawrence M. Bryant, *The King and the City in the Parisian Royal Entry Ceremony: Politics, Ritual, and Art in the Renaissance* (Geneva: Librairie Droz, 1986), fig. 31.

321. Reproduced by Pignatti, *Veronese*, II: fig. 276.

322. Reproduced by Andrew Morrall, *Rubens* (London: Chartwell Books, 1988), 51.

323. Alain de Lille, *The Plaint of Nature*, trans. James J. Sheridan (Toronto: Pontifical Institute of Mediaeval Studies, 1980), 196, 197.

324. George Chapman, *Hero and Leander*, in *Elizabethan Minor Epics*, ed. Elizabeth Story Donno (London: Routledge & Kegan Paul, 1963).

325. Phineas Fletcher, "An Hymen at the Marriage of my most deare Cousins Mr. W. and M. R.," in *The Purple Island, or The Isle of Man: Together with Piscatorie Eclogs and Other Poeticall Miscellanies* (Cambridge, 1633), pt. 2, 55.

326. Thomas Heywood, *A Marriage Triumphe Solemnized in an Epithalamium, in Memorie of the happie Nuptials betwixt the High and Mightie Prince Count Palatine, and the most Excellent Princesse the Lady Elizabeth* (London, 1613), sig. C3r.

Conclusion

1. Reproduced by Erna Auerbach and C. Kingsley Adams, *Paintings and Sculpture at Hatfield House: A Catalogue* (London: Constable, 1971), illustration 97 (the entire tomb).

2. Ibid., illustration 98 (detail).

3. Monuments depicting the body in a state of decomposition following death are known as transi tombs. Their history has been traced by Erwin Panofsky, in *Tomb Sculpture: Four Lectures on Its Changing Aspects from Ancient Egypt to Bernini*, ed. H. W. Janson (New York: Harry N. Abrams, 1964). Panofsky observes that the double-decker tomb "was the arrangement favored by the great in France for about two centuries, from the end of the fourteenth century to that of the sixteenth" (64). Today those royal tombs may be visited at the abbey church of St.-Denis, near Paris. Kathleen Cohen has also provided a detailed treatment of transi tombs, in *Metamorphosis of a Death Symbol: The Transi Tomb in the Late Middle Ages and the Renaissance* (Berkeley, Los Angeles, London: University of California Press, 1973). Cohen does not actually treat Cecil's tomb, though she includes it in her list of transi tombs. Peggy Muñoz Simonds and Roger T. Simonds, in "The Aesthetics of Speaking Stones: Multi-lingual Emblems on a 17th-century English Transi Tomb," in *European Iconography East and West, Selected Papers of the Szeged International Conference, June 9-12, 1993*, ed. György E. Szönyi (Leiden: E. J. Brill, 1996), observe that "most English examples of such double-decker *transi* monuments date from the fifteenth century" (52).

4. Colt, "a sculptor from Arras, settled in England at the close of Elizabeth's reign and was appointed master carver to the King in 1628. In 1633 he had the post of Master Sculptor to the King." See Margaret Jourdain, *English Interior Decoration 1500–1830: A Study in the Development of Design* (London and New York: B. T. Batsford, 1950), 7.

5. Auerbach and Adams reproduce a detail of Temperance (illustration 99).

6. Henry Peacham, *The Art of Drawing with the Pen, and Limming in Water Colours* (London, 1606), 17.

7. Ibid., 21.

8. Lucy Gent, in *Picture and Poetry 1560–1620: Relations between Literature and the Visual Arts in the English Renaissance* (Leamington Spa: James Hall, 1981), observes that "Peacham retitles his 1612 version *Graphice*, as though the term used by Aristotle might dispel his readers' prejudice against the practice of drawing" (10, n.23).

9. Henry Peacham, *Graphice or The Most Auncient and Excellent Art of Drawing and Limming* (London, 1612), 105. Peacham's work was also issued with an alternate title: *The Gentleman's Exercise.*

10. *Graphice* contains three sections: the first essentially reproduces *The Art of Drawing*; the second deals with personifications; and the third treats "the Blazon of Armes." The section on personifications represents, according to Alan R. Young, "the first English version, hitherto unnoticed so far as I am aware, of the *Iconologia*" (*Henry Peacham* [New York: Twayne, 1979], 66).

11. In his address to the reader at the beginning of the book, Peacham speaks of the additional material only in the most general terms: he says that he has written

Graphice "that I might *hanc ornare Spartam*, and finish with a more polished hand the modell, which before I had so rawly begun" (sig. A3r).

12. Despite this appeal to artificers of all kinds, John Peacock suggests that some of the changes in the revised book may be owing to Peacham's relationship to the royal court: "Between the two editions of his book (1606 and 1612), Peacham had made contact with the court of Prince Henry. The second edition is dedicated to Henry, to whom, Peacham writes, he had recently presented a book of emblems painted by himself, based on 'his fathers *Basilicon Doron*, which I had turned a little before throughout into Latine verse.' We can see how *The Art of Drawing* has become a more courtier-like book." See "The Politics of Portraiture," in *Culture and Politics in Early Stuart England*, ed. Kevin Sharpe and Peter Lake (London: Macmillan, 1994), 203.

13. For the connection between Hilliard and Peacham, see Young, *Henry Peacham*, 62. Young observes that although Hilliard's work was not published in the seventeenth century, it earlier circulated in manuscript.

14. Nicholas Hilliard, *A Treatise Concerning the Arte of Limning*, ed. R. K. R. Thornton and T. G. S. Cain (1981; reprint, Ashington: The Mid Northumberland Arts Group; Manchester: Carcanet Press, 1992), 53.

15. See Young, *Henry Peacham*, 62.

16. Haydocke's *Tracte Containing the Artes of curious Paintinge, Carvinge and Buildinge* (Oxford, 1598) is a partial translation of Lomazzo's work.

17. Hilliard, *The Arte of Limning*, 55.

18. Michael Leslie, "The Dialogue between Bodies and Souls: Pictures and Poesy in the English Renaissance," *Word and Image* 1 (January–March 1985): 22.

Bibliography

Primary works

Alciato, Andrea. *Emblematum Liber*. Augsburg, 1531.

Allen, Don Cameron, ed. *The Owles Almanacke*. Baltimore: Johns Hopkins University Press, 1943.

Ashley, Robert. *Of Honour*. Ed. Virgil B. Heltzel. San Marino, CA: The Huntington Library, 1947.

Averell, William. *A mervailous combat of contrarieties*. London, 1588.

Bacon, Francis. *The Essayes or Counsels, Civill and Morall*. Ed. Michael Kiernan. Oxford: Clarendon Press, 1985.

  The Wisedome of the Ancients. Trans. Arthur Gorges. London, 1619.

Batman, Stephen. *The Doome warning all men to the Judgemente*. London? 1581.

  The Golden Booke of the Leaden Goddes. London, 1577.

Beaumont, Francis, and John Fletcher. *The Dramatic Works in the Beaumont and Fletcher Canon*. Gen. ed. Fredson Bowers. 10 vols. Cambridge: Cambridge University Press, 1966–96.

  The Maid's Tragedy. Ed. T. W. Craik. The Revels Plays. Manchester: Manchester University Press; New York: St. Martin's Press, 1988.

  Philaster or Love Lies-a-Bleeding. Ed. Andrew Gurr. The Revels Plays. London: Methuen, 1969.

Boguet, Henry. *An Examen of Witches Drawn from various trials of many of this sect in the district of Saint Oyan de Joux*. Trans. E. Allen Ashwin. Ed. Montague Summers. London: John Rodker, 1929.

Brooks-Davies, Douglas, ed. *Edmund Spenser: Selected Shorter Poems*. London and New York: Longman, 1995.

Bullough, Geoffrey, ed. *Narrative and Dramatic Sources of Shakespeare*. 8 vols. London: Routledge and Kegan Paul; New York: Columbia University Press, 1957–75.

  Poems and Dramas of Fulke Greville, First Lord Brooke. 2 vols. Edinburgh and London: Oliver and Boyd, 1939.

Burkhead, Henry. *A Tragedy of Cola's Furie, or Lirenda's Miserie*. Kilkenny, 1646.

Camden, William. *The Historie of the Most Renowned and Victorious Princesse Elizabeth, Late Queene of England*. Trans. R. N[orton]. London, 1630.

  Remaines concerning Britaine. Fifth impression. London, 1636.

Campbell, W. E., et al., ed. *The English Works of Sir Thomas More*. 2 vols. London: Eyre and Spottiswoode; New York: Dial Press, 1931.

Campion, Thomas. *The Works of Thomas Campion*. Ed. Walter R. Davis. Garden City, NY: Doubleday, 1967.

Cartari, Vincenzo. *The Fountaine of Ancient Fiction, Wherein is lively depictured the Images and Statues of the gods of the Ancients, with their proper and perticular expositions*. Trans. Richard Linche. London, 1599.

    Le imagini de i dei degli antichi. Venice, 1571.

    Le vere e nove de gli dei delli antichi. Padua, 1615.

Case, John. *Lapis Philosophicus*. Oxford, 1599.

Castiglione, Baldassare. *The Book of the Courtier*. Trans. Charles S. Singleton. Garden City, NY: Doubleday, 1959.

Cavendish, Margaret. *The Life of the Thrice Noble, High and Puissant Prince William Cavendishe, Duke, Marquess and Earl of Newcastle*. London, 1667.

Chapman, George. *The Revenge of Bussy D'Ambois*. Ed. Robert J. Lordi. Salzburg: Institut für Englische Sprache und Literatur, Universität Salzburg, 1977.

    The Widow's Tears. Ed. Akihiro Yamada. The Revels Plays. London: Methuen, 1975.

Colonna, Francesco. *Hypnerotomachia Poliphili*. Venice, 1499.

    Hypnerotomachia: The Strife of Love in a Dreame. Trans. R. D. [Robert Dallington]. London, 1592.

Combe, Thomas. *The Theater of Fine Devices*. London, 1614. [A translation of Guillaume de la Perrière's *Théâtre des bons engins* (Paris, 1539).]

Conti, Natale. *Mythologie, ou explication des fables, edition nouvelle illustrée*. Trans. Jean de Montlyard. Revised and edited by Jean Baudoin. Paris, 1627.

    "Mythologies": A Select Translation. Trans. Anthony DiMatteo. The Renaissance Imagination. New York and London: Garland, 1994.

Cooper, Thomas. *Thesaurus Linguae Romanae & Britannicae*. London, 1565.

Copley, Anthony. *A Fig for Fortune*. London, 1596.

Corbin, Peter, and Douglas Sedge, *Three Jacobean Witchcraft Plays*. The Revels Plays Companion Library. Manchester: Manchester University Press; New York: St. Martin's Press, 1986.

Corrozet, Gilles. *Hecatomgraphie*. Paris, 1540.

Cunliffe, John, ed. *Early English Classical Tragedies*. Oxford: Clarendon Press, 1912.

Dallington, Robert. *Aphorismes Civill and Militarie: Amplified with Authorities, and exemplified with Historie, out of the first Quarterne of Fr. Guicciardine*. London, 1613.

Daneau, Lambert. *A Dialogue of Witches, in foretime named Lot-tellers, and now commonly called Sorcerers*. Trans. Richard Watkins. London, 1575.

Daniel, Samuel [translator]. *The Worthy tract of Paulus Jovius, contayning a Discourse of rare inventions, both Military and Amorous, called Imprese. Whereunto is added a Preface contayning the Arte of composing them, with many other notable devises*. London, 1585.

David, Jan. *Veridicus Christianus*. Antwerp, 1601.

Day, Richard. *A Booke of Christian Prayers, collected out of the auncient writers, and best learned in our tyme*. London, 1578.

Dekker, Thomas. *The Dramatic Works of Thomas Dekker*. Ed. Fredson Bowers. 4 vols. Cambridge: Cambridge University Press, 1953–61.

Drayton, Michael. *The Works of Michael Drayton*. Ed. J. William Hebel, Kathleen M. Tillotson, and Bernard H. Newdigate. 5 vols. Oxford: Blackwell, 1931–41.

Dutton, Richard, ed. *Jacobean Civic Pageants*. Ryburn Renaissance Texts and Studies. Keele: Keele University Press, 1995.

Elyot, Thomas. *The Boke named the governour*. London, 1531.

Estienne, Henri. *The Art of Making Devises: Treating of Hieroglyphicks, Symboles, Emblemes, Ænigma's, Sentences, Parables, Reverses of Medalls, Armes, Blazons, Cimiers, Cyphres and Rebus*. Trans. Thomas Blount. London, 1648.

Felltham, Owen. *Resolves, A Duple Century*. 3rd edn. London, 1628.

Ferne, John. *The Blazon of Gentrie: Devided into two parts. The first named The Glorie of Generositie. The second, Lacyes Nobilitie. Comprehending discourses of Armes and of Gentry*. London, 1586.

Fletcher, Phineas. *The Purple Island, or The Isle of Man*. Cambridge, 1633.

Ford, John. *Love's Sacrifice*. Ed. A. T. Moore. The Revels Plays. Manchester: Manchester University Press; New York: Palgrave, 2002.

Fraunce, Abraham. *The Third part of the Countesse of Pembrokes Ivychurch, Entituled Amintas Dale, Wherein are the Most Conceited Tales of the Pagan Gods*. London, 1592.

Fulwell, Ulpian. *The Flower of Fame, Containing the bright Renowne, and moste fortunate raigne of King Henry the viii*. London, 1575.

Gibson, Charles. *The Praise of a good Name, The reproch of an ill Name, Wherin every one may see the Fame that followeth laudable Actions, and the infamy that cometh by the contrary*. London, 1594.

Gifford, George. *A Discourse of the subtill Practises of Devilles by Witches and Sorcerers*. London, 1587.

Giovio, Paolo. *Dialogo del imprese militari et amorose*. Rome, 1555.

Goffe, Thomas. *The Couragious Turk*. Ed. David Carnegie. Malone Society Reprints. Oxford: Oxford University Press, 1974 [for 1968].

Gohory, Jacques. *Livre de la conqueste de la toison d'or, par le Prince Jason de Tessalie: faict par figures* [by René Boyvin] *avec exposition d'icelles*. Ed. Jean de Mauregard. Paris, 1563.

Gosson, Stephen. *Playes Confuted in five Actions, Proving that they are not to be suffred in a Christian common weale*. London, [1582?].

Greene, Robert. *The Scottish History of James the Fourth*. Ed. Norman Sanders. The Revels Plays. London: Methuen, 1970.

Hall, Edward. *The Union of the two noble and illustre famelies of Lancastre & Yorke*. London, 1548.

Harrison, Stephen. *The Arches of Triumph Erected in honor of the High and mighty prince James the first*. London, 1604.

Harrison, William. "The Description of Britaine." In Raphael Holinshed's *The Firste volume of the Chronicles of England, Scotlande, and Irelande*. London, 1577.

Harsnett, Samuel. *A Declaration of egregious Popish Impostures*. London, 1603.

Haydocke, Richard. *A Tracte Containing the Artes of curious Paintinge, Carvinge & Buildinge written first in Italian by Io: Paul Lomatius painter of Milan*. Oxford, 1598. [A partial translation – the first five books – of Giovanni Paolo Lomazzo's *Trattato dell'arte della pittura, scoltura, ed archittetura* (Milan, 1584).]

Hentzner, Paul. *A Journey into England . . . in the Year MDXCVIII*. Trans. R. Bentley. Ed. Horace Walpole. Strawberry Hill, 1757.

Herford, C. H., and Percy Simpson, and Evelyn Simpson, eds. *Ben Jonson*. 11 vols. Oxford: Clarendon Press, 1925–52.

Heylen, Peter. *Microcosmos, a Little Description of the Great World*. Augmented and revised edition. Oxford, 1625.

Microcosmos, or a Little Description of the Great World. London, 1621.

Heywood, Thomas. *The Brazen Age*. London, 1613.

A Critical Edition of Thomas Heywood's "The Wise Woman of Hogsdon." Ed. Michael H. Leonard. New York and London: Garland, 1980.

The Dramatic Works of Thomas Heywood. Ed. R. H. Shepherd. 6 vols. London: John Shepherd, 1874.

Gunaikeion: or, Nine Bookes of Various History Concerninge Women. London, 1624.

The Hierarchie of the blessed Angells, Their Names, orders and Offices. London, 1635.

A Marriage Triumphe Solemnized in an Epithalamium, in Memorie of the happie Nuptials betwixt the High and Mightie Prince Count Palatine, and the most Excellent Princesse the Lady Elizabeth. London, 1613.

The Rape of Lucrece. Ed. Allan Holaday. Illinois Studies in Language and Literature 34, no. 3. Urbana: University of Illinois Press, 1950.

Thomas Heywood's Pageants: A Critical Edition. Ed. David M. Bergeron. The Renaissance Imagination 16. New York and London: Garland, 1986.

Troia Britanica: or, Great Britaines Troy. London, 1609.

A Woman Killed with Kindness. Ed. R. W. Van Fossen. The Revels Plays. 1961; reprint. London: Methuen, 1970.

Heywood, Thomas, and Richard Brome. *An Edition of "The Late Lancashire Witches."* Ed. Laird H. Barber. New York and London: Garland, 1979.

Hilliard, Nicholas. *Nicholas Hilliard's "Art of Limning," A New Edition of "A Treatise Concerning the Arte of Limning."* Transcription by Arthur F. Kinney; commentary and apparatus by Linda Bradley Salamon. Boston: Northeastern University Press, 1983.

A Treatise concerning the Arte of Limning. Ed. R. K. R. Thornton and T. G. S. Cain. 1981; reprint. Ashington: The Mid Northumberland Arts Group; Manchester: Carcanet Press, 1992.

Holinshed, Raphael. *The Chronicles of England, Scotland, and Ireland*. 3 vols. in 2. London, 1587.

The Firste volume of the Chronicles of England, Scotlande, and Irelande. London, 1577.

Holland, Henry. *A Treatise against Witchcraft: or A Dialogue, wherein the greatest doubts concerning that sinne, are briefly answered*. Cambridge, 1590.

Hooker, Richard. *The Folger Library Edition of The Works of Richard Hooker*. Ed. W. Speed Hill. 7 vols. Cambridge, MA, and London: Belknap Press, 1977–98.

Hughes, Thomas, and others. *"The Misfortunes of Arthur": A Critical, Old-Spelling Edition*. Ed. Brian Jay Corrigan. New York and London: Garland, 1992.

James I, King of England. *Daemonologie, in Forme of a Dialogue*. Edinburgh, 1597.

Jonson, Ben. *Ben Jonson: The Complete Masques*. Ed. Stephen Orgel. The Yale Ben Jonson. New Haven and London: Yale University Press, 1969.

Every Man In His Humour. Ed. Robert N. Watson. 2nd edn. New Mermaids. New York: W. W. Norton; London: A & C Black, 1998.

The Magnetic Lady. Ed. Peter Happé. The Revels Plays. Manchester: Manchester University Press; New York: St. Martin's Press, 2000.

Sejanus His Fall. Ed. Philip Ayres. The Revels Plays. Manchester: Manchester University Press; New York: St. Martin's Press, 1990.

The Staple of News. Ed. Anthony Parr. The Revels Plays. Manchester: Manchester University Press; New York: St. Martin's Press, 1988.

Volpone. Ed. R. B. Parker. The Revels Plays. Manchester and Dover, NH: Manchester University Press, 1983.

Junius, Franciscus. *The Painting of the Ancients, in three Bookes: Declaring by Historicall Observations and Examples, The Beginning, Progresse, and Consummation of that most Noble Art*. London, 1638.

Kinney, Arthur, ed. *Elizabethan Backgrounds: Historical Documents of the Age of Elizabeth I*. Hamden, CN: Archon Books, 1975.

Kramer, Heinrich, and Jakob Sprenger. *Malleus Maleficarum: The Hammer of Witchcraft*. Trans. Montague Summers. Ed. Pennethorne Hughes. London: The Folio Society, 1968.

Kyd, Thomas. *The Spanish Tragedy*. Ed. Philip Edwards. The Revels Plays. 1959; reprint. London: Methuen, 1969.

Kynaston, Francis. *Corona Minervae, or a Masque Presented before Prince Charles His Highnesse, the Duke of Yorke, his Brother, and the Lady Mary his Sister*. London, 1635.

Lancre, Pierre de. *Tableau d l'inconstance des mauvais anges et demons*. Paris, 1613.

Le Loyer, Pierre. *A Treatise of Specters or straunge sights, visions and apparitions appearing sensibly unto men*. Trans. Zachary Jones. London, 1605.

Linche, Richard. *The Fountaine of Ancient Fiction, Wherein is lively depictured the Images and Statues of the gods of the Ancients, with their proper and perticular expositions*. London, 1599. [A partial translation of Vincenzo Cartari's *Imagini de i dei de gli antichi* (1580 edition).]

Lindley, David, ed. *Court Masques: Jacobean and Caroline Entertainments, 1605–1640*. Oxford Drama Library. Oxford: Clarendon Press, 1995.

Lucan, M. Annaeus. *Lucan's Pharsalia: or The Civill Warres of Rome, betweene Pompey the great and Julius Caesar*. Trans. Thomas May. London, 1627.

Lyly, John. *Endymion*. Ed. David Bevington. The Revels Plays. Manchester: Manchester University Press; New York: St. Martin's Press, 1996.

 Galatea. Ed. George K. Hunter. The Revels Plays. Manchester: Manchester University Press; New York: St. Martin's Press, 2000.

 Sappho and Phao. Ed. David Bevington. The Revels Plays. Manchester: Manchester University Press; New York: St. Martin's Press, 1991.

Machiavelli, Niccolò. *The Prince*. Trans. James B. Atkinson. Library of Liberal Arts. Indianapolis: Bobbs–Merrill, 1976.

Marlowe, Christopher. *"Dido Queen of Carthage" and "The Massacre at Paris."* Ed. H. J. Oliver. The Revels Plays. Cambridge, MA: Harvard University Press, 1968.

 Edward the Second. Ed. Charles R. Forker. The Revels Plays. Manchester: Manchester University Press; New York: St. Martin's Press, 1994.

 Tamburlaine the Great. Ed. J. S. Cunningham. The Revels Plays. Manchester: Manchester University Press; Baltimore: The Johns Hopkins University Press, 1981.

Marston, John. *Antonio's Revenge*. Ed. G. K. Hunter. Regents Renaissance Drama Series. Lincoln: University of Nebraska Press, 1965.

 Antonio's Revenge. Ed. Reaveley Gair. The Revels Plays. Manchester: Manchester University Press; Baltimore: Johns Hopkins University Press, 1978.

Marston, John, and others. *The Insatiate Countess*. Ed. Giorgio Melchiori. The Revels Plays. Manchester and Dover NH: Manchester University Press, 1984.

 The Malcontent. Ed. George K. Hunter. The Revels Plays. London: Methuen, 1975.

 The Plays of John Marston. Ed. H. Harvey Wood. 3 vols. Edinburgh and London: Oliver and Boyd, 1939.

Middleton, Thomas. *The Ghost of Lucrece*. Ed. Joseph Quincy Adams. New York and London: Charles Scribner's Sons for the Trustees of Amherst College, 1937.

 Michaelmas Term. Ed. Gail Kern Paster. The Revels Plays. Manchester: Manchester University Press; New York: St. Martin's Press, 2000.

 The Witch. Ed. Elizabeth Schafer. New Mermaids. New York: W. W. Norton; London: A. & C. Black, 1994.

 The Witch. Ed. W. W. Greg and F. P. Wilson. Malone Society Reprints. Oxford: Oxford University Press, 1950 [for 1948].

 Women Beware Women. Ed. J. R. Mulryne. The Revels Plays. 1975; reprint. London: Methuen, 1983.

Munday, Anthony. *Pageants and Entertainments of Anthony Munday: A Critical Edition*. Ed. David M. Bergeron. The Renaissance Imagination 11. New York and London: Garland, 1985.

Nabbes, Thomas. *Microcosmus, A Morall Maske*. London, 1637.

Nichols, John, ed. *The Progresses and Public Processions of Queen Elizabeth*. 2nd edn. 3 vols. 1823; reprint. New York: Burt Franklin, [1966].

  The Progresses, Processions, and Magnificent Festivities of King James the First. 4 vols. 1828; reprint. New York: AMS Press, 1967.

Norgate, Edward. *Miniatura or the Art of Limning*. Ed. Jeffrey M. Muller and Jim Murrell. New Haven and London: Yale University Press for the Paul Mellon Centre for British Art, 1997.

Ovid. *The Metamorphoses*. Trans. Frank Justus Miller. 2nd edn. Loeb Classical Library. 2 vols. 1921; reprint. London: William Heinemann; Cambridge, MA: Harvard University Press, 1966–68.

Peacham, Henry. *The Art of Drawing with the Pen, and Limming in Water Colours*. London, 1606.

  The Compleat Gentleman. London, 1622.

  The Compleat Gentleman. 2nd edn. London, 1634.

  The Gentlemans Exercise [another issue of *Graphice* with a canceled title-page]. London, 1612.

  Graphice or The Most Auncient and Excellent Art of Drawing and Limming disposed into three bookes. London, 1612.

  Minerva Britanna or a Garden of Heroical Devises, furnished, and adorned with Emblemes and Impresa's of sundry natures. London, 1612.

Peele, George. *The Life and Works of George Peele*. Gen. ed. Charles Tyler Prouty. 3 vols. New Haven: Yale University Press, 1952–70.

Perkins, William. *A Discourse of the Damned Art of Witchcraft; So Farre Forth as it is revealed in the Scriptures, and manifest by true experience*. Cambridge, 1608.

Perrière, Guillaume de la. *Le théâtre des bons engins*. Paris, 1539.

Pett, Peter. *Times journey to seeke his Daughter Truth: and Truths Letter to Fame of Englands Excellencie*. London, 1599.

Peyton, Thomas. *The Glasse of Time, in the second Age*. London, 1620.

Platt, Hugh. *The Jewell House of Art and Nature*. London, 1594.

Plutarch. *The Lives of the Noble Grecians and Romanes*. Trans. Thomas North. London, 1579.

  The Philosophie, commonlie called, The Morals. Trans. Philemon Holland. London, 1603.

Potts, Thomas. *The Wonderfull Discoverie of Witches in the Countie of Lancaster*. London, 1613.

Pricket, Robert. *Honors Fame in Triumph Riding or, The Life and Death of the Late Honorable Earle of Essex*. London, 1604.

Razzell, P. E., ed. *The Journals of Two Travellers in Elizabethan and Early Stuart England: Thomas Platter and Horatio Busino*. London: Caliban Books, 1995.

Rich, Barnaby. *The Honestie of this Age*. London, 1614.

Ripa, Cesare. *Iconologia overo descrittione di diverse imagini cavate dall'antichita, & di propria inventione*. Rome, 1603.

Iconologie, ou explication nouvelle de plusieurs images, emblemes, et autres figures. Trans. Jean Baudoin. Paris, 1641.

Roberts, Alexander. *A Treatise of Witchcraft, Wherein sundry Propositions are laid downe, plainely discovering the wickednesse of that damnable Art.* London, 1616.

Scot, Reginald. *The discoverie of witchcraft, Wherein the lewde dealing of witches and witchmongers is notablie detected.* London, 1584.

Scot, Thomas. *The Second Part of Philomythie, or Philomythologie.* London, 1625.

Shakespeare, William. *As You Like It.* Ed. Alan Brissenden. The New Oxford Shakespeare. Oxford: Clarendon Press, 1993.

As You Like It. Ed. Michael Hattaway. The New Cambridge Shakespeare. Cambridge: Cambridge University Press, 2000.

As You Like It. Ed. Agnes Latham. The Arden Shakespeare. London: Methuen, 1975.

Cymbeline. Ed. Roger Warren. The New Oxford Shakespeare. Oxford: Clarendon Press, 1998.

Hamlet. Ed. Philip Edwards. The New Cambridge Shakespeare. Cambridge: Cambridge University Press, 1985.

Henry IV, Part 1. Ed. David Bevington. The New Oxford Shakespeare. Oxford: Clarendon Press, 1987.

Henry IV, Part 2. Ed. René Weiss. The New Oxford Shakespeare. Oxford: Clarendon Press, 1998.

Julius Caesar. Ed. David Daniell. The Arden Shakespeare, 3rd Series. Walton-on-Thames: Thomas Nelson and Sons, 1998.

King Henry VIII (All is True). Ed. Gordon McMullan. The Arden Shakespeare, 3rd Series. London: Thomson Learning, 2000.

The Life of Timon of Athens. Ed. G. R. Hibbard. The New Penguin Shakespeare. 1970; reprint. Harmondsworth: Penguin, 1981.

Love's Labour's Lost. Ed. G. R. Hibbard. The New Oxford Shakespeare. Oxford: Clarendon Press, 1990.

Love's Labor's Lost. Ed. Peter Holland. The Pelican Shakespeare. New York and London: Penguin, 2000.

Love's Labour's Lost. Ed. John Kerrigan. The New Penguin Shakespeare. Harmondsworth: Penguin, 1982.

Love's Labour's Lost. Ed. H. R. Woudhuysen. The Arden Shakespeare, 3rd Series. Walton-on-Thames: Thomas Nelson and Sons, 1998.

Macbeth. Ed. A. R. Braunmuller. The New Cambridge Shakespeare. Cambridge: Cambridge University Press, 1997.

Macbeth. Ed. Nicholas Brooke. The New Oxford Shakespeare. Oxford: Clarendon Press, 1990.

Pericles. Ed. F. D. Hoeniger. The Arden Shakespeare. 1963; reprint. London: Methuen, 1969.

The Riverside Shakespeare. Ed. G. Blakemore Evans with the assistance of J. J. M. Tobin. 2nd edn. Boston and New York: Houghton Mifflin, 1997.

The Second Part of King Henry IV. Ed. Giorgio Melchiori. The New Cambridge Shakespeare. Cambridge: Cambridge University Press, 1989.

The Tempest. Ed. David Lindley. The New Cambridge Shakespeare. Cambridge: Cambridge University Press, 2002.

The Tempest. Ed. Stephen Orgel. The New Oxford Shakespeare. Oxford: Clarendon Press, 1987.

The Tempest. Ed. Virginia Mason Vaughan and Alden T. Vaughan. The Arden Shakespeare, 3rd Series. Walton-on-Thames: Thomas Nelson and Sons, 1999.

Timon of Athens. Ed. Karl Klein. The New Cambridge Shakespeare. Cambridge: Cambridge University Press, 2001.

Timon of Athens. Ed. H. J. Oliver. The Arden Shakespeare. Cambridge, MA: Harvard University Press, 1959.

Titus Andronicus. Ed. Jonathan Bate. The Arden Shakespeare, 3rd Series. London and New York: Routledge, 1995.

Titus Andronicus. Ed. Alan Hughes. The New Cambridge Shakespeare. Cambridge: Cambridge University Press, 1994.

Titus Andronicus. Ed. J. C. Maxwell. The Arden Shakespeare, 3rd edn. 1961; reprint. London: Methuen, 1963.

Titus Andronicus. Ed. Eugene M. Waith. The New Oxford Shakespeare. Oxford: Clarendon Press, 1984.

The Two Noble Kinsmen. Ed. N. W. Bawcutt. The New Penguin Shakespeare. 1977; reprint. Harmondsworth: Penguin, 1987.

The Two Noble Kinsmen. Ed. Lois Potter. The Arden Shakespeare, 3rd Series. Walton-on-Thames: Thomas Nelson and Sons, 1997.

The Two Noble Kinsmen. Ed. Eugene M. Waith. The New Oxford Shakespeare. Oxford: Clarendon Press, 1989.

William Shakespeare: The Complete Works. Ed. Stanley Wells and Gary Taylor, with John Jowett and William Montgomery. Oxford: Clarendon Press, 1986.

The Winter's Tale. Ed. Stephen Orgel. The New Oxford Shakespeare. Oxford: Clarendon Press, 1996.

The Winter's Tale. Ed. J. H. P. Pafford. The Arden Shakespeare. London: Methuen, 1963.

The Winter's Tale. Ed. Ernest Schanzer. The New Penguin Shakespeare. 1969; reprint. Harmondsworth: Penguin, 1981.

Spencer, T. J. B., and Stanley W. Wells, ed. *A Book of Masques in Honor of Allardyce Nicoll*. 1967; reprint. Cambridge: Cambridge University Press, 1970.

Spenser, Edmund. *The Faerie Queene*. Ed. A. C. Hamilton. 1977; reprint. London and New York: Longman, 1984.

Sprenger, Jacobus, and Heinrich Kramer. *Malleus Maleficarum: The Hammer of Witchcraft*. Trans. Montague Summers. Ed. Pennethorne Hughes. London: The Folio Society, 1968.

Stockwood, John. *A Sermon Preached at Paules Crosse on Barthelmew day, being the 24 of August 1578*. London, [1578].

Stowe, John. *The Annales of England, Faithfully collected out of the most autenticall Authors, Records, and other Monuments of Antiquitie.* London, 1605.

Strype, John. *Annals of the Reformation and Establishment of Religion, and Other Various Occurrences in the Church of England, During the First Twelve Years of Queen Elizabeth's Happy Reign.* London, 1709.

Stubbes, Philip. *The Anatomie of Abuses, Containing A Description of such notable Vices and enormities, as raigne in many Countries of the world, but especiallie in this Realme of England.* 4th edn. "Lately corrected and inlarged." London, 1595.

Taylor, John. *Heavens Blessing, and Earths Joy, or A true relation of the supposed Sea-fights & Fire-workes, as were accomplished, before the Royall Celebration, of the al-beloved Mariage, of the two peerlesse Paragons of Christendome, Fredericke & Elizabeth.* London, 1613.

Taylor, Thomas. *The Second Part of the Theatre of Gods Judgments, Collected out of the writings of sundry Ancient and Moderne Authors.* London, 1642.

Tempesta, Antonio. *Metamorphoseon sive transformationum Ovidianarum libri quindecim.* Antwerp, 1606.

Tomkis, Thomas. *Lingua.* In *A Select Collection of Old English Plays.* 4th edn. Ed. W. Carew Hazlitt. 15 vols. London: Reeves and Turner, 1874–76. Vol. IX.

Tourneur, Cyril [or Thomas Middleton]. *The Revenger's Tragedy.* Ed. R. A. Foakes. The Revels Plays. 1966; reprint. London: Methuen, 1975.

Udall, Joanna, ed. *A Critical Old-Spelling Edition of "The Birth of Merlin."* London: Modern Humanities Research Association, 1991.

Valeriano Bolzani, Giovanni Pierio. *Hieroglyphica sive de sacris aegyptiorum literis commentarii.* Basel, 1556.

Vasari, Giorgio. *Lives of the Artists.* Trans. George Bull. 2 vols. 1965; reprint. London: Penguin, 1987.

Veen [Vaenius], Otto van. *Amorum Emblemata . . . Emblemes of Love, with verses in Latin, English, and Italian.* Antwerp, 1608.

  Q[uinti] Horatii Flacci Emblemata. Antwerp, 1607.

Virgil. *Virgil: Eclogues, Georgics, Aeneid.* Trans. H. Rushton Fairclough. Rev. G. P. Goold. Loeb Classical Library. 2 vols. 1935; reprint. Cambridge, MA: Harvard University Press, 1999.

Webster, John. *The White Devil.* Ed. John Russell Brown. The Revels Plays. 1960; reprint. London: Methuen, 1967.

Weyer, Johann. *Witches, Devils, and Doctors in the Renaissance: Johann Weyer, "De praestigiis daemonum."* Ed. George Mora. Trans. John Shea. Medieval & Renaissance Texts & Studies 73. 1991; reprint. Tempe, AZ: Center for Medieval and Renaissance Studies, 1998.

White, Robert. *Cupid's Banishment.* Ed. C. E. McGee. In *Renaissance Drama* 19 (1988): 227–64.

Whitney, Geoffrey. *A Choice of Emblemes, and other Devises, For the moste parte gathered out of sundrie writers, Englished and Moralized.* Leiden, 1586.

Williams, Roger. *A Briefe Discourse of Warre*. London, 1590.

Wilson, Jean, ed. *Entertainments for Elizabeth I*. Woodbridge: D. S. Brewer; Totowa, NJ: Rowman and Littlefield, 1980.

Wilson, Thomas. *The Arte of Rhetorique*. London, 1553.

Wither, George. *A Collection of Emblemes, Ancient and Moderne*. London, 1635.

Wotton, Henry. *A Parallel betweene Robert late Earle of Essex, and George late Duke of Buckingham*. London, 1641.

 Reliquiae Wottonianae, Or, A Collection of Lives, Letters, Poems; with Characters of Sundry Personages: and other Incomparable Pieces of Language and Art. London, 1651.

Wright, Thomas. *The Passions of the Minde*. London, 1601.

Yarington, Robert. *Two Lamentable Tragedies*. London, 1601.

Secondary works

Abrams, Richard. "Rumor's Reign in *2 Henry IV*: the Scope of a Personification." *English Literary Renaissance* 16 (Autumn 1986): 467–95.

Adams, Robert M. *Shakespeare: The Four Romances*. New York and London: W. W. Norton, 1989.

Adamson, John, ed. *The Princely Courts of Europe: Ritual, Politics and Culture under the Ancien Régime 1500–1750*. London: Weidenfeld and Nicolson, 1999.

Adelman, Janet. "'Born of Women': Fantasies of Maternal Power in *Macbeth*." In *Cannibals, Witches, and Divorce: Estranging the Renaissance*. Ed. Marjorie Garber. Baltimore and London: Johns Hopkins University Press, 1987. Pp. 90–121.

Aghion, Irène, Claire Barbillon, and François Lissarrague. *Gods and Heroes of Classical Antiquity*. Trans. Leonard N. Amico. Flammarion Iconographic Guides. New York and Paris: Flammarion, 1996.

Airs, Malcolm. *The Tudor and Jacobean Country House: A Building History*. London: Sutton Publishing in association with The National Trust, 1995.

Allen, Don Cameron. *Mysteriously Meant: The Rediscovery of Pagan Symbolism and Allegorical Interpretation in the Renaissance*. Baltimore, MD, and London: Johns Hopkins University Press, 1970.

Anglo, Sydney. *Spectacle, Pageantry, and Early Tudor Policy*. Oxford: Clarendon Press, 1969.

Apostolos-Cappadona, Diane. *Encyclopedia of Women in Religious Art*. New York: Continuum, 1996.

Arthos, John. "*Pericles, Prince of Tyre*: A Study in the Dramatic Use of Romantic Narrative." *Shakespeare Quarterly* 4 (July 1953): 257–70.

Astington, John H. *English Court Theatre, 1558–1642*. Cambridge: Cambridge University Press, 1999.

 "*Macbeth* and the Rowe Illustrations." *Shakespeare Quarterly* 49 (Spring 1998): 83–86.

Aston, Elaine, and George Savona. *Theatre as Sign-System: A Semiotics of Text and Performance*. London and New York: Routledge, 1991.

Aston, Margaret. *England's Iconoclasts*, vol. I: *Laws Against Images*. Oxford: Clarendon Press, 1988.

   The King's Bedpost: Reformation and Iconography in a Tudor Group Portrait. Cambridge: Cambridge University Press, 1993.

Auerbach, Erna, and C. Kingsley Adams. *Paintings and Sculpture at Hatfield House: A Catalogue*. London: Constable, 1971.

Axton, Marie. *The Queen's Two Bodies: Drama and the Elizabethan Succession*. London: Royal Historical Society, 1977.

Barber, C. L. *Shakespeare's Festive Comedy: A Study of Dramatic Form and Its Relation to Social Custom*. Princeton: Princeton University Press, 1959.

Barkan, Leonard. "Making Pictures Speak: Renaissance Art, Elizabethan Literature, Modern Scholarship." *Renaissance Quarterly* 48 (Summer 1995): 326–51.

Barroll, Leeds. *Anna of Denmark, Queen of England: A Cultural Biography*. Philadelphia: University of Pennsylvania Press, 2001.

   Politics, Plague, and Shakespeare's Theater: The Stuart Years. Ithaca, NY, and London: Cornell University Press, 1991.

Bartrum, Giulia. *German Renaissance Prints, 1490–1550*. London: British Museum Press, 1995.

Bate, Jonathan. "The Performance of Revenge: *Titus Andronicus* and *The Spanish Tragedy*." In *The Show Within: Dramatic and Other Insets, English Renaissance Drama (1550–1642)*. Ed. François Laroque. Collection Astraea 4. Montpellier: Centre d'Etudes et de Recherches Elisabethaines, Université Paul-Valéry, 1992. Pp. 267–83.

   "Staging the Unspeakable: Four Versions of *Titus Andronicus*." In *Shakespeare: from Text to Stage*. Ed. Patricia Kennan and Mariangela Tempera. The Renaissance Revisited 1. Bologna: Cooperativa Libraria Universitaria Editrice Bologna, 1992. Pp. 97–110.

Bath, Michael. "The Iconography of Time." In *The Telling Image: Explorations in the Emblem*. Ed. Ayers L. Bagley, Edward M. Griffin, and Austin J. McLean. AMS Studies in the Emblem 12. New York: AMS Press, 1996. Pp. 29–68.

   Speaking Pictures: English Emblem Books and Renaissance Culture. London and New York: Longman, 1994.

Bax, Dirk. *Hieronymus Bosch: His Picture-Writing Deciphered*. Trans. M. A. Bax-Botha. Rotterdam: A. A. Balkema, 1979.

Beck, James. *Raphael: The Stanza della Segnatura*. New York: George Braziller, 1993.

Beresford, Richard. *A Dance to the Music of Time*. London: The Wallace Collection, 1995.

Berger, Harry, Jr. "Sneak's Noise or Rumor and Detextualization in *2 Henry IV*." *Kenyon Review* n.s. 6 (Fall 1984): 58–78.

Bergeron, David M. *English Civic Pageantry, 1558–1642*. Columbia: University of South Carolina Press, 1971.

Practicing Renaissance Scholarship: Plays and Pageants, Patrons and Politics. Medieval and Renaissance Literary Studies. Pittsburgh, PA: Duquesne University Press, 2000.

"The Restoration of Hermione in *The Winter's Tale*." In *Shakespeare's Romances Reconsidered*. Ed. Carol McGinnis Kay and Henry E. Jacobs. Lincoln and London: University of Nebraska Press, 1978. Pp. 125–33.

Pageantry in the Shakespearean Theater. Athens: University of Georgia Press, 1985.

Berry, Francis. *The Shakespeare Inset: Word and Picture.* London: Routledge and Kegan Paul, 1965.

Berry, Herbert. "The Globe Bewitched and *El Hombre Fiel*." *Medieval and Renaissance Drama in England* 1 (1984): 211–32.

Berry, Philippa. *Of Chastity and Power: Elizabethan Literature and the Unmarried Queen.* London and New York: Routledge, 1989.

Bethell, S. L. *"The Winter's Tale": A Study.* London: Staples Press, 1947.

Bevington, David. *Action is Eloquence: Shakespeare's Language of Gesture.* Cambridge, MA: Harvard University Press, 1984.

"*The Tempest* and the Jacobean Court Masque." In *The Politics of the Stuart Court Masque*. Ed. Bevington and Peter Holbrook. Cambridge: Cambridge University Press, 1988. Pp. 218–43.

Blissett, William. "This Wide Gap of Time: *The Winter's Tale*." *English Literary Renaissance* 1 (Winter 1971): 52–70.

Blomfield, Reginald. *A History of Renaissance Architecture in England, 1500–1800.* 2 vols. London: George Bell and Sons, 1897.

Boitani, Piero. *Chaucer and the Imaginary World of Fame.* Totowa, NJ: Barnes and Noble, 1984.

Booth, Stephen. *"King Lear," "Macbeth," Indefinition, and Tragedy.* New Haven and London: Yale University Press, 1983.

Bowers, A. Robin. "Emblem and Rape in Shakespeare's *Lucrece* and *Titus Andronicus*." *Studies in Iconography* 10 (1984–86): 79–96.

"Iconography and Rhetoric in Shakespeare's *Lucrece*." *Shakespeare Studies* 14 (1981): 1–21.

Bowles, Edmund A. *Musical Ensembles in Festival Books, 1500–1800: An Iconographical and Documentary Survey.* Ann Arbor, MI: UMI Research Press, 1989.

Bradbrook, M. C. "The Politics of Pageantry: Social Implications in Jacobean London." In *Poetry and Drama, 1570–1700: Essays in Honour of Harold F. Brooks*. Ed. Antony Coleman and Antony Hammond. London and New York: Methuen, 1981. Pp. 60–75.

Shakespeare and Elizabethan Poetry: A Study of His Earlier Work in Relation to the Poetry of the Time. London: Chatto and Windus, 1951.

Braudy, Leo. *The Frenzy of Renown: Fame and Its History.* New York and Oxford: Oxford University Press, 1986.

Braunmuller, A. R. "Thomas Marsh, Henry Marsh, and the Roman Emperors." *The Library* 6th Series, 6 (March 1984): 25–38.

Briggs, K. M. *The Anatomy of Puck: An Examination of Fairy Beliefs among Shakespeare's Contemporaries and Successors.* London: Routledge and Kegan Paul, 1959.

   Pale Hecate's Team: An Examination of the Beliefs on Witchcraft and Magic among Shakespeare's Contemporaries and His Immediate Successors. London: Routledge and Kegan Paul, 1962.

Brissenden, Alan. *Shakespeare and the Dance.* London: Macmillan, 1981.

Brooke, Nicholas. *Shakespeare's Early Tragedies.* London: Methuen, 1968.

Broude, Ronald. "Revenge and Revenge Tragedy in Renaissance England." *Renaissance Quarterly* 28 (Spring 1975): 38–58.

Brown, Cedric C. "Courtesies of Place and Arts of Diplomacy in Ben Jonson's Last Two Entertainments for Royalty." *The Seventeenth Century* 9 (Autumn 1994): 147–71.

Brownlow, F. W. *Two Shakespearean Sequences.* Pittsburgh, PA: University of Pittsburgh Press, 1977.

Brumble, H. David. *Classical Myths and Legends in the Middle Ages and Renaissance: A Dictionary of Allegorical Meanings.* Westport, CN: Greenwood Press, 1998.

Bryant, Lawrence M. *The King and the City in the Parisian Royal Entry Ceremony: Politics, Ritual, and Art in the Renaissance.* Geneva: Librairie Droz, 1986.

Bryson, Norman. "Two Narratives of Rape in the Visual Arts: Lucretia and the Sabine Women." In *Rape.* Ed. Sylvana Tomaselli and Roy Porter. Oxford: Blackwell, 1986. Pp. 152–73.

Bullough, Geoffrey, ed. *Narrative and Dramatic Sources of Shakespeare.* 8 vols. London: Routledge and Kegan Paul; New York: Columbia University Press, 1957–75.

Burlingham, Cynthia, Marianne Grivel, and Henri Zerner. *The French Renaissance in Prints from the Bibliothèque Nationale de France.* Los Angeles: Grunwald Center for the Graphic Arts, UCLA, 1994.

Buxton, John. *Elizabethan Taste.* London: Macmillan, 1963.

Calmann, Gerta. "The Picture of Nobody: An Iconographical Study." *Journal of the Warburg and Courtauld Institutes* 23 (January–June 1960): 60–104.

Caro Baroja, Julio. *The World of Witches.* Trans. Nigel Glendinning. London: Weidenfeld and Nicolson, 1964.

Carroll, Eugene A. *Rosso Fiorentino: Drawings, Prints, and Decorative Arts.* Washington, D.C.: National Gallery of Art, 1987.

Carroll, William C. *The Great Feast of Language in "Love's Labour's Lost."* Princeton: Princeton University Press, 1976.

Cary, Cecile Williamson, and Henry S. Limouze, eds. *Shakespeare and the Arts: A Collection of Essays from the Ohio Shakespeare Conference.* Washington, D.C.: University Press of America, 1982.

Cast, David. *The Calumny of Apelles: A Study in the Humanist Tradition.* New Haven and London: Yale University Press, 1981.

Catty, Jocelyn. *Writing Rape, Writing Women in Early Modern England: Unbridled Speech.* London: Macmillan; New York: St. Martin's Press, 2000.

Cavanagh, Dermoth. "'Possessed with Rumours': Popular Speech and *King John.*" *Shakespeare Yearbook 6: Shakespeare and History.* Ed. Holger Klein and Rowland Wymer. Lewiston, NY, Queenston, Lampeter: Edwin Mellen Press, 1996. Pp. 171–94.

Chakravorty, Swapan. *Society and Politics in the Plays of Thomas Middleton.* Oxford: Clarendon Press, 1996.

Chambers, Douglas. "'A Speaking Picture': Some Ways of Proceeding in Literature and the Fine Arts in the Late-sixteenth and Early-seventeenth Centuries." In *Encounters: Essays on Literature and the Visual Arts.* Ed. John Dixon Hunt. New York: W. W. Norton, 1971. Pp. 28–57.

Chambers, E. K. *The Elizabethan Stage.* 4 vols. 1923; reprint. Oxford: Clarendon Press, 1951.

    William Shakespeare: A Study of Facts and Problems. 2 vols. Oxford: Clarendon Press, 1930.

Cheney, Liana De Girolami. "Fame." In *Encyclopedia of Comparative Iconography: Themes Depicted in Works of Art.* Ed. Helene E. Roberts. 2 vols. Chicago and London: Fitzroy Dearborn, 1998. I: 307–13.

Chew, Samuel C. "The Iconography of *A Book of Christian Prayers* (1578) Illustrated." *Huntington Library Quarterly* 8 (May 1945): 293–305.

    The Pilgrimage of Life. 1962; reprint. Port Washington, NY, and London: Kennikat Press, 1973.

    The Virtues Reconciled: An Iconographic Study. Toronto: University of Toronto Press, 1947.

Cho, Kwang Soon. *Emblems in Shakespeare's Last Plays.* Lanham, MD, New York, and Oxford: University Press of America, 1998.

Clark, Stuart. *Thinking with Demons: The Idea of Witchcraft in Early Modern Europe.* Oxford: Clarendon Press, 1997.

Clements, Robert J. *Picta Poesis: Literary and Humanistic Theory in Renaissance Emblem Books.* Temi e Testi 6. Rome: Edizioni di Storia e Letteratura, 1960.

Coghill, Nevill. "Six Points of Stage-craft in *The Winter's Tale.*" *Shakespeare Survey* 11 (1958): 31–41.

Cohen, Kathleen. *Metamorphosis of a Death Symbol: The Transi Tomb in the Late Middle Ages and the Renaissance.* California Studies in the History of Art 15. Berkeley, Los Angeles, London: University of California Press, 1973.

Cohen, S. "The Early Renaissance Personification of Time and Changing Concepts of Temporality." *Renaissance Studies* 14 (September 2000): 301–28.

Comensoli, Viviana. "Witchcraft and Domestic Tragedy in *The Witch of Edmonton.*" In *The Politics of Gender in Early Modern Europe.* Ed. Jean R. Brink, Allison P.

Coudert, and Maryanne C. Horowitz. Sixteenth Century Essays and Studies 12. Kirksville, MO: Sixteenth Century Journal Publishers, 1989. Pp. 43–59.

Cook, Olive. *The English Country House*. London: Thames and Hudson, 1974.

Corbett, Margery, and Ronald Lightbown. *The Comely Frontispiece: The Emblematic Title-Page in England, 1550–1660*. London, Henley, Boston: Routledge and Kegan Paul, 1979.

Coughlan, Patricia. "'Enter Revenge': Henry Burkhead and *Cola's Furie*." *Theatre Research International* 15 (Spring 1990): 1–17.

Coursen, H. R. *"Macbeth": A Guide to the Play*. Westport, CT, and London: Greenwood Press, 1997.

Cox, J. D. "*Henry VIII* and the Masque." *ELH* 45 (Fall 1978): 390–409.

Cox, Lee Sheridan. *Figurative Design in "Hamlet": The Significance of the Dumb Show*. Columbus: Ohio State University Press, 1973.

Craik, T. W. *The Tudor Interlude: Stage, Costume, and Acting*. Leicester: Leicester University Press, 1962.

Crupi, Charles. "*The Winter's Tale* and *The Thracian Wonder*." *Archiv für das Studium der Neueren Sprachen und Literaturen* 207 (January 1971): 341–47.

Curry, Walter Clyde. *Shakespeare's Philosophical Patterns*. 1937; reprint. Baton Rouge: Louisiana State University Press, 1959.

Cutts, John P. "'When were the *Senses* in such order plac'd?'" *Comparative Drama* 4 (Spring 1970): 52–62.

Czobor, Agnes. "'The Five Senses' by the Antwerp Artist Jacob de Backer." *Nederlands Kunsthistorisch Jaarboek* 23 (1972): 317–27.

Daly, Peter M. *Literature in the Light of the Emblem: Structural Parallels between the Emblem and Literature in the Sixteenth and Seventeenth Centuries*. 2nd edn. Toronto, Buffalo, London: University of Toronto Press, 1998.

Daly, Peter M. "Shakespeare and the Emblem: The Use of Evidence and Analogy in Establishing Iconographic and Emblematic Effects in the Plays." In *Shakespeare and the Emblem: Studies in Renaissance Iconography and Iconology*. Ed. Tibor Fabiny. Szeged: Attila József University Press, 1984. Pp. 117–87.

"Trends and Problems in the Study of Emblematic Literature." *Mosaic* 5 (Summer 1972): 53–68.

Danson, Lawrence. *Tragic Alphabet: Shakespeare's Drama of Language*. New Haven and London: Yale University Press, 1974.

Davidson, Clifford. "Death in His Court: Iconography in Shakespeare's Tragedies." *Studies in Iconography* 1 (1975): 74–86.

Drama and Art: An Introduction to the Use of Evidence from the Visual Arts for the Study of Early Drama. Kalamazoo, MI: The Medieval Institute, 1977.

The Primrose Way: A Study of Shakespeare's "Macbeth." Conesville, IA: John Westburg, 1970.

"*Timon of Athens*: The Iconography of False Friendship." *Huntington Library Quarterly* 43 (Summer 1980): 181–200.

Dees, Jerome S. "Recent Studies in the English Emblem." *English Literary Renaissance* 16 (Spring 1986): 391–420.

Demaray, John G. *Shakespeare and the Spectacles of Strangeness: "The Tempest" and the Transformation of Renaissance Theatrical Forms*. Pittsburgh, PA: Duquesne University Press, 1998.

Dessen, Alan C. "Recovering Shakespeare's Images." *Word & Image* 4 (July–December 1988): 618–25.

  Recovering Shakespeare's Theatrical Vocabulary. Cambridge: Cambridge University Press, 1995.

  Titus Andronicus. Shakespeare in Performance. Manchester: Manchester University Press; New York: St. Martin's Press, 1989.

Dessen, Alan C., and Leslie Thomson. *A Dictionary of Stage Directions in English Drama, 1580–1642*. Cambridge: Cambridge University Press, 1999.

Diehl, Huston. "Iconography and Characterization in English Tragedy, 1585–1642." *Comparative Drama* 12 (Summer 1978): 113–22.

Diehl, Huston. *An Index of Icons in English Emblem Books, 1500–1700*. Norman and London: University of Oklahoma Press, 1986.

  "Observing the Lord's Supper and the Lord Chamberlain's Men: The Visual Rhetoric of Ritual and Play in Early Modern England." *Renaissance Drama* n.s. 22 (1991): 147–74.

  Staging Reform, Reforming the Stage: Protestantism and Popular Theater in Early Modern England. Ithaca, NY, and London: Cornell University Press, 1997.

Doebler, John. *Shakespeare's Speaking Pictures: Studies in Iconic Imagery*. Albuquerque: University of New Mexico Press, 1974.

Dolan, Frances. *Dangerous Familiars: Representations of Domestic Crime in England, 1550–1700*. Ithaca, NY, and London: Cornell University Press, 1994.

Donaldson, Ian. *The Rapes of Lucretia: A Myth and Its Transformations*. Oxford: Clarendon Press, 1982.

Doran, Susan. "Juno versus Diana: The Treatment of Elizabeth I's Marriage in Plays and Entertainments, 1561–1581." *The Historical Journal* 38 (June 1995): 257–74.

Dubrow, Heather. *Captive Victors: Shakespeare's Narrative Poems and Sonnets*. Ithaca, NY, and London: Cornell University Press, 1987.

Dundas, Judith. *Pencils Rhetorique: Renaissance Poets and the Art of Painting*. Newark: University of Delaware Press; London and Toronto: Associated University Presses, 1993.

Dutton, Richard, ed. *Jacobean Civic Pageants*. Ryburn Renaissance Texts and Studies. Keele: Keele University Press, 1995.

Edwards, Philip. "Thrusting Elysium into Hell: The Originality of *The Spanish Tragedy*." *The Elizabethan Theatre* 11 (1990): 117–32.

Eisenbichler, Konrad, and Amilcare A. Iannucci. *Petrarch's "Triumphs": Allegory and Spectacle*. University of Toronto Italian Studies 4. Ottawa: Dovehouse, 1990.

Elton, O. "Literary Fame: a Renaissance Study." *Otia Merseiana* 4 (1904): 24–52.

Erickson, Peter, and Clark Hulse, eds. *Early Modern Visual Culture: Representation, Race, and Empire in Renaissance England*. New Cultural Studies. Philadelphia: University of Pennsylvania Press, 2000.

Erler, Mary C. "Sir John Davies and the Rainbow Portrait of Queen Elizabeth." *Modern Philology* 84 (May 1987): 359–71.

Esler, Anthony. *The Aspiring Mind of the Elizabethan Younger Generation*. Durham, NC: Duke University Press, 1966.

Evett, David. *Literature and the Visual Arts in Tudor England*. Athens and London: University of Georgia Press, 1990.

Ewbank, Inga-Stina. "'More Pregnantly Than Words': Some Uses and Limitations of Visual Symbolism." *Shakespeare Survey* 24 (1971): 13–18.

  "The Theatre Language of Thomas Middleton." *The Elizabethan Theatre* 12 (1993): 77–91.

  "The Triumph of Time in 'The Winter's Tale.'" *Review of English Literature* 5 (April 1964): 83–100.

Fairchild, Arthur H. R. *Shakespeare and the Arts of Design (Architecture, Sculpture, and Painting)*. University of Missouri Studies 12. Columbia: University of Missouri Press, 1937.

Farmer, Norman K., Jr. *Poets and the Visual Arts in Renaissance England*. Austin: University of Texas Press, 1984.

Farnham, Willard. *Shakespeare's Tragic Frontier: The World of His Final Tragedies*. 1950; reprint. Berkeley and Los Angeles: University of California Press, 1963.

Ferber, Michael. *A Dictionary of Literary Symbols*. Cambridge: Cambridge University Press, 1999.

Ferguson, George. *Signs and Symbols in Christian Art*. 1954; reprint. London, Oxford, New York: Oxford University Press, 1972.

Findlay, Alison. *A Feminist Perspective on Renaissance Drama*. Oxford: Blackwell, 1999.

Finney, Paul Corby, ed. *Seeing beyond the Word: Visual Arts and the Calvinist Tradition*. Grand Rapids, MI: William B. Eerdmans, 1999.

Fischlin, Daniel. "Political Allegory, Absolutist Ideology, and the 'Rainbow Portrait' of Queen Elizabeth I." *Renaissance Quarterly* 50 (Spring 1997): 175–206.

Fleischer, Martha Hester. *The Iconography of the English History Play*. Elizabethan and Renaissance Studies 10. Salzburg: Institut für Sprache und Literatur, Universität Salzburg, 1974.

Foakes, R. A. *Illustrations of the English Stage, 1580–1642*. Stanford, CA: Stanford University Press, 1985.

Foakes, R. A. and R. T. Rickert, eds. *Henslowe's Diary*. Cambridge: Cambridge University Press, 1961.

Fowler, Alastair. *Time's Purpled Masquers: Stars and the Afterlife in Renaissance English Literature*. Oxford: Clarendon Press, 1996.

Freedberg, David. *The Power of Images: Studies in the History and Theory of Response*. Chicago and London: University of Chicago Press, 1989.

Freeman, Rosemary. *English Emblem Books*. London: Chatto and Windus, 1948.

Frye, Northrop. "Recognition in *The Winter's Tale*." In *Essays in Shakespearean Criticism*. Ed. James L. Calderwood and Harold E. Toliver. Englewood Cliffs, NJ: Prentice-Hall, 1970. Pp. 357–67.

"Romance as Masque." In *Shakespeare's Romances Reconsidered*. Ed. Carol McGinnis Kay and Henry E. Jacobs. Lincoln and London: University of Nebraska Press, 1978. Pp. 11–39.

Fulton, Robert C. *Shakespeare and the Masque*. New York and London: Garland, 1988.

"Timon, Cupid, and the Amazons." *Shakespeare Studies* 9 (1976): 283–99.

Fumerton, Patricia. *Cultural Aesthetics: Renaissance Literature and the Practice of Social Ornament*. Chicago and London: University of Chicago Press, 1991.

Fumerton, Patricia, and Simon Hunt, eds. *Renaissance Culture and the Everyday*. New Cultural Studies. Philadelphia: University of Pennsylvania Press, 1999.

Gent, Lucy. *Picture and Poetry 1560–1620: Relations between Literature and the Visual Arts in the English Renaissance*. Leamington Spa: James Hall, 1981.

Renaissance Bodies: The Human Figure in English Culture c. 1540–1660. London: Reaktion Books, 1990.

Gilbert, Allan H. *The Symbolic Persons in the Masques of Ben Jonson*. Durham, NC: Duke University Press, 1948.

Gilbert, Miriam. *Love's Labour's Lost*. Shakespeare in Performance. Manchester: Manchester University Press; New York: St. Martin's Press, 1993.

Gilman, Ernest B. *The Curious Perspective: Literary and Pictorial Wit in the Seventeenth Century*. New Haven: Yale University Press, 1978.

Iconoclasm and Poetry in the English Reformation: Down went Dagon. Chicago: University of Chicago Press, 1986.

Givry, Grillot de. *The Illustrated Anthology of Sorcery, Magic and Alchemy*. Trans. J. Courtenay Locke. New York: Causeway Books, 1973.

Goldsworthy, William Lansdown. *Shakespeare's Heraldic Emblems: Their Origin and Meaning*. 2nd and rev. edn. London: H. F. and G. Witherby, 1928.

Gombrich, E. H. *Art and Illusion: A Study of the Psychology of Pictorial Representation*. New York: Pantheon Books, 1960.

Symbolic Images: Studies in the Art of the Renaissance. 1972; reprint. London: Phaidon, 1975.

Gordon, D. J. "Name and Fame: Shakespeare's Coriolanus." *Papers Mainly Shakespearian*. Ed. G. I. Duthie. Aberdeen University Studies 147. Edinburgh: Oliver and Boyd, 1964. Pp. 40–57.

The Renaissance Imagination: Essays and Lectures. Ed. Stephen Orgel. Berkeley and Los Angeles: University of California Press, 1975.

Gore, Alan and Ann. *The History of English Interiors*. Oxford: Phaidon, 1991.

Gossett, Suzanne. *The Influence of the Jacobean Masque on the Plays of Beaumont and Fletcher*. New York and London: Garland, 1988.

Graves, R. B. *Lighting the Shakespearean Stage, 1567–1642.* Carbondale and Edwardsville: Southern Illinois University Press, 1999.

Green, Henry. *Shakespeare and the Emblem Writers: An Exposition of Their Similarities of Thought and Expression.* London: Trübner, 1870.

Greenfield, Thelma. *The Induction in Elizabethan Drama.* Eugene: University of Oregon Books, 1969.

Greenwood, John. *Shifting Perspectives and the Stylish Style: Mannerism in Shakespeare and His Jacobean Contemporaries.* Toronto: University of Toronto Press, 1988.

Griffiths, Antony. *The Print in Stuart Britain, 1603–1689.* London: British Museum Press, 1998.

Gurr, Andrew. *Playgoing in Shakespeare's London.* 2nd edn. Cambridge: Cambridge University Press, 1996.

"Shakespeare and the Visual Signifier." In *Reclamations of Shakespeare.* Ed. A. J. Hoenselaars. DQR Studies in Literature 15. Amsterdam and Atlanta, GA: Rodopi, 1994. Pp. 11–20.

The Shakespearian Playing Companies. Oxford: Clarendon Press, 1996.

The Shakespearean Stage, 1574–1642. 3rd edn. Cambridge: Cambridge University Press, 1992.

"*The Tempest*'s Tempest at Blackfriars." *Shakespeare Survey* 41 (1988): 91–102.

Gurr, Andrew, and Mariko Ichikawa. *Staging in Shakespeare's Theatres.* Oxford Shakespeare Topics. Oxford: Oxford University Press, 2000.

Haaker, Ann. "*Non sine causa*: The Use of Emblematic Method and Iconology in the Thematic Structure of *Titus Andronicus.*" *Research Opportunities in Renaissance Drama* 13–14 (1970–71): 143–68.

Hale, John. "Women and War in the Visual Arts of the Renaissance." In *War, Literature and the Arts in Sixteenth-Century Europe.* Ed. J. R. Mulryne and Margaret Shewring. London: Macmillan, 1989. Pp. 43–62.

Hamilton, Donna B. *Virgil and "The Tempest": The Politics of Imitation.* Columbus: Ohio State University Press, 1990.

Hammer, Paul E. J. *The Polarisation of Elizabethan Politics: The Political Career of Robert Devereux, 2nd Earl of Essex, 1585–1597.* Cambridge: Cambridge University Press, 1999.

Harris, Anthony. *Night's Black Agents: Witchcraft and Magic in Seventeenth-Century English Drama.* Manchester: Manchester University Press; Totowa, NJ: Rowman and Littlefield, 1980.

Harris, John, Stephen Orgel, and Roy Strong. *The King's Arcadia: Inigo Jones and the Stuart Court: A Quatercentenary Exhibition Held at the Banqueting House, Whitehall.* London: Arts Council of Great Britain, 1973.

Harthan, John. *The History of the Illustrated Book: The Western Tradition.* London: Thames and Hudson, 1981.

Härting, Ursula. *Frans Francken der Jüngere (1581–1642): Die Gemälde mit Kritischem Oeuvrekatalog.* Flämische Maler im Umkreis der grossen Meister 2. Freren: Luca Verlag, 1989.

Hartwig, Joan. *Shakespeare's Tragicomic Vision*. Baton Rouge: Louisiana State University Press, 1972.

Hattaway, Michael. "Allegorising in Drama and the Visual Arts." Tudor Theatre 5: *Allegory in the Theatre*. Tours Round Tables on Tudor Drama 7. Bern: Peter Lang, 2000. Pp. 187–205.

Elizabethan Popular Theatre: Plays in Performance. London: Routledge & Kegan Paul, 1982.

Hazard, Mary E. *Elizabethan Silent Language*. Lincoln and London: University of Nebraska Press, 2000.

"Shakespeare's 'Living Art': A Live Issue from *Love's Labour's Lost*." In *Shakespeare and the Arts: A Collection of Essays from the Ohio Shakespeare Conference*, ed. Cecile Williamson Cary and Henry S. Limouze. Washington, D.C.: University Press of America, 1982. Pp. 181–98.

Heckscher, William S. *Art and Literature: Studies in Relationship*. Ed. Egon Verheyen. Durham, NC: Duke University Press; Baden-Baden: Verlag Valentin Koerner, 1985.

"Shakespeare in His Relationship to the Visual Arts: A Study in Paradox." *Research Opportunities in Renaissance Drama* 13–14 (1970–71): 5–71.

Hedrick, Charles W., Jr. *History and Silence: Purge and Rehabilitation of Memory in Late Antiquity*. Austin: University of Texas Press, 2000.

Heinemann, Margot. *Puritanism and Theatre: Thomas Middleton and Opposition Drama under the Early Stuarts*. Cambridge: Cambridge University Press, 1980.

Heninger, S. K., Jr. *Touches of Sweet Harmony: Pythagorean Cosmology and Renaissance Poetics*. San Marino, CA: The Huntington Library, 1974.

Henkel, Arthur, and Albrecht Schöne. *Emblemata: Handbuch zur Sinnbildkunst des XVI. und XVII. Jahrhunderts*. Stuttgart: J. B. Metzler, 1967. (*Supplement*, 1976.)

Hoak, Dale. "Witch-Hunting and Women in the Art of the Renaissance." *History Today* 31 (February 1981): 22–26.

Hodgdon, Barbara. *Henry IV, Part Two*. Shakespeare in Performance. Manchester: Manchester University Press; New York: St. Martin's Press, 1993.

Hodges, C. Walter. *Enter the Whole Army: A Pictorial Study of Shakespearean Staging, 1576–1616*. Cambridge: Cambridge University Press, 1999.

Holderness, Graham, Nick Potter, and John Turner. *Shakespeare Out of Court: Dramatizations of Court Society*. London: Macmillan, 1990.

Hollstein, F. W. H. *Dutch and Flemish Etchings, Engravings and Woodcuts, c. 1450–1700*. Vols. I–XXXI. Amsterdam: M. Hertzberger, 1949–87. Vols. XXXII–XLIII: Roosendaal, 1988–93. Vols. XLIV–: Rotterdam, 1995–.

German Engravings, Etchings and Woodcuts, c. 1450–1700. Amsterdam: M. Hertzberger, 1954–.

Höltgen, Karl Joseph. *Aspects of the Emblem: Studies in the English Emblem Tradition and the European Context*. Kassel: Reichenberger, 1986.

"The Reformation of Images and Some Jacobean Writers on Art." In *Functions of Literature: Essays Presented to Erwin Wolff on his Sixtieth Birthday*. Ed. Ulrich Broich et al. Tübingen: Max Niemeyer Verlag, 1984. Pp. 119–46.

Homan, Sidney, ed. *Shakespeare's "More Than Words Can Witness": Essays on Visual and Nonverbal Enactment in the Plays.* Lewisburg, PA: Bucknell University Press; London: Associated University Presses, 1980.

Shakespeare's Theater of Presence: Language, Spectacle, and the Audience. Lewisburg, PA: Bucknell University Press; London and Toronto: Associated University Presses, 1986.

Hopkins, Lisa. "Play Houses: Drama at Bolsover and Welbeck." *Early Theatre* 2 (1999): 25–44.

Howard, Jean E. "Scripts and/versus Playhouses: Ideological Production and the Renaissance Public Stage." In *The Matter of Difference: Materialist Feminist Criticism of Shakespeare.* Ed. Valerie Wayne. London and New York: Harvester Wheatsheaf, 1991.

Howard, Skiles. *The Politics of Courtly Dancing in Early Modern England.* Amherst: University of Massachusetts Press, 1998.

Hoy, Cyrus. "Artifice and Reality and the Decline of Jacobean Drama." *Research Opportunities in Renaissance Drama* 13–14 (1970–71): 169–80.

Hulse, Clark. "Recent Studies of Literature and Painting in the English Renaissance." *English Literary Renaissance* 15 (Winter 1985): 122–40.

The Rule of Art: Literature and Painting in the Renaissance. Chicago: University of Chicago Press, 1990.

Hunt, John Dixon. "*Pictura, Scriptura,* and *Theatrum*: Shakespeare and the Emblem." *Poetics Today* 10 (Spring 1989): 155–71.

"Shakespeare and the *Paragone*: A Reading of *Timon of Athens*." In *Images of Shakespeare.* Ed. Werner Habicht, D. J. Palmer, and Roger Pringle. Newark: University of Delaware Press; London: Associated University Presses, 1988. Pp. 47–63.

"The Visual Arts in Shakespeare's Work." In *William Shakespeare: His World, His Work, His Influence.* Ed. John F. Andrews. 3 vols. New York: Charles Scribner's Sons, 1985. II: 425–31.

"The Visual Arts of Shakespeare's Day." In *Shakespeare: Pattern of Excelling Nature.* Ed. David Bevington and Jay L. Halio. Newark: University of Delaware Press; London: Associated University Presses, 1978. Pp. 210–21.

Hunter, G. K. "Flatcaps and Bluecoats: Visual Signals on the Elizabethan Stage." *Essays and Studies* n.s. 33 (1980): 16–47.

Hutson, Lorna. "Chivalry for Merchants; or, Knights of Temperance in the Realms of Gold." *Journal of Medieval and Early Modern Studies* 26 (Winter 1996): 29–59.

Hyde, Thomas. *The Poetic Theology of Love: Cupid in Renaissance Literature.* Newark: University of Delaware Press; London and Toronto: Associated University Presses, 1986.

Iwasaki, Soji. *Icons in English Renaissance Drama.* Tokyo: The Renaissance Institute of Sophia University, 1992.

"The Stage Tableau and Iconography of *Macbeth*." In *Japanese Studies in Shakespeare and His Contemporaries.* Ed. Yoshiko Kawachi. Newark:

University of Delaware Press; London: Associated University Presses, 1998. Pp. 86–98.

"*Veritas Filia Temporis* and Shakespeare." *English Literary Renaissance* 3 (Spring 1973): 249–63.

Jackson, MacDonald P. *Studies in Attribution: Middleton and Shakespeare.* Salzburg Studies in English Literature. Salzburg: Institut für Anglistik und Amerikanistik, Universität Salzburg, 1979.

Jackson-Stops, Gervase, ed. *The Treasure Houses of Britain: Five Hundred Years of Private Patronage and Art Collecting.* New Haven and London: Yale University Press; Washington, D.C.: the National Gallery of Art, 1985.

Jacobowitz, Ellen S., and Stephanie Loeb Stepanek. *The Prints of Lucas van Leyden and His Contemporaries.* Washington, D.C.: National Gallery of Art, 1983.

Jacquot, Jean. "The Last Plays and the Masque." In *Shakespeare 1971: Proceedings of the World Shakespeare Congress, Vancouver.* Ed. Clifford Leech and J. M. R. Margeson. Toronto: University of Toronto Press, 1971.

James, Heather. *Shakespeare's Troy: Drama, Politics, and the Translation of Empire.* Cambridge: Cambridge University Press, 1997.

Jardine, Lisa. *Worldly Goods.* London: Macmillan, 1996.

Jed, Stephanie H. *Chaste Thinking: The Rape of Lucretia and the Birth of Humanism.* Bloomington and Indianapolis: Indiana University Press, 1989.

Jeffrey, David L., and Patrick Grant. "Reputation in *Othello.*" *Shakespeare Studies* 6 (1970): 197–221.

Jeffreys, M. D. W. "The Weird Sisters in *Macbeth.*" *English Studies in Africa* 1 (March 1958): 43–54.

Jestaz, Bertrand. *Art of the Renaissance.* Trans. I. Mark Paris. New York: Harry N. Abrams, 1995.

Johnson, Anthony. "Number Symbolism in *Macbeth.*" *Analysis: Quaderni di Anglistica* 4 (1986): 25–41.

Johnston, Sarah Iles. *Restless Dead: Encounters between the Living and the Dead in Ancient Greece.* Berkeley, Los Angeles, London: University of California Press, 1999.

Jones, Ann Rosalind, and Peter Stallybrass. *Renaissance Clothing and the Materials of Memory.* Cambridge: Cambridge University Press, 2000.

Jones-Davies, Marie-Thérèse. *Inigo Jones, Ben Jonson et le masque.* Paris: Marcel Didier, 1967.

Jourdain, Margaret. *English Interior Decoration 1500–1830: A Study in the Development of Design.* London and New York: B. T. Batsford, 1950.

Jowett, John, and Gary Taylor. "'With New Additions': Theatrical Interpolation in *Measure for Measure.*" In *Shakespeare Reshaped, 1606–1623.* Oxford: Clarendon Press, 1993. Pp. 107–236.

Judson, J. Richard, and Carl van de Velde. *Book Illustrations and Title-Pages.* Corpus Rubenianum Ludwig Burchard 21. 2 vols. London and Philadelphia: Harvey Miller-Heyden & Son, 1978.

Kay, Carol McGinnis, and Henry E. Jacobs, eds. *Shakespeare's Romances Reconsidered*. Lincoln and London: University of Nebraska Press, 1978.

Kendrick, A. F. "The Hatfield Tapestries of the Seasons." *Annual Volume of the Walpole Society* 2 (1912–13): 89–97.

Kennedy, Gwynne. *Just Anger: Representing Women's Anger in Early Modern England*. Carbondale and Edwardsville: Southern Illinois University Press, 2000.

Kermode, Frank. "The Banquet of Sense." In *Shakespeare, Spenser, Donne: Renaissance Essays*. New York: Viking Press, 1971. Pp. 84–115.

Kernodle, George R. *From Art to Theatre: Form and Convention in the Renaissance*. 1944; reprint. Chicago and London: University of Chicago Press, 1964.

Kerrigan, John. *Revenge Tragedy: Aeschylus to Armageddon*. Oxford: Clarendon Press, 1996.

Keyishian, Harry. *The Shapes of Revenge: Victimization, Vengeance, and Vindictiveness in Shakespeare*. Atlantic Highlands, NJ: Humanities Press, 1995.

Kiefer, Frederick. *Fortune and Elizabethan Tragedy*. San Marino, CA: Huntington Library Press, 1983.

  Writing on the Renaissance Stage: Written Words, Printed Pages, Metaphoric Books. Newark: University of Delaware Press; London: Associated University Presses, 1996.

King, John N. *Tudor Royal Iconography: Literature and Art in an Age of Religious Crisis*. Princeton: Princeton University Press, 1989.

Kinney, Arthur F., ed. *A Companion to Renaissance Drama*. Oxford: Blackwell, 2002.

Kipling, Gordon. *Enter the King: Theatre, Liturgy, and Ritual in the Medieval Civic Triumph*. Oxford: Clarendon Press, 1998.

Klein, Holger, and James L. Harner, eds. *Shakespeare Yearbook* 11: *Shakespeare and the Visual Arts*. Lewiston, NY, Queenston, Lampeter: Edwin Mellen Press, 2000.

Kliman, Bernice W. *Macbeth*. Shakespeare in Performance. Manchester: Manchester University Press; New York: St. Martin's Press, 1992.

  "Rowe 1709 *Macbeth* Illustration Again." *The Shakespeare Newsletter* 48:3 (Fall 1998): 59–60.

Knight, G. Wilson. *The Crown of Life: Essays in Interpretation of Shakespeare's Final Plays*. London: Oxford University Press, 1947.

  The Shakespearian Tempest. 1932; reprint. Oxford: Oxford University Press; London: Humphrey Milford, 1940.

Knipping, John B. *Iconography of the Counter Reformation in the Netherlands*. 2 vols. Nieuwkoop: B. de Graaf; Leiden: A. W. Sijthoff, 1974.

Kogan, Stephen. *The Hieroglyphic King: Wisdom and Idolatry in the Seventeenth-Century Masque*. Rutherford, Madison, Teaneck, NJ: Fairleigh Dickinson University Press; London and Toronto: Associated University Presses, 1986.

Kolin, Philip C., ed. *"Titus Andronicus": Critical Essays*. New York and London: Garland, 1995.

Lake, David J. *The Canon of Thomas Middleton's Plays: Internal Evidence for the Major Problems of Authorship*. Cambridge: Cambridge University Press, 1975.

Lancashire, Anne. "*The Witch*: Stage Flop or Political Mistake?" In *"Accompaninge the players": Essays Celebrating Thomas Middleton, 1580–1980*. Ed. Kenneth Friedenreich. New York: AMS Press, 1983. Pp. 161–81.

Landau, David, and Peter Parshall. *The Renaissance Print, 1470–1550*. New Haven and London: Yale University Press, 1994.

Larner, Christina. "Witch Beliefs and Witch-hunting in England and Scotland." *History Today* 31 (February 1981): 32–36.

Laroque, François. *Shakespeare's Festive World: Elizabethan Seasonal Entertainment and the Professional Stage*. Trans. Janet Lloyd. Cambridge: Cambridge University Press, 1991.

Laroque, François, ed. *The Show Within: Dramatic and Other Insets, English Renaissance Drama (1550–1642)*. Proceedings of the International Conference held in Montpellier, 22–25 November 1990. Collection Astraea 4. 2 vols. Montpellier: Centre d'Etudes et de Recherches Elisabethaines, Université Paul-Valéry, 1992.

Latham, Jacqueline E. M. "The Magic Banquet in *The Tempest*." *Shakespeare Studies* 12 (1979): 215–27.

Lawrence, W. J. "The Mystery of 'Macbeth': A Solution." *Fortnightly Review* n.s. 108 (November 1920): 777–83.

Lees-Milne, James. *Tudor Renaissance*. London and New York: B. T. Batsford, 1951.

Leslie, Michael. "The Dialogue between Bodies and Souls: Pictures and Poesy in the English Renaissance." *Word and Image* 1 (January–March 1985): 16–30.

Levey, Michael. *Painting at Court*. New York: New York University Press, 1971.

Levey, Santina M. *Elizabethan Treasures: The Hardwick Hall Textiles*. New York: Harry N. Abrams, 1998.

Levi D'Ancona, Mirella. *The Garden of the Renaissance: Botanical Symbolism in Italian Painting*. Arte e Archeologia: Studi e Documenti 10. Florence: Leo S. Olschki, 1977.

Limon, Jerzy. *The Masque of Stuart Culture*. Newark: University of Delaware Press; London and Toronto: Associated University Presses, 1990.

Lincoln, Evelyn. *The Invention of the Italian Renaissance Printmaker*. New Haven and London: Yale University Press, 2000.

Lindley, David, ed. *Court Masques: Jacobean and Caroline Entertainments, 1605–1640*. Oxford: Clarendon Press, 1995.

Linthicum, M. Channing. *Costume in the Drama of Shakespeare and His Contemporaries*. Oxford: Clarendon Press, 1936.

Lippincott, Kristen, with Umberto Eco, E. H. Gombrich, and others. *The Story of Time*. London: Merrell Holberton (in association with the National Maritime Museum), 2000.

Lubbock, Jules. *The Tyranny of Taste: The Politics of Architecture and Design in Britain, 1550–1960*. New Haven and London: Yale University Press for the Paul Mellon Centre for British Art, 1995.

Luborsky, Ruth Samson, and Elizabeth Morley Ingram. *A Guide to English Illustrated Books, 1536–1603*. 2 vols. Medieval and Renaissance Texts and Studies. Tempe: Arizona Center for Medieval and Renaissance Studies, 1998.

Lunney, Ruth. "Transforming the Emblematic: The Dramatic Emblem in the Plays of Marlowe." *Essays in Theatre* 9 (May 1991): 141–58.

McConnell, Sophie, and Alvin Grossman. *Metropolitan Jewelry*. New York: The Metropolitan Museum of Art; Boston: Little, Brown, 1991.

McCorquodale, Charles. *The History of Interior Decoration*. Oxford: Phaidon, 1983.

McCoy, Richard. *The Rites of Knighthood: The Literature and Politics of Elizabethan Chivalry*. Berkeley, Los Angeles, London: University of California Press, 1989.

McGee, Arthur R. "'Macbeth' and the Furies." *Shakespeare Survey* (1966): 55–67.

McGowan, Margaret M. "Pierre de Lancre's *Tableau de l'inconstance des mauvais anges et demons*: The Sabbat Sensationalised." In *The Damned Art: Essays in the Literature of Witchcraft*. Ed. Sydney Anglo. London, Henley, Boston: Routledge & Kegan Paul, 1977. Pp. 182–201.

MacIntyre, Jean. *Costumes and Scripts in the Elizabethan Theatres*. Edmonton: University of Alberta Press, 1992.

MacIntyre, Jean, and Garrett P. J. Epp. "'Cloathes worth all the rest': Costumes and Properties." In *A New Literary History of Early English Drama*. Ed. John D. Cox and David Scott Kastan. New York: Columbia University Press, 1997. Pp. 269–85.

MacKenzie, Clayton G. *Emblems of Mortality: Iconographic Experiments in Shakespeare's Theatre*. Lanham, MD, New York, and Oxford: University Press of America, 2000.

McLay, Catherine M. "The Dialogues of Spring and Winter: A Key to the Unity of *Love's Labour's Lost*." *Shakespeare Quarterly* 18 (Spring 1967): 119–27.

McMillin, Scott, and Sally-Beth MacLean. *The Queen's Men and Their Plays*. Cambridge: Cambridge University Press, 1998.

Manning, John. "Whitney's *Choice of Emblemes*: A Reassessment." *Renaissance Studies* 4 (June 1990): 155–200.

Maquerlot, Jean-Pierre. *Shakespeare and the Mannerist Tradition*. Cambridge: Cambridge University Press, 1995.

Marillier, H. C. *The Tapestries at Hampton Court Palace*. Rev. edn. London: HMSO, 1962.

Martin, John Rupert. *The Decorations for the Pompa Introitus Ferdinandi*. Corpus Rubenianum Ludwig Burchard 16. London and New York: Phaidon, 1972.

Mehl, Dieter. *The Elizabethan Dumb Show: The History of a Dramatic Convention*. London: Methuen, 1965.

"Emblematic Theatre." *Anglia* 95, nos. 1/2 (1977): 130–38.

"Emblems in English Renaissance Drama." *Renaissance Drama* n.s. 2 (1969): 39–57.

"Visual and Rhetorical Imagery in Shakespeare's Plays." *Essays and Studies* n.s. 25 (1972): 83–100.

Mercer, Eric. "The Decoration of the Royal Palaces from 1553–1625." *The Archaeological Journal* 110 (1953): 150–63.

Merchant, W. Moelwyn. "*Timon of Athens* and the Visual Conceit." In *Shakespeare and the Artist*. London: Oxford University Press, 1959. Pp. 167–77.

Metz, G. Harold. *Shakespeare's Earliest Tragedy: Studies in "Titus Andronicus."* Madison, Teaneck, NJ: Fairleigh Dickinson University Press; London: Associated University Presses, 1996.

"*Titus Andronicus*: A Watermark in the Longleat Manuscript." *Shakespeare Quarterly* 36 (Winter 1985): 450–53.

Michalski, Sergiusz. *The Reformation and the Visual Arts: The Protestant Image Question in Western and Eastern Europe*. London and New York: Routledge, 1993.

Midelfort, E. C. Erik. "Heartland of the Witchcraze: Central and Northern Europe." *History Today* 31 (February 1981): 27–31.

Miola, Robert S. *Shakespeare's Rome*. Cambridge: Cambridge University Press, 1983.

"Timon in Shakespeare's Athens." *Shakespeare Quarterly* 31 (Spring 1980): 21–30.

Mitchell, W. J. T. *Iconology: Image, Text, Ideology*. Chicago: University of Chicago Press, 1986.

Mowl, Timothy. *Elizabethan and Jacobean Style*. London: Phaidon, 1993.

Moxey, Keith P. F. "Pieter Bruegel and *The Feast of Fools*." *Art Bulletin* 64 (December 1982): 640–46.

Mulryan, John. "Venus, Cupid and the Italian Mythographers." *Humanistica Lovaniensia* 23 (1974): 31–41.

Nagler, A. M. *Theatre Festivals of the Medici, 1539–1637*. New Haven and London: Yale University Press, 1964.

Neill, Michael. "Broken English and Broken Irish: Nation, Language, and the Optic Power of Shakespeare's Histories." *Shakespeare Quarterly* 45 (Spring 1994): 1–32.

Newton, Stella Mary. *Renaissance Theatre Costume and the Sense of the Historic Past*. London: Rapp and Whiting, 1975.

Nicoll, Allardyce. *The Development of the Theatre: A Study of Theatrical Art from the Beginnings to the Present Day*. 5th edn. Revised. New York: Harcourt Brace Jovanovich, 1966.

Stuart Masques and the Renaissance Stage. 1938; reprint. New York: Arno Press, 1980.

Norbrook, David. "*Macbeth* and the Politics of Historiography." In *Politics of Discourse: The Literature and History of Seventeenth-Century England*. Ed. Kevin

Sharpe and Steven N. Zwicker. Berkeley, Los Angeles, London: University of California Press, 1987. Pp. 78–116.

Nordenfalk, Carl. "The Five Senses in Flemish Art before 1600." In *Netherlandish Mannerism: Papers Given at a Symposium in Nationalmuseum Stockholm, September 21–22, 1984.* Ed. Görel Cavalli-Björkman. Nationalmusei Skriftserie n.s. 4. Stockholm: Nationalmuseum, 1985. Pp. 135–54.

"The Five Senses in Late Medieval and Renaissance Art." *Journal of the Warburg and Courtauld Institutes* 48 (1985): 1–22.

"Les Cinq Sens dans l'art du Moyen Age." *Revue de l'art* 34 (1976): 17–28.

"The Sense of Touch in Art." In *The Verbal and the Visual: Essays in Honor of William Sebastian Heckscher.* Ed. Karl-Ludwig Selig and Elizabeth Sears. New York: Italica Press, 1990. Pp. 109–32.

North, Helen F. *From Myth to Icon: Reflections of Greek Ethical Doctrine in Literature and Art.* Ithaca, NY, and London: Cornell University Press, 1979.

Nosworthy, J. M. *Shakespeare's Occasional Plays: Their Origin and Transmission.* London: Edward Arnold, 1965.

Nurse, Julia. "She-Devils, Harlots and Harridans in Northern Renaissance Prints." *History Today* 48 (July 1998): 41–48.

O'Connell, Michael. *The Idolatrous Eye: Iconoclasm and Theater in Early-Modern England.* New York and Oxford: Oxford University Press, 2000.

O'Dell, Ilse. *Jost Ammans Buchschmuck-Holzschnitte für Sigmund Feyerabend.* Wiesbaden: Otto Harrassowitz, 1993.

Orgel, Stephen. "Acting Scripts, Performing Texts." In *Crisis in Editing: Texts of the English Renaissance.* Ed. Randall M. Leod [Randall McLeod]. New York: AMS Press, 1994. Pp. 251–94.

The Illusion of Power: Political Theater in the English Renaissance. Berkeley: University of California Press, 1975.

The Jonsonian Masque. Cambridge, MA: Harvard University Press, 1965.

"Textual Icons: Reading Early Modern Illustrations." In *The Renaissance Computer: Knowledge Technology in the First Age of Print.* Ed. Neil Rhodes and Jonathan Sawday. London and New York: Routledge, 2000. Pp. 59–94.

Orgel, Stephen and Roy Strong. *Inigo Jones: The Theatre of the Stuart Court.* 2 vols. Berkeley: University of California Press; London: Sotheby Parke Bernet, 1973.

Orlin, Lena Cowen. "'The Causes and Reasons of all Artificial Things' in the Elizabethan Domestic Environment." *Medieval and Renaissance Drama in England* 7 (1995): 19–75.

Private Matters and Public Culture in Post-Reformation England. Ithaca, NY, and London: Cornell University Press, 1994.

Ornstein, Robert. *Shakespeare's Comedies: From Roman Farce to Romantic Mystery.* Newark: University of Delaware Press, 1986.

Orrell, John. *The Theatres of Inigo Jones and John Webb.* Cambridge: Cambridge University Press, 1985.

Palfrey, Simon. *Late Shakespeare: A New World of Words*. Oxford: Clarendon Press, 1997.

Panofsky, Erwin. *Studies in Iconology: Humanistic Themes in the Art of the Renaissance*. 2nd edn. New York: Harper and Row, 1962.

Tomb Sculpture: Four Lectures on Its Changing Aspects from Ancient Egypt to Bernini. Ed. H. W. Janson. New York: Harry N. Abrams, 1964.

Parke, H. W. *Sibyls and Sibylline Prophecy in Classical Antiquity*. Ed. B. C. McClung. London and New York: Routledge, 1988.

Parry, Graham. *The Golden Age Restor'd: The Culture of the Stuart Court, 1603–42*. Manchester: Manchester University Press, 1981.

The Seventeenth Century: The Intellectual and Cultural Context of English Literature, 1603–1700. London and New York: Longman, 1989.

Paul, Henry N. *The Royal Play of "Macbeth."* 1948; reprint. New York: Octagon Books, 1978.

Peacock, John. "Ben Jonson's Masques and Italian Culture." In *Theatre of the English and Italian Renaissance*. Ed. J. R. Mulryne and Margaret Shewring. Warwick Studies in the European Humanities. London: Macmillan, 1991. Pp. 73–94.

"The Politics of Portraiture." In *Culture and Politics in Early Stuart England*. Ed. Kevin Sharpe and Peter Lake. London: Macmillan, 1994. Pp. 199–228.

Peck, Linda Levy. "Building, Buying, and Collecting in London, 1600–1625." In *Material London, ca. 1600*. Ed. Lena Cowen Orlin. Philadelphia: University of Pennsylvania Press, 2000. Pp. 268–89.

Pennington, Richard. *A Descriptive Catalogue of the Etched Work of Wenceslaus Hollar, 1607–1677*. Cambridge: Cambridge University Press, 1982.

Perry, Curtis. *The Making of Jacobean Culture: James I and the Renegotiation of Elizabethan Literary Practice*. Cambridge: Cambridge University Press, 1997.

Phillips, John. *The Reformation of Images: Destruction of Art in England, 1535–1660*. Berkeley, Los Angeles, London: University of California Press, 1973.

Pincombe, Michael. *The Plays of John Lyly: Eros and Eliza*. The Revels Plays Companion Library. Manchester: Manchester University Press; New York: St. Martin's Press, 1996.

Pinkus, Karen. *Picturing Silence: Emblem, Language, Counter-Reformation Materiality*. Ann Arbor: University of Michigan Press, 1996.

Praz, Mario. *Studies in Seventeenth-Century Imagery*. 2nd edn. Rome: Edizioni di Storia e Letteratura, 1964.

Purkiss, Diane. *The Witch in History: Early Modern and Twentieth-Century Representations*. London and New York: Routledge, 1996.

Rabb, Theodore K. "Play, not Politics: Who Really Understood the Symbolism in Renaissance Art?" *TLS* 10 November 1995: 18–20.

Reid, Jane Davidson. *The Oxford Guide to Classical Mythology in the Arts, 1300–1990s*. 2 vols. New York: Oxford University Press, 1993.

Riggs, Timothy, and Larry Silver. *Graven Images: The Rise of Professional Printmakers in Antwerp and Haarlem, 1540–1640*. Evanston, IL: Northwestern University Press, 1993.

Roberts, Helene E., ed. *Encyclopedia of Comparative Iconography: Themes Depicted in Works of Art*. 2 vols. Chicago and London: Fitzroy Dearborn, 1998.

Roberts, Jeanne Addison. "Shades of the Triple Hecate in Shakespeare." *Proceedings of the PMR Conference* 12/13 (1987–88): 47–66.

"Types of Crone: the Nurse and the Wise Woman in English Renaissance Drama." *Renaissance Papers, 2000*. Ed. T. H. Howard-Hill and Philip Rollinson. Rochester, NY: Camden House, 2000. Pp. 71–86.

Roesen, Bobbyann [Anne Barton]. "*Love's Labour's Lost*." *Shakespeare Quarterly* 4 (October 1953): 411–26.

Ronayne, John. "Totus Mundus Agit Histrionem [The Whole World Moves the Actor]: The Interior Decorative Scheme of the Bankside Globe." In *Shakespeare's Globe Rebuilt*. Ed. J. R. Mulryne and Margaret Shewring. Cambridge: Cambridge University Press, 1997. Pp. 121–46.

Rosenberg, Marvin. *The Masks of Macbeth*. Berkeley, Los Angeles, London: University of California Press, 1978.

Roston, Murray. *Changing Perspectives in Literature and the Visual Arts, 1650–1820*. Princeton: Princeton University Press, 1990.

Renaissance Perspectives in Literature and the Visual Arts. Princeton: Princeton University Press, 1987.

Rouse, E. Clive. "Elizabethan Wall Paintings at Little Moreton Hall." *National Trust Studies 1980*. London: Sotheby Parke Bernet, 1979.

Rowland, Beryl. *Birds with Human Souls: A Guide to Bird Symbolism*. Knoxville: University of Tennessee Press, 1978.

Rubin, Patricia Lee. *Giorgio Vasari: Art and History*. New Haven and London: Yale University Press, 1995.

Rundus, Raymond J. "Time and His 'Glass' in *The Winter's Tale*." *Shakespeare Quarterly* 25 (Winter 1974): 123–25.

Russell, Daniel. "Emblems and Hieroglyphics: Some Observations on the Beginnings and Nature of Emblematic Forms." *Emblematica* 1 (Fall 1986): 227–43.

Russell, H. Diane, with Bernadine Barnes. *Eva/Ave: Woman in Renaissance and Baroque Prints*. Washington, D.C.: National Gallery of Art (with The Feminist Press at CUNY), 1990.

Russell, Jeffrey B. *A History of Witchcraft: Sorcerers, Heretics, and Pagans*. 1980; reprint. London: Thames and Hudson, 1987.

Saunders, Alison. "When Is It a Device and When Is It an Emblem: Theory and Practice (but Mainly the Latter) in Sixteenth- and Seventeenth-Century France." *Emblematica* 7 (Winter 1993): 239–57.

Saxl, Fritz. "Veritas Filia Temporis." In *Philosophy and History: Essays Presented to Ernst Cassirer*. Ed. Raymond Klibansky and H. J. Patton. 1936; reprint. New York: Harper & Row, 1963. Pp. 197–222.

Schama, Simon. *Rembrandt's Eyes*. New York: Alfred A. Knopf, 1999.

Schleuter, June. "Rereading the Peacham Drawing." *Shakespeare Quarterly* 50 (Spring 1999): 171–84.

Schmidgall, Gary. *Shakespeare and the Courtly Aesthetic*. Berkeley, Los Angeles, London: University of California Press, 1981.

Schoenbaum, S. *William Shakespeare: A Compact Documentary Life*. New York: Oxford University Press, 1977.

Schuman, Samuel. "Emblems and the English Renaissance Drama: A Checklist." *Research Opportunities in Renaissance Drama* 12 (1969): 43–56.

Seng, Peter J. *The Vocal Songs in the Plays of Shakespeare: A Critical History*. Cambridge, MA: Harvard University Press, 1967.

Seznec, Jean. *The Survival of the Pagan Gods: The Mythological Tradition and Its Place in Renaissance Humanism and Art*. Trans. Barbara F. Sessions. New York: Pantheon Books, 1953.

Shapiro, H. A. *Personifications in Greek Art: The Representation of Abstract Concepts 600–400 B.C.* Zurich: Akanthus, 1993.

Shaw, Catherine M. *"Some Vanity of Mine Art": The Masque in English Renaissance Drama*. 2 vols. Salzburg: Institut für Anglistik und Amerikanistik, Universität Salzburg, 1979.

  "The Visual and the Symbolic in Shakespeare's Masques." In *Shakespeare and the Arts: A Collection of Essays from the Ohio Shakespeare Conference*. Ed. Cecile Williamson Cary and Henry S. Limouze. Dayton, OH: University Press of America, 1982. Pp. 21–34.

Shaw, William P. "Text, Performance, and Perspective: Peter Brook's Landmark Production of *Titus Andronicus*, 1955." *Theatre History Studies* 10 (1990): 31–55.

Shorr, Dorothy. "Some Notes on the Iconography of Petrarch's Triumph of Fame." *Art Bulletin* 20 (March 1938): 100–07.

Sill, Gertrude Grace. *A Handbook of Symbols in Christian Art*. New York: Macmillan, 1975.

Simonds, Peggy Muñoz. *Iconographic Research in English Renaissance Literature: A Critical Guide*. New York and London: Garland, 1995.

  Myth, Emblem, and Music in Shakespeare's "Cymbeline": An Iconographic Reconstruction. Newark: University of Delaware Press; London and Toronto: Associated University Presses, 1992.

Simonds, Peggy Muñoz, and Roger T. Simonds, "The Aesthetics of Speaking Stones: Multi-lingual Emblems on a 17th-century English Transi Tomb." In *European Iconography East and West, Selected Papers of the Szeged International Conference, June 9–12, 1993*. Ed. György E. Szönyi. Symbola et Emblemata: Studies in Renaissance and Baroque Symbolism 7. Leiden: E. J. Brill, 1996. Pp. 49–62.

Simpson, Percy, and C. F. Bell. *Designs by Inigo Jones for Masques and Plays at Court*. Oxford: Walpole and Malone Societies, 1924.

Sinfield, Alan. *Faultlines: Cultural Materialism and the Politics of Dissident Reading*. Berkeley, Los Angeles, Oxford: University of California Press, 1992.

Smith, Eric. *A Dictionary of Classical Reference in English Poetry*. Totowa, NJ: Barnes & Noble, 1984.

Smith, Irwin. *Shakespeare's Blackfriars Playhouse: Its History and Its Design*. New York: New York University Press, 1964.

Smuts, R. Malcolm. *Court Culture and the Origins of a Royalist Tradition in Early Stuart England*. Philadelphia: University of Pennsylvania Press, 1987.

Soellner, Rolf. *"Timon of Athens": Shakespeare's Pessimistic Tragedy*. Columbus: Ohio State University Press, 1979.

Sohmer, Steve. *Shakespeare's Mystery Play: The Opening of the Globe Theatre 1599*. Manchester: Manchester University Press, 1999.

Spencer, Theodore. *"The Two Noble Kinsmen." Modern Philology* 36 (February 1939): 255–76.

Stallybrass, Peter. *"Macbeth* and Witchcraft." In *Focus on "Macbeth."* Ed. John Russell Brown. London, Boston, Henley: Routledge and Kegan Paul, 1982. Pp. 189–209.

Stapleton, M. L. *Fated Sky: The "Femina Furens" in Shakespeare*. Newark: University of Delaware Press; London: Associated University Presses, 2000.

Steadman, John M. "Iconography and Renaissance Drama: Ethical and Mythological Themes." *Research Opportunities in Renaissance Drama* 13–14 (1970–71): 73–122.

Nature into Myth: Medieval and Renaissance Moral Symbols. Pittsburgh, PA: Duquesne University Press, 1979.

Steen, Sara Jayne. *Ambrosia in an Earthen Vessel: Three Centuries of Audience and Reader Response to the Works of Thomas Middleton*. New York: AMS Press, 1993.

Straten, Roelof van. *An Introduction to Iconography*. Rev. English edn. Trans. Patricia de Man. Documenting the Image 1. Yverdon, Switzerland, and Langhorne, PA: Gordon and Breach, 1994.

Strong, Roy. *The English Icon: Elizabethan and Jacobean Portraiture*. London: The Paul Mellon Foundation for British Art (with Routledge & Kegan Paul); New Haven: Yale University Press, 1969.

The English Renaissance Miniature. London: Thames and Hudson, 1983.

Gloriana: The Portraits of Queen Elizabeth I. London: Thames and Hudson, 1987.

Henry Prince of Wales and England's Lost Renaissance. New York: Thames and Hudson, 1986.

Portraits of Queen Elizabeth. Oxford: Clarendon Press, 1963.

The Renaissance Garden in England. London: Thames and Hudson, 1979.

Studing, Richard. "'That rare Italian Master' – Shakespeare's Julio Romano." *Humanities Association Bulletin* 23 (Summer 1971): 22–26.

Suhr, Elmer G. *The Spinning Aphrodite*. New York: Helios Books, 1969.

Sullivan, Margaret A. "The Witches of Dürer and Hans Baldung Grien." *Renaissance Quarterly* 53 (Summer 2000): 332–401.

Sutherland, Sarah P. *Masques in Jacobean Tragedy*. New York: AMS Press, 1983.

Sykes, H. Dugdale. "The Problem of Timon of Athens." In *Sidelights on Elizabethan Drama*. 1924; reprint. London: Frank Cass, 1966. Pp. 1–48.

Sypher, Wylie. *Four Stages of Renaissance Style: Transformations in Art and Literature, 1400–1700*. Garden City, NY: Doubleday, 1955.

   "Painting and the Other Fine Arts." In *William Shakespeare: His World, His Work, His Influence*. Ed. John F. Andrews. 3 vols. New York: Charles Scribner's Sons, 1985. I: 241–56.

Talbot, Charles W. "Baldung and the Female Nude." In *Hans Baldung Grien, Prints and Drawings*. Ed. James H. Marrow and Alan Shestack. New Haven: Yale University Art Gallery, 1981. Pp. 19–37.

Tassi, Marguerite A. "Lover, Poisoner, Counterfeiter: The Painter in Elizabethan Drama." *The Ben Jonson Journal* 7 (2000): 129–56.

Taylor, Gary, and John Jowett. *Shakespeare Reshaped, 1606–1623*. Oxford: Clarendon Press, 1993.

Taymor, Julie. *"Titus": The Illustrated Screenplay*. New York: Newmarket Press, 2000.

Teague, Frances. *Shakespeare's Speaking Properties*. Lewisburg, PA: Bucknell University Press; London: Associated University Presses, 1991.

Tervarent, Guy de. *Attributs et symboles dans l'art profane, 1450–1600*. 2nd edn. Geneva: E. Droz, 1997.

Thomson, Leslie, ed. *Fortune: "All is but Fortune."* Seattle and London: University of Washington Press for the Folger Shakespeare Library, 2000.

Thomson, Peter. *Shakespeare's Theatre*. 2nd edn. London and New York: Routledge, 1992.

Thorne, Alison. *Vision and Rhetoric in Shakespeare: Looking Through Language*. Basingstoke and London: Macmillan; New York: St. Martin's Press, 2000.

Thornton, Peter. *Form and Decoration: Innovation in the Decorative Arts, 1470–1870*. London: Weidenfeld & Nicolson, 1998.

   Seventeenth-Century Interior Decoration in England, France and Holland. New Haven and London: Yale University Press for the Paul Mellon Centre for Studies in British Art, 1978.

Tinkle, Theresa. *Medieval Venuses and Cupids: Sexuality, Hermeneutics, and English Poetry*. Stanford: Stanford University Press, 1996.

Traister, Barbara Howard. *Heavenly Necromancers: The Magician in English Renaissance Drama*. Columbia: University of Missouri Press, 1984.

Truax, Elizabeth. "Emblematic Pictures for the Less Privileged in Shakespeare's England." *Comparative Drama* 29 (Spring 1995): 147–67.

Tuve, Rosemond. *Allegorical Imagery: Some Mediaeval Books and Their Posterity*. Princeton: Princeton University Press, 1966.

Ungerer, Gustav. "An Unrecorded Elizabethan Performance of *Titus Andronicus*." *Shakespeare Survey* 14 (1961): 102–09.

Ure, Peter. "John Marston's *Sophonisba*: A Reconsideration." In *Elizabethan and Jacobean Drama: Critical Essays by Peter Ure*. Ed. J. C. Maxwell. Liverpool: Liverpool University Press, 1974. Pp. 75–92.

Vandenbroeck, Paul. "Verbeeck's Peasant Weddings: A Study of Iconography and Social Function." *Simiolus* 14, no. 2 (1984): 79–124.

Veevers, Erica. *Images of Love and Religion: Queen Henrietta Maria and Court Entertainments*. Cambridge: Cambridge University Press, 1989.

Veldman, Ilja M. *Maarten van Heemskerck and Dutch Humanism in the Sixteenth Century*. Trans. Michael Hoyle. Maarsen: Gary Schwartz, 1977.

The New Hollstein: Dutch and Flemish Etchings, Engravings and Woodcuts, 1450–1700: Maarten van Heemskerck. Ed. Ger Luijten. 2 pts. Roosendaal: Koninklijke van Poll, 1993–94.

"Seasons, Planets and Temperaments in the Work of Maarten van Heemskerck." *Simiolus* 11, nos. 3/4 (1980): 149–76.

Venezky, Alice S. *Pageantry on the Shakespearean Stage*. New York: Twayne, 1951.

Vinge, Louise. *The Five Senses: Studies in a Literary Tradition*. Publications of the Royal Society of Letters at Lund 72. Lund: CWK Gleerup, 1975.

Wall, Wendy. *The Imprint of Gender: Authorship and Publication in the English Renaissance*. Ithaca, NY, and London: Cornell University Press, 1993.

Watkins, Ronald, and Jeremy Lemmon. *Macbeth*. In Shakespeare's Playhouse Series. Totowa, NJ: Rowman and Littlefield, 1974.

Watkins, Susan. *In Public and in Private: Elizabeth I and Her World*. London: Thames and Hudson, 1998.

Wells, Stanley, and Gary Taylor. *William Shakespeare: A Textual Companion*. Oxford: Clarendon Press, 1987.

Wells, William. "'Timon of Athens.'" *Notes and Queries* 6 (5 June 1920): 266–69.

Wells-Cole, Anthony. *Art and Decoration in Elizabethan and Jacobean England: The Influence of Continental Prints, 1558–1625*. New Haven and London: Yale University Press for The Paul Mellon Centre for Studies in British Art, 1997.

Welsford, Enid. *The Court Masque: A Study in the Relationship between Poetry and the Revels*. 1927; reprint. New York: Russell and Russell, 1962.

Wheeler, C. F. *Classical Mythology in the Plays, Masques, and Poems of Ben Jonson*. Princeton: Princeton University Press, 1938.

White, Lynn, Jr. "The Iconography of *Temperantia* and the Virtuousness of Technology." In *Action and Conviction in Early Modern Europe: Essays in Memory of E. H. Harbison*. Ed. Theodore K. Rabb and Jerrold E. Seigel. Princeton: Princeton University Press, 1969. Pp. 197–219.

"Indic Elements in the Iconography of Petrarch's *Trionfo della Morte*." *Speculum* 49 (April 1974): 201–21.

White, Martin. *Renaissance Drama in Action: An Introduction to Aspects of Theatre Practice and Performance*. London and New York: Routledge, 1998.

Wickham, Glynne. "The Emblematic Tradition." In *Early English Stages, 1300–1660*. Vol. II, pt. 1: *1576 to 1660*. New York: Columbia University Press; London: Routledge & Kegan Paul, 1963. Pp. 206–44.

   "Masque and Anti-masque in 'The Tempest.'" *Essays and Studies* 28 (1975): 1–14.

   "To Fly or Not to Fly?: The Problem of Hecate in Shakespeare's 'Macbeth.'" In *Essays on Drama and Theatre: Liber Amicorum Benjamin Hunningher*. Amsterdam: Moussault's; Antwerp: Standaard, 1973. Pp. 171–82.

Wiggins, Martin. *Journeymen in Murder: The Assassin in English Renaissance Drama*. Oxford: Clarendon Press, 1991.

Wilbern, David. "Rape and Revenge in *Titus Andronicus*." *English Literary Renaissance* 8 (Spring 1978): 159–82.

Willis, Deborah. *Malevolent Nurture: Witch-Hunting and Maternal Power in Early Modern England*. Ithaca, NY, and London: Cornell University Press, 1995.

Wilson, Jean, ed. *Entertainments for Elizabeth I*. Woodbridge: D. S. Brewer; Totowa, NJ: Rowman & Littlefield, 1980.

Wind, Edgar. *Pagan Mysteries in the Renaissance*. Rev. edn. New York: W. W. Norton, 1968.

Withington, Robert. *English Pageantry, An Historical Outline*. 2 vols. 1918; reprint. New York and London: Benjamin Blom, 1963.

Wolfthal, Diane. *Images of Rape: The "Heroic" Tradition and Its Alternatives*. Cambridge: Cambridge University Press, 1999.

Woodman, David. *White Magic and English Renaissance Drama*. Rutherford, Madison, Teaneck, NJ: Fairleigh Dickinson University Press, 1973.

Yates, Frances. *Astraea: The Imperial Theme in the Sixteenth Century*. London and Boston: Routledge & Kegan Paul, 1975.

Young, Alan R. "The Emblematic Art of Ben Jonson." *Emblematica* 6 (Summer 1992): 17–36.

   Henry Peacham. Twayne's English Authors Series 251. New York: Twayne, 1979.

   Tudor and Jacobean Tournaments. London: George Philip, 1987.

Zapalac, Kristin Eldyss. *"In His Image and Likeness": Political Iconography and Religious Change in Regensburg, 1500–1600*. Ithaca, NY, and London: Cornell University Press, 1990.

Zika, Charles. "Fears of Flying: Representations of Witchcraft and Sexuality in Early Sixteenth-Century Germany." *Australian Journal of Art* 8 (1989–90): 19–47.

   "She-Man: Visual Representations of Witchcraft and Sexuality in Sixteenth-Century Europe." In *Venus and Mars: Engendering Love and War in Medieval and Early Modern Europe*. Ed. Andrew Lynch and Philippa Maddern. Nedlands: University of Western Australia Press, 1995. Pp. 147–90.

Index